CLINICAL ANTHROPOLOGY

A New Approach to American Health Problems?

Edited by

Demitri B. Shimkin
Peggy Golde

Research Report 7
Department of Anthropology
University of Illinois at
Urbana-Champaign

UNIVERSITY
PRESS OF
AMERICA

LANHAM • NEW YORK • LONDON

TABLE OF CONTENTS

Demitri B. Shimkin and Peggy Golde

The Book's Goals and Contents

Clinical Anthropology: A New Approach to American Health Problems? is a systematic exploration of the activities, rationale, contributions, potentials and problems of a new, innovative vocation. Since both of the editors are involved in this vocation and believe it has much to offer, this work has a positive bias. But it also presents many of the problems encountered by Clinical Anthropology, such as the difficulties inherent in social and intellectual innovation in a period of reaction, and the continuing hesitations of many anthropologists to engage too deeply in clinical settings and especially in intervention--the defining concern of Clinical, as opposed to more general Medical, Anthropology.

This study has been designed, in first order, to inform those in anthropology and in the recognized health disciplines who are concerned with the nature, potentials and limitations of Clinical Anthropology. It also is relevant to all concerned or interested in the interfaces between the social sciences, the humanities and medicine. In editing this work, we have sought a clarity and simplicity of exposition, and a solid substance of illustrative materials and selected references. In consequence, we feel that Clinical Anthropology: A New Approach to American Health Problems? will be of interest to a wide range of professionals, students, and general readers. At the same time, the book's scope is limited to developments in the United States; the important yet barely attacked issues for Clinical Anthropology in countries with national health services, and in the lesser developed countries, await further research.

Clinical Anthropology: A New Approach to American Health Problems? includes seven parts, which form an analytical sequence.

Part I evaluates Clinical Anthropology and, in part, the essays comprised in this volume, from the standpoint of the medical profession. The two papers are each by an eminent authority. Mark Lepper, one of the nation's great pioneers in community health and a former colleague in the Holmes County investigations, is concerned with the medical challenges of forthcoming decades. Larger elements of the American population are reaching their biological lifespans but with soaring costs in health care. The potentialities of the biomedical approach have been largely attained and progress in life expectancies, human functionality and the lowering of medical costs must come basically from the social sciences, especially anthropology. Harold Swartz, both a physician and a biophysicist and a present colleague in medical education, also sees significant roles for clinical anthropologists in research, education and consultation but is dubious about the viability of the direct delivery of services by clinical anthropologists. He urges that the field develop as a small, high quality discipline rather than moving toward major application on the model of Social Work.

Part II is the core of the volume, discussing in detail the characteristics of Clinical Anthropology as a field, and the work of four significant clinical anthropologists, as well as that of a social worker, Catherine Alter, whose perspective is truly cross-cultural. It is not coincidental that most of the contributors to this Part are women. While the roots of Clinical Anthropology are largely male, the vocation today expresses the moral concerns, the new questions, and the depth of personal involvement which have been a hallmark of the woman anthropologist since the days of Margaret Mead. This Part includes the following: an introductory statement by Peggy Golde; a statistical review by Robert Gern, a graduate in Anthropology and a health worker, and Demitri Shimkin; a research paper on problems in maternal and child health by Rochelle Shain and her colleagues in the Department of Obstetrics and Gynecology in San Antonio, Texas; Golde´s formulation of the rationale of Clinical Anthropology in counselling and psychotherapy; Catherine Alter´s remarkable case analysis demonstrating the enormous significance of cultural factors in behavioral diagnosis and intervention strategies; Leonard Borman´s appraisal of the significance of self-help groups in health, a development in which he has been a founder; and Hazel Weidman´s insightful summation of twelve year´s work in the extension of health services to a multi-ethnic population in Miami.

Part III approaches Clinical Anthropology through the detailed review of a large undertaking in health

viii

research and services, the Holmes County (Mississippi) Health Research Program (1969-74) and its successor, the Community Control of Hypertension in Central Mississippi (1980-85). Throughout its history, this undertaking has combined anthropological and medical leadership. It is important for four reasons. First, it constitutes a rigorous, large scale identification of social and environmental factors in the epidemiology of a major disease, hypertension. Second, it illustrates the productive effectiveness of community control in applied research. Community insistence led to shifts in direction from general ecological and clinical research to focussing upon a presssing problem, and from clinical observations to a pilot effort at intervention. Community control has continued, although its locus has changed: it no longer represents the Black population of one county alone, but now represents both races in five counties. Today it is associated with the University of Mississippi, thus broadening its resource base and public health affiliations. And it is applied to improving health services outreach, raising the quality of health for the target population, and health research, as opposed primarily to combating practical denial of services to the Black poor, the key issue in the 1960s. Third, this experience has proven that intelligent, motivated, but not highly educated people can be trained to do complex clinical and other tasks very well indeed. The recruitment and development of local staff remains at the heart of this program. And, fourth, the biosocial and ecological perspectives have facilitated new approaches in research and services, notably the use of extended families, Black and White, as vehicles of health education and disease management.

After a brief foreword, Part III begins with Shimkin's description of the origins and general history of the Holmes County project. Edward Eckenfels, a key figure in that project's clinical planning and training, then considers the ethical and health issues that have dominated both the earlier and later efforts. The initial perspectives and methods of the new project are then presented by Dennis Frate, Eddie W. Logan and Charlie Wade, Sr. These are analyzed in a lively discussion led by Sidney Johnson, a Mississippi physician who is Co-Principal Investigator. Part III concludes with a summary by Dennis Frate of organizational and substantive developments in this project in 1982-1983. This discussion culminates in an assessment of continuing and variable factors in the establishment of resources and services in a poor, rural area, 1965-1983.

ix

Special attention needs to be paid to the similarities and contrasts of Dr. Weidman's undertakings and the Mississippi projects as illustrations of large-scale community health work. In the first instance, the critical problem has been a general articulation of a number of ethnic populations with the varied services of a primary-to-tertiary care system. The emphases were necessarily upon procedures of cultural research and their applications to clinical communication. In the second instance, the essential goal has been a progressive attack upon a severe health problem in which the differences of understanding between physicians and the communities served were not great but in which fundamental barriers to access and improved treatment had to be reduced step by step.

In Part IV, the central concern is evaluation. From the perspectives of persons active in health services, how Useful is Clinical Anthropology? In eliciting these discussions, we have tried both to gain the opinions of experienced and successful health workers, and to have those opinions concretely supported. This Part begins with the overall assessment of Thomas Tourlentes, a psychiatrist, director of an important community mental health program, and friend of self-help groups. The essays of two other physicians follow. Dorothea Leighton, one of the creators of culturally sensitive psychiatry, stresses how the shift from old fashioned general practice to hospital based specialty medicine has created a need for anthropology which, to be successful in resolving health needs, must be medically literate. Paul Friedman also sees a place for the social sciences in clinical settings, through selective training for clinicians, and through direct participation in appropriate, ambulatory cases. He warns, at the same time, of the need to re-structure social science anticipations and behavior to fit into the imperatives of clinical reality.

The next contribution, by a nurse-anthropologist, Toni Tripp-Reimer, specifies the clinically important information on human variability that biological anthropologists have developed. Hope Isaacs, an anthropologist in nursing education, describes her innovative training program in a kind of "clinical ethnography" which has been effective in sensitizing nurses to cultural factors affecting patient health and therapeutic regimes.

While the problems of the individual patient in a diagnostic and therapeutic setting have commanded central attention in the perspectives of Medicine and Nursing, Public Health and Health Education primarily address the needs of populations, and are especially concerned with prevention through environmental and social changes. Miriam Rodin, an anthropologist and epidemiologist, sees Public Health as a social science practiced by people with clinical and technical training. Its primary tasks are to discover the causes of morbidity and mortality in particular populations, to link these causes into population-environment systems, to analyze the adequacy of existing health systems, and to devise ways, particularly through prevention, of making these systems more effective. Today, with the general conquest of infectious diseases, social factors are of central concern--in behavioral disorders, heart disease, and, in part, cancer. In the United States, more hospital beds are occupied by psychiatric patients than any other group. In Public Health, anthropologists conduct field work, examine the influence of cultural values on health-related behavior, and aid in developing intervention systems that are both more effective and acceptable to those served.

A basic link between Public Health findings and improved health is through Health Education, the theme of Thomas O'Rourke's discussion. This vocation has a dual orientation. On one hand, it seeks to help people to adopt more healthful lifeways. On the other, it must deal with the negative influences of, say, tobacco and alcohol promotion coupled with government self-interest in tax returns. It must play an advocacy role to sensitize the public to the limitations of "sick care" systems heavily oriented toward benefits for producers. Clinical Anthropology in Health Education broadens research techniques and models, as well as providing new approaches to communication and self-help group development.

Lillian Pickup, the former director of an outstanding de-toxification center in Chicago, is the anchor person of this session. Her comments, based on the realitites of huge case loads and intractable addictions, parallel Catherine Alter's pleas, noted earlier, for interdisciplinary efforts, clearly including an important role for anthropology.

Part V turns to a basic developmental problem for Clinical Anthropology, the need now and in the future for comprehensive, carefully evaluated, and accessible documentation. This technical question is reviewed by a panel of experts. After a general foreword by Shimkin, Barton Clark, an information specialist and anthropologist, assesses the limited degree of information handling now extant in anthropology. Richard W. Thompson, a psychological anthropologist much involved in quantitative research, discusses key needs in the development of data sets for Clinical Anthropology. David Klass, a psychiatrist engaged in treatment systems research, cautions that statistical "facts" may reflect administrative needs as well as diagnostic or therapeutic realities. Turning to the future, S. B. Sells, a clinical psychologist and pioneer in drug abuse research, insightfully discusses the value and limitations of the Drug Abuse Epidemiology Data Center as a model for documentation in Clinical Anthropology. Allan Levy, a physician and expert in biomedical information, adds to future possibilities the use of computer conferencing and allied techniques. Finally, Clark summarizes the panel's findings in terms of advisable short and longer term strategies of documentation.

Part VI, by Shimkin and Golde, summarizes the findings of our investigation. It deals with the contributions of Clinical Anthropology to research, services and training in the health disciplines. It identifies key problems in the future development of this field. And it suggests some wider perspectives.

The Appendix, by Clark, with the assistance of Romy Borooah, identifies bibliographic and allied resources useful for the deeper study of Clinical Anthropology.

How the Book Developed

With one exception, Hope Isaac's thoughtful paper, all the contributions in this volume were expansions of papers, presentations or discussion in a three-day invitational Planning Conference on Documentation in Clinical Anthropology at the University of Illinois in Urbana, July 22-24, 1980. Because of delays in publication, these papers have been brought up to date in key instances. We sought, in our invitations, to gain a deep and balanced view of Clinical Anthropology from practitioners, researchers and teachers in that field, other health workers, and specialists in documentation. We were concerned with generating a review that would come to grips with key ideas and

xii

issues. Consequently, we adopted a rather loose format, depending on a combination of submitted papers, tape recordings and notes by student assistants to develop a valid record.

To translate these materials into a reasonably coherent book has required much editorial effort in cooperation with each author. We have sought--we believe, successfully--to retain and even enhance diverse viewpoints. Our editorial efforts have been directed primarily toward clarity of exposition, on the one hand, and convincing documentation on the other. In some cases, we have re-arranged the order of papers in order to improve logical developments. And we have added introductory and summary materials, as well as the Appendix, to yield overall structure and continuity for the book.

The Planning Conference generating this book represented the convergence of three distinct concerns with Clinical Anthropology. The first was the long continued involvement of the Society for Applied Anthropology in community health, on the one hand, and new career opportunities for anthropologists, on the other. The second was the strong interest of the State of Illinois Department of Mental Health and Developmental Disabilities in the use of anthropology in mental health research and services. And the third was the desire of Illinois faculty, supported strongly by the School of Social Sciences and the University of Illinois College of Medicine at Urbana, to explore issues in the improved clinical applications of the social sciences and humanities.

Beyond this, both editors have long been active in the interface between anthropology and health. Peggy Golde contributed, as an associate of Herbert Leiderman, to the Pheasant Run conference of 1967, which was critical to the formation of the Holmes County Health Research Project in Mississippi. Demitri Shimkin's involvement goes back to 1937-40 when, as an anthropologist and as a Fellow of the Institute for Child Welfare, he sought to assess the survival and development problems of Wind River Shoshone children.

Acknowledgments

In addition to the work of its authors and discussants, this volume has been made possible through the continued interest and support of Drs. Louis

Aarons, Research and Development Executive, State of
Illinois Department of Mental Health and Developmental
Disabilities; Robert Crawford, formerly Director,
School of Social Sciences, University of Illinois at
Urbana-Champaign; Linda Wilson, Associate Vice
Chancellor for Research, University of Illinois at
Urbana-Champaign; and Eugene Giles, former Head,
Department of Anthropology, University of Illinois,
Urbana-Champaign. The conduct of the Planning
Conference was greatly aided by Rose Davis, R.N.,
Clinical Assistant Professor of Public Health Nursing,
and by J. Kevin Doolen, Research Assistant for the
Conference. Edith M. Shimkin, Associate, Russian and
East European Center, and Carolyn A. Sprague, Research
Assistant, have been indispensable in our final
editorial work. Mrs. Peggy Hills, Ms. Judi Kutzko and
Roland R. Stone helped in the preparation of the
manuscript.

The funding of this volume and the Planning
Conference have come from the School of Social Sciences
and the Graduate College of the University of Illinois
at Urbana, the State of Illinois Department of Mental
Health and Developmental Disabilities, and the National
Heart, Lung and Blood Institute (via Central
Mississippi, Inc.).

AUTHORS, EDITORS AND COMMENTATORS

Catherine Foster Alter, M.S.W., is Assistant Professor School of Social Work, University of Iowa. She teaches human service administration, and social planning and policy. Her experience over ten years includes regional planning as well as program development and evaluation in aging and child abuse.

Ricardo H. Asch, M.D., is Jane and Roland Blumberg Professor in Obstetrics and Gynecology, Chief, Division of Human Reproduction, Department of Obstetrics and Gynecology, University of Texas Health Science Center, San Antonio. He investigates control of pituitary hormone secretion, corpus luteum function, and the effects of drugs of abuse on human and other primate reproductive systems. Reproductive endocrinology and infertility are his clinical fields.

Leonard D. Borman, Ph.D. (University of Chicago), is Founder and Director of the Self-Help Center, a national research and information clearing house located in Evanston, Illinois. An "action anthropologist," he has studied and helped North American Indians, Buddhist Kalmuck (Mongols resettled in the U.S. from the U.S.S.R.), the mentally ill, and numerous self-help/mutual aid groups.

Romy Borooah received her M.A. in anthropology at the University of Illinois, Urbana-Champaign, in 1975. She is presently writing her Ph.D. dissertation, based on fieldwork in India.

Barton M. Clark is Assistant Director of Public Services for Social Science Libraries and Associate Professor of Library Administration, University of Illinois, Urbana-Champaign. He has graduate degrees in Library and Information Science, and in Anthropology, from Illinois. His research interests are computer-based information systems in the social sciences, and anthropological documentation.

Susan L. Dalterio, Ph.D., is Research Assistant Professor of Pharmacology, University of Texas Health Science Center, San Antonio. Her research during the past 6 years has involved cannabinoid effects on the development and function of the reproductive system in male mice, particularly alterations in steroid hormone levels, testis function and sexual behavior.

Edward J. Eckenfels is Assistant Dean for Academic Counseling and Associate Professor, Department of Preventative Medicine, Rush Medical College. He organized pilot hypertensive services in the Holmes County (Mississippi) Health Research Project, and has long been active in Black health problems. He has co-authored (with Irene Turner and Tom Madden) Health Care Fact Book, U.S.A., Raven Press, 1982.

Dennis A. Frate, Ph.D., is Principal Investigator of "Community Control of Hypertension" supported by the National Heart, Lung, and Blood Institute and a Research Associate Professor, Research Institute of Pharmaceutical Sciences, The University of Mississippi. A Fellow of the Council on Epidemiology, American Heart Association, his research in rural Mississippi has centered on hypertension epidemiology and control, geophagy, and family structure. Prior to coming to Mississippi he was Director of the Office for Community Health Research, Rockford School of Medicine, University of Illinois.

Paul C. Friedman, M.D., trained in social science and medicine, practices in Helotes, Texas, and edits Introduction to Clinical Family Medicine and Current Literature Review. He was formerly Assistant Professor, Research Co-ordinator and Director of the Clinical Social Science and Family Medicine Programs, University of Texas, Health Science Center, San Antonio. He consults on applying social-science concepts to the provider-recipient relationship in clinical settings.

Robert Gern, B.S. (Genetics and Developmental Biology), B.A. (Anthropology), and a former medical student at the University of Illinois, Medical Center. Currently a community organizer with the Champaign County Health Care Consumers, Illinois. Eventually plans to incorporate concepts of Clinical Anthropology into graduate studies in Public Health.

Peggy Golde, Ph.D. Born in St. Louis. B.A. (Creative Arts), Antioch College; graduate study in Social Relations, Harvard University. Fieldwork in Mexico led to Women in the Field (Aldine, 1970). Taught ethno-art, medical anthropology and social psychiatry at Stanford, 1968-1974. In private practice since 1975 as a Licensed Marriage, Family and Child Counselor.

Hope L. Isaacs, Ph.D. Studying Seneca Iroquois health-directed behavior at home and in urban medical centers stimulated her interest in clinical anthropology. Over 10 years, her work has focused on course development in Medical Anthropology, and on teaching clinicians in training, first at State University of New York at Buffalo, and currently at San Diego State University.

Sidney A. Johnson, M.D., is Co-Principal Investigator of "Community Control of Hypertension" and also Clinical Assistant Professor in the Research Institute of Pharmaceutical Sciences, The University of Mississippi. After receiving his medical education at The Unversity of Mississippi, he was Director of Emergency Medical Services, Hinds General Hospital, Jackson, Mississippi. Since 1974 he has been in private general practice in Goodman, Mississippi.

David D. Klass, M.D., is currently Coordinator of Research and Director of Evaluation of the Illinois Department of Mental Health and Developmental Disabilities. He has been working for the last few years with a group attempting to improve the data base in a large service delivery bureaucracy so that decisions and planning may take place in a data informed climate.

Dorothea C. Leighton, M.D. As psychiatric residents, her husband and she sought exposure to other cultures to see if psychiatrists would find relevant data in anthropology. This led to noticing problems in cross-cultural medical practices, and eventually to helping organize The Society for Medical Anthropology, of which she was the first president.

Mark H. Lepper, M.D., is Vice President, Interinstitutional Affairs, Rush-Presbyterian-St. Luke's Medical Center (Chicago) and Professor of Internal Medicine and Preventive Medicine (Rush Medical College). An original interest in research and teaching in infectious diseases led to work on associated chronic diseases (rheumatic fever, endocarditis) and disabling residues from acute infections (poliomyelitis, post-meningitic brain damage). As chairman of Preventative Medicine (University of Illinois), he favored epidemiological and control activities in coronary artery and chronic bronchopulmonary disease, and in the general provision of health care. The O.E.O. program in Chicago permitted the development of a neighborhood health center affiliated with Rush, and a later opening of a new medical college there. In 1970, a three-year leave from the college deanship allowed service as the governor's health adviser and director of the State health planning agency for Illinois. Since then, a major responsibility has been developing a network of affiliated hospitals for a comprehensive care program for 1.25 million people.

Allan H. Levy, M.D., a graduate of Columbia University and Harvard Medical School, trained at Boston City Hospital (in internal medicine) and at the National Cancer Institute. On the faculty in medicine at Johhs Hopkins and later Baylor, he worked to apply computers in medicine and biology. At Illinois' College of Medicine in Urbana since 1975, he teaches medical computing and investigates artificial intelligence in medicine.

Eddie W. Logan, M.S., is Executive Project Officer of the research project "Community Control of Hypertension" supported by the National Heart, Lung, and Blood Institute (NIH'. From 1970-1975 he directed the Holmes County (Mississippi) Health Research Project funded by the National Center for Health Services Research. His training and previous work centered on science education.

Warren B. Miller, M.D., is Principal Research Scientist and Associate Director of the Transnational Family Research Institute in Palo Alto. His primary research interests include the psychology of reproduction and contraceptive use.

Thomas W. O'Rourke, Ph.D., M.P.H., Associate Professor, Department of Health Education and School of Clinical Medicine, University of Illinois at Urbana-Champaign, is concerned with health educational policy at national, state and local levels. His research focuses upon the understanding and modification of health-related behavior; he seeks to integrate social-science orientations into health education.

Lillian E. Pickup, R.N., Certified Alcoholism Counselor, Strategic Planning Task Force, Division of Alcoholism, State of Illinois. Consultant to community based alcoholism treatments units. Member of faculty, Central Y.M.C.A. Community College, Chicago. Formerly Director, A.T.A. Community Detox Center, Chicago. Who's Who of American Women.

Miriam B. Rodin, Ph.D, (Illinois, Urbana-Champaign), is Associate Professor of Epidemiology at the University of Illinois School of Public Health in Chicago. Her doctoral work was in urban and medical anthropology. Her current research focuses on the epidemiology of drinking and alcoholism.

S.B. Sells, Ph.D. (Psychology, Columbia, 1936) is (1958 -) Research Professor and Director of the Institute of B havioral Research, Texas Christian University. In 1948-1958, he was Professor of Medical Psychology, Air Force School of Aviation Medicine. Fellow, American Psychological Association and Aerospace Medical Association; President, Society for Multivariate Experimental Psychology; Managing Editor, Multivariate Experimental Behavioral Research. He has published 20 books and 350 papers.

Rochelle Shain, Ph.D. (California, Berkeley), is Associate Professor, Department of Obstetrics and Gynecology, University of Texas Health Science Center, San Antonio. Her postdoctoral training is in reproductive physiology and fertility control. She teaches medical students and postdoctoral fellows, and conducts research in reproduction and fertility regulation. Her recent book is <u>Fertility Control: Biologic and Behavioral Aspects</u> (Harper and Row).

Marguerite K. Shepard, M.D., is Professor, Department of Obstetrics and Gynecology and Chief, Section of Reproductive Endocrinology, Indiana School of Medicine, Indianapolis. Her primary research areas are amenorrhea and galactorrhea. Her clinical activities focus on infertility and endocrinology.

Demitri B. Shimkin, Ph.D. (California, Berkeley), is Professor of Anthropology and of Geography and Adjunct Professor of Epidemiology (School of Public Health), University of Illinois. He was a student of Lowie, Kroeber, Brunswik and Erikson. A human ecologist and systems analyst, he has worked with community health, child development, tuberculosis, hypertension and alcoholism. He has written about 200 scientific papers.

xix

Edith M. Shimkin, Associate, Russian and East European Center, University of Illinois at Urbana-Champaign, is an editor, technical translator and culture historian. Among her publications are The Extended Family in Black Societies (1978), edited with D.B. Shimkin and D.A. Frate; "The Upper Paleolithic in Central Eurasia," in Views of the Past, edited by Leslie Freeman (1978); and Contributions to Inner Asian Anthropology (Journal of the Steward Anthropological Society 12:356-506, 1981).

Gary S. Sorock, Ph.D., is Assistant Professor, Department of Health Sciences, William Paterson College (Wayne, N.J). His researches have dealt with hypertension, organ transplants in end-stage renal disease, and the epidemiology of falls among the elderly.

Carolyn A. Sprague, a graduate student in anthropology at the University of Illinois at Urbana-Champaign, is finishing her dissertation on Nevada Ranch Women, A Study in Isolation. She has written, with D.B. Shimkin, How Midwesterners Cope: The East Urbana Energy Study (1981).

Harold M. Swartz, M.D., M.S.P.H., Ph.D., is Associate Dean for Academic Affairs and Professor of Biophysics and Medicine, University of Illinois College of Medicine at Urbana. His primary interest is the relationship of the social sciences and humanities to medicine. The College of Medicine at Urbana emphasizes the education of M.D.-Ph.D. candidates in the humanities, social sciences, biological sciences and physcial sciences.

Richard W. Thompson, Ph.D., is an independent contractor. Formerly, he was Assistant Professor of Anthropology, University of Illinois at Urbana-Champaign; former Associate Editor, American Ethnologist. He has conducted fieldwork in Mexico, East Africa and the United States. He has published on social change and deviance, and on qualitative-quantitative research strategies, including "Methods in Social Anthropology" (American Behavioral Scientists, 1980).

Thomas T. Tourlentes, M.D., is Executive Director of the Comprehensive Community Mental Health Center of Rock Island and Mercer Counties, Rock Island, Illinois. He is also Associate Clinical Professor of Psychiatry, University of Illinois College of

Medicine. He was formerly Superintendent of the Galesburg State Research Hospital and Regional Administrator of the Department of Mental Health and Developmental Disabilities, State of Illinois.

Toni Tripp-Reimer, B.S., M.S. (Nursing), M.A., Ph.D. (Anthropology), is Associate Professor, University of Iowa, and President of the Council on Anthropology and Nursing. She has published articles and chapters on cross-cultural gerontology, physical assessment of racially distinct clients, and health behaviors of the following ethnic groups: Appalachians, Old Order Amish, Czech-Americans, Greeks, and Indochinese Refugees.

Charlie F. Wade, Sr. is the County Agent for Holmes County, Mississippi, Cooperative Extension Service, U.S. Department of Agriculture. He is also President of the Board of Directors of Central Mississippi, Incorporated, the community service agency initially sponsoring the research project "Community Control of Hypertension." He has been actively involved and a participant in all past research conducted in this central Mississippi area.

Hazel Hitson Weidman, Ph.D., is Professor of Social Anthropology and Director, Office of Transcultural Education and Research, Department of Psychiatry, University of Miami School of Medicine. Working at the interface of community and health institutions across departmental lines, she has sought to transform unicultural approaches and perspectives to transcultural ones, thus improving the delivery of health services in a multi-ethnic environment.

PART I

INTRODUCTION: MEDICINE AND THE SOCIAL SCIENCES

THE ROLE OF ANTHROPOLOGY IN HEALTH CARE: AN IMPERATIVE AT THE RESEARCH AND PRACTICAL LEVEL

Mark H. Lepper

The aim of this paper is to confirm that the social sciences including anthropology have in the past made contributions to the art and science of health care directed toward optimizing the health status of each individual and of whole societies. Moreover, it is postulated that because of the changing nature of the problems, particularly as they have been skewed by the dominant and successful use of the basic and applied biologic sciences, anthropology and kindred sciences will make a multifold greater contribution in the future. Such developments are imperative to long term improvement in the nation's health status.

In this volume, the current status and immediate past history of the application of anthropology to health care are well presented. It is demonstrated that anthropology has expanded the base of scientific knowledge essential to understanding the health statuses of various contemporary societies and their individual memberships. This knowledge exlains much of the failure of contemporary health care services developed in the Western European and North American cultures to serve well other cultures, including immigrant groups into westernized societies. In addition, clinical anthropology has achieved a measure of success in rendering services to these immigrant groups and to other groups. Public health practices are also heavily dependent upon the cultural milieu; hence anthropology is and will continue to provide basic understandings for the care of whole societies through public health activities.

The purpose of this chapter is to provide a frame of reference for what I consider will be a major expansion of anthropology and some other social and human sciences into health care because existing problems demand it. Based upon analogies with the outcome when the biologic sciences were systematically applied to health problems, my premise is that a similar utilization of anthropology by the health care community will result in its fruitful integration into the existing paradigm for service activities.

3

The U.S. Health Services Paradigm

In its simplest form, the belief upon which that paradigm is based is that the services which have been or will be developed, and which can and should be provided to each individual depend on his or her health status (Dever 1980:25-40). They may, of course, be applied directly or indirectly through community-wide services such as educational or public health programs. Thus two related bodies of knowledge, each derived from research over many years, are brought together in this construct.

1. Each individual at any point in time has a unique health status based upon the impact of cumulative life experiences impinging upon an ever changing yet relatively stable biologic substrate genetically pre-conditioned and environmentally influenced from conception onward. There are usually strong and weak aspects in each individual's health status. Weak aspects are not only the individual's perceptions of not feeling well or being "ill" but also the presence of risk factors, life style errors and problems uncovered by examination and laboratory screening.

2. Scientifically accurate therapeutic trials and field studies, applying concepts and techniques developed in the basic sciences, have established sets of services designed to meet the needs of the weaker aspects of health statuses. Over a period of time, usually less than a year and rarely longer than two years, essentially every individual's health status can be benefitted by one or more service.

   a. A service is an abstraction that is defined from studies and is ultimately performed by individuals taught to provide it at an operational level. Services may, of course, by performed directly or through an organized indirect service program as in public health activities.

   b. Since services may vary from life saving crisis care for critically ill or injured individuals to health education or physical examinations in relatively well individuals, various resources are needed.

c. Resource allocations, both quantitative, and qualitative, depends primarily upon individual health statuses.

There is, of course, a vast amount of evidence that application of this construct has accomplished a marked improvement in individual health statuses as well as in those of whole populations. However, there is even more to be done. Nothing less than a utopian concept of appropriate intervention with professional services throughout the life span of each individual to guarantee his or her optimal health status should be the ultimate goal.

The definition of health by the World Health Organization (1964) agrees with such a goal. It is that health is a state of complete physical, mental and social well being and not mere absence of disease and infirmity. In no population is it even closely approached. This positive, albeit utopian, goal would permit fuller expression of human intellectual and emotional capacities throughout the life span of each individual.

Mortality Reduction: Current Limits and Results

Historically, health care services have had to focus on the reduction of mortality and acute morbidity since they were such obvious and emotionally laden aspects of human experiences. Even in the "health wise" more advanced countries, progress is still measured primarily by reduction in death rates and the absence of the acute episodic diseases which are caused by easily definable environmental elements such as microbes or parasites or nutritional deficiencies.

However, in countries with the most favorable situations new health problems have become dominant concerns of the majority of the population. Most morbidity results from chronic persistent diseases which lead to reductions in functional capacity and somewhat premature deaths. With high incidence and prolonged duration, these conditions have very high prevalences. Thus a burden of illness persists for most people and illness is a dominant concern for the majority of the population. Multiple, interacting biologic and environmental variables have been shown to be responsible. Some of them are:

5

1. Genetic predispositions toward particular diseases which are expressible throughout the life span generally but with increased vulnerability as age increases.

   a. Experiences with migrant populations such as Japanese-Americans have been a major tool in studying genetic-environmental relationships.

   b. Polygenetic predispositions are more common than single gene diatheses but neither has been as important quantitatively in disturbances of the health status as environmental stressors.

   c. In populations with improved health statuses genetic predispositions are becoming more easily demonstrated, particularly throughout a life span.

2. Environmental stressors which were originally easily definable, approaching all-or-none characteristics, have now also been shown to be one or more of the following:

   a. Active in low amounts over prolonged periods of time.

   b. Active intermittantly with cumulative results.

   c. Active in an all-or-none manner but infrequently effective, dependent on low likelihood of the precise mechanisms of interaction. In this situation there may be only a few diseases in spite of much environmental contamination but the two are roughly proportional over a portion of the curve.

   d. Able to interact with other environmental and/or host factors with compounding, synergistic, protective or purely additive results.

   e. Selectively active: solely in individuals with previously determined susceptibility which may have been genetic, caused by residuals from prior disease, an existing predisease state, or a previously unexpressed pathologic process.

In the long run the genetic impact not only is important in chronic diseases but also in mortality. Studies with genetically inbred animal colonies in optimally controlled environments coupled with cell cultures from them indicate a predetermined life span exists for each species observed (Cutler 1976). Such colonies show maximum survival rates until a rather abrupt termination of life occurs for all members of the cohort. The duration of average life of the individuals in the cohort is uniform and is genetically determined for each distinct breeding population. This type of survival pattern is described as the "squaring" of the survival curve. In a completely optimal environment each individual would live out his or her genetic potential and the curve for such a population would be completely "squared."

It is important to note that, along with the increasing problem of chronic disease has come a massive increase of life expectancies. Among the more affluent populations, human survival curves are approaching "squared" configurations with the terminal phase generally after eighty, but a duration somewhat longer in some populations than others. The curve for women is much more "squared" than for men. In these populations, a further reduction of 80% in deaths from all causes among persons under 65 years old would result in no more than a five year increase in average life span.

This partial control of deaths from specific causes has uncovered the fact that in previous eras the manifest causes of death were superimposed upon a massive amount of latent morbidity as well as the potential for the kinds of disease currently observed to develop. Age corrected statistics help to evaluate the trend and reveal the following:

1. There are some conditions which have increased in prevalence even when age adjustments are made, i.e., cancer of the lung, and seem to represent true increases in risks.

2. Previously, estimation of health in the present positive sense was simply not feasible within the then existing level of understanding and the basic complexities of health problems. Even so, experiences with disease control and concomitant increases in the understanding of the roots of disease have allowed estimates of health status even among the less developed countries and the

7

disadvantaged sub-populations at the practical level. The more complex health statuses of such groups have required more sophisticated analytic techniques.

a. Studies of health status in communities in the more affluent segments of developed countries indicate that only a small percentage among their populations believe themselves to be free of symptoms and among these a much smaller percentage perceive themselves to be well in a broad sense.[1]

1. At age 20-40 years, 35-40% of the population are symptom free and 8-10% consider themselves well. By age 60 the ranges are 10-15% and 4-5% respectively.

2. Forty percent of twenty year olds report some type of persistent symptom, 15% some one of the chronic diseases, 5% more than one chronic disease and 4-5% a permanent disability. About one-third of the disabilities are severe.

3. There is a progressive decline in the percentage of persons who do not have chronic symptoms to about 10% by the age of 60. They enter the group of those with a single chronic disease which increases to 20% and those with two or more chronic disease which showed a four-fold increase by that age. By this age 20% have permanent disabilities, about half of which are severe.

b. Health status studies among the lower socioeconomic groups such as the population of an urban "poverty area" in Chicago (Chicago Board of Health 1966) or in an underadvantaged rural population like the one in Mississippi reported in this volume find few if any truly well, symptom-free or even disease-free individuals. The percentages in the more severely diseased categories and the most accentuated and multiple problems are considerably more frequent.

8

Since the human survival curve even in the most
favorable situations is still not as long as would be
expected genetically, it is likely that some
environmental forces are still detracting from
longevity even in such instances. These environmental
stressors are more subtle than many associated with the
spread of infection. Some have been shown by
epidemiologic studies to be associated with life
styles, occupation and general stressors within the
socioeconomic environment.

The skewing of the survival curve in a favorable
direction is so large that the chances of losing ground
in the race against mortality and morbidity are quite
large. Even a return to the conditions of 1960 for the
population under age 65 would decrease total U.S. life
expectancy by about three years. It is, therefore,
necessary to continue present activities simultaneously
with adding new ones or substituting those which appear
potentially better for those existing, all this at
growing cost and with major problems of maldistribution
in services.

Health Services

Health services can be classified into one of
several levels. Included are services provided to the
total population or a segment of it, and are indirect
in the sense that the provider has no direct contact
with the recipient. Other services are provided
directly and may be part of a planned program of
services such as screening for early disease or risk
factors, or individualized as is generally done in
treating patients recognized as ill.

Mass approaches to disease control and health
promotion have been documented to have success varying
from great to realtively small. They include
sanitation, food and water technologies, health
education, accident control and numerous others.
Obviously, such mass approaches have not reached a
level of success sufficient to replace the need for
individualized scheduled services. But they can
greatly reduce the intensity of services needed by the
population as a whole because of the better health
statuses among numerous individuals therein. In less
developed countries with limited resources, mass
approaches are by far the most cost effective initial
steps.

Mass approaches should include correction of scioeconomic factors leading to problems like malnutrition and obviously should be a first priority. Combating the whole impact of poverty, relative and absolute, in the social and cultural context of the cohort in question may be the most important of all mass approaches.

In spite of much activity in health education as a mass approach to the control of the major causes of morbidity and mortality in a country at the level of development presently enjoyed by the U.S.A., there is little agreement as to its worth and content. Epidemiologic studies have defined predictors of much morbidity in a variety of behaviors, habits, occupational exposures, urban atmospheres, etc. In the last decade, a beginning has been made to approach the control of these through educational programs but these are preliminary attempts and need evaluation. In the area of social pathologies such as child abuse and neglect the programs are even less well developed.

Much of the improvement in health status achieved in the last decade has been associated with markedly increased intensity of provision of direct services from highly trained providers to individuals. The model which has evolved around the use of remedial services to prevent or delay premature deaths has become increasingly expensive as the nature of the diseases has shifted toward progressive chronic deterioration and great complexity. The appropriate responses to their more manifest stages have become based upon technologies which similarly have become quite complex.

Even though in some areas the technologies are being simplified and becoming more acceptable to the patient, costs are still increasing at a rate that is straining other societal activities. In addition, there is a problem of lack of uniform access to the system which provides individualized services. Many of the technologies successfully used earlier to control some types of deaths in the developed countries are proving to be inadequate in other areas. Often, cultural and socioeconomic factors are impediments to their application. Persistence of the problem of premature deaths is a correlate of lower socioeconomic status in all populations available for study, whether whole nations or sub-classes within the more technically developed countries.

Thus the implication which results from analysis of populations, even those with the most favorable situation, is that the present service package is inadequate and/or inadequately applied to achieve a level of health which individual experimental and field studies suggest as potentially feasible for individuals in all populations. In fact, health problems are still so extensive in each country that provision of appropriate services is a major drain on resources. Even among the most affluent countries in which other necessities such as food, shelter and education are satisfactorily provided, the cost of an optimal service package based on current knowledge and/or operating system is more than can be allocated. There is no indication that either those receiving services or those providing them are satisfied with the overall situation.

Need for Change

This lack of satisfaction calls for change. In my opinion this should be qualitative and not just more of the same kind of expansion of technologies which has recently been predominant.

The history of the development of appropriate services to date has been one of a simultaneous expansion of available technologies (covering an ever widening number of problems) and an increased depth of understanding of the clinical problems. Because of the very large number and variety of conditions involved, the sum of the expansions of services has greatly exceeded reductions from areas where new services have replaced complex and expensive methods, i.e., immunization for poliomyelitis versus hospital care. Only in one area, smallpox, has the need for services been entirely eliminated. Services are furnished by individuals with various levels of training in many separate disciplines, individually or in groups. The expansion of services has therefore been accomplished by a qualitative and quantitative expansion of the manpower pool. This has for the most part been a haphazard process. Until recently shortages were perceived in almost all fields, hence, there was little consensus about the need for making the process more precise.

The lead sciences in the definition of the health statuses and appropriate services to meet the deficiencies have been the biologic sciences supported

11

by the physical, chemical and mathematical fields, but the catalogue of present problems now requires a change. The forces which have driven the changes in health status to their present state have been conditioned by the biases of those who have participated. Therefore, most of the residual problems are dominated by needs for new insights that may be brought to bear by a science such as anthropology and its clinical derivative. The contents of this volume make crystal clear that need. For example, the vigorous study of alcoholism is overdue. It requires more than the biologic sciences have had to offer. Yet it is only a small part of the total life style factor in health and disease, the understanding of which is rooted in the sciences studying man's behavior, culture and social structure. Thus, there is now a need to bring in the whole range of the sciences which have the capacities and information base to lead in the closing of the remaining service-health status gap.

The biologic sciences entered the health field essentially on their own initiative and achieved a spread of activities ranging from providing the theoretical constructs needed for understanding processes, including those functioning sub-optimally to those demonstrating ways of quantifying these processes and establishing the effects of remedial actions. In the same way, other sciences must bring to bear their entire capabilities over an equally broad range of health related activities. They should be invited in but, even if not, they should enter the field on their own initiative as they seem to be doing.

Recent critical analyses by the Office of the Surgeon General of the United States (1979, 1980) provide good catalogues of the needs for anthroplogists, along with their sister or brother social and behavioral scientists, to enter the health field on their own initiative. While there has been some effort to invite them into provider efforts, the terms have been restrictive. Nevertheless, a significant group of scientists are spontaneously entering the field. From this study, it appears to be a two way street. Providers in conventional medical areas are seeking new insights by using anthropological methods, and anthroplogists are directly applying their insights to some highly specific health and disease problems. This is a most logical outgrowth of the present health status globally and, specifically, in the United States.

12

Its essence is the attainment of both longevity and functional capacity throughout life, at a cost societies can bear. This brings with it resolving the many social problems of new age structures and longer work lives. It mandates, in essence, a new paradigm of health services.

The need is like a vacuum; it will be filled. The sooner the better.

Summary

Provision of health care in its present form has produced a health status in the public which is increasingly refractive to further improvement based upon the biologic sciences alone.

A major deficiency has been the small scale of involvement of the behavioral and social sciences in health services design and provision, even though most of the need is generated by social and behavioral problems impacting on health statuses. The problems of aging further accentuate the need. Because of historical omissions there is need now to expand the numbers and scope of professionals from these sciences avaialable to health care. Anthropologists are particularly needed and their entry into the health field is not only welcome but imperative. Existing health care providers, particularly physicians, should support, encourage and even demand the expansion of these professions so that together they can tackle the major problems. The information in this book will facilitate the understandings needed to bring about these changes.

NOTE

1. The data presented on the prevalence of symptoms
    and disease are summarized from a study of 10,000
    "healthy" persons in Alameda County, California, in
    1972 by Lester Breslaw, M.D. and associates.

REFERENCES

Chicago Board of Health
    1966   Medical Care Report: Preliminary Report on
            Patterns of Medical and Health Care in
            Poverty Areas of Chicago, prepared by Mark H.
            Lepper, M.D., and Joyce Lashof, M.D.
            Chicago: Office of the Mayor.

Culter, Richard G.
    1976   Nature of Aging and Life Maintenance
            Processes. Interdisciplinary Topics in
            Gerontology 9: 83-113.

Dever, G.E.A.
    1980   Holistic Health--An Epidemiological Model for
            Policy Analysis in Community Health Analyses.
            Germantown, MD: Aspen Systems Corporation.

Surgeon General of the U.S.
    1979   Healthy People. Washington, D.C.: Department
            of Health and Human Services.

    1980   Promoting Health, Preventing Diseases.
            Objectives for the Nation. Washington, D.C.:
            Department of Health and Human Services.

World Health Organization
    1966   Constitution of the World Health
            Organization, 1948. In Basic Documents of
            the World Health Organization. Geneva,
            Switzerland.

THE FUTURE DEVELOPMENT AND ROLE OF CLINICAL ANTHROPOLOGY--THE PERSPECTIVES OF A MEDICAL EDUCATOR

Harold M. Swartz

This essay is written with some trepidation because I am so clearly distant from clinical anthropology, distant in both theory and practice--and yet I am attempting to write about the potentials and limitations of this still-to-be-defined field. But I shall approach my task with the same fatalism that has allowed me to persist in the unsettling world of administration in medical education and shall, in fact, rely in great part on the perspectives that come from that field. I also write from three other, interrelated perspectives which I feel may be relevant to this task: clinician (I have spent part of eight years in general practice and several more in specialty practice in Nuclear Medicine), biophysicist and researcher. Each of these provides me with some insight into both the potential for, and limitations of, clinical anthropology. I will first consider clinical anthropology from these four viewpoints and then provide a summary of what I see as the critical issues affecting the future development of this field.

The Viewpoint of the Medical Educator

First, from the viewpoint of a medical educator, I believe that we are only beginning to realize the full potential of the contributions of the social sciences and humanities to the practice of medicine. A number of medical schools, including ours (University of Illinois College of Medicine, Urbana, Illinois), are spending more time and paying more attention to the systematic inclusion of these fields into the basic education of medical students. This is occurring because of the increasing awareness of the impact of social factors on the diagnosis and treatment of individual patients and the organization of the entire health care delivery system. A simple but perhaps convincing argument for the increasing recognition of the role of these fields is the table of contents of prominent medical journals such as the New England Journal of Medicine (NEJM). My own classification of the contents of the last six months of the NEJM

15

indicates that topics ordinarily considered social sciences or humanities play a prominent role in 25% of the major articles and 50% of the editorials of this journal (NEJM, Volume 305, 1981). At our own medical school our faculty have become convinced of the need 1) to provide a systematic education for our students in these areas and 2) to initiate and encourage inter-disciplinary research by faculty and students to expand our knowledge in these areas. Our educational program now includes a series of approximately 25 two-hour seminars devoted to "sociomedical" topics such as the impact of organizational factors on health care delivery, ethics and medicine, law and medicine, health economics, etc. The principal exposure to these topics, however, occurs in an eight-week full-time course required for all medical students. In this course various aspects of "sociomedicine" are studied intensively without the distractions of any other courses. In one component of the course the students consider the sociomedical disciplines in the context of one or two particular diseases, e.g., end-stage renal disease, in which students study the ethical, economic, cultural, legal, political, and other aspects of patients requiring long-term kidney dialysis. At the faculty level we have initiated an interdisciplinary "Health and Society Faculty Development Seminar" in which faculty from various departments have an active exchange of disciplinary perspectives and research in the interfaces of clinical medicine, social sciences, and humanities. The goal of this interchange is to develop interdisciplinary research and teaching that have solid bases in both medicine and traditional university disciplines such as anthropology. It is from this viewpoint, then, that I view the potential contributions of clinical anthropology with considerable enthusiasm. Clearly, there are major contributions that can be made by the deliberate application of the concepts and methodology of anthropology to medical problems. Because of this viewpoint I welcomed Professor Shimkin's and Dr. Golde's efforts in organizing the symposium that gave rise to this book. But, as indicated in the remarks that follow, my enthusiasm and appreciation for the emerging field of clinical anthropology force me to look critically at its proposed focus and form, because it seems quite possible for the participants in this field to go off in directions that may be unproductive or even counter-productive. My considerations are influenced by the fact that I anticipate that the physician will remain at the center of the actual delivery of health care and that the other individuals now involved in day-to-day care of the patient (i.e., nurses, allied health occupations, social workers, and clinical psychologists) will retain or even moderately increase their roles. In order for these individuals to interact optimally with patients they need to develop better understanding of the factors that affect an individual's perception of and response to health, illness, and therapy. It follows then, that as a medical educator, a critical aspect of my judgment of the value of clinical anthropology is the extent to which experts in this field can increase the understanding and use of anthropological concepts in the activities of traditional providers of health care.

The Potential Contributions of Clinical Anthropolgy to the Clinician

As a clinician, especially with the advantages of hindsight and the benefits of association with colleagues in the humanities and social sciences, I also see great potential for the field of clinical anthropology. We have only begun to scratch the surface of understanding the influence of the patient's (and the doctor's!) cultural background on the eitiology, development and therapy of illness. The examples provided in other chapters in this book point out the potential impact of cultural background on a patient's understanding of disease and the proposed treatment, and the impact that these understandings have on the patient's cooperation and response to the diagnostic and therapeutic measures employed by the health care practitioners. The examples are usually based on dramatic differences in cultural background and language, for instance patients from the West Indies whose perception of the etiology of disease is based on Voodoo and therefore whose interactions with the health care system are effective only when these beliefs are taken into account. The fact that in this example we clinicians needed clinical anthropologists to make us understand why our attempts to communicate were ineffective indicates some profound gaps in contemporary medical education and clinical thought processes. Here certainly is a fertile ground for important roles of clinical anthropologists in the education and socialization of physicians. Ideally, the involvement of clinical anthropologists would be in the early stages of the medical education process--so that the awareness of the clinical implications of

17

different cultural backgrounds becomes built into the regular thinking processes of physicians.

Nevertheless, the vast majority of patients in this country are not from cultures with concepts of disease and therapy that are so obviously and radically different from ours. Consequently a focus on examples involving exotic differences can have the negative connotation that the insights of clinical anthropology are limited to such unusual and special situations and irrelevant to most clinical practice. But the participants in the symposium also alluded to a much more extensive set of cultural differences (or more properly, subcultural differences) which are encountered more often in modern clinical practice in the United States: the cultural patterns of drug addicts, alcoholics and alcohol abusers, migrant workers, certain religious groups, various minorities, etc. Because these subcultures include components with significant implications for health and disease, these differences provide very fertile grounds for clinical anthropologists to find both teaching and research opportunities. The analytic bibliographic review prepared by Borooah and Clark in the Appendix provides information on many of the extant studies.

Virtually all health care professionals will deal with at least some of the above subcultural segments of America, and therefore the need for the clinical anthropologist is more substantive than may appear at first glance. But, in fact, I believe that considerations of the distinctive subcultures described above only begin to touch the potential contributions of the clinical anthropologist to help health professionals understand the cultural environment of their patients. Even within the "homogeneous" middle classes of the United States there are profound but often unrecognized strong cultural differences that affect the perception of disease (e.g., is high blood pressure a "real" disease?), the response to diagnostic procedures (e.g., varying concepts of privacy and modesty), the response to medical history questions (e.g., what information is "proper" to disclose to or with which to "bother" a physician?), the response to dietary manipulations (e.g., the relative importance attributed to various foods and differences in the normal content of the patient's diet), the response to disease (e.g., for some individuals some diseases have strong moral implications) and the response to treatment (e.g., whether it is necessary to follow in detail all instructions on the taking of medications).

The more I think about these aspects, the greater and the more important it appears to me that we develop systematic understanding of the social factors that lead to and activate very different perceptions and responses in the area of health and disease. From my clinical perspective, I have observed significant cultural differences which affect the delivery of health care in a number of population groups, including: 1) rural populations compared to urban populations, 2) small children, who often develop within their circle of friends a complex and fairly definite set of concepts and expectations that differ in some important aspects from those of their parents, 3) teenagers, who seem to develop continually varying norms and expectations which significantly affect their perception of both the authority and content of the practice of medicine, and 4) males and females, especially when patients take extreme positions in their definition of the proper roles of women and men. Such a list compiled by an expert in this field, it seems, could go on and on.

I recognize that some of the differences I have mentioned involve aspects that are the province of sociologists and psychologists as well as anthropologists but it seems to me that we, in the health care profession, are especially lacking in expertise in the areas that are included in anthropology. We now have an excellent opportunity to eliminate this deficiency because there is a group of anthropologists who are openly offering to help us.

Clinical Anthropology--Problems of Definition

Turning to my viewpoint as a biophysicist, I can view clinical anthropology with the sympathy and understanding that comes to a member of another interdisciplinary academic specialty which has had to seek a generally accepted identity. Clinical anthropology is currently at a stage that biophysics occupied for a number of years--a stage in which there was no commonly agreed upon definition of the discipline or even delineation of the boundaries of potentially overlapping academic areas. In the case of biophysics this uncertain identity persisted for a number of years, leading to several negative effects. Although a large number of scientists identify themselves as biophysicists (e.g., the current membership of the American Biophysics Society is 3570 [Biophysical Society, Directory of Members, 1980]),

19

they have had reduced academic mobility because of the
limited number of formal departments of biophysics and
the vast differences among many of those departments.
Similarly the lack of a definition of biophysics has
limited recruitment of excellent graduate students into
biophysics departments and even into interdisciplinary
biophysics programs. This problem exists to some
extent even today, in spite of the general recognition
of the leading role of biophysical techniques and
biophysics in many of the most active and promising
biomedical research areas. As a biophysicist the
lesson to me is clear--if a new academic specialty
wishes to prosper it should define its boundaries as
soon as possible with as broad an agreement as
possible. I feel that this should be done even at the
risk of excluding from the new specialty some possible
areas of involvement. This means that some hard
choices need to be made and some potential members of
clinical anthropology lost. But the advantages of a
specialty with recognizable and agreed upon credentials
and areas of common knowledge should, in the long run,
result in a healthier and more productive discipline of
clinical anthropology. If any really pertinent areas
have been left out of the original boundaries, I
suspect that they can be brought in at a later date.

Wearing my hat as a researcher, it seems clear to
me that there are a large number of very promising
research areas in clinical anthropology. It is not
clear that this potential has been recognized as an
important aspect of clinical anthropology by all of
those who attended the Symposium. There is a wealth of
problems whose solutions will have practical as well as
theoretical implications and which therefore provide
opportunities to do research in applied areas of health
care. There is a tremendous amount of money, effort,
and emotional involvement in the health care system of
the United States. Clinical anthropologists have a
valuable and often unique way of viewing many aspects
of this system and can affect it profoundly by solid
research that demonstrates the validity of their
insights. I cannot think of a single major health
problem that would not benefit significantly from a
carefully documented analysis of how cultural factors
affect that problem--in its etiology, its course, its
management, and its social and economic implications
for the patient and family. In addition to education,
research seems to me to be the other major activity
that clinical anthropology should emphasize as it
defines its activities. In this way the new discipline
could make major contributions to the health care

system using a mechanism that is already in place and acceptable. If the research emphasis of clinical anthropology is focused on areas with significant clinical input and applications, the results of the research could have significant effects on the health care of virtually all individuals.

Conclusions

Based on the preceding brief considerations, on my observations of clinical anthropology and clinical anthropologists at the Symposium and, mostly, on my lack of inhibition at making such pronouncements on inadequate data, I offer the following conclusions and comments regarding the future of clinical anthropology:

1. The field has great potential for making valuable and sometimes unique contributions to health and health care.

2. It is properly distinguished and distinguishable from medical anthropology and other social sciences by virtue of its focus on using the concepts of anthropology to explain and suggest changes for the health care system and patients within the systems. A useful perspective may be obtained by comparing trends in anthropology with those of sociology (cf. Twaddle and Hessler 1977:25-26; Mechanic 1978:516-520). At this time Clinical Anthroplogy appears to encompass the perspectives and orientations analogous to Clinical Sociology and Sociology In Medicine, while Medical Anthropology is analogous to Sociology of Medicine.

3. The major contributions are likely to be in the areas of research, teaching and consultation. Virtually all health professions and health professionals would benefit greatly by having a more thorough understanding of how cultural factors affect health and illness. There also is a profound need for further research in this area, with an emphasis on those problems for which the results may have direct implications for the health care system.

4. The intensive involvement of clinical anthropologists in the actual delivery of health care on a one-to-one basis is an attractive seduction that I feel should be thoroughly

21

resisted. The health care field is already overpopulated with well meaning individuals with modest educations in specialized areas. The addition of individuals with the level of sophistication of a bachelor's or even an master's degree in clinical anthropology would add little but would have a very significant effect on the academic standing of clinical anthropology. The best way for clinical anthropologists to become involved effectively in clinical care is via teaching and consultation. The viewpoint of the clinical anthropologist needs to be incorporated in the education and attitudes of all health professionals via teaching by clinical anthropologists rather than by providing direct clinical care administered by the clinical anthropologist. Only rarely, and then most often in the context of a specialized and in-depth set of skills, developed by extensive postdoctoral training, will the clinical anthropologist be involved in direct medical care. The experience of Dr. Golde (Part II, this volume) appears to be a good example of the exceptional instance in which a clinical anthropologist has a strong direct involvement in actual delivery of health care. My interpretation of her activities is that her day-to-day involvement appears to involve skills and experience more parallel to clinical psychology, albeit clinical psychology with an unusuallly strong anthropological flavor. This appears to me to be a noteworthy exception rather than a prototype for many other prospective clinical anthropologists. Similarly, in my estimation, the most important contribution of anthropology to the Central Mississippi hypertension project was the establishment of the etiological role of cultural and social factors in the disease (Pt. III). When that project turned toward direct care of the residents, the anthropologists continued to play a significant role in advising the health care delivery team but they had no essential role in the actual delivery of the health care. I recognize that in regard to direct clinical involvement of clinical anthropologists, my views clearly contrast with those of some of the attendees of the Symposium. Professors Shimkin and Golde have effectively summarized the viewpoint of those who feel that involvement in direct clinical care is a viable option for clinical anthropologists, with a role that is parallel to that of social workers (D.B. Shimkin and P. Golde, Part VI, this volume).

5. While arguing that most clinical anthropologists should not have continuing direct involvement in the delivery of clinical care, I believe their education should include realistic and thorough exposure to clinical medicine. Even, or perhaps especially, because most clinical anthropologists will be located in a nonclinical setting, he or she should be cognizant of the health professional's subculture and work environment. This familiarity should be sufficiently extensive so that through the balance of his or her career, the clinical anthropologist will retain a realistic understanding of the limitations and challenges of the clinical setting. Recurrent exposure to clinical medicine should be a regular aspect of the careers of most clinical anthropologists.

6. Considerable attention and effort should be spent in delineating the field and arranging for educational programs of clearly defined quality. Emerging disciplines in the health care area have a very high probability of becoming a haven for the well-intentioned but poorly equipped person who has not achieved success in his or her own academic discipline. The potential for major contributions in clinical anthropology is too great to allow the field to become dominated by those who move into it because they cannot compete effectively in the parent field. There already are classical, excellent examples of successful clinical anthropology such as the Central Mississippi project. The future of the field is in well-educated, positively selected individuals pursuing similarly excellent projects in a thorough and scholarly manner.

Finally, I turn to a topic for which I am even less prepared than the preceding analyses--namely, my initial assignments to provide perspectives on today's and tomorrow's sociopolitical and intellectual climates as they bear on clinical anthropology. I believe we are going to have a rather long and painful period in which the contributions of newcomers to the health care field will be rigorously and critically scrutinized.

Concern abut rising cost of health care coupled with
concerns about a potential oversupply of physicians
will lead to an intensive scrutiny of any proposed
alterations in the health care system. I suspect that
in the context of cost-benefit analysis many of the
"innovative" approaches to complex medical and social
problems will fall into disfavor and that there will be
a swing back towards administration and domination of
health care by more traditional and conservative
approaches. If this forecast is correct, it will be a
special challenge to clinical anthropology to develop
and grow in this basically inhospitable climate. I
believe that it can do so because it has a valid and
valuable point of view to contribute. Whether it does
achieve this promise may depend to a great extent on
the willingness and ability of the leaders in this
field to establish it as an academically legitimate
specialty that produces excellent research and teaching
that somewhat remotely but effectively makes an impact
on clinical care.

REFERENCES

Mechanic, David
   1978   Medical Sociology. New York: MacMillan.

Twaddle, A.C. and R.M. Hessler
   1977   A Sociology of Health. St. Louis:
           C.V. Mosby.

PART II

CLINICAL ANTHROPOLOGY: SOME DIMENSIONS OF

AN EMERGING VOCATION

FOREWORD: CLINICAL ANTHROPOLGY
AS A COMMITTED VOCATION

Peggy Golde

Prologue

"Clinical: 1. pertaining to a clinic. 2. pertaining to direct observation and treatment of patients. 3. analytical, highly objective" (American Heritage Dictionary, 1969).

Taking a cue from the third meaning of clinical, "analytical and highly objective," we begin a definition of Clinical Anthropology with a consideration of its major modes of inquiry as scientific, replicable and based on the separation of a whole into its constituent parts. Many who call themselves clinical anthropologists work as therapists for people defined as needing help, or in the area of community health, while still others are involved in direct observations from which they draw conclusions. Though these researchers may seem to function as academic anthropologists, their interest is motivated chiefly by the wish to do preventive intervention that ultimately results from the implications of their researches. It is this motivation, this commitment to immediate or longer range outcomes in health, joined with the rigor of a strong research orientation that distinguishes the emerging area of Clinical Anthropology.

Applied anthropology, the wedding of two sets of goals--pure research and direct offers to help those who ask--is asserting its moral claim in the present state of the world. Pure, untarnished research has come to be too great a luxury, I believe, in the face of the need to "educate" the uneducated and to help the helpless and impotent. Each prospective student of Clinical Anthropology will have, in my opinion, to evaluate where he or she stands on a continuum of commitment to a therapeutic or helping role or some combination of research and interventive activity. At the very least, an assessment will have to be made about what constitutes a meaningful life-work.

It must have struck others, as it has me, that the word "care" has many synonyms--not all of equivalent meaning--from "painstaking or watchful attention" as "under a doctor's care," to having affection or interest as in "to care for." The word, despite its several connotations, is an apt noun-verb to describe the essence of clnical anthropology, a specialization in which people do more than study or research--they attempt to intervene actively in some helpful way, to express "caring" through doing.

Clinical Anthropology as Communication and Role Taking

The papers that follow sample a broad spectrum from research to active therapy. They may be classified as follows, in terms of major topic and relatedness to Clinical Anthropology:

1. Primarily research, setting the stage for what follows (Gern and Shimkin);

2. Primarily research on maternal and child health (Shain et al.).

3. Anthropological contributions to counselling and psychotherapy (Golde);

4. Counselling from a social worker's cross-cultural perspective (Alter);

5. Reaching those in need through organizing individuals with problems, illness or addictions (Borman); and

6. Using social anthropology to improve medical outreach in a highly differentiated, multi-ethnic population (Weidman).

By chance, the papers represent a range of different work settings: medical school and university, community agency, and private practice in the home. Other clinical anthropologists work in a variety of government agencies and programs, community mental health clinics and other non-academic positions. Despite the diversity that is shown, these few papers cannot adequately represent the diversity that we know exists. For example, we had no paper to represent the important area of trauma and rehabilitation.

What is compelling is that these unrelated and
varied papers share a common attribute: they all
demostrate the paramount importance of
"communication"--to be understood, to send clear
messages, the difficultly of achieving clarity when
there are myriad ways of perceiving reality. It might
be argued that any six papers written by social
scientists would share the same commonality. Maybe,
maybe not. Though all the papers were written
ultimately to be read, not heard, we suggest that
clinical anthropologists have become "rainmakers," not
in the sense of being charlatans, but in the importance
placed on being able to talk, convince, persuade,
create in others faith in their effectiveness,
experience, and conviction of what they espouse. Part
of this is done by the example of their life
commitment, part by the sincerity they convey, and part
by attempting something new.

Some, the therapists in particular, need to be
especially good at this type of interaction. Others,
who are teachers or organizers or researchers, need to
go to the heart of understanding others so they can
tailor their communications to seem artless yet be
immediately understood. This is particularly
challenging when working with people from other
cultures or age groups. The best communicators must
first be consummate actors. The essence of clear
exchange must be what George Herbert Mead (1934:256-7)
called "taking the role of the other."

Hugh Dalziel Duncan (1962), an insightful
sociologist, has written about "the emergence of the
self" in Mead's work. As he interprets Mead, social
life is described as if it were a game with rules,
predictable responses and inevitable conflicts. When
he describes the role of the umpire who is "given power
to make decisions which preserve the organic relations
between players," my mind saw a close parallel to the
role of the marriage counselor. Duncan also refers to
the umpire as the actor whose role personifies the
"generalized other," reminding us the "the umpire does
not create rules, he applies them" (op. cit., p. 78).

As Duncan interprets him, Mead believes "the self
and society originates and develops in communication,"
and we all come to understand each other through the
process of sociation. Then, writing of some
generalized individual, Duncan adds: "for when he
speaks he hears his own words and thus learns what
words mean because he can observe how they affect
others as well as how they affect him" (ibid, p. 79).

Let me continue my consideration of Mead through his own words (Straus 1956:218). He explains that social expressions of intelligence depend on the given individual's "ability to take the roles of or put himself in the place of other individuals implicated with him in given social situations . . . the nature of intelligence is social to the very core . . . putting one's self in the place of others."

Duncan (1962:96) explicates Mead's position: "taking the role of others is the characteristic human act of communication, for only in role taking do we take into account the attitudes of others toward us and toward the situation we share." Duncan comments, "certainly his [Mead's] concept of communication as the process in which the self and society emerge is one of our greatest contributions to social thought" (ibid., p. 103).

I have been using the ideas of George Herbert Mead, almost a half century old yet still fresh, to highlight what I found common in the papers below. I am also struck that Mead intended communication to be understood not as any actual verbal exchanges, but as the countless acts of perception and imagination that make up the experience of being acculturated into a human society.

I have made this extended excursion to stress that the critical concept of clinical anthropology, whether in one-to-one therapy, or community health, or research, is interaction, in behavior and in cognition. Also, it is important to point out that the basic assumptions of clinical anthropologists—and of many other applied anthropologists as well—are current expressions of American philosophical and scientific pragmatism. By re-examining the thoughts of George Herbert Mead, Louis Wirth, John Dewey and others, there can be both a clarification of shared assumptions and an intellectual stimulus through contact with these creative and committed minds of the living past.

What Clinical Anthropologists Do--
A Review of the Papers

Let me now turn, having outlined my general point of view, to a more detailed consideration of the papers that follow.

Gern and Shimkin

"Clinical Anthropology and Clinical Anthropologists, A Preliminary Survey," by Robert Gern and Demitri B. Shimkin, is a mapping of this emerging field, based on responses from perhaps a quarter of the nation's clinical anthropologists. An earlier version of some results has been published in Golde and Shimkin (1980).

The factual materials of this paper are extensive; here I want to point out only the major areas of clinical anthropology which emerged from the survey. Over a quarter of the clinical anthropologists are in community health and social epidemiology. Nearly as many are in mental health and counselling. The third largest category is chronic disease, trauma, and rehabilitation; the fourth, maternal health and child development. Small numbers of clinical anthropologists are in many other areas.

Shain, Miller, Shepard, Dalterio, and Asch

"Cultural Dimensions in Obstetrics, Gynecology and Neonatology," a joint effort from the Department of Obstetrics and Gynecology of the University of Texas Health Center in San Antonio, is a model of anthropologically informed clinical research. In both problems considered, female tubal ligation and the developmental effects of fetal marijuana exposure, the critical fact is the inability of physicians to provide full and reliable information regarding consequences to patients. The specific elements involved are complementary. In tubal ligation, it is essential to define the range of psychosexual consequences of an act that, while physically minor, impinges upon truly basic values and inter-relationships between couples. In marijuana use, the need is to know what danger it may or may not pose to the child, and to advise the mother accurately and responsibly.

I wish to stress the excellence of Rochelle Shain's research design. In 1980 she, Miller and Shepard designed a controlled prospective study with two

31

control groups--something rarely done. One group was women who had completed their child bearing and had no immediate plans for drastic medical measures, and the other a group of wives of vasectomy patients. Also, the combination of an anthropologist, psychiatrist and gynecologist has provided the best of two worlds: anthropological field work and the viewpoints of clinicians accustomed to think from the perspective of individual patients. The field work considered the "fields" of obstetricians' and gynecologists' offices as well as vasectomy clinics.

Golde

My own paper, "Anthropological Contributions to Psychotherapy, An Overview," attempts to analyze and present the basic features of an approach to mental health which has arisen particularly from the work of Gregory Bateson and Virginia Satir. This formulation I have also found to be the most compatible with developments in clinical social work, an area in which I received my training as a Marriage, Family and Child Counselor. In general terms, the paper illustrates some tenets of a major area of clinical anthropology, especially from the viewpoint of a private practitioner.

In addition to these formal remarks, I need to communicate at this point my deep satisfaction and my optimism in my chosen work. In 1975, when I was licensed as a Counselor, Clinical Anthropology did not exist as a meaningful field. Today, as our studies and my personal experience have shown, there is both increasing interest and entry into the field. People not only say it is a good thing to do; many--relatively speaking--are now being trained to do it.

What is most important to me here is that this emergence is far more than a simple response to a poor academic job market. I think it reflects a high valuation of health, mental and physical, in American society. But I feel it also expresses a growth of motivations within anthropology, motivations that appear to have long been submerged in our discipline's mainstream, but which are very meaningful to me, to do good, to be helpful, to create some new therapeutic mode for a wide range of human distress.

Alter

"A Case of Child Medical Neglect and a Plea for Interdisciplinary Research," by Catherine Alter, exemplifies her social work training, albeit from a cross-cultural perspective. Having been trained in a social work agency myself, much of the philosophy, values and techniques of that training have rubbed off on my perceptions and methods. What is so special about Alter's casework role is how neatly it fitted into our thinking when this conference was first organized. Her focal example, the choice of problem to illustrate and her viewpoint were entirely hers before she heard the other papers in this section on Clinical Anthropology. Her paper sharply demonstrates how communication about a client is affected by the stereotypical perceptions of helping persons or agencies. Communication is not only through words but by means of symbolic acts; what the client is trying to communicate through the nature of her problems with her children, her inadequate "caring" behavior and through being overwhelmed by the demands being made on her. Professionals, whether or not they had been trained in cross-cultural perspectives, would undoubtedly judge the client to be an inadequate coper on the one hand, but deprived of adequate support, affection and reassurance from the outside world, on the other.

Clinical Anthropology is a specialization in which people express or exhibit their underlying care for others; Alters's paper reveals the same fundamental concern. She is aware of the mistakes made by people trained primarily to appreciate individual differences but unaware of cultural differences. Both can be powerful influences in shaping values and behavior. Her point of view recognizes that culture is not just an abstract concept standing for a multiplicity of beliefs. It is a concept that embraces how a whole group reacts to stress, attempts to solve problems and may even fail in specific ways.

Borman

Moving now to a more community-oriented paper, Leonard B. Borman's "Self-Help Groups, Professionals, and the Redefinition of Pathological States" deals with groups of people confronting sets of individual problems or afflictions. From what he has written, I would strongly support the position of Integrity, a group that views personal disturbance in terms of interpersonal relations.

33

Borman provides a useful enumeration of "helping mechanisms" that operate in the group situations he has observed: the shared feelings of universality and acceptance; the voluntary nature of these groups; an element of altruism in helping others (something I have seen among clinical anthropologists too); and the sharing of a "relatively fixed community of belief."

His analysis of the ways professionals have played a role in these self-help groups is particularly insightful:

1. Some took issue with existing theories and formulated new concepts.

2. Many altered the "specification of the condition or affliction."

3. They utilized a wider repertoire of skills and techniques.

4. And refocused on stages overlooked by their colleagues.

5. They were concerned with populations usually neglected by conventional service delivery systems.

6. They created new roles for themselves as professionals.

7. And they have gone beyond conventional boundaries in supporting new auspices that were more relaxed than traditional, institutional settings.

This list echoes the conclusions in Thomas S. Kuhn's book, The Structure of Scientific Revolutions (Kuhn 1962). Both Borman and Kuhn call attention to cultural blind spots or, if you will, culturally induced inhibitions of creativity. Borman himself has made a major sociocultural contribution by recognizing a process while it was still just a process and furthering its growth as a genuine social movement of international scope.

Weidman

The last paper, "Research, Service and Training Aspects of Clinical Anthropology: An Institutional Overview," by Hazel Weidman reveals her singular role

34

in anthropology as the creative force that first organized the subfield of Medical Anthropology. She is playing a similar role in the development of Clinical Anthropology because of a dual skill: perceiving an unmet need and having the forbearance, ability and dedication to organize professionals who share interests and goals. Though she does little direct therapy, most of her daily activities involve communication--with patients, students, members of several departments in the university, and representatives of different cultural groups who have immigrated to Miami.

She is a "compleat" anthropologist engaged in studying the multiplicity of nearby ethnic groups each with its own language and health belief systems. She is looking at the nature of the relationship between ethnicity and health in five particular groups in Miami, studying people's pains, symptoms, definitions of disease and differences in the way symptoms are organized.

Even when this diversity is organized by a model for the community mental health program, it is a staggering feat to contemplate "full comprehension of the types of transactions between ethnic patient and orthodox practitioner that would be required to achieve full comprehension and communication about health problems . . . "

Clarification can be accomplished through four concepts: culture, health culture, co-culture and culture brokerage, which are interlocking keys to understanding the service program she has created.

What is particularly important is that this is research with a clear social purpose--to improve access to adequate medical care for poor and often confused people. The use of terms drawn from these very populations assures both acceptance and the validity of effective interactions and feedback.

My earlier remarks specifying "communication" as the unifying feature in these six presentations are made even more vivid when Weidman details the many settings in which she actively communicates: discussions at faculty meetings, interviews of patients in their homes which are videotaped for later training purposes, consultation in groups of health educators, exchanges in social science units or among nursing faculty.

Apposite to what has been said earlier in this section is her description of role playing which, in my terms, exhibits the "drama" of acting: displaying through the imagination of the actor/"role player" what has been understood and what still requires futher communication to others.

This final paper presents and represents twelve years of clinical anthropological activities that have evolved into an ideal program of teaching, research, supervision and the promotion of mental health. Not the least of her contributions is the informed, preventive practices that can be seen as giant shadows cast by all her other activities.

REFERENCES

American Heritage Dictionary
   1969   New York: Dell Publishing Company.

Duncan, Hugh D.
   1962   Communication and Social Order. New York:
            Oxford University Press.

Golde, Peggy and Demitri B. Shimkin
   1980   Clinical Anthropology--An Emerging Health
            Profession? Medical Anthropology Newsletter
            12:15-16.

Kuhn, Thomas S.
   1962   The Structure of Scientific Revolutions.
            Chicago: University of Chicago Press.

Mead, George Herbert
   1934   Mind, Self and Society From the Standpoint of
            a Social Behaviorist. Chicago: University of
            Chicago Press.

Strauss, Anselm
   1956   The Social Psychology of George Herbert Mead.
            Chicago: University of Chicago Press.

CLINICAL ANTHROPOLOGY AND CLINICAL ANTHROPLOGISTS:
A PRELIMINARY SURVEY

Robert Gern and Demitri B. Shimkin,
with the assistance of Richard W. Thompson

Background

In July 1979, Drs. Peggy Golde and Demitri Shimkin initiated a systematic assessment of Clinical Anthropology as part of the assignment of the Committee on Anthropology for the Future of the Society for Applied Anthropology (Shimkin, Tax and Morrison 1978; Shimkin and Tax 1979). This assessment was designed to clarify the status and potentials of a new area of anthropological activity on which data were very scarce but which appeared to have genuine significance for the usefulness of anthropology in both developed and developing countries.

The letter of instruction to Dr. Golde (Shimkin 1979) asked that the assessment include " . . . the scope, current status, conceptual framework, problems and potentials of Clinical Anthropology, that is, the use of anthropological approaces to problem solving, therapy and the development of competence for client individuals and families. This assessment should be developed in the broadest possible international frame of reference . . ."

A key part of this project included a survey of clinical anthropologists and their activities and ideas.

We encountered some difficulties in gaining resources for this effort. Funding from the Division of Associated Health Professions, Bureau of Health Manpower (Department of Health, Education and Welfare), was unsuccessful, although a proposal had been encouraged by that agency. The National Institute of Mental Health also proved to be indifferent. Finally, very modest funds were awarded in the Spring of 1980, as part of a more general investigation of the clinical applications of the social sciences by the Office of Interdisciplinary Projects and Studies of the University of Illinois at Urbana-Champaign.

The Survey Instrument

To identify clinical anthropologists and to gain from them key ideas about the field and their interest in participating in a cooperative effort of exploration and possible development, Shimkin and Golde developed a thirty-question instrument. Its major parts include name and address; professional self-identification and nature of clinical activities engaged in; type and place of employment; anthropological and health training and licensure; publications of clinical relevance; ideas about clinical anthropology; possible participation in cooperative efforts; and, to facilitate the organization of workshops and joint activities, professional meetings attended and clinical field(s) of specialization. In this instrument, we deliberately chose an open-ended formulation, so that a full range of responses could be secured. While this required laborious reworking into 111 computer variables, it produced many answers that had not been anticipated. It should be noted that the instrument deliberately omitted a variety of questions, such as those on age and income, which were felt to be intrusive and extraneous.

It may be of interest to state the five questions on "Your ideas about Clinical Anthropology." They included:

1. What is it?

2. What does it contribute practically?

3. What does it contribute intellectually?

4. What do you feel is your role in this field?

5. What are the needs of Clinical Anthropology?

Survey Procedures

In conducting this survey, the essential problems were to identify potential respondents, and to gain their cooperation in a joint activity. Because Clinical Anthropology is at most an emergent activity or specialization, the processes of identification and elicitation of responses were visualized as continuing over a considerable period of time. They included workshops, published reports, distributed rosters, and renewed cycles of response.

The keys to our survey were the kind cooperation of professional anthropological groups, especially the American Anthropological Association, the Society for Medical Anthropology and the Society for Applied Anthropology (S.F.A.A.), in publishing in the Spring of 1980 a statement by Golde and Shimkin on the study of clinical anthropology and in providing rosters of possible respondents to the survey. About 900 names were placed on our list, which did not cover such important groups as the Council on Nursing and Anthropology. In addition, a workshop on clinical anthropology was held in March, 1980, at the S.F.A.A. meetings in Denver, and another in Washington, D.C. in December, 1980, at the joint meetings of the American Anthropological Association and the Society for Medical Anthropology. A report on our findings has been published in the November issue of the Medical Anthropology Newsletter (Golde and Shimkin 1980).

Such publicity was augmented by referrals through personal networks, with most of our respondents suggesting one or several persons to be contacted. This had been especially important because of the mobility of young anthropologists, which makes society rosters quickly obsolete, and because of the high efficiency of personal referrals in gaining responses.

The findings that follow came from 122 questionnaires returned up to October 1, 1980. About 400 letters had been sent out up to that date, sampling almost half of our reference panel. Assuming that we achieved a 50 percent response rate, it is our working estimate that the national number of graduated professionals active in all areas of clinical anthropology in 1980 was about 500. This estimate does not include students, foreign anthropologists or health professionals with secondary interests in anthropology, e.g., cross-cultural psychiatrists.

Findings

Our questionnaire breaks itself logically into four basic sections. The first is the background and self-description of the respondents, while the second gives information concerning their training. The third deals with the nature and status of Clinical Anthropology, while the fourth gives some general characteristics of the population of respondents.

Who do the respondents feel they are, with what do
they affiliate, and do they intend to participate
further in a cooperative project in Clinical
Anthropology? Among our respondents the distribution
of professional self-identifications was as follows:

Anthropologists 80.5%

    Including: clinical   36.5%

               medical   22.0%

               cultural   8.5%

               biological
                 specialities   7.6%

               other   5.9%

Health specialists (M.D., nurses, other) . 10.2%

Psychologists and others 9.3%

As far as affiliation with professional societies was
concerned, 57 percent of all respondents attended
meetings of the American Anthropological Association.
Also, and with much overlap, 28 percent affiliated with
the Society for Applied Anthropology. Other
anthropological groups such as the American Association
of Physical Anthropologists and the South West
Anthropological Association attracted about 9 percent
of the respondents each. The American Psychological
Association accounted for a similar percentage. On the
question of further participation in a cooperative
project in Clinical Anthropology, 80 percent said
"yes."

     Let us now turn to questions concerning the level
and pattern of training and professional activity,
specialization, and clinically relevant publications.
The largest category of employment was at a university
or college--40 percent of all respondents. Twenty-four
percent of the respondents worked primarily at a
teaching hospital or medical center at a university.
Other areas of work included private practice (10%),
government agencies or programs (11%), and other public
and private hospitals (8%). Eight percent of those
surveyed indicated that their primary occupation was as
a student in higher education.

40

Almost three-quarters (74%) of all respondents had a Ph.D. in some area of anthropology. Overall, 92 percent indicated some formal training in anthropology. Another very interesting point is when the respondents completed their most recent formal training in anthropology. Three-fourths graduated from 1971 to the present; 21 percent between 1956-1970, and only 5 percent prior to 1956. These figures do not indicate the youth of the participants--since many have gone back for additional or re-training--as much as they highlight the general recency of the development of Clinical Anthropology.

Training in clinical and health-related areas was broken into two categories; degrees in health fields, and specialized clinical training and/or certification. The first group consisted of Post-docs, Ph.D.´s, Masters, Bachelors, M.P.H., M.S.W., R.N., and M.D. degrees, and accounted for 39 percent of the total sample. The second group accounted for 28 percent of the respondents and included the following proportions of respondents in every category: 1) certified in psychiatry, psychoanalysis, and/or marriage, family, child, and sex counseling and therapy (10%); 2) trained but not certified in these fields (7%); and 3) trained with other hospital programs and clinical field experience (11%). Overall, 67 percent of all respondents had some form of specialized clinical health training. However, in contrast to degrees in anthropology, only 61 percent of all respondents who answered obtained their most recent training in health-related areas within the past decade. Virtually all others had gained the training in 1956-1970.

Four-fifths of the respondents answered the question on specialization of activities and interests, indicating an average of two areas each. The total responses had the following distributions:

25% in mental health and counseling services;

11% in maternal health and child development;

14% in chronic diseases, trauma, and rehabilitation;

26% in community health and social epidemiology; and

24% in all other areas.

41

The major areas of concern can be aggregated into those of primarily clinical orientation (the first three) and that of public health orientation (community health and social epidemiology).

Publications of clinical relevance showed a relatively modest output. Only 54 percent of the respondents indicated any publication dealing with clinical matters. This shows, as may have been expected, that this group of people is not primarily research oriented. And this brings us to a consideration of the orientations and prospects which people visualize for Clinical Anthropology.

When asked "What is it?" in reference to Clinical Anthropology, 58 percent of the responses included the idea that it involves some type of intervention in health care; in other words, a direct application of anthropological concepts in a clinical situation. One-fifth of those stressing intervention specifically mentioned counseling, consulting, or therapy as the preferred mode. On the other hand, only 20 percent of those replying thought that Clinical Anthropology should be defined primarily in terms of research.

Seventy percent of the respondents replied to the question: "What does Clinical Anthropology contribute intellectually?" The distribution of responses was as follows: the synthesis of research and application (34%), the understanding of cultural dimensions in health and illness (33%), a deeper understanding of change in holistic terms (17%), and improved communications between practitioners and patients (16%). The practical contributions of this field were seen to be closely related to the intellectual ones. Among the 80 percent of those who replied, the most frequent answer, given by one-third, was the reduction of barriers to the delivery and acceptance of health services. Seventeen percent of the respondents answering gave "expansion of knowledge of diseases and therapeutic approaches"; 14 percent, improved therapy through a better understanding of clients; 11 percent, interfacing between physicians' and patients' models of illness; 9 percent, integrating theory and practice; and 16 percent, all other answers.

Regarding the role respondents perceive themselves in vis-a-vis Clinical Anthropology, 24 percent of the respondents called themselves researchers. However, 40 percent were clinical practitioners. Another 29 percent felt their role to be that of a teacher or promoter of this interdisciplinary field. Seven percent were other or uncertain.

Answers about the needs of Clinical Anthropology were varied. In general, many people felt that the needs are multiple. Three-fourths of the sample answered, giving an average of two suggestions each. The distribution of responses was as follows:

32 percent called for what could be described as an identity search within the field. Mainly this calls for definition and description of what is and what is not Clinical Anthropology. This also includes legitimization professionally and publicly.

26 percent stressed the need for some form of communication through literature (i.e., journal, text, directory), workshops, conferences, or other direct contact.

16 percent emphasized training in clinical areas for social scientists and the creation and revision of certification programs and curricular positions in Clinical Anthropology.

5 percent stated that further research is among the principal needs of Clinical Anthropology.

21 percent were miscellaneous suggestions.

Finally, some general characteristics of the population surveyed may be of interest. Almost exactly half were men and half were women. In regard to residence, only 3 percent were from outside of the United States. Within this country, the respondents were widely distributed. Specifically, 13.9 percent came from New England; 9.6 percent from New York, New Jersey and Pennsylvania; 20.0 percent from the Midwest and Plains states; 11.3 percent from the South Atlantic states; 4.3 percent from Kentucky, Tennesse, Alabama and Mississippi; 6.9 percent from Arkansas, Louisiana, Oklahoma, and Texas; 6.9 percent from the Mountain states; and 27.0 percent from the Pacific coast, especially California.

Comparisons and Conclusions

This survey has elicited a clearly defined vocational pattern, Clinical Anthropology, from a sample of 122 respondents. The predominant characteristic of clinical anthropology is seen as intervention in health care, including counseling and therapy. Most of the respondents see their own roles to be in a service context, as practitioners or as intermediaries between patients and practitioners, or researchers and practitioners. They feel that clinical anthropology particularly contributes an intellectual and humanitarian orientation to health care.

In pursuit of their vocation, almost 40 percent of the clinical anthropologists have had a primary health degree, or post-doctoral training; another 28 percent have had specialized clinical training, largely in psychotherapy. But basically they are anthropologists, with three-fourths of the respondents holding the doctorate in that discipline. Finally, this group is new, although not necessarily young. Three-fourths of its members have received their highest level of training in anthropology, and over sixty percent in the health fields, only since 1971.

We believe that the total number of persons engaged in clinical anthropology, although not necessarily using that term, was about 500 in 1980. Perhaps half of them were members of anthropological organizations and the remainder affiliated with a variety of health professions, or were isolated. Our survey sample was large enough and of sufficiently diverse origin to be fairly representative.

Important contrasts arise when our data are compared with those of Michael Logan's (1979) survey of academic medical anthropologists. The population covered comprised 330 anthropologists listed in the 1976/77 American Anthropological Association Guide to Departments as having interests in medical anthropology or related subjects such as nutrition. A third of this group, or 112 persons, replied to an inquiry in September, 1978.

Of these medical anthropologists, 62 percent specialized in geographical areas outside of the United States and Canada. Topically, 54 percent were involved in ethnomedicine; 50 percent in the epidemiology and ecology of disease. Only 27 percent gave primary significance to applied anthropology or planned behavioral change. Moreover, while almost all felt that diet and nutrition should receive more attention, only a third were engaged in research in that field. Sixty-one percent urged more research in drugs and alcohol, but fewer than 5 percent were engaged in such work.

Only half of the medical anthropologists had ever worked in a medical setting or elsewhere outside academia; fewer than 5 percent wanted nonacademic employment full time.

Yet these medical anthropologists were critical of their own field. The majority felt that much more attention was need to nutrition and diet, fertility-related behavior, disease epidemiology and ecology, health of the elderly and American ethnic groups, and drug and alcohol abuse. A sizeable minority criticized publications in medical anthropology for lack of applied significance, esoteric orientation, and technical defects.

It appears to us that Clinical Anthropology, a few pioneers apart, is a new trend in anthropology and the health fields fostered by the somewhat older generation of academic medical anthropologists surveyed by Logan. Clinical anthropology is still small and insecure. Yet its promise bears serious investigation, its participants deserve active aid, because it is seeking to attack important human needs in innovative ways. It will unquestionably be a significant choice of younger anthropologists and of younger health workers, especially in Medicine and Nursing. With proper development, it could become an element of Anthropology for the Future--and of the health professions for the future. Such a development promises neither to be easy nor quick. But the potential benefits, particularly for the control of chronic diseases in developed countries and for community health in developing ones, as well as for the continued vitality of anthropology, justify the effort needed.

45

REFERENCES

Golde, Peggy, and Demitri B. Shimkin
  1980   Clinical Anthropology--An Emerging Health
           Profession? Medical Anthropology Newsletter
           12:15-16.

Logan, Michael
  1979   Directions of Research in Medical
           Anthropology: Implications Concerning
           Non-academic Employment. Medical
           Anthropology. Summer 1979:353-363.

Shimkin, Demitri B.
  1979   Letter to Dr. Peggy Golde, July 27, 1979 in
           re: Leadership in Assessment of Clinical
           Anthropology.

Shimkin, Demitri B. and Sol Tax
  1979   Anthropology for the Future: The Status and
           Prospects of a Program of International
           Cooperation. Human Organization 38:326-330.

Shimkin, Demitri B., Sol Tax and John W. Morrison
  1978   Anthropology for the Future. Research Report
           No. 4. Department of Anthropology. Urbana:
           University of Illinois.

46

CULTURAL DIMENSIONS IN OBSTETRICS, GYNECOLOGY AND NEONATOLOGY[1]

Rochelle N. Shain, Warren B. Miller,
Marguerite K. Shepard, Susan Dalterio
and Ricardo H. Asch

Introduction: Responses to Consumer Demand in Today's Obstetrics

Unlike most medical fields, obstetrics and gynecology provide certain services and products which are basically unrelated to treating illness or correcting or preventing deficiencies, notably those pertaining to family planning and routine obstetrical care. Although contraceptive use is medically indicated for women whose health would be endangered by an additional pregnancy, family planning is primarily a socioeconomic phenomenon. More so than in other areas, family planning patients are consumers: they select and purchase goods and services over which they have ultimate control. Compliance with a contraceptive regime is placed in their hands because pregnancy, the outcome of non-compliance, is not a disease state and, in the great majority of cases, is not life-threatening. Similarly, women with normal pregnancies are given responsibility for the outcomes of their behavior. They are told to avoid medication without consulting a physician, moderate or eliminate alcohol consumption and cigarette smoking, but otherwise to lead normal lives.

Although family planning and obstetrical care are included in the "Medical Model" within the United States, both areas are undergoing considerable change. Nurse practitioners are being successfully introduced into family planning services and it is not uncommon for nurses to supervise obstetric clinics without physician assistance. Some private physicians now employ nurses to supervise routine obstetric care whereas the physician attends only to high risk patients. Patients's feelings are being considered more and increasing numbers of physicians and hospitals are accommodating women who want to be awake, undergoing little or no anesthesia, during delivery. Provisions are also being made for the husband's presence in the delivery room; in fact, the father's presence at a Caesarian birth is no longer unheard of. Birthing rooms are becoming commonplace in many major

47

hospitals and a growing tide of resentment against the regular use of fetal monitoring equipment may soon diminish its popularity among obstetricians. In summary, both family planning and obstetrics are becoming less restrictive; women, in turn, have more choice in their care and treatment than they do in any other area of medicine.

Women's Informed Decisions:
Tubal Ligation and Marijuana Use as Cases

Whereas women are given greater freedom, they are not necessarily given sufficient information, particularly within their given individual and cultural contexts, to appropriately exercise that freedom.

Cases in point are contraceptive sterilization and marijuana use during pregnancy. These instances illustrate contrasting problems: the first is assessing the psychosocial consequences of a surgical intervention; the second is assessing the need for intervention in regard to a widespread personal practice. Physicians are unable to provide women with full information regarding the physical aftereffects of female tubal sterilization because, as will be discussed in greater detail later, there are no conclusive data. Information on the possible pyschosocial consequences of tubal sterilization, particularly relating to what the underlying meaning of sterilization may be for that particular woman in her particular culture, is not provided. First of all, this information is unavailable; most importantly however, tubal sterilization is commonly conceptualized by the medical profession as the burning, banding, or ligating of tubes, i.e., a mechanical change with no symbolic significance. While many patients undoubtedly also feel this way, others may feel very differently. In order to make an informed decision, women need to be apprised of the possible physical consequences of sterilization and to explore if and how the surgery may affect their self-concepts, particularly their feelings of wholeness and femininity. Moreover, the choice of tubal sterilization by a married woman involves a decision-making process with her spouse. Her husband may dominate the decision, may participate equally with her, may have a secondary role or none at all. The way this decision is handled may affect satisfaction or result in regret on the part of both spouses. It ultimately may affect the marriage itself.

The study of contraceptive (including sterilization) acceptability is becoming commonplace outside western cultures. We know why the female villagers of Bunkipur rejected the IUD (Marshall 1973) and why the villagers in a Mexican village (Shedlin 1977; Shedlin and Hollerbach 1978) rejected the pill in favor of the injectable medication. We also know that in some cultures vasectomy is believed to increase ones's strength, while in others it is thought to decrease it (Shain 1980). However, we know very little about the way men and women in our culture conceptualize underlying meanings of contraceptive use, particularly contraceptive sterilization.

The second issue discussed in this paper is marijuana use during pregnancy. Physicians can advise a woman not to smoke marijuana as they would advise her to abstain from any drug or substance that she abolutely does not require. However, there are no hard data to indicate that marijuana is actually harmful to the human fetus. In obtaining such data, it is important to consider the individual and cultural factors which contribute to a woman's smoking, the amount she smokes, why she smokes, the effects of smoking, the conflict she perceives regarding her smoking and her feelings toward pregnancy and motherhood in general. This type of information is necessary in order to offer culturally appropriate intervention mechanisms, should we or others find that in-utero exposure to marijuana has short or long-term adverse consequences for the child.

Contraceptive Sterilization

Surgical sterilization has been gaining increasing acceptance in the United States as an alternative method of contraception. Results of the National Fertility Studies conducted in 1965, 1970, and 1975 and the National Survey of Family Growth conducted in 1973 indicate that both the approval of contraceptive sterilization and its prevalence have risen. For example, among continuously married White women, contraceptive sterilization had been choosen by 31.5 percent of contracepting couples by 1975 (16.3 percent opted for female sterilization and 15.0 percent for vasectomy) compared to 22 percent in 1973, 14 percent in 1970, and 8.8 percent in 1965 (Westoff and Jones 1977). Futhermore, among contracepting couples who want no more children, 43.5 percent had selected surgical sterilization by 1975, compared to 31.9

percent in 1973, 20 percent in 1970, and 13.7 percent in 1965. The oral contraceptive, in contrast, was adopted by only 24.1 percent of these couples in 1975 (ibid.).

Despite the increasing demand for tubal sterilization, there is a dearth of well-founded data regarding the long-term physical and psychosocial consequences of this surgery. Some information is available; however, it is either incomplete or is the result of poorly designed research.

Physical Aftereffects

The two major physical aftereffects that have been attributed to tubal sterilization are intermenstrual or increased menstrual bleeding and previously unexperienced pelvic pain. This combination is commonly termed the post-tubal ligation syndrome. Studies of this phenomenon gained momentum in the 1950s as tubal sterilization increased in popularity. Early sterilizations were performed largely for medical (for example, heart disease) and obstetric (for example 3 or more previous Caesarean sections) indications. Consequently, the early investigations dealt primarily with procedures performed for these reasons.[2] Incidences of irregular vaginal bleeding reported in these studies ranged from a low of 4.8 percent (Prystowsky and Eastman 1955) to a high of 51.8 percent (Lu and Chun 1967) with the remainder averaging approximately 20 percent.

Later studies focused on procedures performed for social and economic reasons as well as medical indications, and ranges with as great a span were evident. Stock (1978), for example, reported as few as 6 percent of subjects complaining of excessive menstrual bleeding after excluding patients who previously used oral contraceptives. On the other hand, Campanella and Wolff (1975) found as many as 65 percent of their subjects under age 26 noting menstrual irregularities at 2 years post-surgery. Other reports from the United States and other parts of the world generally found complaints ranging from between 10 to 40 percent of patients studied.[3] Differences in reporting procedures and sample characteristics account for at least part of these differences.

Pelvic pain has been considerd less frequently in the literature; moreover, it is often unclear whether the pain in question is cyclic or random in occurrence, particularly with relation to menses. Reports of some kind of pelvic pain range from a low of 2 percent (DiMusto, Owens and Klomparens 1974) to highs of 20.5 percent (Lu and Chun 1967), 21 percent (Neil et al. 1975), and 29.1 percent (Madrigal et al. 1975).

Because of gross deficiencies in study design, it is as yet impossible to determine whether the reported complaints of pain and bleeding are related to tubal sterilization and if they are, whether they are organic or functional in nature. "Organic" implies that an identifiable anatomic lesion that is responsible for either pain or bleeding has been created by the procedure itself. "Functional" denotes that the symptoms may reflect somatization of psychic stresses, perhaps those resulting from loss of fertiliy. The woman may integrate the symbolic significance of sterilization into her self-concept and perhaps begin to question her feminine integrity and her role as mother and wife. Symptoms may also be totally unrelated to the procedure other than temporally. Surgical sterilization often represents a critial event in an individual's life to which subsequent outcomes, both good and bad, are attributed (Barglow and Eisner 1966; Miller 1978).

Psychological Aftereffects

Studies of psychosocial outcomes of tubal sterilization have focused primarily upon loosely defined areas of satisfaction and regret, and changes in sexual functioning.

Reports of regret following surgical sterilization tend to be relatively infrequent, that is, the incidence is usually less than 10 percent and generally less than 5 percent.[4] Only one study, that conducted by Ansari and Francis (1976), found a very high incidence of reported regret: 43 percent. Eighteen percent of the subjects, in fact, wanted a reversal. However, the sample consisted of only 49 women.

Regret tends to be correlated with medical or obstetric indications for tubal sterilization or with the simultaneous performance of abortion. In the former group, regret appears to result from a decision forced by external circumstances rather than one made by free choice. In the latter group, regret appears to result either from a double-loss phenomenon, that of the pregnancy and fertility, or from making a decision at a time of stress. It is, however, difficult to

51

evaluate such studies because many cases involved "package deals" in which sterilization was not freely chosen but was a condition for abortion. Postsurgical dissatisfaction also appears to be associated with ambivalence about the sterilization decision, a history of emotional instability or psychological disturbance, and an unstable or unsatisfactory marriage.[5]

Reported deterioration of sexual life, either with respect to quantity or quality of intercourse, ranges from lows of 3 percent (Adams 1964) and 4 percent (Cheng et al. 1977) to a high of 20 percent (Cardenas-Escovar 1975) and 24 percent (Paniagua et al. 1964). The remainder fall in between.[6] Reported improvements in sexual functioning are more frequent. The majority of studies which considered this question reported improvements in some aspects of sexual functioning, ranging from 36 percent to 54 percent of sujects.[7] Both postive and negative changes have also been reported within the same study. This is to be expected because tubal ligation may have different pyschological effects on different people. Positive effects may result from feeling sexually liberated after fears of pregnancy have been removed. Negative effects may result from associating female attractiveness with reproductive integrity.

There is very little information in this area with regard to the sterilized female; however, Rogers and Ziegler have determined among their study group of sterilized males that vasectomy may lead to fears that sterilization may dampen sexual drive. This may lead to overcompensation at least during the first year following the procedure (Rogers and Ziegler 1974). In the absence of in-depth studies with respect to the female, it is difficult to hypothesize whether the woman's sexuality, particularly in different subcultural groups, would be similarly affected. The whole question of what sterilization means to women with respect to self-concept needs to be probed in depth.

Reports of psychosocial outcomes other than sexual behavior are difficult to compare because of the diversity of factors which have been considered. Paniagua and his co-workers (1964), for example, reported that 6.9 percent of their subjects expressed a craving for children, and 47.6 percent and 31.9 percent, respectively, believed they were more irritable and depressed than before. On the other hand, 69 percent of the sample reported they were happier. Watkins et al. (1976) found that althouggh 4.7 percent of their subjects desired children, 31 percent noted an improvement in emotional stability. Wise et al. (1976) also reported a 32 percent improvement in emotional adjustment. Adams (1964) found that, one or two years post-surgery, only one percent of his sample expressed a "poor attitude toward life" and one and a half percent felt their "subsequent maternal health" had declined. Three years later these numbers changed to zero and 6 percent, respectively. DiMusto, Owens and Klomparens (1974) reported that 12 percent of their sample felt more fatigued and 6 percent more nervous than before the operation. However, 32 percent noted an improvement in overall emotional status. Stock (1978) reported that 70 percent of his subjects believed sterilization had a positive effect upon their lives whereas only one percent noted a negative effect. Feelings of emptiness and defeminization (Ekblad 1961) and devaluation by one's spouse (Whitehouse 1971) have also been reported. As in the case of regret, the only study reporting a large proportion of negative psychosocial outcomes was that conducted by Ansari and Francis (1976). Twenty-five of the forty-nine women studied (51%) reported a worsened mental state characterized by depression, headaches, irritability and insomnia. Fourteen percent, in fact, reported an increase in alcohol intake.

Methodological Inadequacies of Previous Studies

Despite the volume of research on long-term physical and psychosocial consequences of tubal ligation, few strong conclusions can be drawn about the impact of this procedure. In particular, two methodological deficiences of previous research must be noted. These are failure to conduct prospective research and the absence of a carefully selected control group.

In retrospective studies respondents are asked, following their surgery, to describe their preoperative status on various outcome variables, such as sexual functioning and pelvic pain. This approach leads to problems because there may be a tendency for women to reevaluate prior experience in the light of that more recent. For example, a woman who regrets having undergone tubal ligation may overestimate her previous sexual pleasure.

Other studies have used women as their own controls, contrasting their postsurgical status with their presurgical status. In this case, the goal is to extablish that the situation existing after their surgery did not predate it. However, such an approach fails to recognize that for many tubal ligation patients, surgery is paired with other medical and psychological occurences. For example, the incidence of irregular vaginal bleeding increases as women approach menopause. Moreover, women who use oral contraceptives rarely report pain accompanying menses, and their menstrual periods are shorter and scantier than what would normally be the case (Chamberlain and Foulkes 1976; Speroff, Glass and Kase 1978). When such women undergo tubal ligation any increase in menstual pain or bleeding may be a result of termination of oral contraceptives rather than a result of contraceptive sugery. In such cases, the effects of tubal ligation cannot be evaluated unequivocally without comparison to a suitable control group.

The overwhelming majority of studies have exhibited both flaws noted above: they have been retrospective and have used no control group. Several studies have been prospective, at least to some degree, but have not employed independent controls and still others have used controls but have selected a retrospective approach.[8] One of the better studies to date was conducted by Neil et al. (1975). They employed a control group of women whose husbands had been vasectomized. The study found significantly greater incidence of menstrual loss in tubal ligation patients, particularly those sterilized by laparoscopic cauterization (burning), than the controls. However, failure to investigate patterns previous to the surgery reduced the impact of these findings.

Tubal Ligation Study: Research Design

In order to study the psychosocial and physical consequences of tubal sterilization, we (Shain, Shepard and Miller) designed a controlled prospective study which began in September, 1980.

The study group consists of 317 women scheduled for tubal sterilization. Two control groups are employed: Group 1 consists of 244 women who have completed childbearing but have no plans for tubal ligation or vasectomy for their partners for at least 12 months and are relying on temporary contraceptive methods. Control group 2 consists of 167 wives of vasectomy patients.

54

Group 1 is employed primarily to control for the effect of the sterilization decision on psychosocial outcomes. Psychosocial aspects of life, such as marital and sexual satisfaction, tend to change with time. It is thus impossible to determine the extent to which the psychosocial aspects of a tubal ligation subject's life are correlated with the sterilization procedure as opposed to the passage of time, unless patterns of change are compared to those of control subjects.

Since the primary difference between the study group and control group 1 is loss of fertility through surgery, changes in psychosocial patterns can be appropriately compared between groups. All major psychosocial differences present from the beginning between these groups are controlled for statistically, as necessary. Measures of all relevant variables are determined prior to the surgery, with respect to the study group, and at a randomly assigned time with respect to control group 1; changes will be documented at one and two years following the initial interview. Changes which appear with significantly greater frequency or greater intensity among tubal ligation subjects may in some way be associated with loss of fertility and/or with the surgical procedure.

Women in control group 1 are also being questioned about their menstrual cycles to ascertain the stability of their initial physical patterns in comparison to the study group. However, because these women are utilizing a variety of contraceptive methods, including the IUD and pill, which are known to affect bleeding and pelvic pain, comparison with the study group on physical variables is of limited value.

The group which appears to be the most suitable control for the physical consequences of tubal ligation consists of wives of vasectomy patients. They are similar to tubal ligation patients in all basic respects except for the actual surgery: 1. for most practical purposes, as part of a couple, they have made a decision to forfeit their future fertility; 2. they are using no method of temporary contraception but, prior to their partner's vasectomy, will have used a random mix of contraceptive methods; 3. they are experiencing a definite change in their lives--an event--which although directly perpetrated on one mate, has important and immediate consequences on both lives. They can and will be interviewed before, and one and two years after, the "event" and questioned about the consequences of sterilization on their lives, including satisfaction and regret. They are not the most appropriate control for some psychosocial changes because, like the study group, they are part of a couple who have decided to be sterilized; thus, consequences of that general decision cannot be controlled for. However, they are ideal controls for study of the physical consequences of tubal ligation and psychosocial consequences regarding choice of female sterilization.

Age, parity, and contraceptive method used prior to surgery are the major variables. Age and parity need to be controlled for because both of these factors may affect the regularily and quantity of menstrual bleeding and pelvic pain, and may also be expected to influence sexual reactions and overall satisfaction.[9]

Women of different age groups may represent different populations, both in terms of general attitudes and the span of time left in their reproductive careers. In a previously mentioned study, for example, women who are under 26 showed more negative symptoms than women over 26 (Campanella and Wolff 1975). This area has not been considered in depth.

It is therefore important to include all women of all ages who seek sterilization. It is anticipated that few subjects will be under 21 or childless; although these groups may be too small for extensive statistical analyses, they are included within the study because they should constitute important sources of variation with respect to both pyschosocial and physical outcomes.

Previous contraceptive usage will be controlled for because different methods have different effects on outcomes. As previously noted, women who used oral contraceptives prior to surgery can be expected to experience increased vaginal bleeding and even pelvic pain as a result of discontinuing the pill. On the other hand, IUD users typically experience a decrease in bleeding and discomfort because the IUD intensifies these conditions.[10] Moreover, women who use coitus related methods such as the diaphram, may represent a different sub-population from those who use the pill and IUD and shun the inconvenient and perhaps "messy" barrier methods, despite their lack of side effects.

In addition to the major control variables
discussed above, the effects of other factors such as
education, religion, work status, marital status and
income will be accounted for. Tubal ligation is more
than cutting or burning of tubes. It is likely to
affect some women's self perception, both cognitively
and emotionally. Some women feel less complete, less
attractive, less youthful and may act accordingly.
Unfortunately the "price" of feeling diminished
attractiveness in our society with its "youth culture"
is particularly steep. It can also be anticipated that
in a small proportion of cases some spouses or partners
may reinforce these women's fears. On the other hand
what, is "normal" for one woman may not be "normal" for
another. Some women may interpret tubal ligation as a
key to freedom and greater "youthfulness." They may
not tie sexual adequacy with reproductive integrity and
feel more whole than previously. It is important to
investigate group differences (such as married versus
single, Catholic versus Protestant, lower versus upper
socioeconomic status) with respect to both the physical
outcomes and symbolic significance of tubal
sterilization. A pilot sample (N=65) of Mexican
American women has also been included so that broad
ethnic differences in physical and psychosocial
outcomes can be examined, albeit, in preliminary
fashion.

Tubal Ligation: Selected Results

To date, analysis has been based on the
preoperative data set, focusing on ambivalence
regarding the decisions to terminate childbearing and
to undergo sterilization as factors likely to
contribute either to post-decision satisfaction or
regret.[11] If sources of regret can be identified
preoperatively and appropriate counseling provided, the
incidence of dissatisfaction could be reduced.

Two areas of analysis have been explored. In the
first, proxy variables (based on two measures of
preoperative ambivalence, and on the interviewers'
assessments) for satisfaction with the termination of
childbearing and sterilization decisions are examined
to identify likely predictors of future satisfaction
with these decisions. The following sets of predictor
variables have been identified: motivational factors,
such as interest in having another baby and ideal
family size; external pressures or constraints, such as
perceptions of social pressure and influence of a
recent experience; and decision-making processual

factors, such as level of conflict with husband, and which spouse favored the decision most.[12] The actual predictive strength of these variables will be explored through analysis of follow-up data.

The second area of analysis focuses on inter-group differences in preoperative ambivalence regarding the decision to terminate childbearing. Although the predictors mentioned above affect both the tubal ligation and vasectomy groups in the same way, there are, nonetheless, significant inter-group differences in preoperative ambivalence: women who undergo tubal ligations are significantly more certain and comfortable with their decision to terminate childbearing than are the wives of men who have undergone vasectomy. These differences remain significant even after controlling for sociodemographic variability between the two groups.

In order to explain this finding, analysis focused on time factors related to the decision; variables related to communication with spouse and others; factors internal to the individual, including interest in another child and motivation for the decision; external constraints on the decision; and couple dynamics in the decision-making process. The only variables which could explain these differences in ambivalence concern differential spousal roles in the decision-making process. The role taken by the wife in the tubal ligation decision is generally much stronger than that assumed by women in their husband's vasectomy. Conversely, the male input is usually much greater in the vasectomy than in the tubal ligation group.

The relation between satisfaction with decisions and roles in decisions is also evident from intra-group comparisons. Couple dynamics variables were examined more closely as indicators of perceived spousal "dominance" over the termination decision including construction of an index measuring extent of control. Detailed analyses indicate that group differences in ambivalence are largely due to the effects of strong male control of the termination decision, as perceived by the wife, and a disproportionate prevalence of this pattern among vasectomy couples. Although extent of male control plays the predominant role in accounting for group differences, there is also an interaction effect between male dominance and group membership, in that vasectomy wives whose husbands exerted extensive control over the decision were more ambivalent than

58

their tubal ligation counterparts. In the tubal ligation sample, 88 percent of the women who either dominated the decision or participated equally with the spouses remained completely certain of the decision to terminate fertility. This compared with 76 percent and 60 percent of those women whose spouses exerted either slight or extensive control, respectively. In the vasectomy sample, the corresponding results were 87 percent certainty among women whose husbands did not dominate the decision, compared to 81 percent for those whose spouses exerted slight, and 39 percent for those whose spouses exerted extensive, control, respectively.

Hypotheses based on these data predict that full participation by both spouses in the termination decision will be related to post-sterilization satisfaction and that tubal ligation women may be less likely to experience regret than vasectomy wives because they exerted more control over the decision-making process. However, in either group, women who totally dominated the decision, as well as those who played little or no role, may experience regret in that their husbands may resent their secondary role in cases of female sterilization or may feel that they were forced into a vasectomy.

Moreover, under conditions of marital dissolution, regret is likely to be experienced most by either those ambivalent tubal ligation women who underwent the surgery, despite mixed feelings, or by vasectomy wives who convinced their reluctant spouses to be sterilized. These hypotheses, if proven correct following analyses of first and second year follow-up data, concern the importance of counseling both partners, and the selection of sterilization by the spouse who wants to end childbearing most. [13] In most general terms, it is clear that the sterilization decisions are not merely bio-medical procedures but sensitive reflections or married couple dynamics.

Future Work

It is hoped that as a result of this study, information will be provided to help 1. identify sources of regret preoperatively and 2. determine if there is an increase in physocial and psychosocial complaints on the part of tubal ligation patients compared to the controls. The conditions related to the surgery (type, timing, and indication for sterilization; private versus clinic setting; and whether or not the tubal ligation was performed alone or in conjunction with another procedure) which are most and least conducive to these problems will be determined. This information is important in itself because it will assist individuals seeking a permanent end to childbearing, and their physicians, in making a choice of sterilization procedures.

Moreover, if tubal ligation is correlated with adverse symptoms, biomedial scientists will be encouraged to conduct sophisticated endocrine studies to determine specific causality. Data provided by such research would establish if tubal ligation, and which types of tubal ligation, are causally related to the development of pelvic pathology and, consequently, if these is any justification for recommending vaginal hysterectomy over tubal ligation for female sterilization in healthy, symptom-free women. On the basis of currently available, poorly-controlled studies, many gynecologists are suggesting that tubal ligation induces pelvic pathology that will require subsequent surgery (Haynes and Wolfe 1970; van Nagell and Roddick 1971). These recommendations are being countered (Hibbard 1972), but until sophisticated endocrine studies are conducted, no definitive evidence will be available. The present research is thus a first step within a larger effort of biological and social scientists combining energies to meet consumer needs.

Marijuana Use During Pregnancy

The second research area discussed in this paper concerns marijuana use during pregnancy: again, another voluntary behavior, this time with potential health consequences not so much for the woman involved, but for her offspring.

Since the 1960s the extent of marijuana use has been increasing among all groups of people, particularly the young. Estimates for 1976 indicate that approximately 25 percent of individuals 18-25 years of age are currently using marijuana and 53 percent have ever used it. In 1977 these figures increased to 28 percent and 60 percent, respectively. Among the 12-17 year olds, 12 perent were currently using marijuana in 1976 compared to 16 percent in 1977; 25.5 percent had ever smoked marijuana in 1976 compared to 28 percent in 1977. These represent 30 and 25 percent increases, respectively. In surveys taken of high school classes in 1979, 60 percent said they had used marijuana sometime in their lives, compared to 47 percent in 1975; moreover, 36.5 percent said they were currently using marijuana compared to slightly over 25 percent in 1975. Additionally, over 10 percent of these seniors said they used marijuana daily compared with only 6 percent in 1975. Equally significant, the potency of street marijuana appears to be increasing. Whereas a representative random sample of marijuana strength is not available, researchers who have been analyzing samples for many years have found that the 1978 and 1979 samples averaged 3-5 percent THC compared to only one percent before 1975 (Secretary, HEW 1980).

Effects of Marijuana on General
Reproductive Functioning

Marijuana is still considered an innocuous substance to use, although some potentially harmful side effects have recently been published.[14] Marijuana and its purified constituents, the cannabinoids, have been reported to exert a wide variety of effects on reproductive function in male and female experimental animals and humans. Marijuana exposure has been reported to depress circulating levels of testosterone, the gonadal hormone responsible in part for spermatogenesis and maintenance of the male secondary sex characteristics, such as beard growth and muscle/fat ratio. Chronic exposure to marijuana has been reported to result in impotence, and a reduction in sperm count in young men and impaired spermatogenesis in mice. Serum concentrations of different pituitary hormones, i.e., FSH, LH, GH, Prolactin and ACTH, are markedly depressed by cannabinoids. Cannobinoids are also known to cross the placental barrier and to accumulate in the milk of lactating mothers of several species (Idanpaan-Heikkila et al. 1969; Jakubovic, Tait and McGreer 1974; and Kennedy and Waddell 1973).

Effects of In-Utero Exposure to Marijuana

Because marijuana is still believed to be relatively innocuous, some women continue to smoke it while pregnant, although they may cease other activities which they consider hazardous. It is not known how many women smoke marijuana while pregnant. One can only assume that the growing use of the substance also involves greater numbers of pregnant females. In our obstetrical clinic, for example, approximately five women a month admit to marijuana use sometime during their pregnancy.

Results of various animal studies indicate there is a need to examine the effects of prenatal exposure to cannabinoids. In rats it has been shown that prenatal exposure to cannobinoids results in impaired learning ability (Fried 1976; Gianutsos and Abbatiello 1972). There is also good evidence that when THC and the other cannabinoids pass the placental barrier, they tend to concentrate in the fetus' fatty tissue, including the brain (Kennedy and Waddell 1972).

Researchers in our own department have found interesting results in male mice, which indicate that both the pyschoactive and the non-psvchoactive constituents of marijuana can alter development of a male offspring if administered prenatally (Dalterio 1980). (Female progeny have not yet been examined.) Whereas transient hyperactivity was noted in young mice, major and apparently permanent changes, such as alteration in body weight regulation, became apparent around the time of puberty. The prenatally exposed males were intially characterized bv reduced body weight; they developed, however, into obese adults. The pituitary-testicular feedback relationship in these males was also altered. The increased pituitary release of luteinizing hormone failed to elicit the usual increased production in testicular steroids. This occurred coincident with a reduction in testes weights. Again, these effects of prior exposure to marijuana did not become evident until the prepubertal period and persisted into adulthood.

These is also some evidence that maturation was delayed in these animals and that the response of other endocrine parameters, such as adrenal function, may have also been altered. Thus, changes in environmental conditions which are not perceived as stressful by a normal male, produced adrenal hypertrophv and atypical behavior patterns, such as withdrawal. Moreover, as adults these animals failed to respond to sexual stimuli and their mating behavior was suppressed. It thus appears that subtle alterations in the hormonal environment during critical periods of fetal development have produced profound and long-lasting effects on offspring which, as was the case with diethylstilbesterol, did not appear until after sexual maturation.

Other studies have been conducted with primates. Increased reproductive loss among marijuana exposed rhesus females and decreased birthweight, hyperactivity, over-responsiveness to environmental stimuli with lack of appropriate avoidance behaviors and enhanced assertiveness in response to peer socialization among the exposed male infants (perhaps as a result of impaired placental circulation and decreased weight gain of the pregnant females) have been noted (Sassenrath, Chapman and Goo 1978). Because the rhesus monkey has proved to be an excellent model for the human being in regard to effects of substance abuse during pregnancy on the neonate, these findings are particularly significant.

These types of observations merit futher study among human populations to determine if there are any behavioral or physical consequences to offspring from in-utero exposure to marijuana. In a unique study, Fried (1979) has already found that in tests of symmetry, marijuana exposed neonates do not exhibit a preference for right of left (unlike the controls) and are hyperactive. Such measures, in addition to many others, need to be obtained and their meanings and implications understood with regard to individual cognitive, emotional, sexual, and physiologic development; mother-infant interaction; and later, social functioning in general.

A Problem Area Requiring Investigation

In view of the above data, we (Shain, Dalterio, Asch and staff) suggest that the following study be conducted: a longitudinal study in which obstetric, sociodemographic, attitudinal and behavioral data from at least 50 pregnant women smoking marijuana regularly (three or more joints a week), but who do not use hard drugs, needs to be compared to equivalent data from 50 controls matched with regard to age, parity and use of other substances, such as tobacco and alcohol. In addition to a comprehensive intake interview, subjects should compile an attitudinal scale, such as the Lederman Acceptance of Pregnancy (this scale has an intertest reliability of .90) and Identification of a Motherhood Role (this test has an intertest reliability scale of .79) Scales. Both types of information can be used to control for differences in mothers' attitudes toward motherhood in general and the child they are carrying. Information on nutrition, changes in acceptance of pregnancy, support systems, and substance use, that is, the amount, frequency, reasons for, and effects of use, should be updated monthly via a telephone interview. During the ninth month the attitudinal scale should be administered again to determine if there have been any changes in the acceptance of pregnancy or perception of the motherhood role. Behavioral, cognitive and physical data from the resultant progeny should be examined at birth and at regular intervals during the first 18 months of life. Substance use by the mother, and whether she is nursng her infant, should be ascertained during this period as well. Infant behavior and intelligence should be assessed on the basis of neonatal scales, such as the Brazelton neonatal assessment scale or the Albert Einstein Neonatal Neurobehavioral Scale, and the Carey Infant Temperament Scale, and tests such as the Bayley Intelligence Test. Observation of mother-infant interaction would also be useful. These children should be followed up through their adolescent years if feasible.

If smoking marijuana during pregnancy is found to have short or long-term adverse consequences for offspring, provision of this information to pregnant women will allow them to make informed choices regarding whether or not to smoke. Moreover, if information on why women smoke marijuana during pregnancy and how marijuana personally affects them, is obtained, culturally appropriate modes of intervention, specifically alternative modes of coping behavior, can be identified and offered. We, in conjunction with staff pediatricians, have already enrolled over ten marijuana-using women into an exploratory study. The offspring are being followed up. Results are not yet available, and, in the absence of funding, adherence to a rigid protocol has proven very difficult.

Summary

In summary, because pregnancy is not a disease state, family planning and routine obstetrical care can and are moving away from the typical medical model of health care in the United States. However, because women have more freedom in these areas, they need sufficient information to make informed decisions.

Anthropologists working in a team with other professionals can help provide such information. Increasing numbers of women are selecting tubal sterilization without knowing or really considering the full impact of that decision. By studying both the physical and psychosocial effects of sterilization in the context of women's personal and sociocultural situations, needed data will be gathered. What sterilization really means to the individual, particularly to her sense of feminine identity, may vary among different groups, as defined by socio-economic status, parity, marital status, type of conjugal relationship and perhaps prior method of contraception used. These issues and how they relate to the wider culture need to be thoroughly explored. For some women, the wider culture may be child oriented. For them the final termination of childbearing may carry negative cosequences. For others, the wider culture may be youth oriented. Because the normal reaction of one female is not the normal reaction for another, some women may feel freer, sexually more invigorated; others who may relate femininity to reproductive integrity may feel less attractive and sexually unresponsive as a result of the procedure. Once these issues are brought to light, once we know of the possible psychosocial consequences of tubal sterilization, we may be able to resolve conflicts prior to surgery or suggest alternative contraceptive methods and thus save regret on the part of certain women. Analysis of preoperative data indicate the importance of counseling both partners and selection of sterilization by the partner who wants to end childbearing most.

Secondly, by carefully studying women who smoke marijuana while pregnant and subsequently working with pediatricians who will thoroughly follow-up their children, anthropologists can help determine the effects of in-utero exposure to the substance. Other contributions relating to identifying cultural variation in smoking and perception of pregnancy and motherhood can be made. If marijuana proves to be harmful to the fetus, knowledge of why a woman feels the need to smoke and under what circumstances she smokes should facilitate the identification of culturally acceptable alternatives.

NOTES

1. The tubal sterilization research is supported by NICHD Grant HD-13459.

2. See Black and Sclare 1968, Lu and Chun 1967, Prystowksy and Eastman 1955, Sacks and Lacroix 1962, and Williams, Jones and Merrill 1951.

3. See Adams 1964, Cardenas-Escovar 1975, Cheng et al. 1977, DiMusto, Owens and Klomperens 1974, Madrigal et al. 1975, Neil et al. 1975, Paniagua et al. 1964.

4. See Adams 1964, Campanella and Wolff 1975, Cheng et al. 1977, DiMusto, Owens and Klomperens 1974, Hampton and Tarnasky 1974, Kopil and Barnes 1976, Lu and Chun 1967, Neil et al. 1975, Paniagua et al. 1964, Stock 1978, Thompson and Baird 1968, Watkins et al. 1975, and Wise, Perkin and Correy 1976.

5. See Ansari and Francis 1976, Barnes and Zuspan 1958, Black and Sclare 1968, Campanella and Wolff 1975, Ekblad 1961, 1963, Hampton and Tarnasky 1974, Kopit and Barnes 1976, Sacks and Lacroix 1962, Schwyhart and Kutner 1975, Thompson and Baird 1968, Winston 1977, and Wise, Perkins and Correy 1976.

6. See Thompson and Baird 1968, Watkins et al. 1976, and Wise et al. 1976.

7. See Cardenas-Escovar 1975, DiMusto, Owens and Klomperens 1974, Hampton and Tarnasky 1974, Neil et al. 1975, Thompson and Baird 1968, Watkins et al. 1976, and Wise et al. 1976.

8. References to the sources are as follows: a: retrospective studies with no control: Adams 1964, Ansari and Francis 1976, Cardenas-Escovar 1975, Chamberlain and Foulkes 1976, DiMusto, Owens and Klomperens 1974, Ekblad 1961, Haynes and Wolfe 1970, Kopit and Barnes 1976, Lu and Chun 1967, Madrigal et al. 1975, Paniagua et al. 1964, Sacks and Lacroix 1962, Watkins et al. 1976 and Winston 1977; b: prospective studies with no control: Campanella and Wolff 1975, Cheng et al. 1977, Stock 1978, and Thompson and Baird 1968; c:

66

retrospective studies with controls: Mehta 1976 and Neil et al. 1975.

9. See Alderman 1977, Campanella and Wolff 1975, Cheng et al. 1977, Miller 1978, and Wise et al. 1976.

10. See Alderman 1975, Chamberlain and Foulkes 1976, Rioux 1977, and Stock 1978.

11. These analyses are based on the married, surgical sub-samples (255 women who had tubal ligation, 167 wives of men who have had vasectomies).

12. Miller and Shain have submitted a paper on these variables to Population and Environment, in 1983.

13. Shain, Miller and Holden submitted a paper on these hypotheses for publication in 1983.

14. In regard to the possible side effects of marijuana see, for reproductive functions, Asch et al. 1979, Dalterio 1980, Kolodny et al. 1974, and Sassenrath, Chapman and Goo 1978; level of testosterone, Dalterio et al. 1978; on reduction in human sperm count, Kolodny et al. 1974; on impaired mouse spermatogenesis, Dixon, Sharma and Lohiya 1974; and on the depression of pituitary hormones, Kokka and Garcia 1974, Kramer and Ben-David 1974, and Symons, Teal and Marks 1976.

REFERENCES

Abbreviations:

AJOG   American Journal of Obstetrics and
            Gynecology

APS   Acta Psychiatrica Scandinavica

BMJ   British Medical Journal

EJP   European Journal of Pharmacology

FS   Fertility and Sterility

IJGO   International Journal of Gynaecology and
            Obstetrics

JAMA	Journal of the American Medical Association
JOG-BC	Journal of Obstetrics and Gynaecology of the British Commonwealth
JRM	Journal of Reproductive Medicine
L	Lancet
LS	Life Sciences
NEJM	New England Journal of Medicine
OG	Obstetrics and Gynecology
PBB	Pharmacology, Biochemistry and Behavior
TAP	Toxicology and Applied Pharmacology

Adams, T.W.
1964   Female Sterilization. AJOG 89:395.

Alderman, B.
1977   Women Who Regret Sterilization. Letter BMJ 2:766.

Ansari, J.M.A. and H.H. Francis
1976   A Study of 49 Sterilized Females. APS 54:315.

Asch, R.H., E.O. Fernandez, C.G. Smith and C.J. Pauerstein
1979   Precoital Single Doses of Δ^9-tetrahydrocannabinol Block Ovulation in the Rabbit. FS 31:331-334.

Barglow, P. and M. Eisner
1966   An Evaluation of Tubal Ligation in Switzerland. AJOG 95:1083.

Barnes, A.C. and F.P. Zuspan
1958   Patient Reaction to Puerperal Surgical Sterilization. AJOG 75:65.

Black, W.P. and A.B. Sclare
1968   Sterilization by Tubal Ligation--A Follow-up
         Study. JOG-BC 75:219.

Campanella R. and J.R. Wolff
1975   Emotional Reaction to Sterilization.
         OG 45:31.

Cardenas-Escovar, A.
1975   Post-operative Evaluation of Tubal Ligation.
         In The Family, Proceedings of the 4th
         International Congress of Psychosomatic
         Obstetrics and Gynecology (Tel Aviv).
         H. Hirsch, ed. Basel: Karger.

Chamberlain, G. and J. Foulkes
1976   Long-term Effects of Laparoscopic
         Sterilization and Menstruation. Southern
         Medical Journal 69:1474.

Cheng, M.C.E., J. Cheong, K.S. Khew and S.S. Ratnam
1977   Psychological Sequelae of Sterilization in
         Women in Singapore. IJGO 15:44.

Dalterio, S., A. Bartke, C. Robertson, D. Watson
S. Burstein
1978   Direct and Pituitary-mediated Effects of
         Δ^9-THC and Cannabinol on the Testis. PBB
         8:673-678.

Dalterio, S.
1980   Perinatal or Adult Exposure to Cannabinoids
         Alters Male Reproductive Functions in Mice.
         PBB 12:143-153.

DiMusto, J.C., E.B. Owens and K.A. Klomparens
1974   A Follow-up Study of 100 Sterilized Women.
         JRM 12:112.

Dixit, V.P., V.N. Sharma and N.K. Lohiya
1974   The Effects of Chronically Administered
         Cannabis Extract on the Testicular Function
         in Mice. EJP 26:111-114.

Ekblad, M.
1961   The Prognosis After Sterilization on
         Social-Psychiatric Grounds, a Follow-up Study
         of 225 Women. APS Supplement 161:37.

1963   Social-Psychiatric Progress After
         Sterilization of Women Without Children: A
         Follow-up Study of 60 Women. APS 39:481.

69

Fried, P.A.
1976   Short and Long-term Effects of Pre-Natal
            Cannabis Inhalation upon Rat Offspring.
            Psychopharmacology 50L285-291.

1979   Maternal Use of Alcohol, Cigarettes and/or
            Marihuana During Pregnancy: Effects upon the
            Offspring. Society of Neuroscience.
            Abstract Volume. Symposium 510 UCLA: Brain
            Information Service/BRI Publications Office.

Gianutsos, G. and E.R. Abbatiello
1972   The Effect of Pre-natal Cannabis Sativa on
            Maze Learning in the Rat.
            Psychopharmacologia 27:117-122.

Hampton, P.T. and W.G. Tarnasky
1974   Hysterectomy and Tubal Ligation: A Comparison
            of the Psychological Aftermath. AJOG
            119:949.

Haynes, D.M. and W.M. Wolfe
1970   Tubal Sterilization in an Indigent
            Population. Report of Fourteen Years'
            Experience. AJOG 106:1044.

Hibbard, L.T.
1972   Sexual Sterilization by Elective
            Hysterectomy. AJOG 112:1076.

Idanpaan-Heikkila, J., G.E. Fritchie, L.F. Englert,
B.T. Ho and W.M. McIsaac
1969   Placental Transfer of Tritiated-1-Δ^9-THC.
            NEJM 281:330.

Jakubovic, A., R.M. Trait and P.L. McGeer
1974   Excretion of THC and Its Metabolics in Ewes'
            Milk. TAP 28:38-43.

Kennedy, J.S. and W.J. Waddel
1972   Whole-Body Autoradiography of the Pregnant
            Mouse After Administration of $^{14}C-\Delta^9$-THC
            (tetrahydrocannabinol). TAP 22:525.

Kokka, N. and J.F. Garcia
1974   Effects of Δ^9-tetrahydrocannabinal on GH and
            ACTH Secretion in Rats. LS 15:324-338.

Kolodny, R.C., W.H. Masters, R.M. Kolodner and G. Toro
1974   Depression of Plasma Testosterone Levels
         After Chronic Intensive Marihuana Use.
         NEJM 290:872:874.

Kopit, S. and A.B. Barnes
1976   Patients' Response to Tubal Division.
         JAMA 236:2761.

Kramer, J. and M. Ben-David
1974   Suppression of Prolactin Secretion by Acute
         Administration of Δ^9-THC in Rats.
         Proceedings of the Society for Experimental
         Biology and Medicine. 147:482-484.

Lu, T. and O.J. Chun
1967   A Long Term Follow-up of Study of 1,055 Cases
         of Postpartum Tubal Ligation. JOG-BC 74:875.

Madrigal, V., D.A. Edelman, A. Goldsmith and
W.E. Brenner
1975   Female Sterilization Via Laparoscopy. A
         Long-term Follow-up Study. IJGO 13:268.

Marshall, J.F.
1973   Fertility Regulating Methods: Cultural
         Acceptability for Potential Adopters. In
         Fertility Control Methods: Strategies for
         Introduction. G. Duncan, E.J. Gilton,
         P. Kraeger and A.A. Lumsdaine, eds.
         New York: Academic Press.

Mehta, P.V.
1976   Ovarian Function in Tubectomized Women
         Studied by Vaginal Cytology. IJGO 14:161.

Miller, W.B.
1978   Psychosocial Aspects of Contraceptive
         Sterilization in Women. In Behavioral Social
         Aspects of Contraceptive Sterilization.
         S.H. Newman and Z.E. Klein, eds. Lexington,
         MA: Lexington Books.

Neil, J.R., G.T. Hammond, A.D. Noble,
L. Rushton and A.T. Letchworth
1975   Late Complications of Sterilization by
         Laparoscopy and Tubal Ligation. A Controlled
         Study. L 2:699.

71

Paniagua, M.E., M. Tayback, J.L. Janer and
J.L. Vasquez
    1964   Medical and Psychological Sequelae of
            Sterilization of Women. AJOG 90:421.

Prystowsky, H. and N.J. Eastman
    1955   Puerperal Tubal Sterilization: Report of 1830
            Cases. JAMA 158:463.

Rioux, J.E.
    1977   Late Complications of Female Sterilization: A
            Review of the Literature and a Proposal for
            Further Research. JRM 19:329.

Rogers, D.A. and F.J. Ziegler
    1974   Effects of Surgical Contraception on Sexual
            Behavior. In Advances in Voluntary
            Sterilization. M.E. Schima, I. Lubell,
            J.E. Davis and E. Connel, eds. New York:
            American Elsevier Publishing Co.

Sacks, S. and G. Lacroix
    1962   Gynecologic Sequelae of Postpartum Tubal
            Ligation. OG 19:22.

Sassenrath, E.N., L.F. Chapman and G.P. Goo
    1978   Marihuana: Biological Effects -- Analysis,
            Metabolism, Cellular Responses, Reproduction
            and Brain. In Advances in the Biosciences.
            G.G. Nahas and W.D.M. Paton, eds. Vol. 22
            and 23.

Schwyhart, W.R. and S.J. Kutner
    1975   A Reanalysis of Female Reaction to
            Contraceptive Sterilization. Journal of
            Nervous and Mental Diseases 56:354.

Secretary of Health, Education, and Welfare
    1980   Marihuana and Health. Ninth Annual Report to
            the Congress. Washington, D.C.

Shain, R.N.
    1980   Acceptability of Contraceptive Methods and
            Services: A Cross-Cultural Perspective. In
            Fertility Control: Biologic and Behavioral
            Aspects. R.N. Shain and C.J. Paverstein,
            eds. pp. 299-312. New York: Harper and Row.

Shedlin, M.G.
1977   Body Image and Contraceptive Acceptability in
        a Mexican Community. Paper presented at the
        Annual Meeting of the American
        Anthropological Association, Houston,
        December 1977.

Shedlin, M.G. and P.E. Hollerbach
1978   Modern and Traditional Fertility Regulation
        in a Mexican Community: Factors in the
        Process of Decision Making. Working Papers,
        Center for Policy Studies. New York:
        Population Council.

Speroff, L., R.H. Glass and N.G. Kase
1978   Clinical Gynecologic Endocrinology and
        Infertility. 2nd ed. Baltimore, MD:
        Williams and Williams Co.

Stock, R.J.
1978   Evaluation of Sequelae of Tubal Ligation.
        FS 29:169.

Symons, A.N., J.D. Teale and V. Marks
1976   Effect of Δ^9-tetrahydrocannobinol on the
        Hypothalmic-Pituitary Gonadal System in the
        Maturing Male Rat. Journal of Endocrinology
        68:43-44.

Thompson, B. and D. Baird
1968   Follow-up of 186 Sterilized Women. L 1:1023.

van Nagell, J.R. and J.W. Roddick
1971   Vaginal Hysterectomy as a Sterilization
        Procedure. AJOG 111:703.

Watkins, R.A., J.F. Corey, D.A. Wise and G.J. Perkin
1976   Social and Psychological Changes after Tubal
        Sterilization: A Reevaluation Study of 425
        Women. Medical Journal of Australia 2:251.

Westoff, C.F. and E.F. Jones
1977   Contraception and Sterilization in the United
        States, 1965-1975. Family Planning
        Perspectives 9:153.

Whitehouse, D.B.
1971   Letter. BMJ 2:707.

Williams, E.L., H.E. Jones and R.E. Merrill
  1951   Subsequent Course of Patients Sterilized by
          Tubal Ligation. AJOG 61:423.

Winston, R.M.L.
  1977   Why 103 Women Asked for Reversal of
          Sterilization. BMJ 2:305.

Wise, D.J., G.J. Perkin and J.F. Correy
  1976   Emotional Adjustment Following Tubal
          Sterilization by Laparoscopy and Laparotomy
          in 1,052 Women. Australian and New Zealand
          Journal of Obstetrics and Gynaecology 16:173.

ANTHROPOLOGICAL CONTRIBUTIONS TO PSYCHOTHERAPY:
AN OVERVIEW

Peggy Golde

Introduction

My purpose in this sketch is to present the strategy and rationale of anthropological psychotherapy as I have come to conceptualize it during my training and private practice. I will place it in the context of interaction approaches influenced by the orientation of Gregory Bateson and Virginia Satir. I will finally make some comparative remarks, calling attention to parallels and contrasts with social work, clinical psychology, psychiatry, and the approach of another clinical anthropologist, John Weakland.

Interaction Therapy: Central Concepts

Before I begin the systematic presentation of the contributions anthropology has made to the kind of psychotherapy I practice, I feel the need to present my personal theory of human problems or interpersonal difficulties.

The basic idea which originally stimulated me was the theorem, now central to social science, conceived by W. I. Thomas, the dean of American sociologists (Merton 1949:179). He said: "If men define situations as real, they <u>are</u> <u>real</u> in their <u>consequences</u>" (underlining mine). Among my clients, I have been able to observe a common thread that stitched them together: some false definition of reality had set in motion a series of subsequent behaviors that culminated in insoluble problems or self-fulfilling prophecies that became dizzying vicious circles. As Jerome D. Frank (1961:33) so persuasively wrote, "Breaking vicious circles is the main goal of psychotherapy." I also assume that every individual reflects in some imperfect way the culture of those significant figures who trained him or her. This reflection also refracts that culture so that each actor's vision of his culture's beliefs, values, attitudes, feelings and behavior becomes a blurred image that requires corrective "spectacles" to perceive reality.

75

I won't spend time here on detailing anthropological examples that bear witness to the validity of this basic theorem, such as voodoo death, or evidence from the medical field of the fact that placebos actually work, or the research of Robert Rosenthal (1966) indicating how experimenter bias affects the performance of experimental subjects. Instead, let me consider the work of Paul Watzlawick in the book Change (Watzlawick, Weakland and Fisch 1974:13) which asserts that one of the principles affecting the final step in the process of psychological change is to translate the chosen tactic for change into the person's own language, or "into a form which utilizes his own way of conceptualizing 'reality'." To continue with Watzlawick in his discussion of reframing, when you "change the conceptual and/or emotional setting or viewpoint in relation to which a situation is experienced and place it in another frame which fits the 'facts' of the same concrete situation equally well or even better, you thereby change its entire meaning" (1974:95).

In sum, I see anthropological psychotherapy as a two-stage process. One stage is the determination of those perceptual errors which cause psychic distress to a client. The other is the joint effort of therapist and client in reframing perception and behavior into more viable modes.

Now I will move this paper to a more general plane that will provide a wider rationale of the several activities encompassed in psychotherapy. It will include 1) anthropological methods, communication theory and the nature of the therapeutic role; 2) the meaning of myths for the therapist; 3) the influence of systems theory; 4) sex therapy; and 5) clinical practice as a source of new research ideas. If I am sufficiently deft, these apparently disparate topics will be interwoven into an oriental carpet with a pattern of overlapping geometric elements.

Anthropological Methods

Interaction as an Anthropological Method

When I was an intern at Family Service, a social work agency, none of my clients directly asked what kind of therapy I did, probably assuming that it was social work. However, when I started my own practice I had to sell my wares, as did any entrepreneur, to nearby doctors likely to make a referral, or at informal talks, lectures, or professional presentations. During these talks I would describe the range of clients I saw, presenting their problems, and the way I actually worked: what I referred to as interaction therapy. My training as a social anthropologist had taught me participant observation, reporting only on what I saw and making inferences only from data on behavior I could see as interactions. In other words I tried to avoid thinking in terms of inner psychological dynamics that weren't clearly visible or at least observable.

Doing therapy, searching for the client's definition of the problem and his or her ideas about how to solve it, felt "natural" and easy because there was no disjuncture in my modus operandi: I talked face to face sitting opposite clients who could scrutinize my facial expression as easily as I could watch theirs. We set goals together, my chief role being to guide their <u>serial</u> goals toward steps achievable in a limited time. This latter stricture is basic because I believe success in small doses supports clients' self-esteem as well as reassuring them that meaningful change <u>is</u> possible.

The main reason for setting serial goals with the client is that the accomplishment of such goals becomes a directional signpost for making ultimate decisions about termination. The client begins to verbalize doubts about continuing because she or he is feeling better, running out of things to complain about, feeling a continuing sense of pleasure and having no further concrete goals. If the client exhibits in speech or new behaviors that he has different attitudes or expectations about his current life situation that approach the definition of reality you as therapist had been attempting to impart, this is also a confirmation that he has "graduated." If there has been an abatement of distress, psychic pain, anxiety, or whatever was emotionally troubling, this is fairly easy to observe. If it continues over time and the client feels good, looks good, is spending time in what he considers a productive or satisfying way, if he reports that others comment on his behavior or mood or energy or whatever others spontaneously notice, this too is a means of validating the therapist's judgment. In a way, this judgment parallels how a painter decides when a painting is finished or that he should stop painting, though the moment of decision might vary for different people, whether therapists or painters. Judging the

moment   sensitively   is   what   distinguishes   a   <u>good</u>
practitioner from a commonplace one.

Communication Theory

    Talking about the visual cues of facial   expression
leads   directly   into   a   discussion   of   non-verbal
communication and communication theory   in general.
Anthropologists cannot   take   credit   for its earliest
formulation; probably Norbert Wiener,   the father of
cybernetics,   is   the   first   figure.   However, Time
magazine's obituary for Gregory Bateson credits him as
one of the founders of this field.   Bateson (1958),
George Devereux (1950), Weston LaBarre (1948), and Ray
Birdwhistell (1970), have used the framework to support
their ideas on gesture, speech, voice, language, and
psychotherapy. The last (Birdwhistell) has specialized
in communication without words but   refocused   on
messages sent along other channels like body movement
(what he calls kinesics or body motion communication).
He has offered a limited conclusion on communication
and culture (1970:250): "The mechanisms of information
transmission   are   but   an   aspect . . . of social
experience." He calls it begging the question to
describe communicative behavior as social behavior,
which as process is "interdependent with other social
processes to form culture" (1970:250).

    Virginia Satir, whom I experienced, observed and
learned from in Menlo Park, California, taught me that
"A person simultaneously communicates by his gestures,
facial expression, body posture and movement, tone of
voice and even the way he is dressed" (Satir 1964:75).
She describes the denotative level of communication as
the literal content and the "metacommunication level as
a comment on the literal content as well as on the
nature of the relationship between the   persons
involved"   (1964:76).   This term of Bateson's
(metacommunication) is a message about a message.   A
powerful idea once all its implications are grasped is
that "people cannot <u>not</u> communicate." Bateson and the
Palo Alto Group at the Mental Research Institute also
coined   the   term   "incongruent"   to   refer   to
contradictions that occur between different levels of
communication" (Bateson 1958:82). They define four
parts of every message: the sender, the message, the
receiver, and the context or the situation of the
communication   (1958:87).   This   incongruence   was
perceived to be at the heart of the etiology of
schizophrenia.

Therapist's Role

At this juncture I would like to shift to my own communication to clients about my role as therapist. As an anthropologist, I perforce present myself as a teacher, lecturer, experienced observer who remains outside the impact of troublesome relations and above the power struggles the participants are emotionally involved in. My role is that of negotiator, interceder, a person trained to be skillful at evading becoming enmeshed in the interaction and able to maintain an impartial, objective position.

Anthropological training heightens sensitivity to unconscious cultural assumptions about how people should be and keeps me vigilant for biases that might enter the therapeutic relation. Foremost is the attitude that the therapist does not behave as the authority who is omnipotent, but only one who is more elaborately trained. What is more, the therapist sometimes freely admits to confusion or conflicting understandings about the client's personal meanings that only the client can clarify.

My therapy is based on Satir's growth model--"that people's behavior changes through process: transactions with other people" (Satir 1964:182). This model is based on premises "that people can be taught to be congruent, to speak directly and clearly, and to communicate their feelings, thoughts, and desires accurately in order to be able to deal with what is" (Satir 1964:182). I must add an addendum to this formulation in order to be congruent with what I propounded earlier in this paper about the nature of therapy and definitions of reality. That is that people can be taught to work in concert with the therapist in uncovering the client's perceptions of reality, in setting appropriate and realistic goals, and in jointly deciding when they have been reached.

In this sketch, both the power and the limitations of the clinician in private practice will be apparent. The unique contours of each case are of paramount importance so that principles and approaches can be constantly reassessed by the therapist. Conversely, because the decisions to undertake or terminate therapy are the immediate consequences of client-therapist interaction, they too differ with each case. In other words, true interaction therapy is based on a process model in which movement is determined by the sensitivity of the therapist to both the client's needs and the flow of the relationship. What this means is that common scientific methods are not necessarily the most appropriate.

At the same time, new kinds of data will be perceived and collected in therapy that bring out productive new categories cross cutting the uniqueness of individual cases. I suggest that such categories for married couples (and valuable for therapeutic inquiry) are the amount of time spent talking, rest and sleep patterns, need for touch, need for stimulation from other couples, and time spent for entertainment.

Myths and the Therapist

In my cross-cultural readings I learned the function and nature of myths for non-literate tribal groups and this has made me aware of how myths can be created in the forge of the family, then passed down through the generations as God-given truths never to be questioned. These become quasi-religious verities that are built into the eventual identities of individuals who may eventually need to be seen in a therapeutic interaction.

The anthropological search for cross-cultural universals in language structure and development, expression of emotions, and economic division of labor, serves in therapy as a means to compare clients, whatever their culture, as they experience comparable social situations like marriage, or crisis rites tied to age-specific occasions that facilitate passage from one social role to the next--be it puberty or getting Social Security. Age-specific sociocultural demarcations of appropriate behavior can be visualized as a kind of stratigraphic layering; this stratigraphy in turn will be crosscut by a central anthropological concept--values. Again anthropologists are not unique among social scientists in focusing on value orientations, but we have elaborated and sharpened this concept. Clyde Kluckhohn, the anthropologist and his wife Florence, a sociologist, made the study of values their trademark.

Values underlie choices, order decision making, and rationalize otherwize inexplicable attractions as well as time and money expenditures. Why cross-cultural marriages fracture can best be understood as insoluble conflicts over deeply-held values that are triggered by psychological sets embedded in each partner's personality.

General Systems Theory

Just as communications theory cannot be seen as a purely anthropological creation, similarly, general systems theory has been appropriated from Von Bertalanffy (Buckley 1968). Systems theory certainly underlay my training in how to perceive, analyze, or think about the interconnection between parts of a community, whatever its size--be it a dyad, family, or group. As a therapist, I have found the concept of systems theory most useful in work I've done with families and in marriage counseling per se or when the marital pair can only be fully understood by including children or aging parents or other significant family members as part of the system that influences decisions.

Sex Therapy

The last therapeutic aspect of the clinical anthropology I do concerns sex therapy. This symptom-oriented practice can encompass all the other pieces of the mosaic I've already mentioned: values, communication, theory, myths about sexuality and performance. Sexual performance is a Geiger counter to measure human problems because of its vunerability and sensitivity. If you ask yourselves to specify the overriding motivational need that most Americans are driven by, whatever their gender, I would guess you would answer: the desire to achieve, and equally, the need to avoid failure. These are not mirror images: the positive need for success is not the equivalent of the negative fear of being ignored or pitied or worse, despised or deprecated.

Books on sex therapy commonly begin with the male concern over premature ejaculation, the counterpart for females being anorgasmia. I see these as parallel dysfunctions that express performance anxieties for each sex. A popular recent sex therapy "manual" is called Disorders of Sexual Desire by Helen Singer Kaplan (1979). She stipulates that "Fear or anxiety is the major etiologic factor in all the sexual dysfunctions, but anger at the partner is also a highly prevalent cause for the loss of sexual interest" (1979:90). (A pregnant aside that she notes in passing is that sometimes it seems that people in our culture are more afraid of intimacy than they are of sex [1979:80].)

The anthropologist-therapist role is prima facie therapeutic because she can say "I have sampled books and articles from the anthropological literature regarding countries around the world--and people somewhere, some time, some place have done or imagined anything that you might now be fearing to tell me. As an anthropologist and a therapist I have been trained to avoid making moral judgments." Despite this preamble, the therapist knows that trust is not communicated easily or instantly, but is erected like a pyramid, stone by stone, over time, by means of diverse but consistently positive reassurances.

Research Ideas

I conclude this catalogue of contributions of anthropological training to the therapeutic process with the observation that clients in therapy are a source of new research ideas. I formulated a study of women's friendships as a bulwark against mental disorder, particularly after divorce. As I conceptualized friendship, the reason it served such a function was that it permitted the development of same-sex intimacy and elevated lagging self-esteem. I have led two, eight-week discussion-discovery groups with men and women aged 30-50 about friendship and its vicissitudes. Such "minicourses" made the participants more thoughtful about unexamined life processes. This I suppose is the primary outcome of such workshops, as well as the opportunity to learn directly from the other participants that they have had the same emotional difficulties and have encountered similar pitfalls. I personally feel my own perception and appreciation of taken-for-granted aspects of social life--like friendship--have been elaborated and deepened as a consequence of my therapeutic work.

To close this talk, I shall briefly discuss papers by a social worker, a culturally oriented psychiatrist, a psychologist, and another clinical anthropologist in order to highlight succinctly the differences between them and myself and to point out where we do overlap. This concluding segment is not a carpet designed in advance, rather it is a patchwork quilt put together after the facts, as clarification.

John A. Brown (1979) discusses clinical social work as focusing on "people who are encountering problems in some aspects of daily living" (1979:258), a theoretical position virtually my own. Brown treats members of society who are involved in faulty interpersonal relations that affect their social-role functioning. He intervenes at three levels: individual, family, and small groups. Brown stipulates the importance of penetrating the "invisible wall" that is culture, i.e., language, religion, values, life experiences and folk beliefs. If the social worker has knowledge of a client´s culture he can offer therapy as if within that cultural context.

From my experience, what he suggests about the need for a new conception of the therapist´s role is most important and not fully appreciated: therapists need to become more informal, to move at the client´s pace, to exhibit warmth, concern and intimacy and eschew professional aloofness. This is what he calls part of the process of removing artificial barriers (Brown 1979:262).

In contrast to Brown, a major difference can be perceived between psychiatrist Arthur Kleinman (1978) and me. He uses a disease model; I talk of problems of living. This difference has basic implications relating to the kind of help the suffering person seeks, the kind of preparation or training that the helper needs or must have, and (depending on the culture), the nature of the outcome goal determined by sufferer and healer. For "disease," this goal is called "cure," while for "problems," the goal may be to devise a solution, to alter the perception of reality, to make new friends, etc. The real difficulties come when a "problem" and a "disease" meet head on.

In evaluating Clinical Anthropology, it is helpful to examine an article by Julian Rotter on "The Future of Clinical Psychology" written in 1973. At that time, clinical psychologists were having problems of identity. Graduates saw their main functions in community psychology or in offering "growth" experiences to self-selected groups. To the extent that this is true of graduates today, I would be hard put to differentiate community psychology from clinical anthropology.

Rotter implied a weak status of clinical knowledge by admitting that individual therapy is under attack for its inefficiency from a social point of view and its unproven outcomes. Despite this, new therapeutic techniques were developing at a surprising rate. Evaluation was a crying need (Rotter 1973:314). (The same strictures could today be levelled at Clinical

Anthropology). What Rotter suggests for future
academic training could apply equally to clinical
anthropologists: courses on human learning, problem
solving and thinking, social psychology, and social
change. Since most of what he suggests for
psychologists was encompassed by my own training, I
begin to think that (1) many new academic rubrics will
have to be created in the passage of time, or (2)
disciplines will have amorphous boundaries, or (3) new
sub-disciplines of parallel kinds will evolve in the
social sciences. We know that by coincidence the same
year Clinical Anthropology was recognized by the
Society for Applied Anthropology, Clinical Sociology
was independently organized.

I bring in the clinical anthropologist John
Weakland at this point as a means of coming to a
symmetrical conclusion. Weakland, in his article on
Family Somatics (1977), speaks as an anthropologist to
the problem of illness--dealing with family
interactions in etiology and therapy. He and Virginia
Satir were both part of the group in Palo Alto which
has made many creative contributions that are still
ramifying through the helping professions and research
oriented clinical practice. Weakland gives a brief
history of the field of family interaction studies in
the 25 years of his work as a clinical anthropologist.

He makes an illuminating observation that human
disease has its own ecology, and the understanding of
disease must comprehend the pertinent aspects of that
ecology; the patient's emotional involvement in the
family system is an aspect of that ecology "we can no
longer afford to ignore" (Weakland 1977:13). He
further specifies the need to identify the family's
conception of the disease, its nature and history,
previous similar diseases in preceding generations, how
the disease affects the family and what they have done
to handle the problems associated with the disease
(1977:296). These are, of course, commonplace
questions that anthropologists naturally ask.

In conclusion, the June 1980 issue of American
Anthropologist in memoriam to Margaret Mead arrived
just as I was writing the final paragraphs of this
talk. Catherine Bateson writes about her mother that
"Central to her work . . . is the clinician's notion
of disciplined subjectivity . . . bringing the
subjective response into consciousness so that it is
part of the available data" (Bateson 1980:272).

84

Lola Romanucci-Ross entitles her chapter on Mead "Anthropological Field Research: Muse of the Clinical Experience" with a subtitle "The Investigator as Clinician--Is It Science?" It is a complicated and revealing piece from which I pull my final sentence, reminiscent as it is of my earlier paragraphs: "We accept that interaction between what is believed and the action sets that follow those beliefs defines them as being as real as anything . . . " (Romanucci-Ross 1980:313).

REFERENCES

Bateson, Mary Catherine
    1980   Continuities in Insight and Innovation:
            Toward a Biography of Margaret Mead.
            American Anthropologist 82(2):270-277.

Bateson, Gregory
    1958   Language and Pyschotherapy--Greida Fromm
            Reichman's Last Project. Psychiatry
            21:96-100.

Birdwhistell, Ray L.
    1970   Kinesics and Context. Philadelphia:
            University of Pennsylvania Press.

Brown, John A.
    1979   Clinical Social Work with Chicanos. Some
            Unwarrented Assumptions. Clinical Social
            Work Journal 7(4):256-266.

Buckley, Walter, ed.
    1968   Modern Systems Research for the Behavioral
            Scientist. Chicago: Aldine.

Devereux, George
    1950   Mohave Voice and Speech Mannerisms. Word
            6:268-272.

Frank, Jerome D.
    1961   Persuasion and Healing. New York: Schocken
            Books (reprinted 1971).

Kaplan, Helen Singer
    1979   Disorders of Sexual Desire. New York: Simon
            and Schuster.

Kleinman, Arthur et al.
1978   Culture, Illness and Care. Annals of
          Internal Medicine 88:251-258.

LaBarre, Weston
1948   The Cultural Basis of Emotions and Gestures.
          Journal of Personality 16:49-68.

Merton, Robert K.
1949   Social Theory and Social Structure. Glencoe,
          IL: The Free Press of Glencoe, Illinois.

Romanucci-Ross, Lola
1980   Anthropological Field Research: Margaret
          Mead, Muse of Clinical Experience.   American
          Anthropologist 82(2):304-317.

Rosenthal, Robert
1966   Experimenter Effects in Behavioral Research.
          New York: Applenton-Century-Crofts.

Rotter, Julian B.
1973   The Future of Clinical Pyschology.   Journal
          of Consulting Clinical Psychology
          40(2):313-321.

Satir, Virginia
1964   Conjoint Family Therapy. Palo Alto, CA:
          Science and Behavior Books.

Watzlawick, Paul, John Weakland and Richard Fisch
1974   Change: Principles of Problem Formation and
          Problem Resolution. New York: W.W. Norton
          and Company, Inc.

Weakland, John H.
1977   Family Somatics--A Neglected Edge.   Family
          Process 16(3):263-272.

A CASE OF CHILD MEDICAL NEGLECT AND A PLEA FOR INTERDISCIPLINARY RESEARCH

Catherine Alter

Introduction

I have listened today with excitement to the many successful examples of cross-fertilization of anthropology and health care. The control and ultimate prevention of hypertension, the improvement in diagnosis and care of ethnic groups by physicians and nurses, the successful implementation of drug treatment in a lower-class urban neighborhood--are all models which demonstrate the real potential of applying anthropological precepts and skill to our efforts aimed at the preventing and healing of human pain.

Unfortunately, I cannot describe for you from my own experience an effective interdisciplinary program or model such as we are concerned with at this conference. My purpose today will be simply to raise a few questions and to suggest an area for cooperative research and practice that would be most useful and is, from my vantage point, most critical. The area that I am suggesting as an important one for collaborative effort is social casework, and more specifically, child protective services. I will outline a number of issues which concern me greatly and then present you with a case which illustrates these ethical and practical questions. Finally, I will attempt to suggest where the anthropologist and social worker might work together with the goal of improving services to dysfunctional families.

Child Protection Services and Cross-Cultural Interventions

As the director of a private, community-based planning and coordinating agency that works to solve problems within the system of publically funded child protective services, I witness daily the outcomes of state intervention in the lives of families. It is important to realize that the field known as child protective services, or CPS, is quite new. It is true that since the turn of the century we have provided child welfare programs--namely, services such as adoption, foster care, family casework--that were designed to overcome barriers to the healthy development of the child. It is only in the past ten to fifteen years, however, that the state has had broad jurisdiction over a child if it can be shown that the child is not receiving care that approximates society's standard of adequate care. The differences between child welfare and child protection are considerable and this is the basis of my concern.

My concern has two dimensions. Social work and mental health services have, over the past 100 years, evolved a set of theories and principles of good practice that define the client/helper relationship. This set of generally accepted procedures and rules, however, guides the work with a voluntary client. Virtually all clients of child protective services are unwilling participants in the relationship and are involuntary recipients of services. Similar in many respects to criminal justice counseling, the goal of CPS is to find ways to motivate the client to engage in a behavior-changing process which will result in normative parental care. It seems to me that anthropology should be contributing to the development of new knowledge and improvements of practice in the area focused on involuntary clients--especially involuntary clients who are members of minority groups or cultures.

The second broad dimension of the problem as I see it pertains to the efficacy, the process and the results of intervening in the lives of lower class and minority families (who make up 90 percent of CPS caseloads). Sociologist Alvin Gouldner has postulated that:

> . . . lower class groups have a relatively high degree of funtional autonomy vis-a-vis the total social system because that system does little to meet their needs. In general the fewer the rewards a society offers members of a particular group, the more autonomous will that group be with reference to the norms of the society (1959:32).

Without undertaking an exploration of subcultural autonomy, I would still like to suggest that the child abuse and neglect laws hold a new potential of intrusive action which can have serious and perhaps undesirable consequences. In the case of lower-class Black families particularly, some scholars fear that this new mandate will injure that autonomy which, in a perverse way, has contributed over time to the ethnogenesis of Black culture. Lee Rainwater in Behind Ghetto Walls says that:

. . . whites have interfered less in the relations between . . . parents and children than in other areas of Black existence . . . and this freedom has been used to create an institutional variant more distinctive perhaps to the Negro subculture than any other. Much of the content of Negro art and entertainment derives exactly from the distinctive characteristics of Negro family life (1970:6).

It seems to me that the involuntary nature of child protective work and its potential, over time, for imposing majority norms of child care on various ethnic groups makes this an important area of study and work that should not be neglected by anthropology and social work.

Let me assure you that most of us in social work believe that child abuse/neglect laws are necessary, although we would not all agree that the present approach is the best option available. Under any child protective system, however, there are questions that must be carefully addressed. In broadest terms, how can we be sure that state intervention will not harm the child more than she or he is already harmed and further dinimish the child's chances for physical health and a sound personal identity? In more specific terms, we have a set of interrelated questions. If state intervention is justified based upon criteria of that parental behavior which results in demonstrable harm to the child, how can we distinguish between pathological or dysfunctional behavior and that which is environmentally or culturally adaptive? How can a White CPS case worker with a middle-class reality and set of values adequately assess the risk to a child in a family possessing a very different reality orientation? And when that child is found to be at risk, how can a counselor or therapist help a client to change a set of behaviors which are very functional within that family's existence?

A diagnosis, evaluation or assessment--whatever we choose to call that decision-making process by which we label and describe dysfuntion--I think we would agree, is a product of the perception of reality held by the helper and in no other area of social work today is

89

this process more important in terms of its impact on family life than in child protective services.

CPS workers receive reports of abuse or neglect, gather information about the child and family in question, and process that data in order to determine the degree to which the child is at risk and the most effective plan of treatment. That diagnostic process will be shaped by the conditioned reality of the worker and will, therefore, influence whether the results of the process will be no action, brief service, foster care placement, or termination of parental rights. I do not believe I am off-base when I state that often the futures of children and families depend far more on the knowledge and cross-cultural sensitivity of the case worker than on objective assessment criteria.

A Case of "Neglect": The Case Worker's Report

In order to illustrate that any one of the above outcomes is possible, depending upon the perception of the diagnostician, I would like to describe for you a single case, one that is in no way unique or remarkable in and of itself. I have chosen it only for illustrative purposes and because it is a case of medical neglect which I thought would hold special interest for you.

Dorothy Miller originally came to the attention of the child protection agency when she sought medical care for one of her children at an urban hospital. Dorothy is Black, 22 years old, and a single, never-married parent with five children. At the time of her first contact, her youngest child (age 2 months) was hospitalized and diagnosed as failure-to-thrive. He was near death. Over the following few months, the CPS worker attempted to give Dorothy help with a number of child-related problems. Day care was found for two of the children in order to provide her with some respite from child care. One child was evaluated by the Special Education District and placed in a preschool which provided speech therapy. Homemaker services and public health nursing were extended. Nevertheless, the youngest child did not progress and was hospitalized a number of times with pneumonia. The case notes indicate that the worker felt that Dorothy was being resistive-- failing to be home for the community nurse, failing to keep medical appointments, requesting termination of the homemakers' services, failing to follow through with medical treatment, leaving her children unattended in the home. When the middle child sustained accidental but very serious injury in the home, the agency petitioned the Court for custody of all the children. The summary statement in the petition reads as follows:

The Agency is requesting temporary custody. The mother has not provided proper supervision of her children. She has refused services of the agency to help her understand and handle the needs of her children. The youngest child has been hospitalized three times since birth. This child falls considerably below the norm for weight for her age and has other critical health problems. Her most recent hospitalization was caused by neglect of the mother as was the recent accident which injured the middle child. Because of having so many children, the mother did not take the proper precautions to prevent this accident from happening.

The Agency is requesting temporary custody to be given to them because the mother has failed to provide adequate physical and mental care to her five children and because she refuses birth control.

The agency was granted temporary custody of the five children. Three months later the three oldest children were returned to Dorothy and the two youngest remained in foster placement--although the baby, because her health problems were so severe, had gone through three placements. During this time period, Dorothy gave birth to her sixth child.

A Case of "Neglect"--Evaluation by a Diagnostic Team

Six months after the custody hearing, the agency referred the family to a multi-disciplinary diagnostic team for the purpose of determining whether Dorothy was able to manage all six children. The case worker stated in the referral material that Dorothy's resistive behavior had continued: she continued not to keep medical appointments, she would not be home for the workers, etc. The agency felt that the home environment lacked proper stimulation as documented by the fact that the three older children were not functioning at their age levels (could not identify colors, numbers, alphabet, nor own name). In general, the agency described Dorothy with negatives: lacking initiative, uncooperative, unable to handle all her children.

The Diagnostic Team (social worker, psychologist, pediatrician, educational specialist), in their report, came to a somewhat different conclusion because they focused on a different set of data. First, the Team pointed out that Dorothy, over the past year, had been suffering from situational depression due to the fact that the man with whom she had lived, and who was the father of her six children, had left her to marry another woman. The Team's report found that Dorothy's lack of energy and initiative was due, in part, to the grief associated with this loss.

Secondly, the Team felt that Dorothy's behavior also could be explained by the fact that she was caught between two cultures. She had been born in Mississippi where she had lived with her mother until childhood and then had been raised by her grandmother. This family pattern was a prevalent adaptation to the exigencies of economic survival. Dorothy had come North at age seventeen and soon after established the relationship with the man with whom she would live for the next six years. In the rural South, large families were an economic asset and family members shared the child-rearing tasks. In the Northern urban center, however, this pattern was no longer functional and Dorothy was seen by the Team as suffering from this cultural bind.

Thirdly, the Team pointed out that Dorothy was not purposefully neglecting her children's medical care. After all, the reason she had been identified in the first place was that she had taken the baby to the hospital. The psychologist explained that:

. . . Dorothy is not an appointment-oriented person. She has little sense of time and probably forgets appointments quite easily. The Team believes that this personality factor, coupled with the fact that there is no public health care facility in the area, is one reason for Dorothy's negligence in seeking consistent medical help for her children.

Finally, the Team found that Dorothy, although she knew she was dependent on support, was a proud woman and, therefore, had strong feelings of resentment, rebellion, anger and hostility toward the White professionals trying to help her. Wanting to do what was best for her children, but feeling "downtrodden" when accepting help, resulted in an ambivalence which manifested itself in her passive/aggressive behavior.

The Team concluded its evaluation by observing that Dorothy truly cared for her children, that there was an emotional bond between them (except possibly between her and the baby who had been removed from her care at two months), that she was a very good housekeeper, and that the two children still in placement should be returned. The Team recommended that Dorothy continue to receive homemaker, nursing and day care services, and that she should attend a self-help group for single mothers in order to improve her parenting skills. Because of the obvious need to provide medical supervision of the children, the Team also recommended that the agency retain guardianship of the children for one year. Because of Dorothy's obvious hostility toward the White case worker who had removed her children, the Team recommended changing case workers. In short, the Team's perception was that Dorothy was a victim of the clash between her past and present environments but that with sensitive and consistent services she could be helped to improve those parenting skills which were in question: namely, consistency in seeking medical care for her children and appropriate age specific cognitive stimulation for her children.

A Case of "Neglect"--A Black Consultant's Viewpoint

Sometime shortly after the Diagnostic Team's work was completed, we were given an opportunity to obtain yet another view of Dorothy Miller. A Black social worker with an MSW from a prestigious eastern university (I will call her Jackie Kelly) came to our area to lead a workshop for local human service professionals which was to focus on working with Black families. Jackie Kelly reviewed the Miller case material and notes in order to use it as a teaching case in the workshop. In addition to her current position as the director of a multi-agency substance abuse program in lower Manhattan, Jackie has been director of a mental health center and family service agency in New York City.

After reviewing the case, Ms. Kelly diagnosed Dorothy Miller not as seriously dysfuntional and not as a victim--but as a fundamentally healthy person who was surviving the stress of living with poverty. Ms. Kelly

pointed out that environmental stress is the major
factor that must be considered when evaluating families
and that its effects are often confused with
intra-familial dysfunction. As she put it to the
workshop:

> We have to get away from this pathology model.
> Because when we see pathology in everything,
> we come at clients with nothing but pathology
> and then we cannot help these families develop
> the insight to find their own inner strength.
> Any Black family that is here, that is alive
> and is not waiting around the corner to mug
> you, that is not in stores stealing, that is
> not running around setting fires, that is not
> running around committing murder, <u>those</u> <u>are</u>
> <u>strong</u> <u>families</u>. Because it means that they
> have not succumbed to the stresses of poverty
> that impact their daily life and that they
> have not succumbed to the accompanying rage.

Ms. Kelly agreed with the Team that Dorothy Miller
had suffered some depression when she lost her man and
that the grief had interfered with her ability to care
for her children. That Dorothy had some level of
interpsychic dysfunction with attendant features of
alienation, depression and low self-esteem was a
diagnosis with which she did not quarrel. But the fact
that Dorothy was coping at all, that she had finished
high school, that she hadn't abandoned her children but
maintained a nurturing bond, and that she was capable
of feeling the pain and rage of losing a loving
relationship was indicative, in Ms. Kelly's view, that
Dorothy had considerable inner strength. Interveners,
Ms. Kelly said, must keep the client's inter-psychic
dimensions in mind. It is the envionment, however,
which acts upon the inner world of the client, and is a
stronger force in influencing behavior. And it is the
environment which must be used by the social worker to
change problematic behavior.

Just as her evaluation of the case was different
from the agency's and the Team's, so, too, was her
suggested treatment plan. First, and foremost, she
stressed the need for more Black social workers, or
more White social workers who have the knowledge and
skill to cross cultural barriers:

> Too many child protection workers are White,
> and they don't understand the dynamics of what
> it is they are reaching out to--and if you

don't get a client at the first point of contact you have lost them. Let me tell you, Black people who receive child protection services are no more open to receiving them from Black professionals than they are from White professionals. However, one thing the Black client does know is that Black professionals understand. They just put us to a test to see if we are going to act upon that understanding. They put us to the test to see if we are going to negotiate and fight the system we're employed by. But they do know that we understand, and they will tell us things they won't tell somebody else even though they put us through a death of a test trying to engage us. "Win me sista," that's what they tell us. But they know that we are on target, and they know that our approach is going to be such that they can be comfortable with it.

Secondly, Ms. Kelly stressed the profound need to accept the client as she or he is and to focus upon pragmatic, environmental needs. In the case of Dorothy Miller, the needs were many. Ms. Kelly discussed two with the workshop participants.

If it had been me, as a Black social worker working with that sister, I wouldn't talk about the medical needs of those kids. I would have said, "Sister, look what we got to do first is see how we can get you another good man and we got to make sure that the man you get is better than that one you had." And as we focused on the things she had to do to get her next good man, that would have taken care of a lot of what she needed to do for the kids. I would have told her, "no brother wants no woman that can't take care of her home, no brother wants no woman that the neighbors are saying are neglecting her children, and if she wants to get a man she got to get her program together."

They tell me that when asked, this mother said that the only thing she needed to be a good mother was a car. Well, if I lived in this community I would want a car, too. It's hard getting around here with five kids--no cabs, few buses. I would have started where she was, I would have said, "listen sista,

okay, fine you want a car, but this is what
you got to do in order to get a car." The
steps that that woman would have had to take
to get a car would have moved her toward
improving how she's handling her life, and
that would have taken care of the kids.

Ms. Kelly's recommendations, then, were to listen
without "cultural biases" to the pragmatic sense of
what the client was saying. She firmly stated that had
the treatment plan been focused on Dorothy Miller
"getting herself together to get a good man and a car,"
the medical needs of the kids would have been met.

A Case of "Neglect"--Unresolved Problems and Research Needs

Who's right? Who owns the truth? It depends, of
course, on your own personal place in the world. We
certainly cannot, at this time, cite any empirical
evidence to validate any of the three assessments. I
began this address by pointing out how recently the
child abuse/neglect laws have been enacted. We have
little research on, or experience in working with,
unwilling families in this field where the potential
for hurting is so great. Was more harm done to Dorothy
Miller's children by the assessment and plan that was
adopted--five of the children were ultimately and
permanently removed from her care by the Court--or
would one of the alternate plans have done less harm?
This is an interdisciplinary research question that I
believe is an important and critical one.

The whole question of adaptive behavior, when it
can be shown to have a grave effect on the child, is
another subject for research. Carol Stack concludes
her wonderful analysis of urban Black families by
saying:

> [the] highly adaptive structural features of
> urban Black families comprise a resilient
> response to the social-economic conditions of
> poverty, the inexorable unemployment of Black
> women and men, and the access to scarce
> economic resources of a mother and her
> children as AFDC recipients (1974).

It certainly cannot be ethical or moral to remove a
child because of the parent's "resilient response
to . . . [racist] . . . conditions." But what if the

96

child's life is in danger? What if the child's potential is severely limited or crushed by these behaviors? When does adaptive behavior become abuse or neglect? Ever?

Finally, I would like to suggest that we had better look together at models of adult learning that will enable baccalaureate level social workers to gain and apply bi-cultural perspectives. Today, when staff development and training funds are the first to go and when the least well-trained workers are most often the ones in the field making the decisions, we should be looking for effective, but inexpensive, ways of helping workers stretch their values. And that, too, is a research question.

REFERENCES

Gouldner, Alvin W.
  1959   Reciprocity and Autonomy in Functional
          Theory. In Symposium on Sociological Theory.
          Llewellyn Gross, ed. p. 32. Evanston, IL:
          Row, Peterson and Co.

Rainwater, Lee
  1970   Behind Ghetto Walls. Chicago: Aldine
          Publishing Co.

Stack, Carol B.
  1974   All Our Kin: Strategies for Survival in a
          Black Community. New York: Harper & Row.

SELF-HELP GROUPS, PROFESSIONALS, AND THE REDEFINITION OF PATHOLOGICAL STATES

Leonard D. Borman

Introduction

Since Alcoholics Anonymous was founded in 1935, a large number of self-help/mutual aid groups has emerged where individuals who are similarly afflicted affiliate with each other. In two recent directories, compiled in large part by the Self-Help Center, nearly 400 self-help groups were identified in the United States and Canada (Evans 1979), and in the Chicago area alone, over 100 were listed (Chicago Tribune, Sept. 7, 1980). Recent studies that I have undertaken with colleagues indicate that these groups are by no means a passing fashion, but represent the emergence of common interest groups or voluntary associations that always have been important forms of social organization on the American landscape (Lieberman and Borman 1979).[1] The fact that groups are forming of those who have common afflictions or conditions, or who are even stigmatized, has become of increasing interest to health and social service professionals and agencies (Gartner and Riessman 1977; Katz and Bender 1976; Robinson and Henry 1977). Some of our findings, which I will report on later, indicate that these groups represent a critical resource for helping their participants in important therapeutic ways. They are by no means superficial in their impact. What I would like to focus on in this paper is not so much the basis for their emergence, nor even their impact, but rather their implications for redefining the pathological states they represent. Advances in our understanding of illness and health have always been based on studies of the diseased state. It would seem to follow that these self-help groups, composed of persons who face a variety of afflictions, can shed light on the nature of the pathology or condition they might represent. However, our "case material" comes not from the laboratory, nor from autopsies, nor from the dead, but the living. It is derived from persons who attempt to thrive and cope, to overcome their afflictions, or improve the quality of their lives, by helping each other in natural situations of everyday life.

Much of our knowledge advances in medicine, as in the other sciences, not in a unilinear manner, as if we were placing a brick of truth on a wall of knowledge. Rather, knowledge is advanced by a zig zag process, in which ideas, theories, or positions, often in opposition to one another, are offered to explain the phenomena under consideration. There may be a dialectic or tug-of-war between various viewpoints. New theories may take some time to gain adherents or recognition. They need to be tested, qualified and refined. Yet, someone must nurture the ideas in their infancy, and draw attention to the ways in which their special viewpoints and findings may be applicable to other persons facing the same afflictions.

This is one way in which self-help/mutual aid groups often become advocates for new ways to think about afflictions. But these groups do not represent the disinterest or objectivity often attributed to the scientist; they have a special vantage point. They represent the self-interest of those for whom the findings become a life or death matter. They may live or die, or their loved ones will live or die, from the condition or affliction.

Accordingly, there is a special role that many human service professionals and researchers have in assisting in the formation of these groups and in learning from them. I shall describe some of these professionals, including my own role as an action anthropologist, later in this paper. First, I would like to consider some of the ways many of these groups are helping to redefine pathological states. Let us consider first, one of the oldest self-help groups, Alcoholics Anonymous.

Redefining Pathological States

In the 1930's, when AA was formed, and perhaps continuing into the present, alcoholism was seen as a character defect representing a personal and moral weakness. It was not essentially viewed as a medical problem. Nevertheless, some early physicians who worked with alcoholics and became associated with the development of Alcoholics Anonymous took a contrary point of view. They viewed alcoholism as a disease that represented a combination of mental obsession and physical allergy. The work of William Silkworth, Harry Tiebout, and others was published in numerous professional journals documenting this view with cases drawn increasingly from their work with Alcoholics Anonymous (Tiebout 1944; AA Comes of Age 1957). While complexities of alcoholism cannot be attributed to any single theory, nevertheless, in over 40 years, AA has grown to the point where it identifies over 1,000,000 persons in 105 countries who are maintaining sobriety as a result of group participation. Their twelve steps, combined with complete abstinence, are based on this special view of the nature of addiction. In most cases, the 44,000 chapters of AA work closely with hospitals and treatment centers in order to coordinate AA programs with professional detoxification services. And related Alanon/Alateen programs, designed for the family and friends of alcoholics, are likewise growing in numbers.

A somewhat reverse example, where a self-help group sought to disengage its condition from being considered a pathological state is provided by the homosexual or Gay groups in American society. Through the national advocacy activities of such groups, they succeeded in convincing the American Psychiatric Association to eliminate homosexuality as a pathological condition recognized as such in the APA diagnostic manual. For many gays, homosexuality is considered a chosen life-style, to be considered distinct from problems of sexual orientations that may require professional help.

In the mental health field, a number of self-help groups have sought to clarify the conditions of those they represent. Recovery, Inc., formed in 1937, maintained that adult life was guided more by will--by how one used brains and muscles--than by instincts. Accordingly, this self-help group took issue with prevailing theories of psychotherapy that were based in great part on psychosexual development. Psychopathology was defined in Recovery terms, not so much in the form of psychological complexes that resulted from earlier development and unconscious conditions, but rather as an inability to exert one's will, thoughts, and mind in controlling rage, temper, or other emotional states. No matter the stress in life, every individual was viewed as having the power of choice represented in a vigilant will (Low 1950).

Likewise, Integrity Groups evolved from a reconceptualization of the conventional causes of neuroses. Instead of relating such disorders of personality to an over-strict superego, conscience or to false fears, an alternative view is developed that focuses on the importance of recovering integrity and identity in the presence of a small group of others with similar objectives. While conventional views of neurosis and mental illness focused essentially on intrapsychic conflict, the position taken by Integrity Groups viewed personal disturbances in terms of interpersonal relations (Mowrer 1968; Mowrer and Vattano 1976).

Both Recovery and GROW, the self-help group developed widely in Australia, likewise focused not so much on the intrapsychic or the organic nature of pathology, but on the stigmatizing conditions mental patients faced in returning to their homes and communities. Psychopathology, from this vantage point, needed to be understood in terms of mental patients' relationships to others.

Many of the consciousness-raising groups founded by women to overcome sexism and to strengthen feminism have had an important influence in re-defining women's health issues. The feminist critique has been applied to practically all problems of living that women face with the "afflictions" viewed generally as results of male-dominated oppression (Lieberman and Bond 1976: Kleiber and Light 1978).

While the health-related goals of the women's movement have focused on infusing the women's experience into health care systems, they have equally been concerned with encouraging women's knowledge and responsibilities for their own bodies.

Schizophrenics Anonymous, and other associations of seriously disturbed individuals and their families, have focued importance on orthomolecular theories of mental illness, which attributed much of pathology to nutritional deficiencies and allergic reactions. Many of these groups related closely to the Huxley Institute which conducts research and disseminates information on the use of appropriate nutritions for reducing the incidence of chronic mental illness, retardation, learning disabilities and related disorders. Many of these groups support professional facilities where schizophrenics and others who have not responded to conventional treatments can be presented with these other options which reduce dependence on medications.

Our recent "action learning" activities with epilepsy self-help groups across the country reveal the critical importance of the nonmedical aspects of this malady. A person who develops seizures faces an increasing atrophy of social ties, frequent fear and rejection by the public, along with increasing psychological stress. These social and personal relations can contribute to a vicious circle in which seizure activity and its consequences grow worse (see Borman, Davies, and Droge, 1980). Findings on the nature of the affliction that emerge from epilepsy self-help groups seem quite consonant with recent epidemiological findings. These suggest that "a whole new understanding of epilepsy must be generated--one that is consistent with the evidence that epilepsy is a societal disease, a disease generated by many of the facets of our modern technological society, a disease that is in large part a product of trauma in our time, a disease that afflicts the poor of our society in disproportionate numbers" (Whitman et al. 1980: 268).

Many self-help/mutual aid groups have formed around conditions that have been ignored by modern medicine and human service agencies. These would include groups formed of persons who face life-threatening illness, including cancer, senile dementia, and sudden traumas. Many of their efforts are directed not so much to change existing practice and theory, as to advocate activities designed to pay attention to their conditions. Accordingly, groups such as the Alzheimer's Association are interested in raising funds for basic research on crippling dementia that affects persons over 50, and providing support for famiies dealing with members so afflicted. Groups formed around such life-threatening illnesses as cancer, e.g., Make Today Count, seek to interest professionals in paying more attention to the psychological, physical, and social conditions that terminal patients find themselves coping with. These groups find that many of the stages of the affliction, including the ways in which treatments are administered, can be importantly affected by both the therapists' and patients' outlook, the support provided by family and friends, and belief systems fostered by specific self-help groups. Many surgeons and cardiologists who are active sponsors of Mended Hearts, the self-help group for persons who have experienced heart surgery, regard this self-help group as one from which they can improve knowledge about conditions and treatments that may be prescribed following surgery. The many physicians who serve on the advisory board of Mended Hearts, and who attend their meetings and conventions, derive valuable information on conditions following surgery.

Results of Outcome Studies

Until recently, there has been little substantive knowledge about self-help group effectiveness. One of the reasons that outcome studies are rare is the fact that the self-help researcher has less control over the intervention system than is ordinarily experienced by outcome or evaluation researchers of traditional, professional helping systems. In addition, many participants in self-help groups may cycle their participation, moving freely to inactive status until a specific period in their lives when the trauma or condition occurs again, at which time, they once again re-enter the group. Such patterns of use add to the problem of studying the impact of the group on individual participants.

Nevertheless, there have been some impressive findings. The studies that Morton Lieberman and I have published indicate significant findings with women's consciousness raising groups, members of Mended Hearts, participants in Theos (a self-help group for widows and widowers), and participants in Compassionate Friends, for parents who have lost children.

In utilizing a variety of measures that focus around mental health, personal values, marital relationship, and attitudes and orientations, there appeared to be a highly specific set of impacts such groups had on their participants. With the women's groups, significant increments were found in self esteem, self concept, and alterations in life style. With Mended Hearts, significant effects were found for those individuals who were forced to retire because of their health. Those who were members of Mended Hearts experienced fewer somatic symptoms, higher self esteem, higher levels of coping mastery, and fewer physical symptoms.

The study of widows and widowers in Theos, comparing participants and non-participants, and using a variety of mental health indices such as depression, anxiety, somatic symptoms, utilization of psychotropic drugs, self esteem, coping mastery and well being, indicated significant effects for active participation. The highest benefit seemed to accrue to widows who became linked to an active, ongoing resource exchange social network that grew out of their relationships established in the self-help group. Likewise, the study of Compassionate Friends found group participation had a significant effect on the strategies participants used to cope with the death of a child. (Elaboration of these findings are found in Lieberman and Borman 1979; Lieberman and Borman 1981; Borman and associates 1982.)

Self-Help Group Helping Mechanisms

One of the major findings in our recent studies of self-help groups that has encouraged greater public and professional interest is the recognition of what participants derive from their experiences. In the past, self-help groups have been criticized as being superficial, worthless, or even harmful to members. Our findings strongly suggest the contrary. We have been impressed with the number of helping mechanisms that operate within self-help groups. Interestingly enough, many of these are usually beyond the purview of conventional treatment. Let me identify some of them.

The importance of universality and acceptance, of choosing to be part of a group of others who share your condition and understand what you are experiencing seems to be central. Voluntary participation is important. In the self-help groups, moreover, you are not isolated, weak, and alone, but are communicating together with others like yourself. You are in the "same boat" together. The mix of participants usually includes persons who are at different stages in the affliction or coping process. Elements of cohesion, involvement and "belongingness" offer important support to participants. Groups focus their attention on fostering communication, providing their members with social support, responding to both emotional and informational needs. These occur in settings which are non-coercive, non-threatening, and under the control and management of peers.

In addition, we have noted the importance of altruism, of helping others who are faced with the condition you are facing or once did. The twelfth step of AA, in which you are encouraged to help other alcoholics, is a good example of this. Similarly, the primary orientation of Mended Hearts is captured in their motto, "It's great to be alive and help others." This finds expression in their visitation program to others about to have heart surgery. This has also been characterized as the "helper therapy principle." Simply stated, it means that in helping other persons, you are helping yourself.

Additional helping mechanisms focus around sharing common values, having opportunities to talk at great length with others like yourself, and developing a sense of hope. This is especially important when members of your "natural support systems"--your family and friends--may not have the interest or patience or capacity to communicate about what you regard as the crucial concerns in your life.

One critical mechanism which has not received sufficient attention is the role of belief systems and ideologies for different conditions and afflictions. This may be one of the most central findings emerging from studies of self-help groups in recent years. Paul Antze (1979) has termed these belief systems "cognitive antidotes." They repreent particular teachings, wisdoms, or beliefs that serve as the persuasive function of self-help groups in addition to their supportive or integrative functions. For example, in his analysis of Recovery, AA and Synanon, Antze sees each of these groups as "relatively fixed communites of belief." Let me paraphrase him. The elements of Synanon ideology may be understood as a concerned attack on all the features of the drug addict´s relapse process. The world of everyday life, known as the "floor," calls for redirecting the addict´s attention away from his own level of stress to the surrounding social environment. While this provides a measure of control over one´s tensions, it does not eliminate them. It is the "game," or what has been called "an emotional bathroom," that serves to purge one´s tensions. Here one shares unconfessed fears, resentments, and misdeeds with the group. The "game" works the opposite of heroin. Where heroin serves to isolate, distance, and detach one, the "game" provides an expressive outlet which establishes a new closeness to one´s fellows. The overall ideology expresses a new theory of stress which relieves feelings once remedied by drugs. The "game" combined with the "floor" shapes the meaning of stress, restores for one a sense of his interpersonal origins, and through sharing with the group, opens him to others. Mutual confessions then become a source of mutual loyalty and establish a new level of closeness (Antze 1979).

(It should be pointed out that while this ideology developed initially at Synanon, it has become the prevailing mechanism in hundreds of "therapeutic communities" across the United States and in over fifty countries where drug-free residential programs have been established. Ironically, Synanon not only does

106

not participate in the annual international conferences of therapeutic communities; it is regarded, by most members of these communities, as an example of the corruption brought about by the absolute power of its founder, Charles Dederich.)

One of the reasons that these helping mechanisms are ignored by conventional therapists is their diminished need for a therapist's involvement. These are peer self-help groups, and as I indicate in the next section, while professionals have frequently played important roles in their formation and development, they do not have integral functions in the groups' helping processes. Another question is the proper use and effectiveness of self-help groups. Since systematic outcome studies are just beginning to be published, many professionals may be guarded in their referrals to many groups.

A number of recent surveys of professional attitudes toward self-help groups indicate, however, that the earlier notion that professionals were somehow hostile to self-help groups is no longer true. For example, in recent survey of 160 professionals in Evanston, Illinois (representing a 40% response) undertaken by the Self-Help Center in cooperation with the Evanston Mental Health Board, indicated the importance and usefulness of self-help groups.

Briefly, these were the findings:

1. Respondents by profession: nurses, 3%; counseling psychologists, 19%: pastoral psychologists, 3%; psychiatrists, 4%; social workers, 36%; physicians, 4%; teachers, 5%; clergymen, 8%; others, 14%; no identification, 2%.

2. Eight-five percent indicated that they made referrals of clients (or students or patients) over the course of a year to self-help groups.

3. Seventy-four percent indicated that self-help groups have something to offer their clients or themselves.

4. Sixty-five percent indicated that there is a kind of understanding and empathy which self-help groups offer that professionals simply cannot provide.

5. Ninety-one percent indicated that self-help groups are a useful adjunct to professional services.

6. Eighty-eight percent felt that self-help groups should be a recognized and utilized part of the total mental health delivery system. (Preliminary Results of Self-Help Center Survey, June, 1983).

This survey confirms similar findings found in Toronto, Canada, and Hamburg, Germany, indicating that professionals are prepared to make referrals to self-help groups, find such groups useful, and hold favorable attitudes toward self-help groups.

Roles of Professionals

The importance of self-help groups in helping to provide new therapies and findings around pathological conditions, and in developing a great range of therapeutic mechanisms, has not been completely ignored by professionals. In our review of ten major self-help groups, we have found that in six groups a seasoned professional played a key role in founding or co-founding the organization. This includes Recovery, Integrity Groups, GROW, Compassionate Friends, Parents Anonymous, and Epilepsy Self-Help Groups. Even with others, professionals have played instrumental roles at various stages of the organization's development. Most of these groups cannot be considered solely indigenous, nor can they be conceived of as anti-professional. Our studies of heart surgery groups, epilepsy groups, consciousness raising groups, widows, and others, indicate that the participants in these groups utilize professional services to a rather great extent and report general satisfaction with these services (Lieberman, Borman and Associates 1979).

How can we characterize those professionals who became actively involved in founding, supporting, or in other ways participating actively in the development and encouragement of self-help groups? Clearly they did not adhere rigidly to the conventional theories or practices within their own disciplines. In the analysis of their roles in the groups listed above, I have found at least nine ways in which these professionals have gone beyond such conventional restraints, leading them to participate actively in the development of self-help groups. These can be identified as follows:

1. Some professionals took issue with theories in their field, and articulated new concepts or approaches that became the basis for the self-help groups with which they were identified. This would apply to Abraham Low, the psychiatrist who founded Recovery, and O. Hobart Mowrer, the psychologist who founded Integrity Groups.

2. Many of these professionals altered the usual specification of the condition or affliction. William Silkworth, one of the physicians who treated Bill Wilson, co-founder of AA, was responsible for helping to identify problems of alcoholics as due to a combination of mental obsession and physical susceptibility. Psychiatrist Harry Tiebout became aware of the role that religion plays in changing alcoholics and anchoring new sets of emotions into the structure of an addictive personality.

3. Most of the professionals involved in self-help groups recognized a broader repertoire of skills and techniques than was conventionally utilized in their fields. Psychiatrist Daniel Casriel recognized the value of "attack therapy" as it was employed in the "game" development of Synanon. Social worker Leonard Lieber encouraged the development of Parents Anonymous chapters for reaching child abusers at all hours of the day or night.

4. These professionals, as mentioned earlier, focused on a stage of the disorder normally overlooked by their colleagues. They were concerend with rehabilitation and after-care, community receptivity to discharged mental patients, problems of relapses in the treatment of alcoholics, and the focus on terminal illness, including social and psychological problems faced by surviving relatives. Reverend Simon Stephens, founder of Compassionate Friends, attacked the "conspiracy of silence" about death that pervaded conventional institutions, including hospitals.

5. These professionals were concerned with populations normally neglected by conventional service delivery systems. Leonard Lieber notes that there was little attention paid to child abusers, apart from efforts at incarceration. What was true of abusive parents applied to drug addicts, alcoholics, formally hospitalized mental patients, widows, persons coping with epilepsy, and others.

6. Many of the professionals involved with self-help groups diverged from their colleagues in recognizing new roles for themselves and their colleagues. Often these roles involved close collaboration with the afflicted population, best characterized by being "on tap, but not on top." Even in the case of Recovery, where Doctor A.A. Low's books and tapes have become the basis for group meetings, management and leadership for the organization are vested with the volunteer leaders and members, while professionals are generally excluded from group leadership positions.

7. Another way in which professionals have gone beyond conventional boundaries of their disciplines is in advocating new auspices under which self-help groups can be formed. They were not limited by the hospital, clinic, or church, and often formed groups in homes, libraries or other settings. In many cases, groups were encouraged to form their own not-for-profit corporations.

8. They relied little on conventional referral, screening, and recruitment procedures. Little emphasis was placed on professionally-derived standards and quality control. Members were frequently contacted through word of mouth, the media, and informal contacts. Group leaders emerged from the general participants.

9. Finally, these professionals were rarely concerned with fees. Moreover, many invested their own funds, in addition to their time, in the early and continuing efforts of self-help group development.

Action Anthropology

I shall conclude this paper by identifying my own experiences as a professional anthropologist in learning about affliction-oriented self-help groups and in helping with their formation. This occurred initially when I helped to organize patient self-help councils at Downey Veteran's Hospital, one of the largest federal mental hospitals in the United States. I served there as Chief of the Anthropology Service, and my methods of operation were derived from action anthropology, defined in the classic paper by Sol Tax in this way:

110

An activity in which an anthropologist has two coordinate goals, to neither one of which he will delegate an inferior position. He wants to help a group of people solve a problem and he wants to learn something in the process. He refuses ever to think or to say that the people involved are for him a means of advancing his knowledge; and he refuses to think or to say that he is simply applying science to the solutions of those peoples' problems. If applied anthropology presupposes a body of scientific knowledge--competent empirical propositions--developed by theoretical anthropologists and awaiting application to particular situations when we are asked to do so by management, government, administrator or organization, then action anthropology is far different...The action anthropologist realizes that his problem is less the application of general propositions than the development and clarification of goals and the compromising of conflicting ends or values. In fact, the action anthropologist finds that the proportion of new knowledge which must be developed in the situation is very great in comparison to old knowledge which he can apply. He is and must be a theoretical anthropologist, not only in background but in practice (1952:103,104).

The combined research and practical mission that I had at Downey focused around the long-term, so-called chronic patients who never were discharged into the community. I hoped to come up with ideas and services that would contribute to the purposes of the hospital, which were to return every veteran to a full and useful life in the outside community. Clearly, my major concern as an action anthropologist was to focus on practical issues rather than historical and theoretical problems, and to participate with both patients and staff in finding ways to achieve some common objectives. Much of my work and observations here foreshadowed the scholarly and practical activities I have subsequently pursued with self-help/mutual aid groups for a variety of afflictions (see Borman 1979).

Some of my experiences at Downey help to explain why self-help/mutual aid groups are becoming so widespread in the United States and abroad. These early experiences also indicate some contributions anthropologists can make in learning about self-help

groups and in encouraging this resource for persons
with a variety of afflictions.

I was frankly surprised with the paucity of theory
that would underlie practical efforts to provide help
for long-term hospitalized patients. A sense of
hopelessness for the long-term patient seemed to
pervade the hospital staff. Acute patients were those
who responded to existing therapies, while chronic
patients, almost by definition, were those who did not.
Moreover, these two kinds of patients were also divided
in terms of their location in the hospital. A
patient's building number and geographical location
signalled both to the patient and the hospital staff a
condition from which few were expected to recover.
There was a general overlay of institutional features
in addition to the geographical location, that had
consequences for patient behavior, demands,
aspirations, and general quality of life. Goffman has
described this so well in papers on the total
institution (1957). Mutually hostile stereotypes were
maintained between patients and staff; distancing
occurred where staff might have contacts with patients
but few therapeutically designed relationships. In
general, custodial principles and managment were
instituted where most therapeutic technologies failed.

The culture of the hospital was a dependent one,
and the social structure or social relations that
existed among staff dovetailed well with these
prevailing views. As a large hospital bureaucracy, the
professional staff were locked into well-defined roles
or position descriptions. By their vary nature, they
limited initiative and imagination and stymied most
efforts for innovation and change.

The staff were technical specialists concered with
job descriptions and boundary lines clearly defined in
terms of services offered, space they laid claim to,
equipment they could utilize, and kinds of patients
they could best deal with. In addition, there was
considerable sparring among professionals that occurred
around issues of authority, responsiblity, and control.

I am suggesting that these professional and
institutional conditions provided the setting out of
which self-help groups emerged. Most theories of
informal, voluntary associations and common interest
groups note that such groups develop when existing
institutions and services simply are not sufficing to
meet people's needs (MacIver 1931; Wolff 1950). Even

112

in a highly controlled total institution, where patients were watched carefully, confined to locked wards, and tranquilized heavily, it was possible for self-help/mutual aid groups to develop. These hospital innovations, however, required professional efforts.

My activities at Downey, through the Anthropology Service, undertook such innovative directions with long-term patients. These focused essentially around the formation of patient self-help councils, initially with patients in the back wards of the hospital. Many professionals were surprised that this was even possible, and a good number joined in the efforts. These included nurses, recreation staff, psychologists, and psychiatrists, and served as a meeting point for both professionals and patients to develop new approaches for helping a neglected population (see Borman 1970).

These pioneering efforts for collaboration with both patients and staff at Downey provided a model for subsequent activities and studies with a variety of other populations formed into self-help groups. In my collaboration with Morton Lieberman (Lieberman, Borman and Associates 1979), where there was a major concern with technical and conceptual problems in assessing the benefits of self-help groups, we noted that new efforts were required at collaboration between professional practitioners, self-help groups, and researchers. The helping-learning models provided by action anthropology not only aided in providing mutual access of professionals to self-help groups and vice versa, but in contributing to our mutual understanding of each other's roles in joint endeavors.

As social scientists, we have too frequently been naive about the potentials for collaboration, and it seems that few have really explored the possibilities of collaborative inquiry. We believe that models of meaningful collaboration can be developed and executed, but they will involve the researcher in activities that do not entirely fit with the archetypal view of what research is and how one conducts it. The kind of research findings that emerge and the way in which they are learned, we believe, will be the product of a genuine partnership between the researchers and the members of the self-help group. Realistic collaborative arrangements that involve important pay-offs

113

to the groups, as well as to science, are essential (Lieberman and Borman 1979:460,463).

An important development of this collaborative activity has not only involved efforts to overcome "archetypal" research roles, but to develop new organization auspices under which joint research and helping activities can be implemented. Nearly a dozen self-help clearinghouses have been established since 1974, as adjuncts to universities and mental health centers. In 1980, the Self-Help Center in Evanston became the first independent research and information clearinghouse in the nation. This followed the recommendations made by several of us who had participated in the work of the President's Commission on Mental Health (1978). Not only were such clearinghouses recommended for every federal region, along with the development and dissemination of local self-help group directories, but emphasis was equally placed on the importance of new knowledge and skills for human service professionals. These were to encompass the value and usefulness of community support, natural networks, and self-help groups for vast segments of our population. Already many professional training programs are beginning to implement these suggestins (see Gartner and Riessman 1977; Vinokur-Kaplan 1979). Moreover, activities in European countries seem to be following a similar pattern (see Bakker and Karel 1979).

Clearly a new vista may be opening up for anthropologists that far exceeds the ethnographic opportunities that began in the nineteenth century. The current direction, moreover, as this essay indicates (along with other contributions to this volume), will combine the "heart" and the "head." Anthropologists will not only continue to contribute to theory and knowledge, but directly engage in promoting the well-being of individuals, groups, and communities as well. The development of Clinical Anthropology will surely accelerate this process, for it will foster communication not only among anthropologists, but with other professionals and segments of society that share the goals of learning and helping.

NOTE

1. The Journal of Applied Behavioral Science 12(3), 1976 is devoted to a comprehensive review of self-help groups.

REFERENCES

Alcoholics Anonymous
1957   Alcoholics Anonymous Comes of Age. New York: Alcoholics Anonymous World Services.

Antze, Paul
1979   Role of Ideologies in Peer Psychotherapy Groups. In Self-Help Groups for Coping with Crisis. Morton A. Lieberman and Leonard D. Borman, eds. San Francisco: Jossey-Bass.

Bakker, B. and M. Karel
1979   Zelfhulp en Welzijnswerk (Self-Help and Welfare Work). Brussels: Samson Uitgevij.

Borman, L.D.
1970   The Marginal Role of a Mental Hospital Innovation. Human Organization 29:63-69.

1979   Action Anthropology and The Self-Help/Mutual Aid Movement. In Currents in Anthropology: Essays in Honor of Sol Tax. Robert Hinshaw, ed. The Hague: Mouton.

Borman, L.D., L. Borek, R. Hess, and F. Pasquale, eds.
1982   Helping People to Help Themselves. New York: Haworth.

Borman, L.D., J. Davies and D. Droge
1980   Self-Help Groups for Persons With Epilepsy. In A Multi-disciplinary Handbook of Epilepsy. Bruce P. Hermann, ed. Springfield, IL: Charles C. Thomas.

Evans, Glen
1979   The Family Circle Guide to Self-Help. New York: Ballantine.

Gartner, A. and F. Riessman
1977   Self-Help in the Human Services. San
        Francisco, Washington, London: Jossey-Bass.

Goffman, E.
1957   The Characteristics of Total Institutions.
        In Symposium on Preventative and Social
        Psychiatry. pp. 43-84. Washington, D.C.:
        Walter Reed Army Institute of Research.

Goodstein, L.D.   (General Ed.), M. Lieberman and
L.D. Borman (Special Editors)
1976   Self-Help Groups. The Journal of Applied
        Behavioral Science 12(3).

Katz A. and E. Bender
1976   The Strength In Us. New York, London:
        Franklin Watts.

Kleiber, N. and L. Light
1978   Caring for Ourselves. National Health
        Research and Development Project No. 610 of
        Health and Welfare Canada.

Lieberman, M.A. and G. Bond
1976   The Problem of Being a Woman: A Survey of
        1,700 Women in Consciousness-Raising Groups.
        The Journal of Applied Behavioral Science
        12(3):363-379.

Lieberman, M.A. and Leonard D. Borman
1981   The Impact of Self-Help Groups on Widows'
        Mental Health. National Reporter 4(7), July.
        Evanston, IL: National Research and
        Information Center.

Lieberman, M.A., Leonard D. Borman and Associates
1979   Self-Help Groups for Coping With Crisis. San
        Francisco: Jossey-Bass.

Low, A.A.
1950   Mental Health Through Will-Training. Boston,
        MA: Christopher Publishing House.

Martin, Paul
1980   Chicago's Grass-Roots Problem Solvers.
        Chicago Tribune, Sept. 7.

MacIver, R.M.
1931   Society and Its Structure and Changes. New
        York: Long and Smith.

116

Mowrer, O.H.
1968   New Evidence Concerning the Nature of
        Psychopathology. In Studies in Pyschotherapy
        and Behavior Change. M.H. Feldman, ed.
        Vol. 1, Buffalo, NY: University of Buffalo
        Press.

Mowrer, O.H. and A. Vattano
1976   Integrity Groups: A Context for Growth in
        Honesty, Responsibility, and Involvement.
        The Journal of Applied Behavioral Science
        12(3):419-433.

President's Commission on Mental Health
1978   Commission Report. Vol. 1, Washington D.C.:
        U.S. Government Printing Office.

Robinson, D. and S. Henry
1977   Self-Help and Health. Great Britain: Chaucer
        Press.

Tax, Sol
1952   Action Anthropology. America Indigena
        12:103-106.

Tiebout, H.M.
1944   Therapeutic Mechanisms of AA. American
        Journal of Pyschiatry 100:473-486.
        (Reprinted in Alcoholics Anonymous Comes of
        Age. New York: Alcoholics Anonymous World
        Services, 1975.)

Vinokur-Kaplan, Diane
1979   The Relevance of Self-Help Groups to Social
        Work Education. Contemporary Social Work
        Education 2(2):29-86.

Wolff, K.H.
1950   The Sociology of Georg Simmel. New York:
        Free Press.

Whitman, S., T. Coleman, B. Berg, K. Lambert and
B. Desai
1980   Epidemiological Insights Into the
        Socioeconomic Correlates of Epilepsy. In A
        Multidisciplinary Handbook of Epilepsy.
        Bruce P. Hermann, ed. Springfield, IL:
        Charles C. Thomas.

RESEARCH, SERVICE AND TRAINING ASPECTS OF CLINICAL
ANTHROPOLOGY: AN INSTITUTIONAL OVERVIEW

Hazel H. Weidman

Introduction

The original title for this presentation was,
"Disease and Symbol in Illness." I believe the
conference organizers saw this as a topic which would
illustrate the relevance of an anthropological approach
to clinical matters. It was intended that I discuss,
from a transcultural perspective, some of the
difficulties in diagnosing and treating conditions
whose symptom clusters are linked by patients to one
symbol system and by physicians (and other health
professionals) to another very different symbolic
structure. Falling-out, a culture specific,
seizure-type disorder identified during our research in
Miami, would have served well as an acceptable case
study within such a framework. However, since this
syndrome has been fully reported in the literature
(Weidman et al. 1978; Weidman 1979:95-112) it seems
less redundant and more in line with the goals of this
meeting to describe the tripartite nature of my
anthropological activities as they have related to
medicine generally and health care specifically.
Disease and symbol in illness will be a recurrent
theme, but it will be within the operational context of
the subdiscipline of Medical Anthropology; more
specifically, in that division of the discipline which
is clinically focused, i.e., Clinical Anthropology.
Inasmuch as my career profile is somewhat atypical for
the picture presented earlier in this volume by Gern
and Shimkin, it seems important to make a few comments
about my preparation for the activities to be
described.

Graduate Training

Unlike many who have been drawn to Clinical
Anthropology following a more traditional
anthropological graduate experience, my graduate
training, by design, was explicitly oriented toward
relationships between anthropology and medicine. This
was in the early 1950´s before the general field of
medical anthropology had fully emerged. During
graduate years in the Department of Social Relations at

119

Harvard Univesity, I had the good fortune to be advised by William Caudill, whose pioneering review article appeared shortly after my arrival there (Caudill 1953). Also, in the School of Public Health across the river, I benefitted from the guidance of Benjamin Paul, whose classic Health, Culture, and Community appeared in 1955 following thorough review and discussion by participants in his seminar on anthropology and public health practice (Paul 1955). Furthermore, psychological anthropologists Clyde Kluckhohn and Cora DuBois both supported my interests in culture and personality; while Daniel Funkenstein, a psychiatrist at the Harvard School of Medicine, helped to extend my curiosity about such interrelationships into the physiological realm as well. It was difficult to select a title for specialty examinations which would encompass a topical area as broad as the one which was speaking to me. "Relationships between Culture, Personality, and Physiological Functioning" met this need, but for purposes of efficiency, it was shortened to "Culture and Physiology." Had there been a subdiscipline such as Medical Anthropology at the time, my training, most certainly, would have been so identified. It is not surprising, therefore, that a major part of my work experience has been as an anthropologist in a medical setting.

Work Experience

Teaching in traditional academic departments of anthropology is not entirely foreign to me; however, there has been something less than a feeling of fulfillment in such settings. Each time I have taught in a College of Arts and Sciences I have introduced a new course into the curriculum related to anthropology and medicine. Today, these courses would be entitled, "Medical Anthropology: Part I, Biomedical Aspects and Part II, Sociocultural Aspects." Although research, service, and education are the functional components of any institution of higher learning, their integration and coherence in professional schools has an immediacy which, to me, is very compelling. Each time I have taught in a College of Arts and Sciences I have either done so from a medical school base or have sought out linkages with a school of medicine.

This brief background sketch may explain why the broad interests of my graduate years could best be pursued and my expertise best utilized in medical settings where research, service, and training form interlocking systems of great dynamism.

120

In what follows, I plan to report on the various facets of my work as it evolved in one medical institution and led increasingly to direct engagement in clinical activities. In this regard, it may be of interest to the reader to note that the first stirrings of organizational activity by medical anthropologists occured within the American Anthropological Association and the Society for Applied Anthropology during the years 1966-1968. The Medical Anthropology Newsletter was founded by the author in 1968 just prior to her move to the University of Miami School of Medicine in November of that year and prior, also, to the formation of the Society for Medical Anthropology in 1970 when its constitution was adopted.

1968--The Problem in Health Care

In view of the current national attention being given the multiethnic character of many urban areas of the United States, it may seem surprising that as recently as 1968 ethnicity in this country was not yet a salient issue in health care. Under-utilization of federally-funded health programs for the poor was an issue. In Miami, for example, a new comprehensive pediatric health care program designed to provide total health services to inner city residents from birth to the age of 18 years was functioning far below its enrollment capacity. The population in the service area was known to be in part Black, in part Hispanic, and in part White, but in what proportions, with what ethnic affiliations, and with what specific problems was not clear. My anthropological assumption was that varying life-problems combined with different cultural traditions and views about health and illness may have been acting as impediments to the successful delivery of this comprehensive health care program in an inner city area of multiethnic character.

In a joint effort by the Department of Pediatrics and the Department of Psychiatry (in which the author held her appointment), it was decided to undertake a research project to evaluate the influence of ethnicity in the delivery of the aforementioned comprehensive pediatric health care program. This was before the federal government became sensitive to minority and ethnic group problems and concerns; consequently, following three years of exploration, our funding was provided by The Commonwealth Fund, a private foundation with an enduring interest in health related issues. We embarked upon this research effort in 1971, and

121

identified the comprehensive pediatric health care service area as the study area. Our first task was to determine with accuracy the predominant ethnic groups in this inner-city section of Miami; following that, to pursue comparative studies of health problems, health beliefs and practices, alternative healing resources and utilization patterns.

Although Miami in 1981 has assumed a burgeoning Latin and Caribbean population profile, Cubans, Haitians, Jamaicans, Colombians, Costa Ricans, Nicaraguans, El Salvadorians, and other immigrants were only beginning to have a visible impact upon the city in 1971. It was known that Bahamians were early settlers in the area, that American Blacks from Georgia and North Carolina had moved to Miami, that Puerto Ricans were identifiable in the migrant labor populations, that Haitians were trickling into the central city and that Cubans, many of them professionals and white collar workers, were fleeing the revolutionary processes in their homeland. In fact, however, we did not know what the cultural or family configurations might be in the area designated for comprehensive pediatric health care.

Research Procedures

We began by mapping the area, literally walking every street to identify gathering places such as supermarkets, laundromats, coffee shops, restaurants, pool halls, etc. As we walked, we noted the ethnic character of each section, and observed language use in speech, in signs, and in advertisements. We asked people in stores, on the streets, and in yards, what kind of people lived in the immediate vicinity, on adjacent blocks and in the general area. We noted differences in residential and industrial sections, established the routes followed by buses, recorded the location of orthodox health care facilities and physician's offices. We also established the name, location, and language used in major denominational churches and store-front churches. We noted the presence of traditional healers who could be identified by immediately observable criteria, as well as the presence of stores selling religious articles. We then put all this information together on a base map with a series of overlays which allowed us to identify ethnic enclaves, the location of orthodox health resources in relation to a) ethnic territories, b) religious institutions, and c) traditional (folk) health resources for each major group in the area, as well as public transportation routes which, in themselves, sometimes functioned to inhibit easy access by particular groups to the medical center in which the pediatric health care clinic was situated.

We determined, on the basis of our mapping, that there were five dominant groups in the area to which the comprehensive pediatric health care program was intended to be responsive. These were Bahamians, Haitians, American Blacks, Cubans, and Puerto Ricans. There were a few elderly persons along with many Caribbean and Latin American peoples scattered throughout the area; however, at that time their numbers were not sufficiently great or sufficiently clustered to acknowledge their presence in any particular section of the study area. Consequently, we decided to work with the five predominant groups in our exploration of the salience of ethnicity in health care.

Our research assistants were representatives of the communities involved. They were women who either had raised children or were still in the process of raising them. Both sociological survey methods and anthropological techniques of participant observation were utilized over the five-year period of the project. Each time a questionnaire was administered, a narrative account was also prepared to describe the circumstances of life in each family at the time of the visit. Health related comments and understandings expressed by members of the dwelling unit were recorded. In addition, a sub-sample of families was followed intermittently over the entire period of investigation, so that extensive histories were accumulated around specific illness phenomena. The wealth of data gathered and research findings have been presented in a report to the funding agency (Weidman et al. 1978), 200 copies of which have been distributed to interested parties in health care settings and to colleagues in medical anthropology. For present purposes, it is important to outline some of our general findings related to clinical matters, and, in this context, not necessarily to pediatric clinics alone.

Analyis of Research Findings

It is significant, for example, that we found culturally patterned differences in the manner in which symptoms were identified and presented to health professionals. It is not necessary to describe such a finding across all five groups. The point may be made by contrasting the global symptom categories utilized by sample families in the three Black groups with the more specific ones offered by the two Hispanic groups. On the one hand, Bahamians, Haitians, and American Blacks, in their respective ways, would refer to pain or discomfort throughout the whole body, in certain regions of the body (stomach, meaning the entire abdominal cavity) or in specific parts of the body (head, back, side, leg). For these groups it was not essential to describe the quality of the pain (sharp, dull, aching) nor its duration in terms that were compatible with orthodox health professional needs for precise information about such matters. Sample families from both Hispanic groups, however, offered far more differentiated sets of symptoms. Cubans, in particular, used great specificity in presenting their complaints. This was the only group in which differentiation occurred between a brain ache and a headache, for example, or a spine ache and a back ache, or in which attention was directed so finely to a "tendon in the heel" or a particular part of the elbow. We found that Cubans, as patients, would not only offer a more extensive and differentiated symptom cluster; they generally were more persistent in probing for full explanations of their illnesses and medications. The response of Cuban health professionals was to provide fairly detailed information, an interactive pattern which also helps to explain the frequency of medical terms that were incorporated into Cuban discussions of health problems.

Culturally Patterned Syndromes

At another level of analysis we discovered that there were culturally patterned differences in the way symptoms were organized into conditions or syndromes. Falling-out, for example, which was mentioned above as a culture-specific syndrome, represents, in Black families[1], a cluster of symptoms which does not fit precisely any orthodox diagnostic category. The state is one in which an individual collapses, usually without warning, occasionally with a degree of salivation but without convulsions, tongue-biting, bowel or bladder incontinence, all criteria which help to differentiate it from epilepsy. The person who experiences such episodes usually hears and understands what is happening around him but is powerless to move. Even though his eyes are often open, the afflicted person tends not to "see" during the seizure-like

124

episode. This set of symptoms may also be differentiated from hysteria of both conversion and dissociative types.[2] Nevertheless, persons who experience faling-out in its chronic form are sometimes diagnosed as epileptics or hysterics. Representatives of the orthodox health care system have no other way to diagnose and treat such a syndrome, the symptom cluster of which is organized differently from those in their own classificatory system. They either use the closest approximations and treat the syndrome accordingly, albeit inappropriately, or they dismiss the patient as having a "functional" (non-organic) disorder, which is essentially untreatable medically.

In every ethnic group under study, conditions were identified with symptom clusters organized in ways that were not identical with the ordering of symptoms required to establish diagnoses in line with orthodox medical categories. Two additional examples will help to make the point.

There is a Haitian syndrome called la congestion, which was very disturbing to some individuals and families in the Haitian sample (Weidman et al. 1978:515 ff.). La congestion is a condition characterized by dizziness, headaches, constriction of the throat, and fullness of the "lungs and chest." It is sometimes caused by mixed emotions related to ambiguous social situations wherein someone has used a "big mouth" or a "bad mouth" but for which no appropriate immediate response is possible. In Haitian eyes, la congestion can be a frightening condition. Some say that their throats tighten so much that they cannot swallow even their own saliva. La congestion can also be an acute condition. In one instance a Haitian patient was taken to the hospital under oxygen because she was in such distress. The syndrome is not synonymous with asthma, hypertension, or any other medical condition recognized by the orthodox health care system.

Another Haitian condition, battement de coeur[3], is the name given to a set of symptoms which include weakness, sometimes profuse perspiration, and unpredictable episodes of a rapidly and sometimes wildly beating heart. Battement de coeur is viewed as a very serious condition. At times patients will go to the Emergency Room feeling that they are very sick and in danger of dying. Some even ask if they can be returned to Haiti so they can die in their home country. The orthodox practitioner's ultimate response to such symptoms and such concern is hardly compatible with the threat perceived by Haitians. After careful examination physicians will frequently offer little other than support. The patients may be given prescriptions for tranquilizers, and sent home with reassurances that the problem is "self-limiting," that they are "not to worry," and that they will be all right. Clearly, there are two very different responses to the same symptom cluster, one by the patient and his family, the other by the Emergency Room staff. The condition diagnosed by Haitians has far more severe consequences than the condition diagnosed by orthodox practitioners. In an attempt to understand more fully the reason for such disparate responses to the same set of symptoms, we moved in our research to yet another level of analysis--that of perceptions of physiological functioning.

Perceptions of Physiological Functioning

On the parameter of perceived functioning of the body, we again observed culturally patterned differences across all five groups. For consistency of presentation, this finding will be illustrated by focusing upon la congestion and battement de coeur, the two syndromes introduced immediately above.

The physiological process which is so disturbing to Haitians when symptoms of la congestion are noticed is related to the behavior of the blood. The blood is believed to actually leave the extremities, limbs, and lower part of the body. It begins to accumulate in the region of the chest, neck, and head, thus causing the symptoms of dizziness, headaches, constriction of the throat, and fullness of the "lungs" and "chest." In mild cases, a home remedy of warm water, castor oil, and a little salt, combined with bed rest, will serve to alleviate the symptoms and help to reduce the "congestion" by assisting the blood to be redistributed throughout the lower parts of the body. In acute cases, the danger of stroke and mental derangement is perceived to be so great (because of the flow, pressure, and congestion of blood in the uppermost part of the body, particularly the head) that emergency procedures must be taken.

In contrast to the Haitian understanding of physiological processes and bodily functioning, we might surmise from an orthodox, medical perspective, that the symptoms are related to physiological processes linked to anger, humiliation, the desire to cry, and, perhaps, depression as a consequence of being

126

"bad-mouthed" in a situation where an appropriate response either is not possible or is inhibited because of social context--such as being confronted by a "big-mouthed" customer in the store where one works as a salesperson. We might surmise, also, from an orthodox, psychological perspective, that even though the constriction of the throat could be linked directly to the intensity of the emotional response, it might be related, in addition, to an attempt to prevent the blood (as it is perceived) from causing damage to the head. in Haitian eyes, however, such constriction is simply part of the symptom cluster of la congestion, and la congestion itself is defined as a disease entity or an illness category.

The Haitian understanding of physiological processes in battement de coeur is also centered on the blood. The perception is that the blood is too weak and lacks sufficient nutrients (strength) to nourish the body. The heart is seen as beating wildly, because there simply is not enough blood in the body. Furthermore, the blood that is available is viewed as pale and mucous-like in character. The heart is seen as overworking in a great effort to help the weakened, insufficient blood to be distributed throughout the body in order to sustain it.

Such culturally patterned differences in the presentation of symptoms, the organization of symptoms into syndromes, and perceptions of bodily functioning clearly have clinical relevance. In battement de coeur, for example, the orthodox diagnosis of "stress-related paroxysmal tachycardia" may be a perfectly acceptable one. A prescription for tranquilizers and verbal reassurance may be entirely appropriate for such a diagnosis. However, when the perceived Haitian clinical reality and diagnosis are such that only a blood tonic would be an appropriate therapy, there is little satisfaction in the entire transaction and certainly no conviction that representatives of the orthodox health care system have even "heard" the complaint, let alone addressed the problem. If the therapy prescribed is considered irrelevant or inappropriate, it is unlikely that the physician's instructions will be followed. Thus, patient compliance and outcome of orthodox health care may be influenced by the variable of ethnicity operating along such parameters as those described here.

Although the study from which these samples were drawn was undertaken in collaboration with a pediatric health care program, its extensive findings had implications, also, for other clinical areas. Psychiatry, in particular, was in a position to build upon this solid empirical foundation in the planning of a community mental health program. This leads us to a second aspect of anthropological activity at the University of Miami School of Medicine: namely, contributing substantially to the design of a major service program now being implemented in an inner-city, multiethnic community.

Contributions to Design of a Service Program

The model for the community mental health program evolved from the research project briefly described above. For example, when we considered the types of transactions between ethnic patient and orthodox practitioner that would be required to achieve full comprehension and communication about health problems, we were struck by the two-way process involved. A genuine effort would be required by the health professional to understand the patient's position within the context of the patient's own culturally-organized cognitive system. The patient would need to be encouraged to provide as full a picture as possible. The health professional would then be in a position to negotiate between the two different conceptual realms in order to: 1) satisfy the needs related to the patient's own understandings and 2) make orthodox medical views and therapies as understandable/meaningful/ acceptable to the patient as possible. We came to the conclusion that, in a multiethnic community, utilization, compliance, and outcome might all be improved if there were more mediation between symbolic systems--the patient's and that of health practitioners, regardless of the type of care involved, e.g., pediatric or psychiatric.

Key Concepts: General. Four key concepts were employed to underline the need for neogtiation between orthodox medical and traditional ethnic cultural realms. They are: culture, health culture, co-culture, and culture-brokerage (Weidman 1975:17-19). Inasmuch as these concepts were central in planning the Community Mental Health Program, they will be described before proceeding with the design of the service program.

128

Culture. Following Harris, the concept of __culture__ was defined as "the learned patterns of thought and behavior characteristic of a population or society--a society's repertory of behavioral, cognitive, and emotional patterns" (Harris 1971:624). The point was made that an understanding of the concept of culture usually generates respect for cultural differences. The reason? When there is an appreciation of the tremendous amount of learning necessary to function adequately within any cultural system, and that system provides life-long coping mechanisms, it makes little sense to assume that one process of learning (and adaptation within that learned context) is superior to another. Often a more relativistic and less judgmental point of view accompanies a full understanding of the concept of culture. And when individual life circumstances change so that new adaptive strategies and coping mechanisms are required, cultural understanding by human resources personnel provides a basis for assisting in such change processes.

Health Culture. Health culture refers to "all the phenomena associated with the maintenance of well-being and problems of sickness with which people cope in traditional ways within their own social networks and institutional structures" (Weidman et al. 1978:13). To fully grasp the significance of this concept, it is necessary to come to terms with its component parts. One part pertains to cognitive processes; the other is related to social system functioning. The __cognitive__ __dimension__ includes values and beliefs, guidelines for health action and the symbolic meanings of therapeutic rituals. This dimension necessitates an understanding of theories of illness prevention, health maintenance, bodily functioning, disease etiology, diagnosis, treatment, and cure. The __social__ __system__ aspect of the concept of health culture refers to the organization of health care or the health care delivery system. This system is predominantly reparative or therapeutic in nature. In order to understand the operation of a health care system one must become familiar with the structure and functioning of organized sets of health/illness-related roles and behaviors. The relationship of this concept to that of the concept of culture is that a particular health culture functions as an integral and essential part of the overall cultural tradition of any ethnic group, even though that group may have left its country of origin many years ago.

Co-culture. The co-culture concept assists in making the transition from a unicultural (single cultural) perspective to a transcultural perspective (across two or more cultures). Its importance lies in its acknowledgement of two systems simultaneously. There is no way to use the term, co-culture, without recognizing that more than one cultural system is included as a referent. In addition, it implies co-equal status for the health cultural traditions (symbolic systems and social structures) which guide and support the coping and health-related behaviors of those who participate in them. In a clinical context, the co-culture concept helps to make the point that the patient's cultural beliefs about health and illness are just as meaningful to him or her as are the orthodox health cultural beliefs to the health professional.

In using the concept of co-culture, one fact must be recognized. The orthodox health cultural system, generally, and each orthodox practitioner, specifically, carries the medical, social, and legal responsibility for improving, if possible, the health status of an individual patient as well as helping to maintain at as high a level as possible the health of the national population. The orthodox practitioner may be rendered powerless, however, if the patient refuses or is unable to "buy into" the orthodox health cultural tradition. Recognizing that co-cultures may be involved in every clinical transaction, however, places the orthodox health care provider in a stronger position to carry out his or her responsibilities and achieve the outcome desired, i.e., an improved health status for the patient, and also, in the long run, better compliance and more appropriate utilization of facilities. In addition, the co-culture concept allows for the possibility of culture brokerage if it should be necessary. In brief, moving from the concept of culture, to that of health culture and then to the concept of co-culture involves a perceptual shift from a unicultural to a transcultural posture. It is the latter stance which makes it possible to engage in culture brokerage.

Culture Brokerage. Culture brokerage is a concept which has not been defined precisely (Wolf 1956; Weidman 1973; Weidman 1976). It is applicable, however, whenever there is need to recognize the existence of separate cultural or sub-cultural systems and to acknowledge a particular person's role in establishing meaningful, strategic, or significant links between them. In the context of clinical activities culture brokerage encourages the following:

130

1. a fuller understanding of the person who is presenting specific complaints;

2. a response to the particular points of concern tied to the patient's symbolic system;

3. the development of more meaningful connections between the requirements of orthodox clinical reality and requirements of the patient's own clinical reality;[4]

4. the establishment of a foundation whereby orthodox health beliefs may be incorporated more easily into the patient's repertory of health-related understandings; and

5. a more humane interactive process which tends to establish a stronger bond between the patient and the health professional.

These, then, were the key concepts related to our clinically-oriented research which provided guidelines for program planning. By expanding upon the type of conceptualization outlined above, culture brokerage assumed even broader dimensions in the community mental health program that was designed for a catchment area which extended beyond but included the study area of the research project described earlier.

Planning a Community Mental Health Program: Structural Principles

In planning the community mental health program, we wished to avoid high drop-out rates and patterns of under-utilization so often associated with such programs in low-income and multiethnic settings. Therefore, we gave full recognition to the community configurations identified during the research mapping procedure. We acknowledged the fact of differing definitions of illness, patterns of health maintenance, and beliefs about the causes and curing of illness. We respected, also, the documented presence of traditional (folk) healers and utilization patterns that led easily, and often simultaneously, to both traditional (folk) and orthodox practitioners (Scott 1975:108-110; Weidman et al. 1978:747 ff.). Consequently, our program incorporated a number of innovative strategies.

In the first place we opted not to rent or erect a mental health center building where patients would come to us. Instead, we decided to deploy Bahamian, Haitian, American Black, Cuban, Puerto Rican, and geriatric teams out into the appropriate areas. Second, we elected to focus first on prevention and then on culturally-appropriate care in the event breakdown occured. Third, the orthodox psychiatric services provided by the large county hospital to which the community program was linked were viewed as back-up services only. Fourth, because of the focus on prevention and culturally-appropriate care, six pivotal positions with research, service, and training components were created for social scientists (preferably anthropologists) of the same ethnic background as the population served. Fifth, the role-set mandated for the social scientist positions included responsiveness to the needs of individuals in the respective communities, the development of new strategies to meet those needs, and brokerage a) between the respective communities and the dominant social and political system on the one hand and b) between traditional and orthodox health cultures on the other hand.

Inasmuch as the program has been described in the literature[5] (Weidman et al. 1978:867-902; Lefley and Bestman, In Press), it will not be necessary to elaborate further. The important points for present purposes are as follows:

1. anthropological research and conceptualization entered into the planning of a large service program in a multiethnic area;

2. anthropologically-oriented positions were incorporated into the structure of the service program;

3. culture brokerage at many levels became an inherent part of the service system;

4. the mandate to innovate in the interest of meeting individual and community needs has generated emergent mental health strategies which vary from group-to-group, but are supportive of an improved mental health status for the low-income populations.[6]

It is noteworthy with respect to tradtional healers in particular, that community support networks easily allow the collaboration of traditional healers and orthodox practitioners when an individual's mental health problem requires it. It is the transcultural perspective supporting this program which makes such linkages not only acceptable but for certain numbers of patients, essential.

In concluding this section it may be said that in Miami the anthropological contribution to service programs is just as important an aspect of clinical anthropology as is research of the type discussed above. A third aspect of clinical anthropology as practiced in this setting relates to the training of clinicians.

Training Techniques

The training component of clinical anthropology at the University of Miami School of Medicine is centered in the Ambulatory Care Center (ACC) of Jackson Memorial Hospital (JMH), its teaching institution. The support of the Dean and Associate Dean have made it possible for the author, with the assistance of an anthropologist colleague, Dr. Clarissa Scott, to undertake a pilot study designed to establish the most efficient and effective ways of introducing cultural factors into the residency training programs of four clinical departments. These are the Departments of Medicine, Pediatrics, Family Medicine, and Obstetrics-Gynecology.

This process, currently underway, was begun in 1979 with a 50 percent time commitment supported by the Community Hospital Education Council of Florida. It was by no means a simple task. It has reflected all the characteristics of ethnographic research ordinarily undertaken by anthropologists in a foreign village, with a comparable amount to be learned. For example, it has been necessary to understand the service system in each of the four departments, the structure of the training program in each, the organization of the ambulatory care clinics in each of the four medical specialty areas, the schedules for such clinics, the assignment of residents rotating through the various clinical areas, the schedule and location of case conferences and lectures attended by residents in each of the four medical specialties, and the meaning of medical symbols, notations, and abbreviations that are part of the medical record of each patient seen in the Ambulatory Care Center. Because many of our exploratory methods are basic to anthropological pursuits in any service-oriented context, they are outlined below. The techniques utilized in Miami have set the stage for and influenced the training process.

Participant Observation

The anthropological method of participant observation is central in this pilot effort. It has focused on both organizational and clinical aspects of residency training. By rotating through each of the four medical divisions in the Ambulatory Care Center and joining residents on their assignments, during ward rounds, at case conferences, and in examining rooms, it has been possible to learn the broader context in which residency training in primary care occurs in each of the four medical specialties.

Interviewing Patients

Interviewing patients is another technique utililzed primarily to assess the various contributions that cultural knowledge might make in the management of a patient with a particular kind of clinical problem. When cultural information elicited by anthropologists seems especially important for a positive therapeutic result, the matter is pursued further with both the attending physician and the resident responsible for that patient's care.

Record Review

Record review has been undertaken in each of the medical specialty areas of the ACC in an effort to identify general medical problems linked to recorded observations of poor compliance. These are then explored for the possible impact of beliefs and traditions divergent from those of the orthodox health care providers. In the pediatric specialty clinics, for example, problems of poor compliance in the medical management of asthma, cardiac conditions, and epilepsy were clearly evident. And, in the continuing care clinic of Pediatrics, nutritional problems were pronounced for infants and toddlers. Dietary control in the management of both obesity and diabetes for older children emerged as a particularly important area for investigating compliance behavior.

When patterns of poor or non-compliant behavior appeared in this type of record review, attempts were made to determine the ethnic representation of both the "problem" group and the general clinic population with the same medical condition. By following this procedure, we learned that obese Hispanic children were over-represented in relation to their percentage of the clinic population during the month-long period of record review. Blacks, on the other hand, were over-represented in the anemia category. Such findings raised the possibility that culturally-patterned food preferences and body-image ideals might be factors contributing to difficulties in the management of obesity and anemia in this pediatric clinic population. This research question is being pursued.

Contextualization

While record reviews in each of the clinical units of the ACC helped to identify general areas in which cultural factors might be contributing significantly to poor compliance, the anthropological technique of contextualization has led us to recognize several structural or organizational impediments which also are interfering with a better outcome from orthodox health care. Contextualization is the process of understanding every component of the unit providing health care and then tracing every step in the patient's movement through that system. For example, contextualization provides as full an understanding as possible of patient/health care interactions from the time nutritional counseling is emphasized by resident physicians to the point that the patient returns and has a notation of "poor compliance" recorded in his or her medical chart. From such an approach we were able to see significant weaknesses in the network of care which could be strengthened to enhance compliance.

We learned, for example, that nutritional counseling was often provided by physicians without referral to the nutritionist. We also learned that when referrals were made to the nutritionist the patients did not always receive such counseling. Many could not wait until she was free to see them. Nutritional counseling was not built into the computerized appointment system, so that there was no systematic way to ensure accessibility to the nutritionist. Furthermore, the location of the nutritionist's desk functioned to undermine the importance of her contribution. It was situated under the clinic loudspeaker in a place where other staff necessarily had to disrupt her conversations with patients in order to gain access to supplies and records needed for their work. Other factors operated once the patient was in the context of home and community, but because of specific organizational features, many patients did not have the reinforcement of nutritional counseling, while others may not have given it much importance because of the setting in which it occurred. These weaknesses in the system had no direct relation to cultural factors in compliance or non-compliance, but by correcting them both patients and health care providers have had a better opportunity to achieve their respective goals, i.e., raised health levels for those entering the orthodox health care system.

The point that needs to be made regarding the technique of contextualization of clinical anthropology is that it is useful in pinpointing structural weaknesses in the health care delivery system as well as in identifying specific points at which cultural factors may be inhibiting a favorable outcome of orthodox care. Cultural beliefs which were influencing poor compliance behavior in diabetes control, for example, emerged from the process of contextualization in an Internal Medicine clinic. They included such Hispanic beliefs as the following: that one might become "dependent" upon insulin if it were taken too long and too regularly; also, that "once you start taking insulin, the eyes go bad."

By utilizing the above outlined approaches in each of the four specialty areas of the Ambulatory Care Center, patients have been identified as having problems in which cultural factors are crucial for a favorable outcome. In some instances their problems have been successfully resolved; at other times they have not been resolved. For example, one of the Haitian patients referred from Obstetric-Gynecology in Internal Medicine for pseudocyesis (false pregnancy) continues to engage our attention. She has been converted from Haitian Catholicism (which holds a lenient attitude toward Haitian Vodun) to fundamentalist Protestantism (which rejects Vodun beliefs and practices as works of the Devil). She, therefore, seeks help from orthodox practitioners for her prolonged "pregnancy," now into its fourth year. She explains her condidtion in traditional terms, i.e., that the baby has been magically bound within her womb. However, because of her religious conversion, she is prohibited from seeking a cure from traditional healers who have the ability to magically "free" the fetus and allow it to be "born." Orthodox psychiatric approaches are not applicable, given her new religious conviction, culturally appropriate therapies, psychologically, are not available to her even though Haitian traditional healers do practice in Miami and are easily accessible. The patient continues to be followed in the Internal Medicine Clinic of the ACC without change in her health status.

In this case, regardless of anthropological insights, it may not be possible to find a solution to the problem of appropriate care for this woman, given the double-bind situation in which providers and patient alike are caught. Nevertheless, such a clinical problem represents just as important a teaching case as those which can be resolved satisfactorily; perhaps it is a more important case, because it illustrates so well the influence of beliefs upon health care.

When acknowledgment of and response to cultural beliefs make a favorable and dramatic difference in medical management and outcome, there is no question but that such an experience has a profound effect upon the clinician involved. For this reason, our teaching strategies have been designed 1) with a potential for diffusion and 2) to allow the learning process to be an experiential one to as great an extent as possible.

Integrated Training Strategies

An early decison was made to focus upon second and third year residents. This was done in order 1) to ensure reinforcement of cultural awareness as second year residents became third year residents and 2) to encourage dissemination to others in the training hierarchy as third and then second year residents supervised those who followed them, e.g., first-year residents and medical students.

Another strategy contitutes the practice of first discussing a particular patient's cultural views with one of the attending physicians and then going with this member of the faculty to the resident responsible for the patient's care. By working with attending physicians as well as residents, we do not undermine medical authority. In fact, we add a dimension which broadens the view and experience of both the physician in training (the resident) and the member of the teaching faculty. Inasmuch as attending physicians are responsible for the quality of the care provided by residents, they are constantly engaged in clinical teaching while supervising the residents' care of patients assigned to them. As this process continues, it is anticipated that the teaching model will become

one of clinical cohorts or team teaching, with the
anthropological view gradually incorporated as a
valuable one in medical diagnosis and patient care.

Dissemniation of the Anthropological Perspective

Although our teaching efforts in the clinical areas
are directed toward second and third year residents,
our work is having an impact, also, on a wider audience
via other mechanisms of instruction. They include the
following:

1. Participation in Staff Meetings

   Results of record surveys have been brought to
   staff meetings for discussion by clinic
   personnel in specific units of the ACC.
   Contextual analyses describing organizational
   impediments to care have also been presented for
   staff consideration. Action has been taken as a
   consequence of some of these reports. For
   example, nutritional counseling appointments
   have been built into the computer system, and
   the nutritionist now works from a different
   location.

2. Videotaping

   Occasionally interviews with patients in their
   homes are so revealing of cultural beliefs
   regarding home management of health problems
   that videotapes have been made with the
   patient´s consent for use in teaching medical
   students. They are available, also, for use in
   other health professional training contexts.

3. Response to Consultation Requests

   As word spreads that cultural factors may have
   important bearing on outcome of health care,
   there are increasing numbers of requests for
   consultation. These are both individual in
   nature and group related. Individual requests
   tend to be for patients whose diagnostic picture
   is confused or who are not responding to
   orthodox therapies for particular complaints.
   Requests for group consultation and assistance
   have come from health educators, social service
   units, and nursing school faculty.

4. Case Conferences

Cases conferences have been used with success for groups of residents and faculty. For example, in Family Medicine three cases have been presented in which cultural factors played a crucial role in the successful treatment of patients. The physicians involved were at different levels of training and responsibility, one a member of the teaching faculty, one an intern, and one a second year resident. Each presented the medical facts, the puzzling aspects of symptoms and treatment, the manner in which cultural information was utilized, the importance of that information, and the successful outcome that occurred as a result of taking both traditional ethnic and orthodox medical views into consideration. In each instance, the entire presentation and the lively discussion which followed were tape recorded. The tapes are being transcribed, edited, and submitted for publication in the <u>Journal</u> <u>of</u> <u>Family</u> <u>Practice</u> as Grand Rounds presentations. For the reader's benefit, these cases will be described briefly later in the last section of this paper.

One additional training format which is becoming more structured in the Department of Family Medicine involves the use of videotapes of resident-patient interactions. We have found that this allows a multi-layered teaching/learning format which can have a broad ripple effect. For example, when a patient's visit with a resident is videotaped (with the patient's permission), the tape is utilized to assess various parameters of interaction such as: interviewing skills, interpersonal behavior, patient education about medical conditions, prescription instructions, counseling in primary care, etc. It is also possible, during such reviews, to introduce cultural information linked directly to medical diagnosis and treatment. Simultaneously, as the attending faculty member and teaching fellows who may be present comment and advise the resident, the anthropologist is able to understand points of particular medical and interactional concern. Everyone benefits, including, ultimately, the patient involved and other patients as well.

This multi-layered teaching/learning process has been futher expanded in the context of the Faculty Development Seminar of the Department of Family

Medicine which meets weekly with 6-8 faculty members (not always the same ones) in attendance. After viewing a segment of such a tape, faculty members engage in role-playing. One faculty member acts as "resident"; while, first a physician and then an anthropologist take turns guiding the "resident" to a more skillful interactive approach prior to sending him or her "back into the examining room" with the patient.

The role-playing exercises are followed by comment and advice from other faculty members present. Such sessions contribute to more efficacious teaching methods on the part of all faculty and function in a powerful way to underscore the importance of cultural factors in health care. We have found, for example, that at times cultural views are clearly expressed by the patient who appears on the videotape. Medical faculty, however, may be unaware of their full meaning and uncertain about utilizing such information in their analyses of the resident's performance. The Faculty Development Seminar allows them to understand more clearly the cultural issues involved. This is sure to influence all levels of residency-training in Family Medicine as more members of the faculty become at ease with a cultural component in their teaching and in the practice of medicine.

The Health Cultural Data Base

Through all of these explorations in the training aspects of clinical anthropology, one remarkable advantage that we have had lies in the amount of information available to us through our prior research on health cultural traditions of the major populations served by the University of Miami School of Medicine-Jackson Memorial Medical Center. The extent of our knowledge about health cultural beliefs and practices in the five dominant ethnic groups in the area gave us general understandings from local communities which served as a springboard for relating more directly to persons from those communities who might be typical or atypical in the views they expressed. The important point is that we recognized general patterns from which to begin our inquiries and from which to judge the patient's position on what might be considered a "bell-shaped curve" of cultural patterning. It was the solid body of data from our community research which allowed us to set forth hypotheses about hidden concerns lying behind particular configurations of symptoms. It also served to encourage therapeutic strategies which might not have been possible otherwise. The importance of such a data base will be apparent, from the sketches presented below of three patients whose problems and treatments were reviewed during case conferences in Family Medicine. In each instance there were many more complexities than can be conveyed here. However, the sense of the problem and the value of the transcultural perspective should be evident.

Case A

Mr. A., a Black male adult from Miami was interviewed by an anthropologist colleague, Dr. Clarissa Scott, while waiting to be seen in the Ambulatory Care Unit of Family Medicine. He had stopped going to another doctor who kept focusing on his obesity, which he did not consider to be his greatest concern. His worries were linked to other major complaints: lost nature (impotence), a skin rash on his arms and legs, nervousness, difficulty sleeping, and voices in the night. He had come hoping one of the doctors in Family Medicine could help him "get to the bottom of these problems."

Following his examination by a second-year resident, we were dismayed to learn from his record that Mr. A. had been considered to be schizophrenic because of his "flat affect" and the voices he was hearing. He had been given Thorazine for these symptoms. His skin rash was diagnosed as impetigo, and he was given a topical ointment to apply locally. He was advised that his sexual potency (his "nature") would return as his nervousness and voices subsided. Following this visit, when Dr. Scott called to ask how the visit had gone, Mr. A. said he was "waiting to see."

On the basis of our previous research findings, we had hypothesized that Mr. A.'s real concerns included the following tentative cultural diagnoses:

1. that the skin rash might be caused by "acid" in the blood, because rashes are seen by many Black Americans as impurities (including acid) which work their way to the surface of the skin--the body's way of cleansing itself;

2. that lost "nature" (impotence) might be caused by "bad blood." Too much acid in the blood for too long a time can spoil it and cause both loss

141

of nature and sores on the skin. Cultural question: Were both the impotence and the skin rash caused by bad blood, one form of which might by syphilis?;

3. that nervousness, sleeplessness, and voices in the night might be caused by evil spirits free to disturb him because of general weakness, loss of strength, and possibly "bad blood";

4. that all of the symptoms together might be caused by someone who wished to harm him magically, bring him down, drive him mad, and/or possibly even cause his death.

We provided to both the attending physician and the resident a description of relevant aspects of American Black world view and health cultural beliefs as we understood them. We then outlined what we believed could have precipitated the various possible interpretations of the symptoms the patient was experiencing. We then suggested that it might be worth exploring such matters with Mr. A. upon his return visit. We prepared a set of questions which would be helpful in guiding the resident physician. We also suggested that if Mr. A. did, indeed feel that a blood problem might be causing the rash (and possibly the impotence), then he would be happier with medication to be taken by mouth in liquid form or by injection rather than relying entirely upon a topical ointment. If he believed someone was trying to harm him magically, then other steps would need to be taken, which were outlined.

During Mr. A.´s second vist, the resident used the questions and the cultural perceptions very skillfully. He elicited a far more informative response from Mr. A., who confirmed that he was, indeed, concerned about the state of his blood. The voices "were leaving," and his nervousness was subsiding. He was regaining his potency, but he had not been able to achieve climax. He did not feel that anyone was trying to harm him. If he had thought that, he would have gone to his mother "who knows what to do."

In order to put Mr. A. at ease about the state of his blood, the resident ordered a blood test, encouraged him to continue the topical ointment for his skin condition, but gave him an injection, also. He continued the Thorazine. When Dr. Scott telephoned following this visit to see how things were going,

142

Mr. A. said he felt that doctor was "on the right track."

Prior to the patient's third visit, we suggested to the resident that if Mr. A. had regained his potency but still could not reach climax, then he would be concerned abut the strength of his blood, and liquid vitamins or some kind of tonic would be reassuring. On this third visit Mr. A. brought his wife and children to meet his doctor. In the examining room he expressed his pleasure that he was feeling so much better. He added, however, before the resident could inquire, that he felt he needed something for a little more strength. The resident responded with a prescription that would meet this need. There was now a very cordial relationship between them. Later, when questioned, the resident expressed the view that he no longer considered Mr. A. to be schizophrenic. And when Dr. Scott called Mr. A. shortly thereafter to ask whether or not the doctor was getting to the bottom of his problem, he replied with conviction, "He's getting to the bottom of all of my problems."

Case B

Mr. B., a Black adult male who lived in a somewhat rural area southwest of Miami was brought to our attention by a member of the Family Medicine teaching faculty assigned to the unviersity affiliated health center in that area. She was of East Indian origin and had an acquaintance with traditional health cultural beliefs in her home country. She discounted them, however, and accepted fully the value system of orthodox medicine. Nevertheless, she had been sufficiently exposed to the various local healing traditions to know that "roots" and "being rooted" were terms used by American Blacks to refer to the uses and effects of malign magic. The physician had been seeing Mr. B. in the Family Medicine Clinic over a period of several weeks because of unexplained weight loss. There was no physical basis for the state in which she found him, and he was not responding to any of her suggestions to improve his appetite and achieve weight gain. Finally, she asked him if he thought he had been "rooted." He denied this on two separate occasions, but as she questioned him yet another time, he finally admitted that, yes, he did feel that he had been "rooted," and he suspected his wife. He thought she was trying to get rid of him so she and a local root doctor could take possession of his house.

Mr. B. explained that he was a deacon in his church and, therefore, should have been protected spiritually by his belief in God and Jesus and also by his high position in the church. Although the church elders had been praying for him, he had not improved, and they had said, finally, that they could not help him--that he would have to find another way to find relief from the evil forces which were making him waste away. On the day he had expressed these fears he had come to the Family Medicine clinic in such a state of anxiety that the physician had become alarmed. But, following Mr. B.´s admission that he did feel he had been "rooted," she was at a loss to know how to handle the situation. She called the author for advice while the patient waited in the examining room.

After a fairly lengthy discussion the following points were agreed upon:

1. Mr. B. must be reassured that he would be all right;

2. that there were some steps she could take to help him;

3. that he could also take specific actions on his own which would help protect him;

4. that we had worked with a spiritual healer from Miami in other cases with good results and the we would be glad to request a consultation from the Miami healer if he wished us to do so.

The plan was carried out. The physician stated emphatically that Mr. B. would be all right and gave him an injection which was designed to "strengthen" him. He was advised to go to a local market, purchase some Red Devil Lye and place some of this traditionally accepted spirit-repelling substance in the four corners of his house, to open his Bible to the 23rd Psalm and place it by his bed (to allow the power of God to fill the room with the goodness of the Holy Spirit, another culturally acceptable protection), and to return the next day when the spiritual healer, who had been contacted, would be able to see him.

As Mr. B. was given the injection to help see him through the night he began to shout, "Hallelujah," "Praise the Lord," etc. Later, the doctor commented that she had never seen anyone so relieved and so grateful. It was pointed out that this was surely the

144

case. Mr. B. had been in such a state of panic that he could not sleep and was beginning to feel that he was doomed. It was explained, moreover, that this shouting behavior is also part of traditional healing modes used to cleanse the person of damaging influences. When medicinal baths are given, for example, it is customary to recite Psalms, to sing religious songs and to shout praises to God and Jesus. The healing power of sacred plants in the bathwater permeates every pore and orifice of the body while the supernaturally derived healng power of worship fills the body and spirit and is augmented further by the sacred sounds which enter the ears. In this way the whole person is purged--cleansed and purified. Whatever evil spirits or forces have been disturbing the patient are thus "sent back" whence they came. This explanation made sense to the orthodox practitioner who agreed that there may have been more to Mr. B.'s behavior than relief and gratitude.

The patient followed the instructions given him but disguised the lye by placing it in his snuff boxes in inconspicuous locations at each corner of the house. He returned the following day after having had a very restful night. He was seen by the spiritual healer in the Family Medicine unit of the local medical facility. The orthodox physician was present throughout. When Mr. B. returned the following week, his anxiety was markedly decreased, and he had gained seven pounds. He had begun to feel that he could withstand any further onslaughts, but wished to be in touch with the spiritual healer about improving his relationship with his wife.

When discussing the traditional healing techniques actually employed by the spiritual healer in her presence, the family physician expressed her surprise that she found them not very spectacular or impressive. There were some prayers, some sprinkling of holy water, a ritual tying of a scarf around the patient's neck and a bottle of some healing oil or other medicine given to Mr. B. to use at home. This provided an opportunity for the two of us to make a comparative analysis of what she had observed and what she does every day in the clinic. From this transcultural stance, the physician was able to acknowledge that much of the drama of healing is invisible. It relates to the importance and complexity of the system of knowledge involved and to the remarkable action of medicines and therapy in whatever form they assume. She conceded that the process of giving an injection or writing a prescription in ambulatory care settings was not all that spectacular either; yet the results were often dramatic.

It is important to note that many of the ethical issues which arose for this family practitioner in her initial unicultural posture became much less problematic when she achieved a transcultural perspective on the clinical problem. In the first instance, she had no way to help the patient. In the second instance, many more strategies were available to her, and the patient improved. Fortunately, there were no areas of conflict or disagreement between the conceptual realms which prohibited meaningful steps from being taken. Both traditional and orthodox techniques worked collaboratively to ensure an acceptable outcome--improved health status for the patient.

<u>Case C</u>

Mrs. C. was a young black woman from Belize (formerly British Honduras) who was brought to our attention by a Family Medicine intern on his surgical rotation. She had come to Miami because her hydrocephalic child required surgery for a shunt. The Lion's Club in Belize had provided funds for her trip, but after her baby had been admitted to the pediatric ward, Mrs. C. developed an acute abdominal pain in the right lower quadrant and had to be hospitalized. She had all the classic symptoms of acute appendicitis even though her laboratory results were largely negative. After considerable discussion the decison was finally made to operate because of the possibility of a ruptured appendix. Following surgery, however, the pathology report showed a normal appendix. Despite some complaints about continuing pain, Mrs. C. was being readied for discharge when she collapsed in the bathroom on the ward.[8] She was observed another day without any distress other than her continuing pain which was attributed to post-operative discomfort. On the second discharge attempt she collapsed again just before leaving the lobby to go to the place she was staying. Once again she was returned to the surgical floor. At this point surgical staff and ward personnel believed that Mrs. C. was, in a sense, "creating" her pain and her episodes of collapse as a way of being close to her baby who was in the pediatric ward one floor below. In other words, they saw her symptoms as motivated by secondary gain.

146

As the Family Medicine intern remarked, however, "things just didn't add up"; so he began to question Mrs. C. about her life in Belize, her baby's condition, and her views about her own problems. Although he was not well-informed on the subject of magical practices, he had heard enough about them to make inquiries along these lines. He asked if Mrs. C. believed in "spiritual things" and the possibility that spirits could have an effect on people's lives. At first she denied such beliefs, but when assured by the intern that many people believed this way and that there was nothing wrong with such a view, Mrs. C. began to respond. She said she "didn't know for sure" but that she would like to see an "obeah man," which is the equivalent of the American Black root doctor.[9] She especially wanted an oil bath. She talked about events in Belize that the intern did not fully understand. It was at this point that he requested anthropological consultation.

When the intern and the author combined information from their respective conversations with the patient, it became apparent that Mrs. C. felt her neighbor in Belize was trying to get rid of her. She had had an argument with this woman, whose mother was an obeah practitioner. Her neighbor had cursed her and said that her baby would be born sick and that she would take her husband away from her. Later, some of her underwear had been taken from the clothes line, and Mrs. C. was sure this had been used for magic that worked against her. Her baby had, indeed, been born sick, and she had lost her husband to the neighbor. She was terrified now that her neighbor (through her neighbor's mother) would try to cause her death in the United States to prevent her return to Belize. Although she did not say so, she obviously felt some protection from such a fate as long as she was in the hospital, presumably through the shielding "power" of othodox medicine. She was noticeably more relaxed and in less pain following these conversations.

It was agreed that we should try to have Mrs. C. seen on the ward by a traditional healer, a Bahamian, who in his home country is also called an "obeah man." The intern checked with his supervising resident, who, in turn took the matter to the chief resident who said, in essence, "Go ahead: just don't let me know about it."

The Bahamian healer was contacted and was perfectly willing to see Mrs. C. in the hospital. He talked with her privately, rubbed her with healing oil, and gave her a small bottle to carry with her. He told her she would be protected and that she need not fear leaving the hospital. It was arranged that she would call him from her quarters, and that he would schedule a time when he could give her a medicinal bath. She was able, then, to cope with her discharge from the hospital. Following her return to the hotel she telephoned to make the appointment for a medicinal bath. Before this could be given, however, her child was discharged from the hospital, and the Lion's Club had flown her back to Belize. It is interesting to note, in this instance, that even though our cultural knowledge was based upon work with Black groups in Miami, there was no difficulty whatsoever in understanding the significant elements in the story presented by Mrs. C.

Summary Observations

The abbreviated case histories presented above provide examples of anthropological contributions in the provison of care as well as in the training of clinicians. It will be apparent that a substantial amount of specific cultural content was transmitted during anthropologist-physician interactions directed toward helping patients get better. It is unlikely that this type of learning will be dismissed very easily.

In the process of responding to each patient's needs, physicians found the transcultural perspective fairly easy to assume. They also found it to be helpful when it was adopted. It allowed them to understand and to mediate between two disparate symbolic systems. Furthermore, although skeptical and possibly hesitant at first, orthodox practiners began to feel good about their part in the cultural negotiations. Their interactions with patients became more person-oriented, and ethical problems which might have existed from a unicultural perspective were minimized or became irrelevant from a transcultural one.

A final training approach which should be made explicit is the overall strategy inherent in our pilot study. The anthropologist as a staff person is free to work across departmental and clinical boundaries. The ready accessibility to such individuals by health professionals allows an immediate and focused response to a specific need. This is entirely compatible with the dominant educational mode in medical institutions.

148

In a sense, the pilot effort, itself, now needs to be formalized into a continuing training program for both clinicians and aspiring clinical anthropologists.

Conclusion

It is noteworthy that three major factors are contributing to the ease of collaboration between clinical anthropologists and orthodox health care providers in Miami. The <u>first</u> may be linked to world-wide social and political forces which are leading professionals in every urban center of the world to recognize the multicultural nature of populations and the pluralisitic nature of societies and communities. The impact of such pluralism on health care is pronounced under any circumstances. In Miami, with wave after wave of large numbers of immigrants from politically unstable regions of Latin America and the Caribbean, it becomes, at times, almost overwhelming. The repercussions are felt in multitudinous ways in every component of the health care system. Consequently the anthropological contribution is welcomed.[10]

A <u>second</u> factor stems from 12 years of clinical anthropological activities in the area. These have provided a solid base of cultural information to draw upon when working with physicians and patients with special needs. In addition, many networks have been built in various ethnic communities of Greater Miami. Such networks allow collaboration with traditional healers even when our own contacts, for one reason or another, do not work out or are not fully compatible with the requirements of a particular patient. There is always access to another resource through such connections. The <u>third</u> and perhaps most important enabling factor is that clinical anthropology in Miami has strong support at the highest administrative levels in both the University of Miami School of Medicine and its teaching facility, Jackson Memorial Hospital. This is not to say that hindrances do not exist. Every series of successes seems to create new problems. A current one, for example, relates to consultation fees for traditional healers whose services are needed by indigent patients. This is unrelated to in-house impediments, but it constitutes a problem, nevertheless.

One final aspect of clinical anthropology needs to be mentioned, although it has not been formalized in

any of the Miami program. This is what might be called
the role of the <u>anthropologist clinician</u>, licensed, as
is Dr. Golde, for example, to engage in individual and
family therapy. Culture-brokers in the Community
Mental Health Program described above often see
patients and, in some respects, function as
"therapists" alongside psychiatrists, nurses and social
workers in community clinics. They are not, however,
certified as therapists, and they are not licensed as
such. It may be predicted that training programs for
anthropologist clinicians most assuredly will emerge in
the near future--not necessarily in Miami, although
there is great need for this--but in almost any setting
where there are sufficient numbers of anthropologist
clinicians to initiate such training programs. It is
the author's opinion that this is not far over the
horizon.

1. "Falling-out" is used here as a general label for variants of what appear to be equivalent syndromes among American Blacks, Bahamians, and Haitians. In our study, it was most often referred to as "falling-out" by American Blacks, as "blacking-out" by Bahamians, and as indisposition by Haitians, cf. Social Science and Medicine 1979, 13B for a series of articles focused upon the syndrome.

2. For a discussion of this point, see Weidman, H.H. 1979:102-103. Persons who "fall-out" chronically are atypical "hysterics" in that they do hurt themselves. Furthermore, their behavior lacks the marked manipulative overtones so often ascribed to hysterical conditions. Also, in contrast to the indifference of individuals showing symptoms of classical conversion hysteria, victims of falling-out show great concern about their health problem.

3. Proper spelling would be battement du coeur; however, Haitian speakers of Creole frequently transform the article du into de. This custom is reflected here. Battement de coeur has been described previously in Weidman 1976b, and also Weidman et al. 1978.

4. Kleinman, Eisenberg and Good (1978) have directed attention to the concept of clinical reality as a useful and relativistic term.

5. The entire issue of Psychiatric Annals 1975, 5(8) is devoted to the Miami program.

6. Documentation is provided in the continuation grant of the Comprehensive Community Health Center of the Mental Health Division of Jackson Memorial Hospital and the University of Miami Department of Psychiatry, 12-19-77.

7. These administrators also carry the respective titles of Vice President for Medical Affairs and Assistant Vice President for Medical Affairs of the University of Miami.

8. There are many similarities in this case history to some of those obtained in Miami with

falling-out. As the story unfolds, the reader will understand the likelihood that Mrs. C. "fell-out" because of overwhelming fear of what might befall her upon leaving the hospital. Cf. Weidman, H.H. 1979, op. cit.

9. Obeah is the term used by Blacks in several former British colonies to refer to the system of malign magic. Obeah men and women who have expertise in manipulating the world of evil spirits are known not only in Belize but also in the Bahamas, Jamaica, Trinidad, and Barbados, for example. For a discussion of "roots" and the probable origin of the the word, see Weidman and collaborators 1978, op. cit., pp. 733-736.

10. What is not yet realized by health professionals is that the transcultural (trans-person) posture is desirable in every clinical transaction. At this point in time Family Medicine is much closer to achieving such a stance than are the other three departments in which we work. This is so despite a discernable philosophical shift in medical fields, generally, toward prevention and primary care. The anthropological approach in Miami focuses upon ethnicity as a teaching strategy designed to lead ultimately to similar considerations of the views of every patient. Such a goal is entirely compatible with the mission of orthodox providers of care to help patients get better and to raise the health level of the national population.

REFERENCES

Caudill, W.
    1953   Applied Anthropology in Medicine. In
            Anthropology Today. Kroeber, A.L., ed.
            pp. 771-806. Chicago: University of Chicago
            Press.

Harris, M.
    1971   Culture, Man, and Nature. New York: Thomas
            Y. Crowell.

Kleinman, A., L. Eisenberg and B. Good
    1978   Culture, Illness and Care. Annals of
            Internal Medicine 88(2):251-258.

Lefley, H.P. and E.W. Bestmann
In   Community Mental Health and Minorities: A
Press   Multi-Cultural Approach. In Community Mental
         Health in a Pluralistic Society. Sue
         S. Moore and T. Moore, eds. New York: Human
         Services Press.

Paul, Benjamin D., ed.
1955   Health, Culture, and Community. New York:
         Russel Sage Foundation.

Scott, C.S.
1975   Competing Health Care Systems in an Inner
         City Area. Human Organization 34(1):108-110.

Weidman, H.H.
1973   Implications of the Culture Broker Concept
         for the Delivery of Health Care. Paper
         presented at the Annual Meeting of the
         Southern Anthropological Society,
         Wrightsville Beach, N.C., March 8-11.

1975   Concepts as Strategies for Change.
         Pyschiatric Annals 5(8):17-19.

1976a   On Getting from "Here" to "There." Guest
         Editorial. Medical Anthropology Newsletter
         8(1):2-7.

1976b   The Constructive Potential of Alienation: A
         Transcultural Perspective. In Alienation in
         Contemporary Society. R.S. Bryce-Laporte and
         C.S. Thomas, eds. pp. 335-357. New York:
         Praeger Publishers.

1979   Falling-out: A Diagnostic and Treatment
         Problem Viewed from a Transcultural
         Perspective. Social Science and Medicine
         13B:95-112.

Weidman, H.H. et al.
1978   Miami Health Ecology Project Report.
         Departments of Psychiatry and Pediatrics,
         University of Miami School of Medicine (off
         print).

Wolf, E.R.
1956   Aspects of Group Relations in a Complex
         Society: Mexico. American Anthropologist
         58:1065-1078.

PART III

THE SOCIAL SCIENCES AND MEDICINE IN COMMUNITY HEALTH:

THE COMMUNITY CONTROL OF HYPERTENSION

IN CENTRAL MISSISSIPPI

FOREWORD

Demitri B. Shimkin

The Holmes County (Mississippi) Health Research
Project of 1965-1975 and the project now funded for
1980-1985 for the Community Control of Hypertension in
Central Mississippi constitute a related pair of
socio-biological investigations and experiments of
general importance for medicine, the social sciences
and, indeed, public policy. Both are focused on a
poor, rural population suffering heavily from
ill-defined diseases and, at least initially, dominated
by social tensions and oppression. Both utilize a
basic ecological model with the fundamental dependent
variables being morbidity (especially hyperendemic
hypertension) and mortality, while major independent
variables derive from the social environment.
Specifically identified as intensifying hypertension in
the early 1970s in the Black population of Holmes
County were social marginality (work as a farm laborer,
residence on plantations, in-migrant status) and the
burdens of household headship for both men and women.
A decade later, large-scale control has introduced new
relationships. The major mediating variable in both
the epidemiology and control of hypertension discovered
thus far has been membership in a "strong" extended
family. This finding seems to apply to both Black and
White families. The catharsis afforded by expressive
religion is also probably important, although
unevaluated empirically. In the physical environment,
endemic streptococcus infections, particularly evident
among Delta children, are a major, still uncontrolled
health problem.

In the conduct of research and of intervention
experiments in maternal and child nutrition, and later,
the control of hypertension, both the earlier and
current project have rested upon direction by a local
governing board and execution by a combined team of
scientific specialists and trained local people. These
projects are not _for_ but _of_ the affected community, a
relationship which has strengthened rather than diluted
their scientific rigor. The combination of research
and services remains crucial.

Since the start of work in Holmes County in
1966-67, important changes have taken place. The

157

earlier efforts began when racial violence still
dominated Mississippi. They had to be confined to the
Black community, and encountered severe opposition from
local physicians. Nevertheless the University of
Mississippi College of Medicine provided important
support both in research and in the care of identified
severe hypertensives.

The current project enjoys massive support, up to
the state government and population served. It serves
both races in a five-county area. Its leadership,
although jointly anthropological and medical as in the
beginning, is now controlled by persons with long-term
local commitments.

Given the present understanding of the effects of
the social environment upon hypertension, it is
important to assess how the significant changes in
Mississippi society since 1965 are affecting the
incidence of hypertension, and the degree to which
other variables are also being expressed. The profound
improvements in the control of the disease since the
1970s also modify larger functional capacities within
the population, biology feeding back to social
dynamics.

The many, only partially solved, problems of health
in central Mississippi have intrinsic significance.
They also merit attention because of the magnitude of
migration out of and, more recently, back to
Mississippi. And they also are representative of a
wide range of health and social problems, including
those of rapid change, which are found widely in the
Third World. One of the direct associations of African
urbanization has been the marked increase of
hypertension. Cooperative efforts between our
Mississippi work and health programs in Tanzania are
currently being explored.

ANTECEDENTS: THE INTERNATIONAL BIOLOGICAL PROGRAM
AND THE HOLMES COUNTY (MISSISSIPPI)
HEALTH RESEARCH PROJECT
1965-1975

Demitri B. Shimkin

Early in 1965, the United States formally entered
the International Biological Program (IBP), a worldwide
cooperative effort designed to provide systematic and
comparable data on the natural environment, on the one
had, and on human adaptability, on the other, which
would be applicable to practical as well as scientific
uses. Specifically the human adaptability component
sought:

. . . to take stock of human adaptability as
it is manifested at the present time in a wide
variety of terrains, climates and social
groups, to deepen our knowledge of its
biological basis and to apply this knowledge
to problems of health and welfare. To do all
of this satisfactorily, for communities
ranging from the very simple to the highly
industrialized, requires an integrated
approach and an application of methods from
many fields, particularly those of human
environmental physiology, population genetics
and developmental biology aided by auxilary
disciplines, for example, medicine,
anthropology, ecology and demography (Weiner
and Baker 1965:7).

By August, 1965, the U. S. National Committee for
the IBP had elaborated approaches to the study of human
adaptability in several respects. "Meaningful
biological units," from the individual to the breeding
population, were to be the units of study. The
investigations were to be "intensive multidisciplinary"
undertakings especially focused on selected groups that
would illuminate human diversity. In addition, less
comprehensive characterizations were to be sought from
groups undergoing biological changes:

. . . [goals were] the biological and
behavioral aspects of population dynamics
within migrant and isolated populations, the
consequences of inbreeding and outbreeding,

159

and the role of disease as a selective agent (USNC IBP 1965:27).

A final consideration was the planned use of research sites as training centers of the "personnel needed to conduct genuinely multi-national collaborative studies" (ibid.).

In subsequent months, the importance of migration and migratory populations as keys to contemporary mechanisms of stress, selection and adaptation became increasingly clear. Also clear was the opportunity for research and services offered by the great disruptions and migrations then underway from the South to the industrial North. Moreover, conversations with civil rights workers made evident that, despite certain hazards, productive communications and research were feasible even in Mississippi and Alabama.

Consequently, I undertook an extensive field trip in the Hill and Delta areas of Central Mississippi in the summer of 1966. Many doors were opened to me through my son, Alec, then a civil rights worker. Among the Black "grass roots" people whom I visited and with whom I stayed, adults and children alike showed great stability and strength, generosity and caring, humor, creativity and hope even in the dire poverty of the temporary camps, such as "Freedom City," of those expelled from the plantations in the brutalities of 1965-1966. The presence of danger, arson and attacks on the road from the Klan generated mature closeness, even from young boys and girls. And, with the terrible lessons of 1964 in mind, the resolution to meet terror with armed strength was widespread: Stokely Carmichael's declaration of Black Power merely reflected an existing consensus. Within this context, local people and the small band of civil rights workers, Black and White, were launching developmental efforts large and small. In Holmes County, in the hamlet of Mileston, the center of Black landownership in the Delta, such a combination had built a community center in 1964. Here lived a white couple, Henry and Susan Lorenzi, he a former physicist and she a computer specialist, now devoted to helping the rise of pre-school education, a health center and much else.

The health center was served by a volunteer White nurse and the weekly visits of Alvin Poussaint, M.D., a Black psychiatrist from Boston. It provided an alternative to local physicians who were segregationalists, often greedy, and an integral part of the plantation credit and control system. Dr. Poussaint served this center and other places from Jackson, a weekly tour of great danger and periodic humiliation from harassing police. He brought to my attention the high prevalence in his patient population of hypertension, ulcers and chronic fatigue. His interviews revealed acute insecurities, self-depreciation and even self-hate. Yet neither suicide nor internally directed violence were in evidence. How the angers associated with oppression, angers which he himself felt intensely, were being released, he could only puzzle over.

The months that followed were devoted to recruiting a working group and to developing project concepts. In particular, Adrian Ostfeld, M.D., then Head of the Department of Preventive Medicine and Community Health, University of Illinois College of Medicine, became my principal project planner. Oscar Lewis and Edward Bruner in my Department were also helpful, while both Alec and Henry Lorenzi helped from the field.

On March 17-19, 1967, at Pheasant Run near Chicago, Dr. Ostfeld and I convened, on behalf of the IBP, a Planning Conference on "The Ecology of Migrant Populations in the United States" (Ostfeld and Shimkin 1967). The project statement, a 27 page document, laid out a number of planning principles and concepts. Some of the most important need to be cited here:

> . . . To develop an adequate bio-social characterization of the nation, intensive work is needed on "non-white," "poor" and "rural" groups, since the great bulk of existing data pertain only to the "white," "middle class," and "urban" portions of the population. Apart from its scientific value, such a characterization would have practical value in defining national medical, economic and educational needs including those for environmental quality (p. 1).

> In research on Human Adaptability especially, the investigation undertaken must be designed and conducted as to guard the welfare and privacy of the individuals and groups studied. In general, acceptance and cooperation by a community, as well as ethical requirements, will necessitate the allocation of measurable resources to medical and social services as well as pure research (p. 8).

161

Bio-social characterization - a quantitative ecological description of a group´s size and composition, biological an socio-psychological characteristics, habitat and major behavior patterns so designed as to identify and measure the group´s constituent biological populations and levels of fitness, adaptive mechanisms and selective pressures of each population (p. 8).

Fitness - the capacity of a population to survive, ultimately measured by the relation of fertility to mortality and also indicated by a variety of cross-sectional and longitudinal measures . . . (p. 9).

Adaptive mechanisms - the behavioral, physiological and ultimately morphological responses stimulated by the pursuit of goals or attempts to manage stresses and identified by the observation and analysis of (1) manifestations of basic drives (hunger, aggression, sexual satisfaction, play, etc.); (2) stressful events (illness, pregnancy, birth, death, conflicts, etc.); and (3) the diagnosis of adaptive breakdowns (physical and mental illness) . . . (p. 9).

Migration - this term embodies a great variety of phenomena, of radically differing adaptive significance. The movement of an isolated individual from a farm to a remote high-density metropolitan area in which he knows perhaps a handful of contacts is scarcely comparable to moving in with kindred in a nearby town. Moreover, since migrations are usually selective, i.e., weighted towards one sex and particular ages, different patterns and intensities of migration have varying effects upon source communities. It is important also to study the non-migrants and those returning to or migrating to the source communities. Who are they? Why do they choose the alternatives they do? What happens to them in comparison to the migrants? Finally, the interconnections between source communities, migrants, and even new kindred and friends in the receiving areas cannot be ignored, for the totality of change may be, in fact, one system . . . (p. 12).

Over forty medical, biological and social scientists, educational specialists, civil rights workers and Federal administrators participated in this conference. Among the better known figures were John Bennett, Cleveland Chandler, Albert Damon, Jack Geiger, Lawrence Hinkle, Everett Lee, P. Herbert Leiderman, Oscar Lewis, Leigh Minturn, Alvin Poussaint, Lee Reeder, Harold Rose, Frederick Sargent, Howard Schneider, Steven Vandenberg and George Wilbur. However, the key presentations for the design and conduct of the future work were given by Alec Shimkin and Henry Lorenzi.

Alec Shimkin sketched the changing structure of Black society in rural Mississippi from the standpoint of potential field research. He emphasized the continuing centrality of White dominance politically, economically, socially and even sexually in shaping Black society. Within this context, Black society was complex. It included plantations, especially in the Delta, where the White landlord makes every decision and survival depended upon his goodwill. It also included Hill areas of small independent Black and White farmers, each group centered on its own church community. In towns, there was marked stratification, among Blacks, from the professionals--largely school teachers dependent upon totally White school boards--to businessmen and craftsmen, to the domestics and handymen. All this had been disturbed in about forty counties out of eighty-two by the greater or lesser impact of the civil rights movement, which had brought out new leaders and attitudes. It was only in these impacted counties that an external scientific program was likely to find acceptance. Even here, there were cautions to be followed. Scientists should remain scientists and not try to be amateur civil rights workers. And acceptance and valid results could come only with respect for local people, poor as they might be. The scientific work, if not necessarily a benefit, should at least not harm the structures and organizations which local people themselves have built through a great deal of struggle in the past five or six years.

Henry Lorenzi expanded these ideas to the organizational principles which should govern work in awakening Black communities. He felt that only a cooperative relationship between scientists and local people could produce sound and valid results. Basic needs were that the program be understood locally and in meaningful terms; that local leaders--and their

163

identification might present a problem--be used for communications, for programmatic suggestions and to develop whatever local employment and services might be feasible; and that training that leadership in program objectives and techniques would be very fruitful in building cooperation. Structurally, the relationship could range from a local advisory board to a delegate agency in which the community undertook field operations under scientific guidance and with veto power, from a research institution.

Much of the summer of 1967 was spent in Holmes County. I sought to assess the styles and capacities of both the new leadership, that of the Freedom Democratic Party, and the old, the heads of extended families in the hills far more than the "teachers and preachers." I elicited perceived health and health services needs. And how ready were the leaders to assume roles in a delegate agency which would be apolitical and colorblind? The vehicle for this was the newly chartered Milton Olive III Memorial Corporation, and the potential Principal Investigator was Mrs. Bernice Montgomery, a former school teacher and Director of a highly successful Head Start operation, the Milton Olive III Memorial Program for Children.

The concept of a delegate agency approach and a commitment to local development and services as well as research appealed to the new National Center for Health Services Research and Development. According, Adrian Ostfeld submitted a five year proposal for almost a million dollars, the direct costs of which would use a locally recruited and trained staff and a local governing body in combination with the scientific direction and training of the University of Illinois. The initial tasks included a thorough census of the Black Population which would provide a reliable basis for sampling and for relating health and social variables. Then the households would be divided into ten random samples and each sample would be asked in random order to participate in a health survey assessing both continuous variables and the presence of abnormalities. In addition, a comparative study would be undertaken in Holmes and adjacent counties to assess the physical and psychological impacts of Head Start. Finally, a limited intervention would take place: women not under medical but midwife care would receive nutritional support, be discouraged from clay and starch eating, and urged to limit weight gain--all as devices to reduce maternal, fetal and neonatal death rates.

A long period of intense difficulty followed this favorable start. The project received no funds until February 1969; until then, a series of desperate hand-to-mouth efforts was needed to keep going. Except for Mrs. Montgomery, all of my initial team had left by mid-1969, impelled by opportunity, felt obligations and exhaustion. But the recruitment of replacements, although difficult, was successful. Two correlated proposals, one on the Chicago end of the migratory stream and the other to manage and handle data for the overall study failed to gain funding, so that we had to proceed with a structurally inadequate design and acute deficits. None of our Northern scientific staff ever received more than partial travel reimbursements, let alone pay. The local physicians in Holmes County opposed our efforts unceasingly; in consequence, services as well as research had to be conducted through long-distance commuting. The International Biological Program, wedded to antiseptic scientism, withdrew its token support.

But the work was accomplished. Basic credit belongs to three men--Kenrad Nelson, M.D., of the University of Illinois College of Medicine; Eddie Logan, Director of the Holmes County Health Research Project; and Edward Eckenfels, of Rush-Presbyterian-Saint Luke´s Medical Center. Nelson carried a huge burden of services as well as doing fruitful research, notably including the discovery of a new strain of endemic streptococcus B in Holmes County (Nelson et al. 1976). He was also able to enlist the participation of Herbert Langford, M.D., and the University of Mississippi College of Medicine in our later research and intervention program on hypertension. Logan, always conscious of scientific rigor and reliablity, trained and directed his staff of 20 to 30 so as to combine effective outreach to the grass roots with well executed technical tasks. Eckenfels also played a major role in survey design and training, in job analysis and simplification, and in overall management.

It must be noted that our original research design had to be changed. While the census was done, randomized health surveys turned out to be both impractical and unacceptable in the presence of many, acute health emergencies. A part of the effort was allocated to services. Health Research was focused on categorical problems--infections, parasitoses, nutrition and hypertension. The neonatal effort was superseded early by a five-county State operation.

Between 1979 and mid-1971, our primary goal was a bio-social assessment of the Black Population in Holmes County. Work in the County, coupled with small investigations in Chicago conducted by Holmes County students in Illinois led by Robert Stewart, permitted a rather full exposition of the demographic and socio-economic correlates of migration (Shimkin 1971). Beginning in 1970, Dennis Frate, then a student at Louisiana State University, conducted extensive research on geophagy in Holmes County (Vermeer and Frate 1975, 1979). As a key by-product, he developed much information on family structure and functioning among the poorest Black people. This work, coupled with the investigation of extended families in migration and urban adaptation by Gloria Louie, a Holmes County student at the University of Illinois, provided the basis for a full evaluation of extended families as basic mediators of stress (Shimkin, Shimkin and Frate 1978).

In 1971, our investigations took a new turn. Our Milton Olive governing board insisted, and we agreed, that defining new, serious health problems without effective attacks upon them was harmful to a population under heavy stress. Moreover, it was clear that we could depend on no new resources--we had to use what we had to maximum advantage. The most promising approach would be a concentration on hypertension, already evident as a major problem from our nutrition survey data. The recruitment of a distinguished specialist, James Schoenberger, M.D., of Rush-Presbyterian-St. Luke's Medical Center and his procurement of free medicines from Abbott Laboratories made feasible a pilot project on the community control of hypertension.

The pilot project, in operation between April 1972 and August 1973, involved setting up a crude clinic, training the local staff as field screeners, health technicians and record managers, and the conduct of mass hypertension screening with about half of the Black households in the County being contacted at least once. The screening measured blood pressure on 4,235 individuals aged five and above. For the population aged 18 and over it revealed 1,101 cases of uncontrolled hypertension out of a total of 2,818 persons screened. These prevalences are higher than those for Blacks in the National Health Survey of 1960-62, almost three-fold so in the age group 25-34 for both sexes. Moreover, the proportions for 800 patients ranged in severity as follows: mild, 49.1%; moderate, 28.6%; and severe, 22.2%.

In contrast to the great success in mass screening and diagnosis, actual control was attained for only 28 patients by the clinic, which was simply overwhelmed by its caseload, with only two physicians being available on a part time basis. Fortunately, both local physicians and the University of Mississippi College of Medicine cooperated in the treatment of patients referred to them (Eckenfels et al. 1977).

What lessons can be chosen from these extensive experiences since 1965?

1. Our efforts have proven that, in the conduct of research on health and human problems, cooperative efforts between scientific institutions and target communities are both feasible and productive

2. High socio-psychological stress in an impoverished community was found to be associated with high levels of physical illness, especially hypertension. Moreover, variations in status and vulnerability within this community, which were pointed out by Alec Shimkin in 1967, were significantly associated with different risks of hypertension. This was particularly true for Delta vs Hill, and for laborers vs other occupations (Schoenberger et al. 1975).

3. Conversely, extended families proved to be the basic institutions facilitating survival under extreme poverty and migration with the least stress (Shimkin, Shimkin, and Frate 1978:25-148). Beyond this, locally identified "strong" families had far lower propensities towards hypertension than "weak" ones, a key to prevention (Frate 1978).

4. In areas of high stress and limited resources, ethical considerations dictate that problem-finding research must be geared in its pace to remedial intervention.

5. Intervention programs, to be effective, require a coordinated use of all local resources. By combining the special mass screening capabilities of a community based effort with the therapeutic capacities of local physicians a joint capacity well beyond that of either alone can be created.

167

REFERENCES

Eckenfels, E.J. et al.
1977   Endemic Hypertension in A Poor, Black,
         Rural Community: Can It Be Controlled?
         Journal of Chronic Diseases 30:499-518.

Frate, Dennis A.
1978   Family Functioning and Hypertension in a
         Black Popultion. Ph.D. Dissertation,
         Department of Anthropology. Urbana:
         University of Illinois.

Nelson, Kenard E. et al.
1976   The Epidemiology and Natural History of
         Streptococcal Pyoderma: An Endemic Disease
         of the Rural Southern United States.
         American Journal of Epidemiology
         103:270-283.

Ostfeld, Adrian and Demitri B. Shimkin
1967   Program Statement. Planning Conference on
         "The Ecology of Migrant Populations in the
         United States" March 17-19 at Chicago,
         Illinois. U.S. National Committee on the
         International Biological Program, National
         Academy of Sciences, Washington D.C.

Schoenberger, James A. et al.
1975   Hypertension in Holmes County,
         Mississippi. In Epidemiology and Control
         of Hypertension. Paul Oglesby, ed.
         pp. 485-501. New York: Stratton.

Shimkin, Demitri B.
1971   Black Migration and The Struggle for
         Equity: A Hundred-Year Survey. In
         Migration and Social Welfare. Joseph
         W. Eaton, ed. New York: National
         Association of Social Workers.

Shimkin, Demitri B, Edith M. Shimkin and
Dennis A. Frate eds.
1978   The Extended Family in Black Societies.
         The Hague: Mouton.

United States National Committee on the
International Biological Program
  1965   Preliminary Framework of the U.S. Program
            of the I.B.P. Publication No. 1.
            Washington D.C.: National Academy of
            Sciences.

Vermeer, Donald E. and Dennis A. Frate
  1975   Geophagy in a Mississippi County. Annals
            of the Association of American Geographers
            65:414-424.

  1979   Geophagy in Rural Mississippi:
            Environmental and Cultural Concepts and
            Nutritional Implications. The American
            Journal of Clinical Nutrition
            32:2129-2135.

Weiner, J.S. with a contribution by Paul Baker
  1965   International Biological Programme. Guide
            to the Human Adaptability Proposals.
            London: International Council of
            Scientific Unions.

RESPONDING TO SOCIAL VALUES IN COMMUNITY
HEALTH RESEARCH AND SERVICES

Edward J. Eckenfels

Introduction

I want to address my remarks to three themes.
First is to look at what we have accomplished in Holmes
County and what we propose to do in the light of
Clinical Anthropology as an emerging discipline. I
hope this will complement other papers, particularly
Leonard Borman's. Second, I want to give you some idea
of the history and significance of the community health
counselor role as a key element of our approach.
Third, I want to discuss the principles of community
control as they apply to our current project in Central
Mississippi.

Let me begin by reviewing a few basic concepts from
a paper that we prepared as an overview of our original
work in Holmes County, entitled, Community Control,
Action Research, and Program Efficacy (Eckenfels et al.
1976). Appropos of what my friend and colleague, Eddie
Logan, said, I believe that the Holmes County Health
Research Project was a true experiment in development
and social change. I would like to quote briefly from
Denis Goulet's Ethical Model for the Study of Values
(Goulet 1979) to give you an idea of what I mean.
Goulet says:

Development is above all a question of values.
It involves human attitudes and preferences,
self-defined goals and criteria for
determining what are tolerable costs to be
borne in the course of change. These are far
more important than better resource
allocation, upgraded skills or the
rationalization of procedures. Moreover,
developmental processes themselves are
dialectical, fraught with contradictions,
conflicts, and unpredictable reversals of
prior trends. At its most profound level,
development is an ambiguous, historical
adventure born of tension between what is
thought and how it is obtained.

Authentic development then, in Goulet's approach,
aims toward realization of human capabilities in all

spheres. Henry Lorenzi, the pioneering civil rights
worker in Holmes County, formulated, and Demitri
Shimkin and Adrian Ostfield wisely adopted the view,
from the very first development of the relationship
between outside consultants with scientific expertise
and the local community base, that open, popular debate
on values must precede significant impingement wrought
by research upon a society's life. I think that
without that kind of groundwork, without that kind of
basis, the original Holmes County Health Research
Project would have failed miserably. We believed, or
we have learned to believe, through the initiatives of
Henry Lorenzi and Alec Shimkin, plus the leadership of
people like Professor Shimkin and Mr. Logan and Mr.
Wade on the local level, that research in poor, rural
communities like Holmes County, and probably in all
human spheres, must be based on reciprocity, and not
domination. In fact, I think we actually applied a
principle of Goulet's, and of Clinical Anthropology;
that is, we made ourselves vulnerable in the conduct of
research. We made it known to the community what we
were doing at all times. They led us to key problems.
They pointed to many solutions and directions we had to
take. In that sense, our research was action research,
closely following, I think, the notion of action
anthropology Leonard Borman was referring to. It was
neither manipulative nor elitist. It was based on
collaboration, cooperation between co-partners,
co-researchers, in advancing science and, at the same
time, human well-being. Scientific and human values
are not mutually exclusive, not in conflict with one
another, but complementary.

Goulet gives a research model that he calls the
basis for permanent synthesis, and I just want to touch
on that very briefly to give you a background here for
appraising our work in Holmes County. This model
consists of four stages.

The Research Model

1. Preliminary Synthesis Stage

This is when there is two-way communication between
researchers and planners, on the one hand, and local
community leaders, on the other, about values, beliefs,
and expectations. It is a stage of mutual education
not only about the specifics but also about the
assumptions and implications of proposed work--in
language both sides understand. Throughout the

172

planning, the detailed design, and the training phases of the Holmes County Health Research Project this is exactly what was done. There was a kind of union between the researchers and the local community, mediated by skilled interpreters of speech and logic, especially Henry Lorenzi, and later, Eddie Logan.

In this process, the community leaders came to understand, agree to and internalize the basic strategies of the project. They, in turn, critically evaluated all protocols. Some, although interesting scientifically, were peripheral to project goals and of little felt value to the community. People in Holmes County felt, for example, quite satisfied with their sex lives, believing research time better spent on other subjects. In other cases, the governing and human subjects boards suggested fruitful modifications. They provided "pilot testing" to integrate science, values and symbols more effectively.

2. Systematic Observations

The basic IBP protocol provided the initial inventory of research questions. But what was essential was a holistic, structural-functional or systemic approach. We undertoook a careful appraisal of community structure, informed by the excellent early insights of Alec Shimkin and Rev. Phillip Rushing. This included primary and integrating groups, activity patterns--extremely important with the multiple occupations characterizing this community--beliefs and values. Out of this somewhat static formulation came questions of stress and the search for mediating mechanisms. This led to the identification and later verification of the Black extended family as the fundamental social unit here (Shimkin, Shimkin and Frate 1978). It provided the key link in understanding the fabric of the community.

As a non-anthropologist, I must say that, without the anthropological perspective we had from Shimkin and Frate, a critical epidemiological dimension of hypertension would have been missed.

3. Reflective Synthesis

While we sought diligently to maintain direction and coherence in our research, all of us engaged in data collection were able to make thoughtful

173

suggestions on the content and procedures of research. This aspect came through very clearly in our critical decisions on data collection, balancing scientific objectives, community needs, costs and acceptability. It involved contributions from all participants, including the local staff. All this took much time in meetings, often hour after hour. But it produced work that was understood and supported. Only once did it stop: our staff, newly raised in dignity, rebelled at having to handle the fecal samples needed for parasitological assessments. These were cut short, although not before the high prevalence of Ascarid infection, particularly in the Delta, had been established.

4. Feedbacks of Reflective Synthesis to and from the Community

Here indeed were the major decision-making processes. Within the Holmes County Health Research Project, this was exemplified in the turn from description and epidemiological research to clinical research centered upon a pilot intervention study. By 1971, we had found a tremendously high prevalence rate of essential hypertension in the population, and we had also learned that it was the principal disease treated, often ineffectually, by the local medical care system. And we know both the possibilities and life-saving significance of the control of blood pressures. It was at this stage that our community governing board simply said:

"Stop the research! You consultants have to do something about this problem. Let´s get out there and set up some kind of service program to help us deal with this disease."

Community control, action-oriented research, and systematic attention to program efficacy have been the inter-related components out of which our work in Mississippi has grown.

The Genesis of the Community Health Counselor Role

Let me now turn to my second topic, the genesis of the community health counselor role in our current approach to hypertension.

In 1974, after five years of data collection and learning how to work effectively with the community, basic funding for our project terminated. We were able to gain another year's funding to analyze the data from the large set collected in the population and housing surveys, along with our hypertension screening and treatment components.

Over the next five years, Dennis Frate and I particularly concentrated our efforts on interpreting our data from the standpoint of an improved program of hypertension control. We oriented our papers for presentation at cardiovascular disease epidemiology meetings. We felt that this group would be a receptive and helpful audience.

General Approaches to Hypertension Control

At that time, two elements comprised the approach to the detection and management of hypertension then in vogue. One was mass community screening to identify the large number of undetected and untreated hypertensives believed to be found. Dr. Jeremiah Stamler and his associates at Northwestern had estimated (Stamler 1973) that out of a population of perhaps 30 million hypertensives nationally, half did not know they had hypertension, half of the remainder were not under treatment, and only half of those under treatment were controlled. In other words, only one out of eight hypertensives was actually having his or her blood pressure normalized. Yet the Veterans Administration studies had both shown that diastolic readings even of 95 mm could be quite predictive of further complications terminating in strokes or kidney failure, and that existing drug therapy could normalize blood pressures in most instances. Because of these studies, the second component of the customary hypertensive management approach was to refer hypertensives found in mass screening to the existing health care system, whatever that system might be. The assumption was the proper therapy would be known and used, with effective compliance by patients.

The Holmes County Situation

We found, in Holmes County, a situation quite different from the general model. We found that two-thirds of the population over 18 whom we screened had diastolic pressures of 90 mm or higher. But very few of these uncontrolled cases were either undetected or untreated. People were highly aware of high blood pressure and most had sought some type of professional care without successful results. Concurrently there was a very high overall level of illness. In the entire population aged 16-74, 18 percent felt "too sick to work," and only half of this disability was associated with definite hypertension (Shimkin 1981:Table 1). This level of illness, both episodic and chronic, burdened the local health system. In addition, inadequate health education and barriers such as poverty and inadequate transportation severely limited compliance with regular, continued medication regimes.

Clearly, problems like those found in Holmes County could be solved neither by additions of physicians nor mass screening alone. They had to be attacked systemically, through the development of outreach based on indigenous health counselors who could carry the major responsibilities of case identification, community health education and, under the direction of physicians, case management.

In our thinking, we moved away from the concept of specialized clinics. Because hypertension is only one aspect of a heavy burden of illness in rural Mississippi, the capabilities of limited clinics are almost always inadequate. Also, the enhancement of the existing health care system, including the addition of resources to bring to local physicians the best new methods of managing hypertension, appeared to be the most economical and long-lasting solution. Given the positive changes in Mississippi over the past decade, this approach appeared to be socially practical. And it was funded for a five-year period.

Community Control

Let me turn to my third topic, community control. In our present project, the tasks and nature of community control are substantially different from those of the Holmes County Health Research Project. We are now concerned with a bi-racial population in five counties, we are depending heavily on local professional and community resources, and we are using external expertise only for specialized, high-skill purposes. Yet the basic strategies remain.

Community accountability rests today in the widely representative Board of Central Mississippi, Inc., a body which speaks for the public interest, for both

176

Black and White. The major technical supporting body is now that of the local physicians, who must learn to use the new health counselors, and who also must gain the advantage of greater effectiveness in this new setting. And the indigenous health counselors, both Black and White, are the component integrating community and health services.

These carefully selected local people are receiving technical training—how to take blood pressures, what hypertension means as a silent killer, the importance of compliance with drug therapy, dietary counseling, elements of patient education, and of behavior modification. But they must be able, through their local knowledge, through their concern and persuasivensss, to gain access to those at risk and to those hypertensive, to get them to gain medical help, to verify their normalization, and to keep on the needed lifetime course of compliance. They will work through three types of social settings: in the extended family, where family caretakers will be identified and trained to monitor, work with, and educate hypertensive relatives; in community settings, where the health counselors will develop volunteer leaders to conduct patient instruction; and on an individualized basis, with people who find difficulty in adhering to treatment plans.

Our program will be a vehicle of change as well as social reinforcement. Dr. Sidney Johnson, a local practitioner, and Dr. James Schoenberger, my chairman and president-elect of the American Heart Association, will work together to provide the practicing physicians of the five-county area with specialized training emphasizing new ideas and methods in the management of hypertension. The Control Data Corporation has provided us with the PLATO system to be used in developing a current hypertension registry for the area. We hope also to use this same system of interactive computation to speed and strengthen our training program for health counselors and other staff.

It is through these means, balancing technical requirements and professional skills with community direction and the maximum use, training and development of local people that we hope both to control a dangerous, endemic disease and to enhance social capacity and cohesion in an impoverished rural area. In doing this, the approaches of Clinical Anthropology and Medicine are mutually reinforcing.

REFERENCES

Eckenfels, Edward J. et al.
1976   Community Control, Action Research, and
          Program Efficacy: The Evolution of the Holmes
          County Health Research Project. 66 pp.
          Lexington, MS: Milton Olive III Memorial
          Corporation.

Goulet, Denis
1979   An Ethical Model for the Study of Values. In
          Education, Participation, and Power: Essays
          in Theory and Practice. p. 35-57.
          Cambridge, MA: Harvard Educational Review
          Reprint Series, No. 10.

Shimkin, Demitri B.
1981   Systems Analysis: A Promising Focus for
          Biosocial Research. Journal of Biosocial
          Science 13:1-11.

Shimkin, Demitri B., Edith M. Shimkin and
Dennis A. Frate eds.
1978   The Extended Family in Black Societies. The
          Hague: Mouton.

Stamler, Jeremiah
1973   High Blood Pressure in The United States--An
          Overview of The Problem and The Challenge.
          In Proceedings of the National Conference on
          High Blood Pressure Education. National
          Heart and Lung Institute. Washington, D.C.:
          U.S. Department of Health, Education and
          Welfare. Pub. No. (NIH) 73-486.

178

THE ORGANIZATION AND IMPLEMENTATION OF
A COMMUNITY-BASED RESEARCH PROJECT:
THE INITIAL PHASE, 1980-1981[1]

Dennis A. Frate, Eddie W. Logan
and Charlie F. Wade, Sr.

This section will focus on three main topics.
First comes a description of the community organization
that sponsered the Community Control of Hypertension in
Central Mississippi between 1980 and 1982. Second, the
research problem itself, including its initial research
design, will be discussed. And, third, the
implementaion of this specific research project within
a community-based structure will be sketched.

Community Organization

Since the orginial Holmes County Health Research
Project was funded in April, 1969, numerous social and
political changes occurred nationally, locally and
within Federal funding agencies that dictated
alterations in the organization and scope of the
proposed research. Several proposals were submitted
unsuccessfully in the late 1970s. When the particular
research proposal which did gain funding was being
developed in 1979, a community-based social action
agency was sought as our local sponsor. At the same
time, because of our own research interests and the
funding priorities of Federal agencies, both Black and
White residents were to be addressed in this research
design. The scope of the project, concurrently, was
expanded to five counties. It was these dictates that
led our project to work within a Community Service
Agency structure, that of Central Mississippi,
Incorporated, rather than the original structure of the
Milton Olive III Memorial Corporation, the activities
of which were restricted to Holmes County.

Central Mississippi, Incorporated, is a Community
Service Agency (CSA), organized to meet the needs of
all residents in the seven counties of its service
area. (When our grant application for the hypertension
project was initially developed in 1977, only five
counties were being served by Central Mississippi,
Inc.) Formally chartered on August 25, 1965, the
organization itself was an outgrowth of the War on

Poverty in the mid-1960s which was launched to attack problems encountered by all poor people throughout this country. Locally, a broad-based organization was needed to address the numerous ills encountered by both races. Since 1965, the organization has expanded and altered its scope and today houses the following service components; aging programs (i.e., nutrition sites); economic guidance and development; weatherization programs (environmental health efforts for housing structures); crisis intervention; youth employment programs; companion programs (i.e., recreational efforts); and Head Start. The administration of these programs is handled through individual directors for each program, an Executive Director, and a broadly based governing board. The Board is composed of 36 members representing all segments of the local population. In fact, as stated in the by-laws, one-third of the Board must represent low-income residents, one-third must represent the private sector, and one-third must represent the public sector.

Central Mississippi, Incoporated, addresses the overall needs of the community. The proposed project on controlling high blood pressure was felt to comply with the goals of the organization. Normally, a Community Service Agency would not sponser a research project. Two factors, however, were critical in the decision of Central Mississippi, Incorported, to undertake sponsorship. First, the organization was well aware of the health problems in its area. Every day, the effects of high blood pressure are felt by the residents. Second, this research project had a service component imbedded within it; research could be conducted while services to the people were being provided. In other words, the project could help those with high blood pressure while investigating the best approaches to controlling this disease. Also, it was felt that if the health of area residents could be improved, possibly some of their other needs would not be as great. Consequently, Central Mississippi, Incorporated, became one of the few Community Service Agencies, if not the only one, involved in such research in this country. It should be restated that the initial sponser for this research was not a major university nor a research corporation but a non-profit community organization dedicated to assisting residents in need.

The Research Problem

Untreated essential hypertension presents an unique problem to the medical community. First, it is one of the leading factors contributing to all major cardiovascular disease mortality, the number one cause of death in this country. Second, hypertension is generally very controllable but sustained adherence to therapeutic regimens has proven difficult for patients. And third, many of the identified risk factors to elevated blood pressure can be reduced through behavior modification. Our 15 years of research in central Mississippi have demonstrated a wide range of findings salient to controlling hypertension here. For example, in 1973, it was demonstrated that the vast majority, 68 percent of hypertensive Blacks in Holmes County, Mississippi, were aware they were hypertensives. However, only 41 percent of those on treatment were under control. Important among the many problems identified in the management of hypertension in Holmes County were a lack of patient education and an overburdened medical care delivery system which could effectively function for acute episodic care but could not provide the continuity demanded by the long-term management of a chronic disease such as hypertension. Therefore, this research project was designed as a comprehensive, specially adapted, approach to controlling hypertension in this poor, rural area of central Mississippi.

One of the most critical components of this research project is that it is community based. The original grantee institution, as previously noted, is a community organization, Central Mississippi, Incorporated. This project is also community based in that a local physician is Co-Principal Investigator. His role centers on the coordination of the existing medical care delivery system in attacking hypertension. With his involvement in this carefully designed hypertension control and education program, the thrust is on articulation with the existing medical care system rather than autonomy from it. In addition, the majority of the staff, especially the health counselors or outreach workers, are local residents. The use of residents as the core staff helps to assure community acceptance as well as provide a basis for continuing feedback from the community. Finally, as will be shown, the overall education and control efforts have been fashioned to interface with the social fabric of this local community.

181

There is "outside" involvement and that centers on the scientific support of the program. At the time it was officially funded, June, 1980, its Principal Investigator, Dennis Frate, was on the Faculty of the School of Pharmacy, The University of Mississippi. But scientific advice and support came primarily from Rush Medical College in Chicago (for cardiovascular and health education expertise), the University of Illinois at Urbana-Champaign (for research in community structure and human ecology), and the University of Michigan (for biostatisical expertise). A private organization, Control Data Corporation, committed resources, including computer hardware and software and personnel, to this project.

On June 1, 1980, the National Heart, Lung, and Blood Institute of the National Institute, of Health, Department of Health and Human Services, awarded Central Mississippi, Incorporated, 2.46 million dollars to conduct research on high blood pressure in five central Mississippi counties: Attala, Carroll, Grenada, Holmes, and Montgomery (see Figure 1). The research has two major thrusts. One centers on testing new models for controlling blood pressure and the other on examining the genetic-enviromental relationships in high blood pressure, i.e., specific epidemiological investigations.

This study is being conducted in a predominantly rural area of central Mississippi. The 1979 population estimates for this area show 84,859 individuals residing here. Approximately 49 percent of that population is White and 51 percent is Black. This distribution provides a unique opportunity to assess the impact of such a program on a truly biracial population. Another unique feature of this area is the impact that cardiovascular diseases have on mortality. For example, in 1975 cerebrovascular mortality was 91.1 per 100,000 in the United States, and 171.9 per 100,000 in the target area. In 1976, the cerebrovascular mortality rose to 208.4 per 100,000 in this area. It was 224.3 per 100,000 for Whites and 194.0 for Non-Whites (Mississippi Health Systems Agency 1978). Consequently, this study area has the unique features of an empirical data base rising from the Holmes County studies, a biracial population, and an extremely high rate of hypertension-related mortality.

Specifically, the component of the research centering on the control of high blood pressures concentrates on the management of hypertensives and not

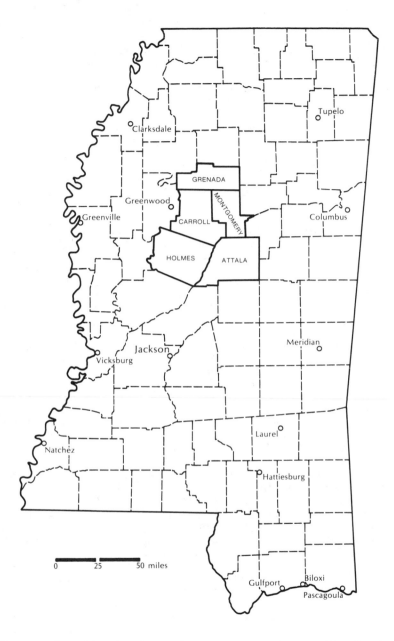

Figure 1.   The Project Study Area: Community Control
            of Hypertension in Central Mississippi
                        1980-1985

183

the prevention of this disorder. It was felt that more inroads on control could be made if the focus was on getting the individual into the medical care system and assisting the physician in the management of that individual. Prevention in an area so economically deprived would be a more tenuous approach to benefiting the health of its population.

The key role within the high blood pressure control component of this project is that of the health counselor. We have devised two separate counselor models. One is a more sophisticated model for a counselor extensively trained in data collection, interviewing techniques, blood pressure measurements, the epidemiology of hypertension, and health education techniques. These Hypertension Health Counselors are local residents hired as full-time staff members and trained as the project's outreach workers. One of the most critical characteristics of these counselors is that they are local residents. Their knowledge of their community (in this case the county), their familiarity with the residents, and their insights into the social structure and behavioral processes of this area make them an indispensable part of the model.

The other counselor model is the Volunteer Health Counselor. These individuals are recruited and trained to monitor the blood pressures of a defined group of hypertensives. There are two different settings where this counselor model will be tested: the extended family and various community (mainly church) settings. The Volunteer Health Counselors from the family settings are recruited from large extended families. They monitor the blood pressures of their own family. The community Volunteer Health Counselors are recruited from other social group settings such as churches, social clubs or any place where individuals congregate on a regularly scheduled basis. A variety of concepts is incorporated into this model of Volunteer Health Counselor. One is that of returning some responsibility for maintaining health to the individual. Another concept embedded in this model is that of social familiarity, as with the Hypertension Health Counselors. Individuals may be more apt to comply with therapeutic regimens if these are conveyed by someone from their own background. Finally, since the management of a chronic disorder of this nature will require an evolution in the structure of the local medical system, now oriented to acute disease, this model provides the regime and close monitoring required. It should be stressed, however, that this

184

project is still relying on the local medical care system for the clinical diagnosis and management of all hypertensives. In fact, the counselors are thoroughly trained not to alter the therapeutic regimen or suggest any therapy not prescribed by the physician. For example, weight loss is only discussed if weight reduction was prescribed by the client's physician.

The other component of this five-year effort centers on a replication of earlier investigations here which showed that blood pressure levels were associated with the relative social cohesion of extended families (Frate 1978). This finding centers on the concept of the relationship that environmental stressors have in the etiology of hyperstension. If environmental stressors do play a role in aggravating blood pressures, support mechanisms present in this community may mediate the etiological loop and result in lower blood pressure for those who utilize available support mechanisms. The social investigations here found that the extended family network within the community provides for its members (Shimkin, Shimkin and Frate 1978). Therefore, the design focuses on blood pressures within various extended families exhibiting both low and high social cohesion. A new feature of the present study is the inclusion of White families, the structure, dynamics and health associations of which are poorly known.

In addition to the study measuring the effects of environmental stressors and social cohesion, two other epidemiological studies are to be conducted. One centers on the familial (sibling and parental) aggregation of blood pressures. The other study examines the role of diet and, more specifically, dietary sodium and potassium, in the etiology of high blood pressure.

As is evident, both components of this research have their roots in the social environment. The management and control of hypertension is tied to the two health counselor models which are imbedded in the community social fabric here. Part of the epidemiological investigation is also tied to the social environment based on the hypothesis that the nature and distribution of this disorder can, in significant part, be explained by environmental factors. Examination of the various social factors, however, is not being done in isolation from the biological characteristics of this disorder. High blood pressure involves the neuroendocrine system, a physiological system that is especially responsive to external stimuli.

Demonstration of effectiveness within the health-services research component, or that centering on managing hypertensives, involves a very detailed, quasi-experimental design. The design incorporates a number of characteristics including random allocation, repeated measures, and a control group. The primary sampling units for this study have been identified; in this case this required identification of all households by race and subsequent randomization of areal sections on county maps. Selection stratified by place of residence and race is made through the randomization of all areal sections. A time series design is to be employed for the evaluation. For this purpose, three successive measures will be taken in the population. Finally, a control group from a neighboring county will be used to determine the direction and magnitude of the change of knowledge and awareness of hypertension, and of diagnostic and therapeutic statuses.

The actual high blood pressure control effort involves a number of chronological phases. The first year, Phase One, centers on identification of community resources, hiring and training of staff, and refinement of the baseline survey instrument. Toward the end of Year One and into Year Two the baseline survey is to be administered. This instrument measures a wide range of facts essential for final outcome evaluation. Phase Two of the program involves community-wide screenings, assignment into the intervention groups (Hypertension Health Counselor management, self-help group, and total community). Also, during Phase Two the epidemiological investigations into the genetic-environmental relationships of hypertension will be initiated. Phase Three of the program centers on a mid-point or formative evaluation of program process and potential alterations in the program elements. The final phase of this multifaceted project involves summative evaluation and the determination of the overall health and cost effectivesness of the control models.

As outlined, within this community-based framework a health service research project and an epidemiological investigation into high blood pressure have been designed. This chronic disorder presents an excellent opportunity to see if a local population can be trained to manage such medical conditions, and to test hypotheses about the role the social environment

186

plays in the etiology of disease. The control of blood pressures has been a somewhat elusive goal for most demonstration projects. Here, however, the model being tested is based not on interjecting a new concept alien to all involved but rather to tap into an already existing structure, in other words, a community-based research project. If proven successful, continuation of the model after funding terminates should be expedited by such a community-based foundation.

Implementing the Research Project

Up to this point the community organization and the research protocols have been discussed. These two descriptions logically lead to the implementation of those research protocols within the community.

The first step taken was to plan and initiate the project. This first step centered on a broad-based educational effort. The Board of Central Mississippi, Inc., and the community had to be educated about research per se. This was not to be simply a service project. The local experience at the multi-county level was based on a service agency model. In such efforts, the needs and subsequent solutions are specifically delineated. Research, on the other hand, is not as clearly defined. Methods and procedures, although outlined, have to be tested and altered if not successful. Also, in research, every step must be documented. The community is, of course, interested in the service component embedded in the research. However, implementation of that service component is a gradual process. Consequently, the community itself has had to be educated about research in general and this project in particular. In this instance the term "community" is being used to describe the sponsoring organization (CMI) and the lay community.

There is, of course, another critical part of the community to consider, and that is the medical community. Any project of this nature must have the local medical community's cooperation or success cannot be realized. This cooperation will be accomplished two ways. First, a local physician is integrally involved in the project. This involvement does not center as much on organizing continuing medical education or coordinating treatment regimens as on communicating the nature of this project to local physicians. This communication is accomplished informally through hospital rounds or other informal mechanisms. (The success of this approach was later evidenced by the fact that over 90 percent of all referral postcards delivered by hypertensive patients to their physicians were mailed by the physicians back to the project.) The second way the local medical care system's cooperation is facilitated is through the model itself. The intervention models implemented are not medical management oriented. The best description of the models is that of a "physician's management advocate in the field." In other words, the models used are nonthreatening to the physicians; this is of critical importance.

Another educational effort has had to be conducted and that is with the scientific research team itself. The project has to orient the community to research and the core staff has to orient the research team to the community. Obviously, this locale is not a "brown bench" research clinical setting. Although adherence to the quasi-experimental design will be adhered to, rigidity in that design must be absent. This project is not a clinical trial. And, finally, like the community, the research team has to be oriented toward specific research protocols in health services and epidemiology, and away from a primarily service orientation.

The final step in the implementation of the project has involved the hiring and training of the staff. Although other specific positions exist (secretary, bookkeeper, data clerks, etc.), the key position to fill has been that of Hypetension Health Counselor. These individuals are the backbone of the project since the public interacts mainly with them. All data for the evaluation are based on their role. Consequently, these positions have been screened most carefully. Six individuals were recruited and hired from the five-county target area. In order to solicit applications, job advertisements, including job descriptions and areas of desired competence, were placed in all the local newspapers for a two-week period. About 350 applications were received. Out of this group, 15 persons were interviewed and six subsequently hired.

The training and experience of these persons varies greatly. One of the counselors is an L.P.N. (Licencsed Practical Nurse) while another does not have a high school diploma. Three are Black, three are White. However, the final choice of these persons was not based on their educational background. Although duties

and responsibilities could easilty be outlined, other
key qualifications were much more difficult to list in
a job description. The following aspects were
critically appraised in the hiring process:

1. indigenous or long-term resident of the area;

2. familiarity with the community, including
   communication networks;

3. ability to work with a wide range and type of
   individuals: Black/White, rich/poor, medical
   provider/consumer; and

4. ability to learn the research protocols,
   including the measurement of blood pressures.

These attributes were generally observed or documented
during the interviewing process; distinct criteria were
not or could not be employed. The total selection
process, altough difficult to describe, was fairly
simple to conduct in reality.

Once hired the Hypertension Health Counselors have
had to receive extensive training. The curriculum has
included the following topics: 1. physiology of the
cardiovascular system; 2. principles of epidemiology;
3. epidemiology and control of high blood pressure;
4. pharmacology of antihypertensive medications;
5. interview techniques; 6. blood pressure measurement
techniques; 7. approaches to health education; and
8. cardio-pulmonary resuscitation. This complicated
curriculum was developed by a wide range of health
professionals. In order to be able to train other
counselors a curriculum document was prepared and is
available. After the formal training a small substudy
was conducted as a field practicum. The response rate
of this first field effort speaks both of the
community's acceptance of the project and the
counselors' ability to conduct field work.

Households Contacted	Household Refused	Response Rate
371	29	93%

Implementation of this research project is not
being accomplished rapidly nor haphazardly. It is
being accomplished through a very deliberate process of
informal community education and awareness, and a very
detailed hiring and training program for the staff.

Conclusions

In summary, efforts to investigate and help meet the health needs of the poor in central Mississippi continued after the termination of the Holmes County Health Research Project in 1974-1975. It was not, however, until 1980, that the National Heart, Lung and Blood Institute awarded funds for a five-year, five-county, bi-racial project on the Community Control of Hypertension. The new project required sponsorship by the relevant Community Service Agency, Central Mississippi, Incorporated. This step gained a broad basis of involvement although it lost the intense, volunteer concerns of the original "grass roots" sponsor, the Milton Olive III Memorial Corporation.

At the same time, research directions became more focused and outcome related. Rather than broad explorations to identify key health problems, rather than experimentation with pilot services designs, the new study has to improve control of hypertension through a new outreach mechanism articulated with existing medical services, to engage local social units (extended families, churches, clubs, etc.) in the processes of health education and management, and to undertake investigations bearing on the epidemiolgy of hypertension.

The epidemiological work of the project has the longer term goal of approaching the still elusvie problem of prevention in hypertension. In the same way, articulation with local physicians and careful evaluations of program effectiveness have as their goals an ultimate transfer of the community control of hypertension from an externally funded project to an internally funded service. Finally, while external scientific support remains important, the development of health research by Mississippians is a desirable objective. The goals of this project, therefore, seek to fulfill the original objectives of the International Biological Programme, as outlined in the article on the antecedents of the project by Demitri Shimkin in Part III of this volume.

In implementing this project, meticulous personnel selection and training are essential. Those involved must combine sensitivities to human needs and concerns; knowledge of local institutions and values for both races; capacities to learn new techniques, to work within precisely stated protocols, and to note problems that justify questioning or modification of procedures;

and, finally, to function harmoniously as a team. It has been a source of great gratification, a measure of the rich human resources of poor communities such as those of central Mississippi, that the remarkable talents we need have been found among local people, both White and Black.

NOTE

1. This represents a consolidation and partial re-working in 1983 of presentations made at the Urbana conference.

REFERENCES

Frate, Dennis A.
1978   Family Functioning and Hypertension in a
        Black Population. Ph.D. Dissertation.
        Department of Anthropology. Urbana:
        University of Illinois.

Mississippi Health Systems Agency
1978   Health Statistics: Mississippi, 1978.

Shimkin, Demitri B., Edith M. Shimkin and
Dennis A. Frate
1978   The Extended Family in Black Societies.   The
        Hague: Mouton.

THE PRACTICING PHYSICIAN'S PERSPECTIVE:
PRESENTATION AND DISCUSSION

Sidney A. Johnson, M.D.

Introduction

In essence, I practive general medicine in a rural community, Goodman, Mississippi. Like Mr. Wade says, him and me argue over who's Mr. Holmes County. Now, look how big he is and how big I am, and you can see that he wins every time we argue about it.

But in truth, our people are ill in our county and adjoining counties. This is an area of hyperendemic hypertension and that's unique. City internists would have coronaries themselves if they worked one day in my office. Can you imagine letting someone go home with a blood pressure of 180/130? We just let them go on home. If we hospitalized every severe hypertensive, we wouldn't have room for anybody else. So, mostly, we take care of them at home.

The people here are sincere in their wish to get their blood pressure lowered, and they are sincere in wanting to come to get it lowered, and they are really sincere in taking the medication. These people will work very well with someone they know, our health counselors or home visitors, folks they know. Our health counselors will talk to them, and they will listen. That's our initial basis of getting to our people. The key is familiarity.

I like to see my part of this project not in any academic fashion whatsoever. I have never written a paper for publication. But it would be most helpful to convert the research knowledge gained here into practicality. If we can do that, and at the end of five years show a reduction of our people's blood pressure, the money will be well spent. We are grateful for the opportunity to help our people. We are selfish, and we are unique, and we are like everybody else--we want the health of our people to be better. We are going to do something about the blood pressure of our area, get it down. Hopefully, then we can come up with some kind of a model that can be used to help other locales with their health problems. All of this can be shifted--it doesn't have to be hypertension, it can be diabetes or whatever disease you want to attack.

If you read the papers, you know that the National Institutes of Health have just spent a whole ton of money—and it looks like salt is real bad news, one of the most critical factors in raising blood pressure. Here, our people eat a lot of pork, and the fat in the pork is not good, but more importantly, most pork has also been salted as a means of preservation. So our people by habit eat much salt.

How will we be working on this and our other problems?

In essence, what we are going to do is to send our health care counselors out into the field. They will find hypertensives. They will check and find out who their doctor is, and they will send them to that doctor and not to me. Their doctor will treat them with drugs of his choice. Our health counselors will make sure that the hypertensives go to the doctor, and they will check blood pressures. If the blood pressures are down, fantastic! If they are not—back to the doctor's office with arrangements for that patient to be seen. We are working in conjuction with the rest of the general practitioners in our area. We also work in conjuction with the Health Department—they too have some blood pressure clinics and screening programs.

This is a community effort as far as the physicians are concerned. Some of them know about this and some of them don't. The ones who don't know about it, soon will. The doctors down there get along together real well, and we don't have any problems among the physicians to speak of. And, if any develop we can work them out.

Discussion

Question: What is there about salt?

Dr. Johnson: It's the sodium, which makes for water retention in the tissues.

Question: Why do they eat so much salt?

Dr. Johnson: It just naturally tastes good! You try eating French fries without salt. Salt is just GOOD.

Question: What about salt substitutes?

Dr. Johnson: They don't taste like salt. If I put my

patients on a salt substitute, the first thing they do is to use twice as much. It's taste and habit.

Question: Is there a very high incidence of secondary problems to hypertension?

Dr. Johnson: Certainly. I have right now four people with strokes at the Lexington hospital. The youngest is 53; I lost a 48-year old last week from heat and stroke. I don't mean to be crude or rude, but if the heart is not really enlarged on the chest x-ray, we don't call it "abnormal." We say "normal for age." A decent radiologist would say "cardiomegaly." Kidney disease and other end organ damage is very prevalent here. There is terrible end organ damage througout this area.

Dr. Frate: In 1976, mortality from stroke in Central Mississippi was two-and-a half times the national average. This was also true for all major cardiovascular diseases.

Mr. Sorock: It sounds like you've been basing a lot of the medical care of the hypertensive patients on the blood pressure readings taken in their homes and blood pressure readings taken in the physician's offices. From some experience I have had, I know how important it is to make sure that you check blood pressure in the same manner in the home and in the physician's office. I think it is important to train your health counselors, who you said will be checking blood pressure, to do it in the same way that the physicians will be doing in their offices. The two things that I think are most important are first, that you give the hypertensive the same amount of time at rest prior to checking the blood pressure reading both at home and in the office. The second point is that you make sure that the health counselors check the blood pressure three times and take an average of the second and third reading.

Dr. Johnson: We are following the guidelines developed by the Joint Commission of the National Heart, Lung and Blood Institute on the confirmation of essential hypertension.

Mr. Sorock: The other thing is, from some work done at Cook County Hospital, I was able to interview some hypertensive patients that I was about to train to be patient educators of other patients. I asked them which way they would prefer to be trained themselves, and I gave them a choice. One of the things that I talked a little about was using a tape recorder to help train patients as patient educators of health counselors, and they seemed to like this idea. I thought that, although I didn't get to do it, it would be great to use a tape recorder to be able to listen to the styles of communication of the patient educator, to be able to play this back for that particular patient who would become a counselor, to help that counselor become more effective. So, although I didn't do it, I thought it would work. Also, it would give you the advantage of having a permanent record of how these patients were trained and how effectively they were trained. You might want to think about that.

Question: What percentage of the population seems to be overweight?

Dr. Johnson: Just off the top of my head, of those above 40 years of age, over half are very overweight.

Mr. Wade: In the South we tend to have a lot of fat people. Do you know why that is? They eat, but they don't eat the right things. We describe this as "hungry fat."

Dr. Johnson: I'm not a nutritionist, but you can eat like crazy all day long, but if you don't get the right kind of food, your craving for food is never satisfied.

Question: Are there normotensives who eat about the same diet as hypertensives?

Dr. Johnson: Certainly.

Question: So it may not be diet alone.

Dr. Johnson: I don't think anyone knows. I think it has to do with environment, with heredity, with the whole socioeconomic picture, with childhood experiences, childhood diets, this, that and the other. It's like some people smoking. I've got an uncle, 95. His wife called to ask if I didn't think he ought to quit smoking those cigars because they will ruin his health. He's been smoking them ever since I knew him. I told her I didn't think so. Yet, some people smoke cigars, and by the time they are 55 they are sick. There is an inherent variability in people. I like to say folks are folks, but each one is different. All machines function exactly the same as each other, but people aren't that way.

Dr. Weidman: In our research in Miami there were just an awful lot of local remedies for "high blood," not hypertension. Are your health educators taking these beliefs into consideration?

Dr. Johnson: If you take away home remedies to start with, you are meddling too much. You take somebody 70 or 80, that hasn't seen a physician many times, and their mother has taught them to do this for that. If you take away the home remedy suddenly, your treatment may be no good either. The home remedy may help not just the "high blood" but perhaps "sugar" (diabetes) or burns. For instance, our best remedy for burns at home is--you'll never guess what it is--it's shoe polish.

To answer your question, we will incorporate home remedies into what we are trying to do, but we will gradually get rid of them if we think they interfere with the medical regimen. If we don't think they are bothering anything, we'll leave them alone.

Dr. Weidman: I'm still a little concerned about your health educators, and I'd be interested in knowing more about the extent to which they do take traditional beliefs and practices into consideration?

Dr. Johnson: The health counselors are the health educators, but they are under the supervision of me. We will follow tradition in our area, as we always have, and we always will. We cannot separate an individual from their heritage nor their environment nor their tradition. If you do, you don't have anything and you lose your impact.

Dr. Weidman: It seems to me that you are really underplaying one element of information, one total system of beliefs, which could provide a great deal of information, helping you to achieve your long range goal of reducing the incidence of hypertension by working with these beliefs.

Dr. Frate: There will be a baseline survey to establish beliefs, attitudes and knowledge about hypertension. In that survey there we will cover folks' beliefs, to see what is happening out there. For example, one of the treatments used is baking soda, which is very high in sodium. We want to find out, as Dr. Johnson was saying, if it is totally damaging (by counteracting the diuretic), then we will attack that. But if it is not injuring the patient, then possibly the health counselor will promote it along with the other treatments.

197

Dr. Johnson: We're going to check diets; we're going to check social habits; we're going to check alcohol intake; we're going to check age; try our best to check all variables. But that's left to the academics. When they find something we can convert to practical use, we'll use it on a practical basis. The first part of your question, are we going to interfere with it (folk belief). No, we are not, unless it is injurious, and then we'll do it gradually, very gradually.

The M.D.'s will do that at their offices so it won't be a part and parcel of the study. That's included in the doctor-patient interaction. In family groups, and at the church groups, those things will be given, by health counselors. But on a one-to-one basis, this will be handled by the doctor or the Health Department or the nurse practitioner, whoever has the ultimate responsibility for the health of the patient. The health of the patient is first; the study is second.

Dr. Weidman: Then what are the health educators doing?

Dr. Johnson: Checking blood pressures, getting names, dietary history, monitoring care, encouraging compliance.

Dr. Weidman: Then they are not actually in education.

Dr. Johnson: They will be in education some, but not so much on a one-to-one basis. The direct patient care will be from the doctor. Now, if they have a meeting at the church, the health counselors will go into diet, they'll go into weight, they'll go into what blood pressure can do to you. It will be group education. Like I say, salt is bad. But on a one-to-one [basis] it will be the doctor's responsibility for the care and education of his patient. And the diet the patient is on is the doctor's responsibility, not the neighbor's, not the health counselor's.

Question: Are you going to use fear to get them to take their medicine?

Dr. Johnson: Fear? I would never use fear. Education and fact, yes, but not fear.

Question: One of the problems I have with these kinds of things is that it is possible, for example, when you say that blood pressure is the silent killer, and one spreads the word about that, that kind of preoccupation has something to do with the fact that it might turn out to be harmful. What sorts of means are you going to be using to get people to comply with taking your medicine?

Dr. Johnson: Persistence, both with clinic care and health education.

Mr. Logan: People will respond to you if they believe in you. We are going to utilize local people. Let me take you to Holmes County. There are about 18 communities in Holmes County, so if we decide to go out into a particular community, we are going to try to train a person in that particular locale, and you don't frighten people into doing anything. You can tell them what they need to do, and they do it on their own, voluntary basis. So there is not going to be a frightening technique. If there is, a lot of people are not going to have anything to do with us. We will train them, and of course they will have a certain area that they will work with. You've got to believe in the person who is making the statement, "Don't step on the snake, he will bite you." So, that's the type of method we are going to use, not the scare technique.

Question: What about radio, newspapers, TV, etc.? Are you going to keep a low profile?

Dr. Johnson: We will initially keep a kind of low profile until we can make ourselves known, because we'd rather let people know ourselves. Up here, you can have on TV that there is going to be something at a fixed place, and they are accustomed to getting their instructions and advice that way. Down home, it's lots different--you see, I didn't even put a note [on my office door] that I was leaving. I just told some people and everybody in town knew. We have an underground system that works better. We will use TV coverage later. Early on, we go very light, and then heavier and heavier, when people are aware of what we are doing. If we are not careful, the people will think they have another bunch of "those folks" coming down here, and going to do something to us again, and we'll not want any part of it. Our people just freeze you right out.

Question: To change directions a little, Dr. Frate mentioned that the Holmes County Health Research Project found two problems above all, one was hypertension and the other was poverty. I just wonder whether you are going to follow up on the poverty part of the earlier study.

Dr. Johnson: The poverty question, we hope, will be answered in our questionnaire. We will try to work it in such a way that we can determine a degree of income without bringing too much pressure to bear. We will have to do that very carefully. We have total acceptance, and down home to get total acceptance you have to mind your own business a little bit. So, we won't tread too deeply, and the fact of the matter is, using the counselors from the local community, we'll all know the poverty level anyway, maybe not in specific detail but in general. But it will be included.

Dr. Frate: In our earlier work on Holmes County, poverty was so widespread it was associated with everything. Now, in Central Mississippi as a whole, we should be able to see some gradients, especially in urban areas such as Grenada. An important problem in assessing poverty in this area is that cash income is a poor measure. There is still much subsistence farming so that someone with no real income but with five acres, a few chickens and a pig might be much better off than many wage laborers.

Dr. Johnson: Let me add. The other day I had a patient come in with diabetic blood sugars of about 600-700, and she was doing quite well, no real problem other than the high blood sugar. So I pitched one of my fits about her diet, and she looked me straight in the eye and said, "Doctor, what I am going to do? I eat what we have." And so, since I didn't have an answer, I just shut up. Here again, I think this is one of the things that also involves hypertension. I don't know. I don't think anybody does. But I would wager that, at the poverty levels, there is a definite association. You can buy fat-back meat, well-salted, a lot cheaper than you can buy a piece of steak.

One other point on poverty and dietary habits. Through Mr. Wade's organization they run the Headstart Program. The physicians down there do physicals on these children every year. Up at Headstart, they go get them, carry them to school, feed them, take care of them, and take them home. Three years ago, if you did physicals on a hundred youngsters, you would expect 30-35 of them to be anemic. After three years or four years with their program in Headstart, if you check one hundred children that's been going to Headstart for a little while, you find maybe five out of a hundred that are anemic. The diet program at Headstart is a part of correcting this problem.

Dr. Lepper: I have been watching the Holmes County program evolve over a long time, and have also been interested in hypertension for many years. As I recall, Dr. Kenrad Nelson found high incidences of nephritis as a sequel to streptococcus infections among Holmes County Headstart children. In my mind, the national declines of nephritis and associated hypertension are as dramatic as those of tuberculosis and scarlet fever.

In a sense, Holmes County appears to be a social relict of the tough days of hypertension. You said that you see quite a bit of renal failure. Even at Cook County Hospital, one does not see renal failure very often, certainly from straight renal disease or malignant hypertension. There was a good study at one of the original hypertension conferences sponsored by the Chicago Heart Association where the health officer from Memphis showed a tremendous decline in uremia all through the thirties and forties. This would be one of the best explanations for the continued decline in deaths from stroke and hypertension, which has been going on ten years longer than the reduction in coronaries. It was continuing all through the fifties, when you couldn't get a doctor interested in treating hypertension unless the patients had malignant hypertension. I think that here are some other social factors at work, tied to poverty and lifestyle, that are as potent variables as the cigarette.

Question: What about people who have migrated out of this area? What is happening to them in relation to blood pressure and other health problems? I'm mindful of the studies about the Orientals. In Japan they have a different rate of hypertension, coronary heart disease and stroke when they move towards the West. In Hawaii, it's higher, and when they get to Los Angeles, it's very much like it is here.

Dr. Frate: We did a study on migrants from Holmes County to Rockford, the second largest city in Illinois. We had measured and then re-measured the same people or at least siblings. In essence, blood pressures rose for five years, then dropped to the levels expected for their age group. These changes took place regardless of all other variables.

Question: Were these people initially normotensive?

Dr. Frate: Some were normal, some were hypertensive. Specific blood presssure were taken in 1972 and 1973.

I met them in 1977-78, and their blood pressures were much higher.

Question: Have you taken any pressures of sub-adults?

Dr. Frate: We took blood pressures on everybody five years of age or older, in a sample of thirty per cent of the households in 1972-73. Very high blood pressure levels were found in adolescents, too.

Dr. Shimkin: I want to do a little commenting and make some suggestions. First, it is pleasant to see a starving infant become a six-foot-one husky. That is what has happened since the start of this work under the old International Biolgoical Program fifteen years ago. I feel that what is here now is going to stick. It represents a new structure with its roots in the local population, both Black and White, and with its extensions through the best of the local doctors to the University of Mississippi and the old system of power. This is a remarkable achievement to which many people contributed.

There are two things that I'd like to sort of bring up here, though. They are really addressed to future directions. One is, there is a very real need to write up not the statistics, but the actual history and development of what has happened, in terms of training and participation, because it is a part which we have not done, and there is a very real need for communication to others who may follow. I'm talking particularly to Ed Eckenfels and Eddie Logan about the volume on that part of the whole project, the bringing in of community personnel, their training, all of this mechanism. I think that this is one of the programmatic needs that you really need to attend to.

The other thing, which I think is of enormous importance, and I hope again that I can stimulate our College of Medicine at Urbana here to think of it, is that the actual achievements, the relation between the nitty-gritty practice of medicine and community participation, are the kind of training which would be of enormous value in clerkships. I hope that it will be possible in the days here to think of how this could be brought at least a step forward.

I would also like to see one of the early meetings of this group take place in the South but not only with academics, but, as we have done in the past again and again, with the direct and active participation of

community people, Black and White. It is only in that
way that we can know whether we are reaching people.
All too often, there are many words. People say:
"That's right. That's right," or people just don't
answer. Mr. Logan has said the words are there but
then there is no communication. You've got to go real
slow, and start all over again, because you know that
you just got off the track.

These are some of the implications. I hope that
through what we are doing now we will not merely have a
report and a nice publication. I'm very much devoted
to defining real end points in health. It isn't the
reports, it's the change in outcomes that is always the
key to what we are doing. In this regard, Dr. Johnson
and I are very much of a mind.

Conclusion

Dr. Johnson: To summarize. We have two primary
purposes. 1. Take the grant that we were fortunate to
get, and do some good for people generally, and more
specifically, help the people in the five county area
of Central Mississippi. 2. Our other function is to
help anybody else, at any time that we can. I speak
for myself but I'm sure that everybody agrees. We
would be interested to receive information. My
colleagues would be interested in giving you
information because they have it, I don't. We will
work with anybody, anywhere, in order to do something
to help folks. If we can answer a question, seek us
out; our model will work in other settings for
different diseases.

THE OPERATION AND REALITIES OF A COMMUNITY-BASED
PROJECT: THE SECOND PHASE, 1982-83,
OF THE COMMUNITY CONTROL OF HYPERTENSION
IN CENTRAL MISSISSIPPI[1]

Dennis A. Frate

        This section covers the past two and one-half years
of this research project. The chapter by Frate, Logan
and Wade (this volume) reviewed the original
organizational structure and the initiation of the
research protocols within this community-based
environment, including the hiring and training of the
local staff. This chapter continues the discussion of
the project and covers the further implementation of
the research design, including the health intervention
models, the necessary changes made in the
organizational structure, and a formative or midpoint
evaluation using both quantitative and qualitative
data.

        Further Implementation of the Research Design

        Once the staff was hired and trained, the actual
implementation of the research design began. The
health services research aspects of this project were
based upon a quasi-experimental design in which the
health and cost effectiveness of the three high blood
pressure control interventions would be compared. The
three intervention strategies were: 1. the
Hypertension Health Counselor-single hypertensive
client; 2. the high blood pressure management
self-help groups; and, 3. community-wide detection,
referral, and educational activities. These three
interventions were to be compared to each other and to
a control county where no significant high blood
pressure control program is operating. The three
interventions were all developed from our accumulated
knowledge of the sociocultural fabric of this area.

        Prior to initiating the interventions two related
tasks had to be accomplished. First, in order to
provide a method of randomly selecting study
participants, the total population had to be
identified. This identification process proved to be a
valuable, albeit, arduous, task as all households in
the rural areas had to be located and identified by

race. Once identified, a five percent household sample was selected in order to conduct the "baseline survey." This second task, the baseline survey, was necessary for the overall evaluation design; an initial point-in-time measure of the population was required before beginning any intervention activities. Also, participants for the interventions would be identified through this randomly conducted survey. In addition to measuring high blood pressure prevalence, treatment status, and awareness and knowledge about the disease, this survey provided data on 216 independent variables including those relating to health status, family health history, health attitudes and beliefs, and extensive social data. Blood pressure measurements were taken on over 2,700 individuals and detailed questionnaires completed on over 1,700 adults. It was from this survey that the majority of individuals participating in the interventions were later selected. By using this method of random selection the final summative evaluation would be more meaningful. In addition to this first random measure of the population a second random midpoint measure was conducted one year later to determine the direction and intensity of any changes occurring in the population.

The initial baseline survey determined two very important facts that would reinforce our perceptions of the problems with high blood pressure confronted by the local consumer and provider communities. First, it found extremely high point prevalence rates for both adult Blacks and Whites. Using the standard criteria of a systolic pressure greater than or equal to 160mm and/or a diastolic pressure greater than or equal to 95mm, the baseline survey found that over 40 percent of adult Whites and over 50 percent of adult Blacks had elevated blood pressures or were on medication for hypertension and had controlled pressures. Obviously, we are dealing with a very serious health problem in this five-county area. Interestingly, we found, however, that the medical care system is achieving great success in controlling this disorder, in fact, achieving a better rate of high blood pressure control than is true nationally. Almost 60 percent of Black hypertensives and 64 percent of White hypertensives are on medication and attaining a controlled blood pressure, or pressures less than 160mm systolic and less than 95mm diastolic (Frate et al. 1983). However creditable that control rate is, the fact remains that about 40 percent of all hypertensives are not under control; this proportion must be viewed in conjuction with the very high prevalence rates. In other words, uncontrolled high blood pressure affecting thousands of individuals is still a serious problem in this area. The frequency of end organ damage referred to by Dr. Johnson (this volume) must also be kept in mind in this connection. The rate of blood pressure control achieved by this community did indicate two important facts to us. One, even though this area is a poor region with a marginally educated adult population, the residents are extremely health conscious and informed about such matters. Two, the provider community could not be dealt with as originally outlined. Continuing medical education seminars would not have a major impact on a group of practitioners achieving such a high rate of success in controlling this chronic disease. More informal communications were decided upon. These communications had to reflect the significant improvements in health care standards in central Mississippi achieved by local medical practitioners over the past decade.

With all this information in hand, the specific intervention strategies were initiated. The two main innovative strategies, the Hypertension Health Counselor and the self-help groups, were based on years of social research in this area. The Hypertension Health Counselor was based on the "granny midwife" model, while the self-help intervention was based on our documentation of the social support available in familial, religious, and community organizations. As mentioned earlier, these two intervention strategies utilized social concepts for specific health outcomes. It should be stressed that these intervention activities focus on disease management and not on health promotion or prevention. Also, the model is health, not medically, oriented in that the counselors comply exactly with the treatment regimens prescribed by the physicians.

In addition to the health services research activities of this project, specific epidemiological investigations were launched during this phase. These epidemiological studies centered on both independent analyses of data already collected, and specifically designed and conducted field efforts. These studies include: an investigation into the aggregation of blood pressure within families, more specifically between siblings and parents-and-siblings; a detailed examination of dietary patterns of Blacks and Whites conducted to determine the role sodium and potassium play in the distribution of blood pressures; and an examination of the increase in the blood pressures of comparably aged adolescents during the past ten years using new data as well as information collected in 1972-73 by the Holmes County Health Research Project.

As stated before, all of these health services research efforts, including the intervention strategies and the epidemiological investigations, were conducted or initiated during this phase of the program.

Organizational Changes

The original community-based model of this project integrated three major, diverse aspects: a local community service agency as sponsor, scientific expertise which initially was mainly external to Mississippi, and an indigenous staff. Even this community-based model was significantly different from the model employed in the original Holmes County Health Research Project (1969-74). The most significant changes were that a broader-based, biracial social agency was now being used as a local sponsor; the Principal Investigator of this study was an accredited scientist residing on-site in Mississippi with an adjunct appointment with The University of Mississippi; and the Co-Principal Investigator was a local General Practitioner.

Also significant, as opposed to the earlier Holmes County Health Research Project, the current grantee institution did not play an influential role in the guidance and administration of the program. All decisions were made internally by the project administrators. The three administrators represented the key units of the new community-based model: a resident research scientist, an indigenous General Practitioner, and an indigenous administrator representing the consumer community. This lack of a prominent role by the community service agency was a result of the highly technical nature of the research protocols and advice from the funding agency. This was a highly visible change from the previous research project. Feedback from the community, both positive and negative, was received by the internal administrative staff through three mechanisms. The first mechanism was from the project staff itself. These individuals not only functioned to staff the program but became informants on the social environment and the implementation of the specific research protocols. The second feedback mechanism came from the provider community (i.e., local physicians). Their cooperation is continually sought through referral of clients and the transmittal of clinical information to the project. If the project was not performing up to the local clinical norms or expectations, the providers' rejection would quickly be noticed. The third feedback mechanism centers on the consumer community. In this case acceptance can be measured indirectly in two ways. First, all studies conducted received a high response rate varying from 80-95 percent. And, second, campaigns for the selection of participants into the various intervention strategies continuously resulted in additional persons offering their participation. Hence the community-based nature of this particular study is not as related to the grantee institution as in the Holmes County Health Research Project conducted here but rather to the internal staff itself and the provider community.

It is important to stress that a maximum practicable responsiveness to community needs and values has continued to be a key factor in the operation of this project. But this project, like Urban Neighborhood Health Centers throughout the United States (Hessler and Beavert 1982), has had to function within increasingly restrictive funding and management guidelines, as well as more technical performance requirements.

Due to the sociopolitical climate encountered in the earlier study of 1969-1974, in-state expertise was then generally not solicited. Because of this political climate, including the local perception of the program as an extension of the Civil Rights Movement, external experts had to be used. In 1980, external experts were again contacted and listed as principal to this study. One negative outcome of the use of such an extensive external consulting network was that the local (state) health and health research institutions were not eager to accept the project as a vital in-state operation. The perceptions of these key institutions were clear--the project was an externally directed operation. Specific changes were made, however, to help alleviate this perception of external control: the Principal Investigator obtained a faculty appointment at The University of Mississippi and became a resident of the area. In addition, an unrelated administrative occurrence resulted in the two major contractual agreements being renegotiated with out-of-state institutions. These contractual agreements were for the services of experts in a variety of fields, including computer analysis, evaluation design, biostatistics, and genetics. The renegotiation of the contracts eventually resulted in these functions being handled by faculty from The University of Mississippi-Oxford and the University of Mississippi Medical Center. Subsequently, over ninety percent of the funds for external consultants were being paid to local institutions, and less than 10 percent by dollar amount was still contracted for through out-of-state institutions. This change, occurring in the middle of the second year of the project, had a critical impact on the perceptions of local institutions. The project no longer had major ties with external institutions, and instead, local experts were now playing a vital role.

The final change in organization occurred on June 1, 1983. As of that date the grantee institution was changed from the local community service agency (Central Mississippi, Inc.) to The University of Mississippi, the major research institution in the state. This change in grantee institutions was considered necessary for two main reasons. First, the federal funding agencies were continuously unsure of providing research funds channeled through a community service agency, and, therefore, future funding would be a very tenuous proposition. Second, the complexities and scope of this research project demanded numerous support systems specific to research; these support systems were not available through the community service agency. All of these reorganizational steps resulted in the legitimization of the project vis-a-vis state institutions. These reorganizational efforts solidified the project within the state and precipitated the involvement by the project staff in other state-wide activities, including teaching at The University of Mississippi, submission of research applications with in-state scientists, placement on the Research Advisory and Policy Committee of the Mississippi Affiliate of the American Heart Association, and co-sponsorship of an eight-state conference on high blood pressure.

The project still remains community-based, but, as is evident, the community base has changed over time. In 1969, the organizational focus was on a race-specific social service agency--external consultants--indigeneous staff triad. In 1980, the focus shifted to a broad-based community service agency--external consultants with an on-site research scientist--indigenous staff triad. And, in 1983, the project's interrelationships had altered to an in-state research institution--local consultants--indigenous staff triad. The transition in organization does reflect the changes and nature of the local sociopolitcal environment. However, no matter how great the change in that environment the reduction in the involvement of external institutions was fundamental in initiating and solidifying relationships with state institutions. The local institutions had to be convinced that the project was indeed a local, community-based effort, and not one directed by experts outside Mississippi. In fact, given the rise of capabilities locally, conflicts with state institutions would have been continually more likely. Each shift in organization then has resulted in a dramatic change in the acceptability of the project, although our ties to the community service agency remain strong. For example, the primary contact for the project previously was the Board President, and this same person is now our consultant for community relations.

Program Evaluation

Obviously, the effectiveness of any health services research and demonstration effort must be based on an outcome evaluation. Three separate issues are involved in the evaluation of the effectiveness of any health intervention program. First, what were the program outcomes? Under this category the effectiveness of this project is being measured in two ways: one, as to the proportion of hypertensives achieving a controlled pressure by intervention strategy, and two, as to the mean blood pressure levels per intervention strategy. The second issue relates to program costs. Even though a health effective intervention strategy can be developed and initiated the cost effectiveness of that stategy must be considered. In other words, what are the costs in controlling a single hypertensive per intervention strategy? And, third, even though a health and cost effective model can be developed and implemented, can a successful program be continued or institutionalized once programmatic funding terminates? Consequently, any program evaluation must consider the short-term effectiveness by evaluating health and cost outcomes and the long-term effectiveness by measuring the continuity of the program over a period of time. Our research project is still in operation. Therefore, cost effectiveness and continuity evaluation cannot as yet be quantified. Qualitative data do exist, howver, on both items. Data are available on health outcomes. The data to be presented, however, represent only a

211

six-month formative evaluation of two of the interventions. Any conclusions are obviously preliminary; a summative evaluation will be conducted in two years.

At the present time the five Hypertension Health Counselors are managing 229 individual clients. This management consists of monthly blood pressure monitoring and specific health education activities focusing on drug therapy, drug side effects, nutritional counseling, including weight loss, and general education on the causes and potential outcomes of uncontrolled high blood pressure. As shown in Table 1, approximately 50 percent of the 229 clients had uncontrolled blood pressure upon entry. By Measurement 6, however, over 75 percent of the client panel had achieved a controlled blood pressure.

Six-month formative data are available on 16 self-help groups, ten in extended family settings, and six in community, mainly church, settings. As shown in Table 1 almost 50 percent of individuals in both groups were uncontrolled hypertensives. However, by Measurement 6 a significant change between the groups had occured. At the sixth measurement, over 90 percent of the 128 individuals participating in family-based self-help groups had achieved a controlled blood pressure and over 70 percent of individuals participating in community (church)-based self-help groups similarly had achieved a controlled pressure. The differences between the proportion controlled in the family-based blood pressure management intervention were statistically significant from the other two interventions. The three interventions units were not significantly different at entry.

Table 2 illustrates mean blood pressure levels. At the time of entry, the mean pressures of individuals in the three interventions were not significantly different. However, one-way analysis of variance found a statistically significant decrease in pressures between Measurement 1 and Measurement 6 in all three interventions. Even though preliminary, these data support the health effectiveness of all three interventions, especially the family-based self-help groups. Their effectiveness is more evident when compared to recent national data which show that only 34.1 percent of those on medication for hypertension are achieving a controlled blood pressure (Rowland and Roberts 1982).

Table 1. Proportions of Patients Achieving a Controlled Blood Pressure by Sequential Measurement

Intervention Unit	Measurement 1 Number A B	Percent	Measurement 2 Number A B	Percent	Measurement 3 Number A B	Percent	Measurement 4 Number A B	Percent	Measurement 5 Number A B	Percent	Measurement 6 Number A B	Percent
Self-Help Group-Extended Family (N=128)	60/128	46.9	91/128	71.6	98/128	78.1	103/128	80.4	112/128	87.5	118/128	92.2
Self-Help Group-Church Setting (N=83)	41/83	49.4	51/83	61.4	64/83	77.1	73/83	88.0	70/83	84.3	59/83	71.1
Hypertension Health Counselor-Single Client (N=229)	113/229	49.3	140/229	61.1	150/229	65.5	152/229	66.4	152/229	66.4	172/229	75.1

Legend: A, Number of clients with controlled hypertension

B, Number of clients in intervention unit

Measurement 1: Chi Square = 0.22   2DF   P > 0.05

Measurement 2. Chi Square = 18.83   2DF   P < 0.01

Table 2. Mean Blood Pressures by Sequential Measurement

Intervention Unit		Measurement 1 (Entry)	Measurement 2	Measurement 3	Measurement 4	Measurement 5	Measurement 6
		Mean Blood Pressures in MM of Mercury					
Self-Help Group- Extended Family (N=128)	Systolic	148.2	138.6	137.6	133.1	133.0	130.6
	Diastolic	91.1	87.3	84.2	82.2	82.4	79.6
Self-Help Group- Church Setting (N=83)	Systolic	152.0	145.9	137.9	134.2	130.6	134.1
	Diastolic	91.6	88.3	82.5	82.0	83.3	85.2
Hypertension Health Counselor- Single Client (N=229)	Systolic	153.6	149.4	146.6	144.9	143.0	140.6
	Diastolic	91.8	90.0	88.7	88.3	87.9	86.8

One-way analysis of variance of blood pressures at time of entry: Systolic   P = 0.122
                                                                  Diastolic P = 0.90

One-way anlaysis of variance in changes in blood pressure between
Measurement 1 and Measurement 6:   Systolic $P < 0.01$
                                   Diastolic $P < 0.01$

214

As mentioned earlier cost effectiveness cannot as yet be accurately quantified, although certain preliminary data exist. For example, the five Hypertension Health Counselors have generated over 1300 new patients for high blood pressure treatment. At the maximum these can be interpreted into 15,600 patient visits per year generated for the local medical care system for this disease (1300 x 12 visits per year). These data have an obvious patient revenue interpretation. Consequently, the Hypertension Health Counselor model generates funds that can offset salary and other operating expenses. The self-help intervention is even less costly to operate as only $150 are neeeded for equipment and three to five hours for clinical training.

Although the continuity of this project is difficult to determine, there are certain indications that these interventions will continue once funding terminates. For example, area physicians have offered to hire specific counselors to perform similar functions in private clinical settings. Also, one "problem" encountered in both of the interventions described is that individuals or groups not randomly selected have continuously offered to participate in the study. Because of time constraints and statistical considerations recruitment of additional clients or self-help groups had to be curtailed. The interest generated, however, does reflect the diffusion of these health intervention schemes to a wide range of audiences. This diffusion of ideas reflects the fact that these interventions are culturally relevant to local residents, both Black and White. These data, however preliminary, do support the fact that the interventions are health effective strategies. Although varying, the two interventions are apparently cost effective. Continuation of the intervention strategies, although much too early to definitively project, is felt to have a high probability of occurring after programmatic funding terminates.

The conduct of this project under conditions of rapid, basic change and with rigorous performance standards has not been easy. It has been most gratifying, therefore, that our project was formally designated by the National Association of Community Health Centers, Inc., an organization representing approximately 1,000 such centers, as an "exemplary health promotion/disease prevention effort" (Cooper/Frate letter, May 4, 1983).

Conclusions

In summary, this research project was designed specifically to articulate with the social fabric of this community. The particular health interventions developed were based on years of empirical health and social research. Consequently, both the consumer and provider communities have accepted these strategies.

The initial organizational structure of this project was based on the model employed in the earlier Holmes County Health Research Project. The focus of that organizational model was a local social service agency sponsor, external scientific support, and an indigenous staff. The realities of operating this project under that model became quite clear after about 18 months. Service agency sponsorship and an external consultant network could not facilitate interrelationships with the major state health and research institutions; therefore, a more viable model had to be sought. The model now being used centers on local University sponsorship and a majority of consultants coming from within the state (including a resident accredited scientist as Principal Investigator and a resident General Practitioner as Co-Principal Investigator); the project is still staffed by area residents. While more citizen participation in the project would be desirable, the principles of community control are still maintained through informal but carefully monitored ways.

As systems alter over time adaptation to various changes must also occur. The current model reflects both an adaptation to todays sociopolitical environment and a realistic appraisal of how that system is actually organized and operated. The obvious objective of this project on the Community Control of Hypertension is to develop high blood pressure control intervention strategies that are both successful, and that have a high probability of existing long after the health services research project terminates. The careful design of the intervention strategies and implementation within a socially acceptable organizational model create a favorable environment for that success.

NOTE

1. As of June, 1983, the current staff and their professional titles include:

Dennis A. Frate, Ph.D., Principal Investigator; Sidney A. Johnson, M.D., Co-Principal Investigator; Eddie W. Logan, M.S Executive Project Officer; *Thomas R. Sharpe, Ph.D., Investigator; *Robert Freeman, Ph.D, Investigator; *Robert Buchanan, Ph.D., Investigator; Juliet B. Frate, Research Associate; Margaret Cannon, M.S.N., Clinical Field Supervisor; Dorothy Garnett, Hypertension Health Counselor; Henrene Johnson, Hypertension Health Counselor; Margaret Lomax, Hypertension Health Counselor; Sandra Pinkard, Hypertension Health Counselor; Brenda Simmons, Hypertension Health Counselor; Bessie Foster, Financial/Administrative Recorder; Janey Ginn, Research Project Coordinator; Iola Anderson, Data Clerk; Donna Ingold, Data Clerk; *Beverly Butts, Acounting Coordinator; *Bonnie Varner, Computer Programmer; *Sherry Whitehead, Secretary.

(*Off-site at the Research Institute of Pharmaceutical Sciences, The University of Mississippi, Oxford.)

As of June 1983, the current consultant network, their institutional affiliations, and areas of expertise include:

Demitri B. Shimkin, Ph.D., University of Illinois at Urbana-Champaign, Social Structure/Human Ecology; Wilbrod St. Amand, Ph.D., University of Mississippi, Human Genetics; Adolph Greenberg, Ph.D., Miami University, Social Structure/Self-Help; Marshall McLeod, Ed.D., Rappahanock College, Allied Health Professional Development; Edward F. Meydrech, Ph.D., University of Mississippi Medical Center, Biostatistics; David A. Walsh, Ph.D., University of Mississippi Medical Center, Biostatistics; John Downer, M.D., Lexington, Mississippi, Local General Practitioner; Johnny Bills, M.D., Lexington, Mississippi, Local General Practitioner; Millard Costilow, M.D., Carrolton, Mississippi,

217

Local General Practitioner; Charlie F. Wade, Sr., Lexington, Mississippi, Community Relations.

As of June, 1983, the current colaborative arrangements include:

Herbert G. Langford, M.D., University of Mississippi Medical Center: an investigation into the racial differences in dietary sodium and potassium and urinary excretion;

Sylvia Wassertheil-Smoller, Ph.D., Albert Einstein College of Medicine, Bronx, New York: an investigation into the racial differences in dietary sodium and potassium and urinary excretion;

Robert Watson, Ph.D., D.V.M., University of Mississippi Medical Center: development of research investigation into the relationship between lifestyle changes and cardiovascular risk factors in an 18-49 year-old population;

Mississippi State Board of Health, University of Mississippi Medical Center, American Heart Association--Mississippi Affiliate: co-sponsorship of the Ninth Southeastern High Blood Pressure Conference;

Dean W.J. Makene, Faculty of Medicine, University of Dar es Salaam, Tanzania: collaboration on cardiovascular diseases in a Third World country.

REFERENCES

Cooper, Barry A.
    1983   Letter to Dennis A. Frate, Ph.D. May 4,
            1983. Washington, D.C.: National Association
            of Community Health Centers, Inc.

Frate, Dennis A., Sidney A. Johnson, Edward F. Meydrech
and Thomas R. Sharpe
    1983   The Status of High Blood Pressure Control in
            Central Mississippi. The Journal of the
            Mississippi State Medical Association
            24:124-127.

Hessler, Richard M. and Carolyn Sue Beavert
    1982   Citizen Participation in Neighborhood Health
            Centers for the Poor: The Politics of Reform
            Organizational Change, 1965-77. Human
            Organization 41:245-255.

Rowland, Michael and Jean Roberts
    1982   Blood Pressure Levels and Hypertension in
            Persons Aged 6-74 Years: United States,
            1976-80. Advance Data from Vital and Health
            Statistics, No. 84, DHHS Pub. No.
            (PHS)82-1250. Washington D.C.: National
            Center for Health Statistics.

PART IV

HOW USEFUL IS ANTHROPOLOGY?

VIEWPOINTS BY HEALTH WORKERS

221

AN OVERVIEW OF ANTHROPOLOGY AND
COMMUNITY MENTAL HEALTH

Thomas T. Tourlentes

Prologue

The strong common bonds between anthropology and
psychiatry are neither new nor novel. Both obviously
are concerned with overlapping aspects of human
behavior. Psychiatry looks at individuals clinically.
Anthropology takes a broader cultural view of man.
Community mental health clearly must borrow liberally
from both to serve its diverse clientele's many needs
effectively.

Wittkower and Dubreuil (1971), in their historical
review of the interface between psychiatry and
anthropology, define anthropology as simply "the long
range study of mankind," and psychiatry as "the short
range study of the individual." The more formal and
complete dictionary definition of pyschiatry, of
course, is "a medical specialty dealing with mental
disorders," while anthropology is "the science of man
in relation to physical character, distribution,
origin, environmental and social relations, and
culture." It is interesting to note that one
definition is rather specific while the other one seems
very general.

Emil Kraepelin, who is best known for his early
classification schemes of mental disorders, was also a
psychiatric pioneer in the comparative study of
behavioral phenomena. He travelled to Java in 1904 to
confirm his views that there were hereditary and racial
differences in human behavior. Others disagreed, and
felt that syndromes like amok, latah, and Arctic
hysteria were culturally determined.

Sigmund Freud, who wrote Totem and Taboo in 1913,
was rejected by the leading anthropologists of that
day, but others soon found merit in psychoanalytic
concepts as applied to their work. These included such
later luminaries as Sapir, Benedict, Mead, and Bateson.
Anthropological/psychiatric teamwork began before World
War II, and involved prominent contributors like
Kardiner, Linton, DuBois, the Leightons, and Kluckhohn.
Dr. Dorthea Leighton is also an important contributor
to this volume.

The perspectives of both disciplines have broadened considerably in the post-World War II period, with anthropology showing greater interest in motivation and the meanings of behavior, and psychiatry becoming more keenly aware of the sociocultural relationships of individuals. This has given rise more recently to the formation of subspecialtly organizations devoted to social psychiatry and trans-cultural psychiatry.

While one discipline stresses the external milieu, and the other emphasizes the internal milieu, it seems difficult to see how the two milieus can be studied separately when they are clearly inseparable and interdependent. Modern behavioral medicine cannot be practiced in isolation, and one must take into account sociocultural factors which affect understanding and impact on communication. Beliefs, values, and traditions are powerful forces which constantly color judgment and shape action, both at the individual and group levels. As we know, these forces can persist and prevail in the face of overwhelming logic and scientific proof that they really do not "work."

The ancient Greek physician Hippocrates notes in one of his more interesting aphorisms that

Life is short and the Art long; the occasion fleeting; experience fallacious and judgment difficult. The physician must not only be prepared to do what is right himself, but also to make the patients, the attendants, and externals cooperate (Clendenning 1960).

This ageless bit of wisdom seems to capture in just a few words the essence of community mental health and modern psychiatric practice.

The rhetoric and reality of community mental health are not always in harmony with each other. The most critical current example is the widespread and opportunistic depopulation of large public institutions in the misguided hope that this would also lead to effective deinstitutionalization of the individuals involved. However, the main achievement thus far has been merely to redistribute and scatter more widely the abandoned and unattended chronically ill. Traditional short term politico-economic expediency has prevailed once again over humanitarian good intentions.

"Rights" advocacy and litigation also have added to this problem by making it possible for very sick younger people to deny illness and refuse treatment, and in effect become chronic through socially sanctioned neglect. What are the long term implications of this massive restructuring of the composition and behavioral norms of the community? Is it in the best interest of all concerned to allow these people to drift aimlessly through our streets and social byways, guided only by their personal fantasies and peculiar perceptions of the world? When we close hospitals and convert them to jails, are we doing so to contain some of these troublesome individuals under a different label through the criminal justice system? Statistics from many places seem to support this thesis. This should be of special interest and concern to our social scientists along with all clinicians.

I hope it is sufficiently evident from the foregoing that anthropology and community health do indeed have much in common and that this is important, and challenging, and well worth pursuing. Both have bodies of knowledge and technologies which can help us develop better working insights. Together the two are greater than their parts. Opportunities for greater collaboration should be seized and assigned high priority, particularly if the ultimate goals are one and the same, namely to help mankind survive successfully in the highly charged atmosphere of our unpredictable atomic era.

This does not necessarily mean that clinicians must become anthropologists, or that basic professional indentities must be blurred or lost in the process. There is adequate room for everyone to make a meaningful contribution within his profession without feeling threatened by other professions working nearby (Doyle 1977; Fink and Weinstein 1979). As Milton Greenblatt (1975a, b) points out in his cogent essays on "Psychopolitics," the mental health field is multifaceted and constantly changing. There are many constituencies and special interests to be juggled and balanced and studied (Panzetta 1971).

This observation is even truer of the larger arena of health services as a whole.

The Papers: A Foreword

Dr. Dorothea Leighton raises interesting questions, for example, about our perceptions of native healers and the actual role they play in facilitating the therapeutic process. She suggests, based on her own work with American Indians in the Southwest, that this can be put into a more scientific framework. The analogy to "indigenous worker" concepts (Lynch and Gardner 1970) as widely advocated and occasionally practiced in community mental health settings should be self evident.

Tripp-Reimer points out the need for more holistic training of all health professionals. She feels that traditional homogenous training values and perceptions, and technically oriented goals are incompatible with the needs of a culturally heterogeneous society. Friedman lends additional support to this thesis by noting that the National Medical Board Part I Examination attempts to test social science "facts" relating to medicine, but that this well intended effort is actually overwhelmed and obscured by the extreme attention paid to basic science subjects.

Friedman also points out the distinctions between "serious" (hosptial based) services and "elective" (outpatient) services, where sociocultural variables frequently play such an important role. The need for better conceptual tools, or "social science microscopes" is stressed. To this end he cites eight basic questions propounded originally by Kleinman, Eisenberg, and Good for evaluating all patients in this area.

Rodin discusses her role as a social anthropologist working on public health issues in an academic setting. She notes that individuals are studied only as representatives of larger public health groups, and aggregate measures and outcomes are the general goal. She attributes gains in life expectancy to social changes and not better public health or clinical practice. Accidents, for example, ranked only seventh as a major cause of death in 1900. Today they are in fourth place, and suicide and cirrhosis are also included now in the top ten. Until the introduction of psychotropic drugs, psychiatric hospitalization accounted for well over half of all occupied hosptial beds in this country. Now this figure has been dramatically reversed. However, the number of patients with chronic mental illness has not declined; only their places of residence have changed.

O´Rourke, a health educator, echoes Rodin by pointing out that the unyielding main factor in mortality rate studies is chronic disease, which is not amenable to great change with more treatment or better prevention. He emphasizes conceptual differences between health care and sick care, and notes the growing size and sophistication of various self-help movements. He sees service availability, accessibility, cost factors, and control issues as legitimate areas for anthropological study.

Isaacs reports on her experience organizing an interdisciplinary graduate course in medical anthropology offered through a school of nursing. Over 50% of the enrollment was outside of nursing, indicating a broader need for this type of teaching. Isaacs' students are required to do field work and produce term papers using the ethnographic reporting method. Some health care providers react defensively, and hide under protective protocols which are administratively paralyzing. The course demonstrates that there are specific cultural factors which impede the delivery of health care, both for providers and for their patients. She suggests that educational approaches such as this one can facilitate the prompt exhange of sociocultural insights between clinical staff members regarding patient behavior.

Pickup is very pragmatic in her contributions to this volume. Her orientation is that of a very busy nurse-administrator trying to run several inner city alcoholism treatment stations with minimal resources. She wants to know how to make an impact on tight-fisted budgetary bureaus and skeptical legislators. She also points out the futility of trying to link rootless people to self-help groups in a crisis setting. She does not think making providers out of anthropologists will be as helpful as expanding the basic curriculum of people already identified as in the health care business.

In summary, it is clear that the significance of anthropology visible to a psychiatrist deeply concerned with community mental health is also evident in many other aspects of health research and services.

Clendenning, Logan
1960   Source Book of Medical History. New York:
        Dover.

Doyle, Marina C.
1977   Egalitarianism in a Mental Health Center: An
        Experiment That Failed. Hospital and
        Community Psychiatry 28(7):521-525.

Fink, Paul J. and Steven P. Weinstein
1979   Whatever Happened to Psychiatry? The
        Deprofessionalization of Community Mental
        Health Centers. American Journal of
        Psychiatry 136(4a):406-409.

Greenblatt, Milton
1975a   Psychiatry: The Battered Child of Medicine.
        New England Journal of Medicine
        292(5):246-250.

1975b   Psychopolitics. American Journal of
        Psychiatry 131(11):1197-1203.

Lynch, Mary and Elmer Gardner
1970   Some Issues Raised in the Training of
        Paraprofessional Personnel as Clinic
        Therapists. American Journal of Psychiatry
        126(10):1473-1479.

Panzetta, A.F.
1971   Community Mental Health: Myth and Reality.
        Philadelphia: Lea and Febiger.

Premo, Frances H. and Louise G. Wiseman
1981   Community Mental Health Centers: Perspectives
        of the Seventies, An Annotated Bibliography.
        DHHS Publication No. (ADM) 81-1074.
        Rockville, Maryland: National Institute of
        Mental Health.

Wittkower, E.D. and Guy Dubreuil
1971   Reflections on the Interface Between
        Psychiatry and Anthropology. In The
        Interface Between Psychiatry and
        Anthropology. Iago Goldston, ed. New York:
        Brunner/Mazel.

ANTHROPOLOGY IN MEDICINE--A PERSONAL HISTORY:
HOW CAN THE HEALTH PROFESSIONALS USE ANTHROPOLOGY?

Dorothea C. Leighton

Medicine and the Social Sciences:
Historical Background

As a starting point for this topic, I would like to
present my perceptions of how social scientists got
mixed up with physicians in recent times. I believe
that it was in the early post-World War II years that
the two disciplines first tried to work together. If I
am not mistaken, doctors took the initiative. I have
always supposed that their experiences with patients of
other cultures during their wartime service gave them
the notion that they might have done a better job if
they had known something about the people they treated.
It is possible that some of their patients were social
scientists who alerted them. In any case, somehow the
word got out that social science might have something
to contribute to the practice of medicine. At that
time it was a rare physician who had had any close
contact with social science, or who would have been
able to define the difference between sociology and
anthropology. In many universities, to be sure, the
two fields were still combined in one department.

When the word reached the proper academic level,
several medical schools recruited a social scientist
and waited expectantly to see what would happen. All
too often, nothing happened. That was at least partly
because the social scientist supposed that the medical
people had hired him because they had something they
wanted him to do. He knew little about medicine,
medical schools or hospitals; he was often young and
insecure, and isolated from other social scientists.
While he waited for someone to tell him what was
wanted, the medical people waited to see what he would
do--what little nugget of information he might add to
their expanding field of knowledge. Communication was
minimal, and if the two sides met, the doctors tended
to use medical jargon and the social scientist
responded in his own jargon. In a few places, either a
doctor knew a little about social science or the social
scientist knew a little about medicine, or about
disease somewhere that he could talk about. Sometimes
this led to collaborative ventures, but all too often
the lonesome scientist left and the medical staff
concluded that the experiment had not paid off.

At about the same time a number of anthropologists began paying more systematic attention to aspects of health and illness in groups they studied, thereby learning much more than had been know earlier about other cultures' ideas of causes and cures, and related attitudes and values. They also took part in many of the outreach programs from the United States to other countries, sometimes working with medical people in public health projects where they might be used to collect data regarding resistance to such activities. Others worked in health programs in the United States as urbanization increased and difficulties developed about how to provide health services to country people now in cities, or to patients of varying ethnic backgrounds. Anthropologists also heard and reported about apparently successful modes of treatment, in various places, which made no use of modern medicine.

Lessons from the Navajo

I had already been sensitized to some of these matters by a sally into anthropology with my husband in 1940. We spent the winter living with some Navajos south of Gallup, New Mexico, and were called on from time to time to treat their ills. We had occasional opportunities to converse with Medicine Men there, and we paid periodic visits to the new Bureau of Indian Affairs (BIA) hospital at Ft. Defiance. This was to replenish our meager medical supplies and to refresh ourselves by a medical interchange with the BIA doctors. We were truly dismayed, however, to note the doctors' ignorance and lack of interest concerning any aspects of Navajo culture beyond the obvious external ones. To them a sick body was a sick body, whatever else it looked like. It simply made them angry that patients sometimes refused a treatment they prescribed, or preferred traditional treatment and left the hospital to get it. By contrast, a Medicine Man had told us that he had noticed that there were some kinds of illness that seemed to do better if they went to the hospital early. When he was called for ceremonial treatment of such a case, he would try to persuade the family to use the hospital first and hold the Sing later.

When we returned to our hospital work and the BIA summoned us to report on our experiences, we described this contrast and went on to recommend utilizing Medicine Men instead of disregarding them. This constituted a truly revolutionary idea to the BIA, which had apparently never received such a suggestion before. We further recommended reducing the ignorance of doctors and other White workers by providing, in palatable form, some pertinent facts about the people they were working with. When this was accomplished in a year or two, it had the effect of at least making medical workers willing to accept the Medicine Men as chaplains, as a starter. Within a few more years, many BIA hospitals permitted ceremonial hogans to be built nearby where Medicine Men could add their treatment to what the hospital was doing to help the patient.

Culture and Medicine: Three Illustrative Cases

1. During the early post-War years, a news item from New York City attracted considerable medical attention. An effort which had been made to establish a pre-natal clinic for one of the ethnic groups was in danger of failing for lack of patients. The reason for this had just been discovered, namely that the ethnic women would not tolerate a pelvic examination made by a male doctor. Doubtless the medical reaction was largely "How ridiculous!" but the clinic group switched to women doctors and nurses with quick success.

2. In 1955 the BIA passed its responsibilities for the medical care of Indians over to the U.S. Public Health Service, which began by mounting a five year study of diseases among Indians and how they were or should be treated. It was done on the Navajo Reservation because of the large population available there and the extensive cultural research that had already been done on that tribe. Doctors in the team were impressed by the large number of people they saw around who had congenital dislocation of the hip, a condition which is rare in the rest of the country. It seemed to them both socially unattractive and occupationally disabling, as well as being a condition which orthopedists could treat. They made arrangements for one or more orthopedists to come out to fuse the floppy joints into nice firm immovable positions, as they would for such a joint in New York City. To the staff's surprise, no Navajos stepped forward for this sophisticated operation, and the Navajo assistants disclaimed knowledge of any one with such a condition.

After a time it was found that a few Navajos had had this kind of operation in the past and that no one admired its results, for it left the patient more

231

crippled than before--he could neither sit on the ground nor get on a horse. Inquiry showed that, furthermore, they did not consider such a hip as either disfiguring or disabling. In fact, the family of such a person felt that they had, in a sense, paid the supernaturals their dues with their member's wobbly hip, and might well be spared further trouble.

The medically alert anthropologists and the culturally sensitive physicians then got together with the orthopedists to consider what could best be done in the Navajo setting. They decided not to fuse any adult hips but rather to focus on prevention and early treatment in children found to have the condition or a tendency toward it. Much was learned about the condition itself because of its high prevalence in the population and the interest engendered in it by the researchers. For early treatment in Eastern hospitals a clumsy device had been invented to keep a baby's legs apart. When this and various modifications proved impractical for use in a hogan, a feasible solution seemed to be to present the new mother of a vulnerable child with a good supply of thick diapers, which served the same purpose and were easier to deal with. Follow-up showed them to be quite effective, and if they did not correct the condition, it could still be treated by an operation which would not impede mobility. In 1969 I visited a Navajo friend who has a congenitally dislocated hip. Nothing had been done to hers, but she pointed out with pride one of her grandsons who had started out with such a hip but was now in perfect shape after an operation.

3. In the 1960s, in Washington, an anthropologist was asked to help new immigrants from Latin America with their health problems. For this purpose she often accompanied them to a clinic, set up for Latinos, and sat in on the patient's interview with the doctor. Once she went with a patient who was most anxious to see a doctor because of her many complaints. Although the doctor she saw spoke Spanish, he was a second or third generation United States citizen, unfamiliar with old-country manners. The anthropologist was amazed to hear the patient assure the doctor that she had no health problems of any account. The doctor examined her, however, and gave her instructions and prescriptions related to malfunctions he found. When they left the clinic the anthropologist quizzed the patient as to why she had not described her complaints to the doctor. She was told that the doctor seemed to be such a nice, educated young man that she didn't like

232

to bother him. Asked if she understood his
instructions, it was quite clear that she had not, so
they were repeated, including certain medicines she
should get right away and take regularly. The patient
commented that she thought she would send back home for
the medicines because they would be cheaper and easier
to get there. Unless the anthropologist reported back
this conversation to the doctor, he might well have
believed that he had provided adequate treatment and
taught the patient how to take care of herself.

   I believve that this last kind of doctor/patient
communication, or lack of it, is still very common
wherever patients of different ethnic or social class
background come for medical help to workers who assume,
like the BIA doctors of yore, that a sick body is a
sick body. Anyone who has worked around health centers
used by people of different backgrounds could add many
stories of the miscommunications and ineffectiveness
that result from even the most humane intentions.
Usually no one has ever told the workers, well trained
in modern medical theory, about the broad and
fascinating differences in beliefs and expectations
regarding health and illness which may counteract their
efforts to help unless understood and taken into
account. Moreover, many an anthropologist, who found
himself in the position of the one in the Latino
clinic, would include the incident in his field notes
but would not feel obliged or inclined to inform the
doctor. The only comment likely to come from a puzzled
patient would be that he might not come back.

Widened Collaboration: What About the Medical Side?

   Before there were many anthropologists, surely
before any called themselves "medical" or "clinical"
anthropologists, doctors did not need their help very
much. Before the advent of antibiotics and other
disease-specific medicines and the numerous technical
advances in medicine, they were much more inclined to
give heed to the patient as a person. People were not
moving about so much then, with the result that the
doctor tended to see the same patients repeatedly and
to become familiar with their family and social
circumstances with little effort. At that time the
doctor´s only hope for diagnosing and treating
correctly was a careful history and examination. Then,
to get the patient well he had to enlist the patient´s
help and encourage him to heal himself, with supportive
help from family and friends. By contrast, nowadays

doctors and patients alike have put their trust in many tests for diagnosis and many chemicals for treatment, some of which are doubtless life-saving.

These new scientific modes of treatment seem to have lowered the level of interpersonal understanding and trust considerably, and have probably contributed to the spate of malpractice suits that developed a few years ago. They may have also reduced the mystique of the medical man to some extent, encouraging a view of him as a technician rather than a healer. Along with these changes there has been a tendency to shift the more nebulous aspects of the patient, such as life situation, cultural values, and expectations, to the attention of the psychiatrist, psychologist or social worker, if they are considered at all. Oddly enough, there has been a concomitant development in the recognition of psychosomatic diseases, biofeedback mechanisms, and the effects which situations that are perceived as threatening can have on the human body. To quite an extent this has led to specialization of some doctors in diseases which can be diagnosed by tests, on one hand, and of other doctors who recognized a larger range of possible causes. Patients may be shuttled back and forth between them. Yet another change has been the great increase in the numbers of people involved in the health and sickness industry. In addition to doctors and nurses there are technicians of many kinds who are required to handle the ever-refined equipment for both testing and treating patients. The old-fashioned doctor has very little place in the new scheme of things and has been replaced by a man who can direct the steps of diagnostic procedure, and then orchestrate the various modes of treatment. The old-fashioned nurse, who did so much for each patient, now often sits in the ward office, directing and keeping track of what goes on, while practical nurses and therapists of many kinds do the jobs that used to be hers. It is certainly easy to see why being sick has become so expensive.

There exist a great many people who do not like the scientific treatment of their illnesses, and even more who can neither afford it nor yet qualify for free services. In addition, many live in places where doctors do not wish to settle, often because there are not enough modern facilities for the kind of medicine they know how to practice, and also because they have been thoroughly urbanized and want to live a city life. There have probably always been a good many non-medical healers at work in our population, even though we

234

usually think of them as belonging to other cultures. They do their healing in many different ways and appear to provide some of the values which have largely disappeared from the practice of scientific medicine. Little is know by the medical fraternity about how these healers operate or how successful they are in helping their clients.

In an effort to deal with the need for better quality medical care without raising the cost still higher, and to supply it where people live without requiring them to travel far, some experiments have been made in training Physicians' Assistants and Nurse Practitioners. They add to the effectiveness of the highly educated physician by doing parts of his work under his official supervision. It is much the same as what Public Health nurses have been doing for several generations, but is being made more explicit and is better compensated, filling part of the gap that has developed.

There are many parts of the world which are very short of scientifically trained doctors, and there is little hope that they will ever have enough native physicians to properly care for their population. Part of the trouble is the same as with us, namely that such doctors choose to stay in large cities rather than in country villages or provincial towns. The British resolved this kind of problem in Fiji, where the population is widely scattered, by educating locally-chosen young people in how to recognize and treat the common diseases. The U.S. Armed Forces did something similar in selecting and training Medical Corpsmen, many of whom have gone on to be Physicians' Assistants. And there are China's "barefoot doctors." But in most societies there still is a supply of people who did the healing work before scientific medicine came along. Why not use them? To do so raises questions, of course: Should people be protected from "untrained" healers? Should healers be licensed? How would licensing affect their treatment methods? Should each healer be associated with an M.D? What limits should be set on their activities? Who would be responsible for them? Would setting limits infringe the rights of healers or their patients? And so on. All there questions have arisen in relation to Physicians' Assistants and Nurse Practitioners as well as to Navajo and other Medicine Men.

Widened Collaboration: Where Does Anthropology Fit In?

In the matter of whether to utilize the native healers of any given culture, a main difficulty is the absence of precise knowledge as to what they actually do. It appears to be clear that there are several different styles of healer, the most congenial to scientific medicine, perhaps, being the herbalist. Could Herbalists be drawn into the orbit of scientific medicine? What do they do besides use herbs? Are their herbs really effective? Other healers rely largely on religious tradition and symbolism but often use herbs also. Does any harm result from their activities? What is the chance of real improvement with any of these methods? What about trances and the use of psychedelics? Are the results good or bad?

There are very few data of value on these matters. Could the treatment be called successful if the disease remains but the patient feels at peace (as with cancer, etc.)? The hullabaloo raised about the use of laetrile in some quarters would immediately indicate a "No" answer here. What are the philosophical and religious views on such questions in different cultures? How can we evaluate whether native healers should be added to the medical armamentarium? It seems to me that a good deal of value would be lost if we simply outlawed their activities as governments have tried to outlaw some religions.

Why couldn't a team of anthropologists and doctors work together on this? Effective collaboration between such a group and native healers is not beyond imagination. For example, a psychiatrist (Robert Bergman) came to the Navajo Reservation about a decade after the improvement in attitude towards Medicine Men took place. He was already convinced that Medicine Men might well prove more effective than he would in dealing with some kinds of psychiatric problems, and he tried to educate a group of them as to the categories used in scientific medicine for various pyschiatric disorders. They would listen politely to his lesson, then take their turn in educating him, showing him that they understood the matter at hand in much the same way. Eventually they told him that they were deeply concerned at the difficultly of continuing the Medicine Man tradition. This was because most of the bright young people spent all their early years going to school, and then got salaried jobs which kept them too busy to learn ceremonials properly. Some modification of their usual teaching pattern for this, plus the procurement of a modest Government grant to fund both teachers and students, has led to the ceremonial education of a number of young people. They will be able to keep the tradition alive for another generation, at least, thus aiding the transition from old ways to new ones and perhaps providing the opportunity to evaluate their treatment techniques.

For the most part, unfortunately, medical anthropologists have not educated themselves extensively in scientific medicine or its practitioners. I would not, by any means, recommend full scale medical training any more than I think it appropriate for most M.D.s to acquire a Ph.D. in anthropology. For effective collaboration, however, each side must learn enough about the field of the other to understand the other's lingo or to develop a common mode of discourse. Too often, ignorance and some awe of each other's probable knowledge inhibit the joint use of talents for the enrichment of knowledge and improvement in handling the whole area of health and illness. The world would benefit from a pooling of knowledge and insight.

REFERENCES

Adair, John and Kurt W. Deuschle
   1970   The People's Health: Anthropology and
           Medicine in a Navajo Community. New York:
           Meridith Corp.

Cohen, Lucy M.
   1980   Stress and Coping Among Latin American
           Immigrants. In Uprooting and Development.
           Geo. V. Coelho and Paul I. Ahmed, eds. New
           York and London: Plenum Press.

Foster, George M.
   1952   Relationships Between Theoretical and Applied
           Anthropology: A Public Health Program
           Analysis. Human Organization 11:5-16.

Leighton, Alexander H. and Dorothea C.
   1944   The Navaho Door. Cambridge, MA: Harvard
           University Press.

Niehoff, Arthur H.
   1966   A Casebook of Social Change. Chicago: Aldine
           Publishing Co.

Paul, Benjamin D.
   1955   Health, Culture and Community. New York:
           Russell Sage Foundation.

THE RELEVANCE OF ANTHROPOLOGY FOR CLINICAL WORK: THE OBSERVATIONS OF A PHYSICIAN-SOCIAL SCIENTIST

Paul Friedman

Introduction

I would like to thank Demitri B. Shimkin and Peggy Golde for bringing together this diverse group, diverse in interest, in training, and in current endeavors, but interested in the common goal of <u>utilizing</u> anthropological knowledge by applying it to the solution of specific, concrete problems in a pragmatic, immediate fashion and usually in relation to specific individuals known as consumers, clients or even patients. I see the overall ferment created by this interest in "clinical anthropology" as potentially beneficial to both anthropology and to the objects of this application. While there are some nettlesome problems touched on in part below, the results of moving out of its academic shell can be a more robust, though less pristine, anthropology and better health services.

I will touch briefly on two aspects of Clinical Anthropology:

1. Discuss my particular focus, which is the problem of systematically developing techniques of teaching anthropology in clinical settings, either actual or simulated; and

2. Share some observations on problems common to all who practice the application of systematic knowledge.

My interest is a mid-ground, semi-theoretical and semi-empirical, effort to alter the behavior of clinicians by teaching and demonstrating the relevance of anthropological (or better, social science) concepts to patient care. The entry of the social and behavioral sciences into the medical curriculum has been formalized for some time by their inclusion in Part I of the National Board of Medical Examiners (NBME) tests for all medical students. However, such classroom teaching is primarily aimed at increasing the student's fund of authoritatively accepted facts, not of altering later clinical behavior. Such teaching also suffers from competition with a deluge of other factual material--anatomy, biochemistry, pharmacology, etc.--which students generally view as more scientific and central. Beyond this, medical students in the first year or two do not have the clinical experience with which they can develop the needed selective mastery of those aspects of social science pertinent to the problems of patient care.

I am sure that many have read the insightful works of Eliot Friedson (1961, 1975) and Renée Fox (1979) and can define the physician's realities. But it is important, nevertheless, to emphasize the clinical context of teaching as the focus of interest, the critical reality, of medical trainees. Their preoccupation with the specific case and requisite intervention places certain imperatives on those who wish to transmit social science concepts in a manner that will have an impact upon health professionals.

The Physician's Clinical Reality

For the clinically-oriented physician, the patient-oriented practitioner, the moment of truth occurs during the doctor-patient encounter when a history is obtained, a physical examination (supported by requisite laboratory tests) is done, a diagnosis is made and a therapeutic intervention undertaken. All of these actions are carried out within the special context of the doctor-patient relationship. That is the moment when all the health professional's training interacts with all that the patient brings. That doctor to patient relationship is the final common pathway for everything a clinician must know.

Immediate resposibility for the patient and mastery of a vast body of recognized fact on disease and therapy, including a highly developed logic of diagnosis and intervention are the heart of today's American medical practice. Medical training involves saturation with these skills and their rigorous testing in NBME, Parts II and III. Because this training works and because of the immense investment in effort, time and money involved in gaining these skills, practicing physicians guard their clinical identification zealously. Most clinicians involved in one-to-one therapy would not consider even community medicine and public health as clinical disciplines, while conceding their immense contributions to health care. Changes in clinical concepts and interventions not centered upon the medical clinician meet great resistance.

240

Today, this medical perception must be accepted, in most areas of practice at least, as a basic reality. The social scientist who wishes to work in this context must face two tasks:

1. The adaptation of social science concepts to clinical requirements; and

2. The adaptation of the social scientist to the clinical setting.

Since it is not possible to create a "mini social scientist" from each health professional, conceptual tools need to be provided which will facilitate the mastery of relevent aspects of social science therapy. I call such tools "social science microscopes." Like other instruments, they can be used both as basic procedures for searching complex problems in unfamiliar areas and in many innovative ways. A prime illustration of such a "microscope" is the set of eight questions devised by Kleinman, Eisenberg and Good (1978:265) to elicit the patient's understanding of his problem.

"1. What do you think has caused your problem?

"2. Why do you think it started when it did?

"3. What do you think your sickness does to you? How does it work?

"4. How severe is your sickness? Will it have a short or long course?

"5. What kind of treatment do you think you should receive?

"6. What are the most important results you hope to receive from this treatment?

"7. What are the chief problems your sickness has caused for you?

"8. What do you fear most about your sickness?"

These questions have proven to be extremely effective. They give medical trainess virtually instant access to and understanding of key anthropological ideas--applied at the level of the individual patient. They are easily memorized, acceptable to patients, and productive in a wide range of cultural backgrounds.

241

Effective Teaching Methodology

In general, the teaching methodology I feel is most effective is a kind of selective training in anthropological field work methods. It includes a variety of approaches, such as the videotaping of actual patients or simulated patients, role playing and written case studies. In all cases, the clinical setting is maintained and each exercise is directed toward broadening understanding of the doctor-patient relationship. Specific materials of particular value have included:

1. the role of the family in health care;

2. the implications of the successes of alternative health-care systems for the practice of scientific medicine; and

3. the impact of cultural variables on adherence to prescribed medication regimens.

The social scientist seeking to work in a clinical setting faces basic requirements of adapting to new patterns of time and urgency of action, and to the necessary eclecticism of the clinician.

In the clinical setting, a major difference exists between hospital and ambulatory care. In the hospital, there is an unspoken understanding that the patient is seriously ill and that he has delegated decisions to the physicians. In the hospital, action must often be prompt and correct--there is no debate with a "hot appendix." Major interventions may be at issue, with high technology and specialized clinical skills essential. The roles of social science are at most auxiliary.

However, in ambulatory cases, the relations between physician and patient are different. It is then that the clinical applicability of social science becomes most evident and relevant. It is also in this less urgent time framework that anthropologists and other social scientists can work most effectively as members of health teams.

In such functioning, it is essential to remember that all clinical activity seeks to solve specific problems for specific patients. Each is in some way unique. Each in some way involves new combinations of facts and intervention strategies. To meet these needs, the clinician must be eclectic, he must use whatever modality of treatment is appropriate for the patient and his case. Such essential flexibility must be shared by all members of the health team, with the consequence that disciplinary boundaries are often blurred. What must be present is an awareness of effective ways to define and solve particular, immediate problems of pressing importance to the human beings seeking medical help.

The Necessity for Concrete Clinical Applicability

That brings up a final point. If anthropology and other social sciences are to have a valid and effective role in clinical settings, they need to be rethought in terms of concrete clinical applicability. Two considerations are central. One is the definition of indications. Just as a physician notes indications for particular drugs or surgery, so he should be able to use the social sciences. In particular, indications can and should be developed for interventions based on anthropological knowledge. Not only would such a development clarify the appropriate nature of a clinical anthropology, it would also help health professionals understand what anthropology has to offer them.

The other side of such indications is the need to understand the limitations of anthropological applications.

The combination of appropriate indications and of limitations must be governed by the development in anthropology of a keen sense of immediate responsibility. Where there are therapeutic interventions, there will also be errors and even malpractice. The development of defined and enforced standards, the acceptance of liability--even anthropological malpractice insurance--are necessary prices for meaningful clinical anthropology.

In all, my attitude as a physician toward the prospect of a clinical anthropology is one of support tempered with needed caution. It will take time and much effort. It will exist in fact when positive answers can be given to two fundamental questions:

Has anyone articulated conceptually and operationally the process which is Clinical Anthropology?

243

Has it been translated into some kind of clinical,
experiential learning process for students of
anthropology?

REFERENCES

Fox, Renée C.
1979   Essays in Medical Sociology: Journeys into
          the Field. New York: Wiley.

Friedson, Eliot
1961   Patients' Views of Medical Practice: A Study
          of Subscribers to a Prepaid Medical Plan in
          the Bronx. New York: Russell Sage
          Foundation.

1975   Doctoring Together: A Study of Professional
          Social Control. New York: Elsevier.

Kleinman, Arthur, Leon Eisenberg and Byron Good
1978   Culture, Illness, and Care. Clinical Lessons
          from Anthropologic and Cross-cultural
          Research. Annals of Internal Medicine
          88:251-258.

HUMAN VARIABILITY AND NURSING:
A NEGLECTED ASPECT OF CLINICAL ANTHROPOLOGY

Toni Tripp-Reimer

Nursing in the Health Professions

Although they are nearly the same age, anthropology and nursing evolved quite differently; anthropology developed primarily as a theoretical field and only recently has given legitimacy to applied aspects. Nursing, on the other hand, developed primarily as an applied field, with major theoretical development coming only in the past twenty years. However, each discpline has much to offer the other. Because the reader is most likely an anthropologist, I will outline the current status as well as trends in the field of nursing.

There are nearly one and one-half million nurses licensed to practice in the United States. Of these, approximately 70 percent are currently employed in nursing. The majority of nurses (about 600,000) work in hospitals. However, the greatest increase in employment of nurses since 1972 involves care of noninstitutionalized persons; the number of nurses employed in public health agencies and other community health settings has nearly doubled since 1972. Other nurses work in extended care facilities or nursing homes, public school systems, occupational health clinics, a variety of general clinics (medical, dental and nursing), or in private practice (NLN [National League for Nursing] 1977).

The nurse is often viewed by lay persons as one who assists the physician and who provides physical care to patients. However, common areas of nursing practice include mental health counseling, midwifery, physical assessment, health teaching, and diet counseling. Thus, the nurse is both an independent as well as collaborative practitioner who assumes a variety of roles depending on her educational preparation and her clinical setting.

Reports identifying the expanding role of the nurse have been well documented for at least a quarter century. Based on a two and one-half year study, a report of the National Commission on Nursing and Nursng Education found three discernible trends which emerged from their analysis of nursing practice: diversification of the levels of nursing practice, increased development of clinical nursing specialization, and restructuring of the traditional relationships between nursing and medicine (Lysaught 1970).

Because all health professionals are in a general sense concerned with the mental and physical well-being of clients, there is considerable overlap in the contribution of each profession to the goal of client health. However, each health professional also offers unique services which complement those of the other professions. To clarify the unique contribution of nursing, we must advance beyond simple commonisms such as "physicians provide medical therapy while nurses provide nursing care."

Perhaps the clearest differentiation in professional goals can be illustrated by the current distinction in the literature of the concepts of disease and illness (see Eisenberg 1977; Kleinmenn 1978). The distinction may be summarized as follows: diseases are abnormalities in the structure and function of body organs and systems, they are problems of biological malfunctioning. Illness, on the other hand, encompasses the subjective experiences of the individual who is sick and includes the way in which this sickness is perceived and experienced by the individual and his social group. In an analogous manner, we can compare medicine and nursing. Medicine primarily focuses on disease: its etiology, pathology, and treatment. Nursing, on the other hand, primarily focuses on the client as he is coping before, during, and after illness.

Nursing is unique in its emphasis on assisting the client to cope with his physical discomforts and to adapt his lifestyle to the illness or treatment. Nursing has reaffirmed its commitment to the concept of holism and it is concerned with the client as a whole person, not merely his pathological part. Because the nurse focuses on the whole client (including his sociocultural environment) the discipline of anthropology is particularly important in nurses´ education and practice.

246

Nursing and Cultural Anthropology

In all nursing settings, the potential for misunderstanding is accentuated when the health provider and recipient are from different ethnic or cultural groups. Misunderstandings may arise from variations in values, beliefs, and customs or patterns of behavior. Because sensitivity to these cultural variables is a requisite for quality health care in multiethnic situations, knowledge borrowed and adapted from cultural anthropology is crucial for the clinical nurse. The following are a few vignettes illustrating the range of situations in which cultural anthropology lends important information to the clinician. Each of these situations arose in clinical practice or in clinically oriented research.

1. Conducting routine physical assessments, a school nurse detected what she suspected as two incidents of child abuse. One involved a Vietnamese refugee, newly arrived in the United States, the other involved a boy of Greek descent. In the first, the nurse identified long bruised areas on the chest and back of the child. In the second, she noticed numerous X-shaped scars on the boy's back. Rather than incidents of child abuse, however, each was the result of parents using culturally sanctioned folk treatments. The Vietnamese parents were using the lay practice of dermabrasion (<u>Cao Gio</u>), a standard home treatment for minor ailments such as fevers, chills and headaches. In this procedure oil is applied to the back and chest with cotton swabs. The skin is massaged until warm. The the skin is rubbed with an edge of a coin until marks (abrasions) appear.

The Greek boy's parents had performed <u>kofte</u> (cut) <u>vendousas</u> on his back for treatment of a severe cold. A cut in the shape of a cross was made on the skin with a sharp instrument (razor). A cotton swab was ignited and placed in an inverted glass. This action created a vacuum in the glass which was then placed on the child's back. When the glass was placed over the cut, blood was drawn into the glass. After removal of the glass, the area was sealed with candle wax. In each of the above cases, the folk treatment left marks that were <u>misinterpreted</u> as child abuse.

2. In Ohio, a public health nurse instructing a hypertensive client discovered that the man had been drinking pickle brine as an adjunct home remedy for his diagnosis of "high blood." Among some Appalachians,

"high blood" is a condition associated with blood volume increase; the mountaineer was following standard folk prescriptions for this condition. In the health clinic, the client had learned that he had high blood <u>pressure</u> and interpreted this phrase as meaning "high blood."

3. In a neighborhood mental health center, a nurse therapist misread a patient's body language (nonverbals) as indicating disinterest in counseling. From his background, the nurse <u>KNEW</u> that good counseling skills include direct eye contact. (Health professionals are generally taught that patients desire this, and that when patients do not engage in direct eye contact they are disinterested or have something to hide.) But in fact, this Appalachian client was being polite by averting her eyes as might an American Indian or an Oriental.

4. In a hospital obstetrical unit, a nurse observed agitation in two mothers. The nurse learned that one of the mothers, a Yoruba foreign student, was distressed because too many individuals had been handling the newborn prior to his "naming" ceremony. The other woman, who was of Greek descent, was agitated because her mother was demanding that the hospital staff allow her daughter to place a <u>phylacto</u> (protective charm) on her newborn. This new mother, sufficiently worn out from delivery, had to mediate between <u>her</u> and the hospital staff.

5. In a surgical unit, a staff nurse identified the fact that many Asian patients tended to be undermedicated for pain, while southern Europeans (Spanish and Italians) tended to be overmedicated for pain. She determined that these situations resulted because Asian patients tend to react stoically to pain, while southern Europeans tend to freely express discomfort. She learned that the intepretation and expression of pain is highly influenced by cultural socialization.

Thus, in a wide range of clinical settings, the potential for misunderstanding is accentuated when nurse and client are from different ethnic or cultural groups. This can occur whether the nurse is engaged in physical assessment, diet counseling, administration or pain medication, discharge planning or direct physcial care. However, incidents such as those just mentioned have been long documented in health science literature. The importance of anthropology to nursing has been evident since the 1960s. It has resulted in curriculum changes incorporating the cultural dimension, the development of master's and doctoral programs in transcultural nursing, and the growth and evolution of two professional groups: the Transcultural Nursing Society and the Council on Nursing and Anthropology. In each of these, the importance of cultural factors in the delivery of effective nursing care has been identified and accepted.

Nursing and Physical Anthropology

Another crucial dimension, but one much less emphasized, is the contribution of physical anthropology to nursing and other health professions. We know that to a great extent cultural diversity accounts for variations in family relationships, food preferences, religion, communication and value patterns, as well as health beliefs and behaviors. However, bio-physiological differences among populations are also crucial factors in the delivery of effective care. Although we know that there is certainly more biological variation within a population than among populations, physical differences are important assessment variables because they indicate particular areas for attention. For example, persons of Mediterranean descent should be routinely screened for glucose-6-phosphate dehydrogenase deficiency, Blacks for sickle-cell anemia and hypertension, and female clients of European descent for breast cancer.

The following are clinically important areas of biological variation among populations documented by physical anthropologists.

1. Growth and Devlopment

Nurses and other health professionals are coming to recognize that standardized growth and development charts have been based on Caucasian norms. From the International Biological Programme, we have learned that persons of African descent tend to be taller and heavier at all ages than their Caucasian counterparts, and that children of Asian descent are generally shorter and lighter (Eveleth and Tanner 1976). In addition, Blacks and Asians tend to reach pubertal maturity more rapidly than do Caucasian (Eveleth and Tanner 1976). Population differences are apparent in newborn weight and head circumference.

249

Newborn reflexes also vary among population groups. Investigating ethnic differences in infants, Freedman (1979; Freedman and De Boer 1979) found that American Indians and Chinese babies showed a reduced Moro response and "defense reaction" (turning away or swiping at a cloth held over the nose) when compared with Caucasian and Black babies.

These population variations in growth and development merit consideration by the practitioner. For example, with the standardized growth charts, Caucasian standards may give false percentile ratings so that a child of Asian descent is ranked at a low percentile when he is actually developing normally. Variations in average pubertal maturity (3+ year differences in onset of menarche) have important implications in school nurses' timing of sex education classes.

2. Cerumen

Ear wax (cerumen) is classified as wet (sticky) or dry (flaky). Wet ear wax is generally found in Caucasian and Black clients, and is tan or brown. Dry ear wax is normal among clients of Asian or American Indian descent (Matsunaga 1962). The nurse examining the ear must remove wax obstructing the view of the tympanic membrane. Knowledge of ear wax type assists the practitioner removing wax. Wet wax is generally best removed with a curette, and flaky wax by irrigation with lukewarm water.

3. Anatomy

There are normal population differences in morphology of various anatomical structures. Epicanthic folds, vertical folds of skin covering the inner canthus of the eye, are found in infants all over the world. They are present at birth in up to 20 percent of children of European descent, although they generally disappear within the first year of life. They are most common among Oriental individuals, usually persisting for life (Alexander and Brown 1979). To the inexperienced examiner, epicanthic folds may give eyes the appearance of strabismus. This fold type may also be mistaken for the eyelid anomaly present with Down's syndrome or fetal alcohol syndrome.

Bone and muscular variations also follow population groups. Lumbar lordosis is normally present in small children with protuberant abdomens, but this normal curvature is most pronounced in Black children. The size of the palmaris longus muscle, whose tendon lies superficially near the center of the flexor surface of the wrist, varies widely among populations. It cannot be detected in 15 to 25 percent of patients of European descent, but is generally observable in Oriental and Black patients (Barnicott 1977). The peroneus tertius muscle assists in dorsiflexion of the foot at the ankle and in elevation of the lateral border of the foot. Its tendon can be felt running from the region of the lateral malleolus at the ankle to the base of the fifth metatarsal. This muscle may be reduced or absent in some populations; absence is more frequent in Black and American Indian populations than in Euopean or Oriental patients (Spuhler 1950). Incidence of cleft uvula varies dramatically among populations: In American Indians it is seen in about 1/10 patients; among Blacks it is extremely rare (1/300); Caucasians are intermediate in frequency (Jarvis and Gorlin 1972).

Many population differences in dentition have also been documented. Gross tooth size of incisors, canines, premolars and molars varies widely from group to group. Some populations have larger anterior teeth; other have larger posterior teeth. Tooth morphology also differs. For example, the rear surfaces of the incisors of many American Indian and Asian populations are "shovel-shaped." Finally, the number of teeth occurring in any individual is also a population variable. Some people from the Pacific have an entire extra set of molars; conversely American Indian and Asian individuals often have congenital absence of the third molars (Poirier 1974).

In all these examples the nurse's knowledge of the range of normal anatomical variation among populations may decrease unnecessary referrals and increase the accuracy of physical assessment in the clinical situation.

4. Pigmentation

The skin is an important assessment site. In the skin melanocytes produce a brown-black pigment called eumelanin and a yellow-red pigment called pheomelanin. In the absence of pathology, skin color depends on the relative proportions of these two melanin compounds and hemoglobin, the red pigment of erythrocytes (Quevado, Fitzpatrick and Jimbow 1975).

Assessing skin color changes may be more difficult in darkly pigmented patients. With pallor, dark skin loses the normal underlying red tones, so that patients with brown skin may appear yellow-brown and the patient with black skin may appear ashen gray particularly around the mouth and on the buccal mucosa. Cyanosis is best detected at the sites of least pigmentation: lips, nail beds, palpebral conjuctiva, palms and soles. Skin color changes which appear red in lighter skinned individuals may also be missed in darkly pigmented ones. In Blacks, the characteristic red flush of fever may be visible at the tips of the ears. Inflammation and rashes may best be detected by palpation in combination with patient's verbal reports (Roach 1972; Rubin 1979; Williams 1976).

Because color changes may be difficult to detect in dark skinned clients, the eye often offers an excellent opportunity for color assessment. The conjunctiva and sclera may show the color change of cyanosis or pallor. Additionally the conjunctiva provide an excellent site for detecting petechiae. However, in dark-skinned individuals yellowish discolorations may occur normally in subconjunctival fat and sclera; in such cases the hard palate of the mouth may serve as an adjunct for the assessment of jaundice. The sclera may also normally have a somewhat brownish cast although this is also more common in highly pigmented individuals (Roach 1972).

Because the buccal mucosa and the tongue may exhibit less pigmentation than other body areas in dark-skinned individuals, these may be good sites to detect cyanosis, jaundice or ecchymosis. However, there are also two frequently occurring non-pathological conditions in the oral mucosa which also exhibit color changes. The first is hyperpigmentation of the oral mucous membranes. While 10 percent of Caucasians will demonstrate hyperpigmentation by age 50, between 50-90 percent of Blacks will show these membrane changes by the fourth decade. In both groups, there is a higher incidence in darker-hued individuals (McDonald and Kelly 1975). A second frequently occurring variation in oral pigmentation results from a condition termed leukoedema. This condition is found in nearly 50 percent of Caucasians and 90 percent of Black individuals (Martin and Crump 1972).

Pigmentation also varies on hands, feet, and nails. In dark-skinned individuals, the palmar surface of the hands and plantar surface of the feet may normally show darkly pigmented creases. While pigmentation of the nails is unusual in healthy Caucasians, it is not uncommon among Blacks, in whom brown or black pigmentation may be found normally along the edge of the nails or in a pattern of longitudinal streaks.

While skin color is an important measure of health status, other skin characteristics also merit consideration when planning nursing care. For example, Blacks tend to have dry skin which may appear ashy or flaky under normal conditions. This condition can be misinterpreted as a sign of systemic dehydration. In addition, it is also important for the nurse to know the life cycle of epidermal tissue. To the experienced care giver the normally sloughing horny layer of highly pigmented patients may appear to be "dirt" which washes off during a bath.

5. Hair Texture

Understanding variation in hair texture is important if proper care is to be given to dependent patients. Hair fibers are formed into straight, wavy, helical or spiral filaments depending on the structure of the protein molecules that make up the hair. This variation in hair fibers makes hair texture range from straight to kinky or wooly (McDonald and Kelly 1975). Spiraled or helical hair, common among Blacks, is more prone to breakage than straight or wavy hair. With Black patients, the standard techniques of shampooing and combing, done for patients with straight or wavy hair, may cause hair loss or tangling.

6. Food Intolerance

In the past, assessment texts have stressed the need for identifying food allergies in the nutritional history. We now recognize the importance of identifying all untoward reactions to food, including not only the type of offending food, but also the patient's response. One such example is urticarial reaction to egg consumption. However, this allergic response has much different intervention implications than the response of a hemolytic crisis when a person with Mediterranean G-6-PD deficiency consumes fava beans, or a response of bloating, flatulence, diarrhea and cramping experienced when a person with lactase deficiency consumes a threshold quantity of milk. The geographical pattern of distribution of these food tolerances has been well documented by physical anthropologists and should be familiar to nurses engaged in nutritional teaching and physical assessment.

7. Drug Metabolism

Another area of population physiological variation is drug metabolism. Differences in population reactions to drugs have long been documented. Among the variations noted are the following: fast or slow isoniazid metabolizers, primaquine sensitivity in patients with G-6-PD deficiency, and population variations in response to alcohol (facial flushing, tachycardia, hypotension). Nurses administering these and other medications must be aware of such population variations in order to be alert for untoward patient response.

Conclusions

While sensitivity to cultural variations is an essential feature in the delivery of effective health care, so too is attention to biological variation among population groups. Physical anthropologists have made important contributions to health assessment and intervention by documenting the normal range of population variation in such factors as growth and development, anatomy, pigmentation, hair texture, food intolerance, and drug metabolism.

Because these contributions by physical anthropologists cross-cut the general curriculum design in nursing education, this content should first be integrated into appropriate introductory courses. For example, variation in hair texture, pigmentation and muscular structure could be introduced in anatomy courses, variation in drug metabolism in pharmacology, and variation in food intolerance in nutrition. However, this content would be reviewed and applied as students take upper division courses in nursing science.

Anthropology, like nursing, stresses the holistic nature of human beings. Recognition of this integrative feature highlights the contributions that both cultural and physical anthropology can make to clinical nursing practice.

REFERENCES

Alexander, M. and M. Brown
   1979   Pediatric History Taking and Physical
           Diagnosis for Nurses. New York: McGraw-Hill.

American Nurses' Association
   1977   Survey of Registered Nurses. Washington,
           D.C: Division of Nursing, Bureau of Health
           Manpower, U.S. Public Health Service (HEW).

Alvear, J. and O. Brooke
   1970   Fetal Growth in Different Racial Groups.
           Archives of Disease in Children 53:27-32.

Barnicot, N.
   1977   Biological Variation in Modern Populations.
           In Human Biology: An Introduction to Human
           Evolution, Variation, Growth and Ecology.
           2nd ed. G. Harrison et al., eds.
           pp. 181-300. Oxford: Oxford University
           Press.

Chioni, R. and C. Panicucci
   1970   Tomorrow's Nurse Practictioners. Nursing
           Outlook 18:32-35.

Eisenberg, L.
   1977   Disease and Illness: Distinctions between
           Professional and Popular Ideas of Sickness.
           Culture, Medicine, and Psychiatry 1:9-23.

Eveleth, P. and J. Tanner
   1976   Worldwide Variation in Human Growth.
           Cambridge: Cambridge University Press.

Freedman, D.
   1979   Ethnic Differences in Babies. Human Nature
           2:36-44.

Freedman, D. and M. DeBoer
   1979   Biological and Cultural Differences in Early
           Child Development. Annual Review of
           Anthropology 8:579-600.

Jarvis, A. and A. Gorlin
1972   Minor Orofacial Abnormalities in an Eskimo
        Population. Oral Surgery 33:417-426.

Kleinman, A.
1978   International Health Care Planning from an
        Ethnomedical Perspective: Critique and
        Recommendations for Change. Medical
        Anthropology 2:71-93.

Lysaught, J.
1970   An Abstract for Action. New York:
        McGraw-Hill.

Martin, J. and E. Crump
1972   Leukoedema of the Buccal Mucosa in Negro
        Children and Youth. Oral Surgery 34:49-58.

Matsunaga, E.
1962   The Dimorphism in Human Normal Cerumen.
        Annals of Human Genetics 25:273-286.

McDonald, C. and P. Kelly
1975   Dermatology and Venereology. In Textbook of
        Black-Related Diseases. Richard A. Williams,
        ed. pp. 513-592. New York: McGraw-Hill.

Poirier, F.
1974   In Search of Ourselves. Minneapolis:
        Burgess.

Quevedo, W., T. Fitzpatrick and K. Jimbow
1975   Role of Light in Human Skin Color Variation.
        American Journal of Physical Anthropology
        43:393-408.

Roach, L.
1972   Color Changes in Dark Skins. Nursing
        2:19-22.

Rubin, B.
1979   Black Skin. RN [Registered Nurse] 42:31-35.

Spuhler, J.
1950   Genetics of Three Normal Morphological
        Variations: Patterns of Superficial Veins of
        the Anterior Thorax, Peroneus Tertius Muscle,
        and Number of Villate Papillae. Cold Spring
        Harbour Symposia on Quantitative Biology
        15:175-189.

Williams, Richard A.
  1976   The Clinical and Physiological Assessment of
          Black Patients. In Black Awareness:
          Implications for Black Patient Care.
          D. Luckraft, ed. pp. 16-26. New York:
          American Journal of Nursing Company.

ON TEACHING MEDICAL ANTHROPOLOGY TO CLINICIANS:
IS IT CLINICAL ANTHROPOLOGY?

Hope L. Isaacs

Introduction

This paper reports on an interdisciplinary graduate
course which I developed and taught as part of a
sequence in medical anthropology in the graduate School
of Nursing at the State University of New York at
Buffalo. The course is listed in the curriculum as
Applied Anthropology of Health: A Clinical Practicum in
Medical Anthropology. Like its prerequisite course,
The Anthropology of Health, this course is open to
graduate students in the Division of Health Sciences,
and characteristically draws about 50 percent of its
enrollment from outside the School of Nursing.

Teaching Transcultural Health Care Delivery

At the outset, the aim of the course was to improve
the awareness and competence of students in the health
professions in the dynamics of transcultural health
care delivery by providing them with opportunities for
problem-oriented participant observation in clinical
settings which served culturally contrastive consumer
populations. A basic assumption was that the
operational premises of Western health care providers
are relatively homogeneous, deriving from a shared
scientific tradition. The problems to be identified
and analyzed for their impact on patient care,
therefore, were initially expected to be those arising
from cultural contrasts between providers and consumers
and/or between consumers with disparate cultural
backgrounds. As it turned out, however, a number of
students identified factors which operate at a level of
the providers themselves, within the shared dominant
culture, and which erect critical impediments to
optimal health care delivery. These observations
proved so fruitful that the requirement of identifying
and analyzing the specifics of cultural differences
which generate care problems was modified to the
broader goal of identifying and analyzing specific
cultural factors which function to impede health care.

The course requirements combined a weekly clinical
practicum with weekly attendance at a seminar. By

following the clinical experience with the seminar we provided students with an opportunity to discuss their clinical observations and experiences when recall is more precise. The seminar thus enabled a prompt exchange of insights into the sociocultural foundations of staff and patient behaviors, and promoted understanding of the universe of cultural forces which cut across clinical specializations and population variations.

The requirement for completion of the course was a term paper based on three phases of study: first, a general ethnographic description of the clinic in which the student did her or his field work; second, identification and detailed description of a particular culture pattern which the student believed to be a significant factor in the etiology either of characteristic health problems presented by many patients at the clinic, or of a unique problem presented by one patient and/or his family. The student was expected to determine whether or not the critical cultural feature noted had been identified by the professional staff, documented in the patient history and assessment, and appropriately evaluated in diagnostic and treatment decisions. Alternatively, the identification and description of an aspect of the culture of the clinic itself, and of its staff, could be choosen as a focus. In this case, it had to be indicated that the cultural pattern identified inhibited or interfered with the transactions between practitioners and patients and the effectiveness of patient care. The third task of the study was analysis of the problem identified and the presentation of a proposition for its resolution. This phase had to incorporate examples of precedence or other supporting data for the proposed solution.

Throughout the course students kept fieldwork records. Initially, these tended to be subjective. Under the stimulus of the assigned readings on fieldwork methodology and seminar dicussions, however, the students quickly improved in objectivity and their ethnographic reporting became more focused and purposeful. The rapidity of this progression was also due to the fact that the students tended to select clinical settings in their own areas of specialization. Since all of the students had had extensive prior clinical experience in their areas of specialization they quickly felt at home in the clinical fieldwork setting even if it was not a practice site with which they were familiar. They understood the functions of their professional informants and had a grasp of the social and power stucture, the roles, norms, values, etc. In addition, since each student brought a considerable degree of clinical competence into the situation, as a participant-observer she or he could be perceived by the clinical staff as potentially an assent rather than "another body," a descriptive term often applied to university students in teaching hospitals.

It should also be pointed out that matching the students' professional competencies to the functions of the clinics in which they do their field work helps to address Kleiman's concern that most medical anthropologists lack "the basic clinical skills needed to do research that integrates biomedical and ethnomedical perspectives" (1977:12). It is my contention that by teaching courses in medical anthropology in schools of nursing, medicine, and other health-related professions, anthropologists who are not clnicians can lay claim to abundant opportunities for such integration. The course described here is only one way of several to utilize the established clinical orientation of the health professional schools in order to expand the reaches of anthropological research, practice and influence into the clinical area. Instances of such reaches will be cited below.

However, lest the impression be given that setting up such a course and getting it moving is all downhill work, the following examples of obstacles we have encountered should be noted. First, the problem of gaining entry for the student into the observation site of his choice is invariably difficult, even when the student offers professional expertise and assistance which is sorely needed in the clinic and to which no request for compensation is attached. Clinic administrators and their superiors downtown typically present such stated objections as "no space is available or appropriate for observing," "the staff has no time for questions," "it makes the patients nervous," etc. There may also be unstated objections, including concerns that the observer may detect incompetence, intrastaff conflict, and the like.

Despite these objections, and the fact that access to administrators is often a problem itself, permission for entry must be gained in the case of each student, and a clinical agreement form must be signed in triplicate. Once in, the student must maintain his objectivity at all costs, and comport himself with discretion, since the staff, however friendly, tends to view the students with suspicion. On the other hand, some members of the staff may rejoice in the opportunity to comment to the student upon the competence of their colleagues.

One of the most intractable barriers to entry invoked by administrators is the body of federal regulation pertaining to the protection of human subjects. In the four year history of this course surveillance over adherence to this regulation has increased in detail and stringency. Clinicians worry about it, staffs are organized around it, and administrators are paralyzed by it.

In addition to these social and political hurdles we encountered some cultural ones. In the culture of nursing, for example, for a course to be defined in the curriculum as "clinical" it must provide a "hands-on" training experience and the presence of a preceptor. Cognitive transactions, whatever the setting and whatever their impact upon health or illness, are not defined as "clinical." What may be clinical to anthropologists, then, may not be clinical to nurses or physicians, including those in academia. A similar problem of definition will be found to obtain in other health disciplines.

Despite these difficulties, however, our clinical anthropology course did get off the ground and consistently produced exciting results. The following abbreviated list (Table 1) of clinical sites in the Buffalo area in which our students have conducted their participant-observations, the foci which they selected, and the cultural problems which they identified and analyzed is presented in order to indicate the range of health-related and health care-related cultural problems which the students investigated.

In several of the cases cited the student continued his or her investigation of the problem identified and expanded it into a full-scale research project. Several of the students were also invited to serve as consultants to their clinics and to give talks on their observations to the staff. One, a nurse practitioner who is a Native American, has been offered a key position in the Alcoholism Clinic of Buffalo as a result of her recommendations for modification of approaches to intractable cases. Perhaps the most exciting outcome to date is to be seen in a program under development by the Pyschoendocrinology Department

Table 1. Clinical Sites in the Buffalo Region

Site of Study	Focus of Study	Cultural Problem
Psychoendocrinology Department (Children's Hospital)	Turner's Syndrome in an Adolescent Girl	Physical Stigmata & Peer Relationships
Pre-school Clinic for Children with Developmental Problems (Children's Hospital)	Hyperactivity in Pre-school children	Labelling by Health Professionals
East Side Clinic	Generational Differences in Health Behaviors Among Polish Americans	Stereotyping by Health Professionals
Alcoholism Clinic	Nurses' Attitudes Toward Alcoholics	Nurses' Attitudinal Variations According to Sex and Age of Patient
Intensive Care Nursery (Children's Hospital)	Staff-Patient Relationships	Health Professional Attitudes Toward Out-of-Wedlock Births
Lackawanna Clinic	Staff Relationships	Competition Among Staff Professionals
Cattaraugus Clinic	Staff-Patient Interactions	Attitudes of Staff Nurses Toward Welfare Patients
West Side Clinic	Interactions Between Medical/Nursing Professionals and Native American Patients	Assignment of Responsibility for Care of Patient
Family Practice Center	Interactions Between Physicians and Patients	Physicians' Modification of Interpersonal Address According to Race of Patient
Student Health Service	Repeated Visits to the Clinic of Students with Minor Aliments	Disruptions in Family Organizations as a Correlate of Number of Visits per Student

of a large local hospital. Based upon the observations of one of our students this program is designed to effect a change in attitudes and behaviors of pre-teen school children toward their physcially impaired or disfigured peers.

The Roles of Anthropologists in Health Care

As a result of my experiences with this course I was particularly interested to read the discussion in the "Open Forum" on Clinical Anthropology (Shiloh et al. 1980). I found that I did not agree with the positions taken either for or against health care interventions by anthropologists. To elaborate, I agree that our task is not hands-on therapy but I'm not certain that what we do isn't intervention. If health professionals who have learned how to detect and interpret the cultural elements in a pathological condition incorporate that understanding into the patient interview and physcial assessment and then proceed to prescribe for and treat the condition on the basis of the inclusive diagnosis, that seems to me to be a continuous, rather than discontinuous, process. Correspondingly, if medical anthropologists working in health care settings participate directly in the diagnostic process by identifying cultural elements in the patient's condition, or in presenting his problem, or in his behavioral responses, then it would seem appropriate to describe such participation in the process as "clinical anthropology." Further, if anthropologists make recommendations which result in bringing the patient and provider together in a working relationship which enhances the therapeutic process, then this participation, too, might be described as "clinical." A familiar instance of this kind of intervention is that of the anthropologist who translates nutritional, pharmaceutical and treatment protocols into regimens which harmonize with the hot-cold system of many Hispanic and other patients while still maintaining the therapeutic valances of Western medicince.

Two phenomena which persistantly engaged my attention in teaching my clinical course are germane to this issue. The first is that once a clinician has learned the uses of anthropological observation, interpretation and analysis, he tends automatically and pragmatically to employ them in the therapeutic process. These uses become part of the tools of his trade.

Secondly, most of the discussions over "Clinical Anthropology" speak to the centrality of research in Anthropology. As the example of the term paper topics listed in Table 1 indicate, all of the students were successful in identifying cultural elements operating both in patient pathologies and in the ineffectiveness of certain instances of treatment and transmission of care. It appears that by teaching anthropology in clinical settings anthropologists will gain access to countless opportunities for research which might otherwise escape our vision or our grasp.

These observations, then, lead to the conclusion that polarization is neither necessary nor pragmatic in this region of Anthropology, and that whatever we name our turf, or, more importantly, however we cultivate it, it is fertile with promise.

REFERENCES

Kleinman, Arthur
    1977   Lessons From a Clinical Approach to Medical
            Anthropological Research. Medical
            Anthropology Newsletter 8(4):11-15.

Shiloh, Ailon et al.
    1980   Open Forum on Clinical Anthropology. Medical
            Anthropology Newletter 8(1):14-24.

ANTHROPOLOGY AND PUBLIC HEALTH:
CULTURE AND POPULATION LEVEL INTERVENTION,
A UNITED STATES PERSPECTIVE

Miriam B. Rodin

Introduction

I am a social anthropologist and I work in a school
of public health, were I am an associate professor of
epidemiology. Although people are rarely surprised
these days to find anthropologists affiliated with
hopitals, clinics, or schools of nursing and medicine,
I encounter a fair amount of perplexity when my job is
explained. The role of anthropologists in United
States clinical settings seems by comparison to be
reasonably well understood. Public health in the
United States on the other hand, suffers from a certain
lack of visibility.

This is all the more perplexing to me, since most
of those who identify with Clinical Anthropology, also
identify a specialty interest within medical
anthropology. Foster and Anderson, in an influential
textbook, trace the roots of medical anthropology to
four sources, one of which was the very early
contribution of anthropologists in the 1940s, through
the present, to public health and development work
overseas (1978:8-9). While much of the literature they
review in a subsequent chapter shows that
anthropologists have participated in clinical settings,
a substantial amount of research is available regarding
public health (planning, technology transfer,
prevention, personnel training, cultural factors
affecting implementation of sanitation and disease
eradication measures, nutrition, family planning and
institutional analyses) in the developing world, and
among cultural enclaves within industrialized
societies.

For these reasons it is likely a useful exercise to
overview public health in the United States so that the
logic of its inclusion in a conference on clinical
applications of anthropology may be more evident.
Following this, I will describe several projects in
Chicago that have combined anthropology and public
health, and then suggest some useful preparations that
an anthropologist interested in pursuing a public
health career might consider.

Public Health and the Clinical Professions

Perhaps the single defining feature of public health that distinguishes it from medicine or nursing or the other clinical professions is that it is concerned with populations, both as objects of study and as objects of intervention. While other health professions deal with individuals as patients or clients or even as consumers in order to identify and solve subjectively experienced problems and complaints, public health does not. Individuals are encountered only as representatives of groups, as sample respondents or as links in chains of transmissible diseases. Thus populations of interest may be the employees of a factory or entire industry, residents of geographically or politically defined communities or cases in registries of particular diseases. The goal of public health is thus to affect aggregate measures of morbidity and mortality, or in research, to identify statistical associations of etiologic import.

The Tasks of Public Health

Public health practitioners are involved in the formulation, enforcement, and evaluation of disease control and of environmental quality measures. They are the people who inspect restaurants, factories and water supplies for compliance with standards. They may work with clinicians in identifying and tracing cases of disease or in evaluating the effectiveness of therapeutics. They do not, however, heal or comfort the sick; their goal rather is to prevent disease. By way of analogy, the relationship between public health and clinical medicine is similar to that between the county agricultural extension agent and the veterinarian. The agent is part policeman, part educator, part financial advisor. A sick cow or blighted crop is his concern only if it may affect the productivity of an entire region. For all of these reasons, I am inclined to think of public health as an applied social science practiced by people with medical and technical training.

Within public health, epidemiology is the discipline which concerns itself with the study of the distribution and determinants of states of health in human populations. In tracing the historical roots of epidemiology, Susser (1973) focused on the evolution of the "epidemiologic triad" of host, agent and environment. Susser credits Hippocrates with the discovery of environment as a critical factor in disease incidence. By the mid-seventeenth century quantitative analyses of distributions of disease were produced by John Graunt, followed by the first published life tables by Halley. Epidemiologic and demographic methods of analysis were reasonably sophisticated by the time of John Snow's application to cholera control. It remained until the latter part of the nineteenth century for Koch and Pasteur to establish a scientific concept of pathogenic agents. Although hinted at by Durkheim's epidemiologic approach to the study of suicide (1897), the third corner of the triad, host characteristics, has remained the most refractory of the triad.

While we have had the development of ecologic models, for example, for malaria control (McElroy and Townsend 1979:85-90; MacDonald 1957) and schistosomiasis (Wilcocks 1962: McElroy and Townsend 1979:389-395), a similar understanding of the social, structural and psychological factors affecting host susceptibility and exposure to organic and pyschiatric disease is not established. Engel's (1977) proposed biopsychosocial model, for example, while accepted in principle, has yet to be operationalized on a wide variety of disorders. Perhaps the most comprehensive investigations using this framework have been on cardiovascular diseases (including hypertension) and on schizophrenia.

Nonetheless, the bulk of the evidence concerning gains in life expectancy and reductions in mortality points to the primary contribution of changing social factors, secondarily to public health interventions, and only to a minor extent, clinical intervention (McKeown 1979). With reference to European populations, McKeown attributes the decline of mortality due to historic epidemics of plague and smallpox during the latter part of the seventeenth century to natural selection. Subsequent decreases in mortality during the latter part of the eighteenth century resulted from improved agricultural methods and systems of distribution and thus the improved nutritional status of the population. The effects of hygienic movements were not to be felt until the late nineteenth century, long after the largest percentage gains in life expectancy had been experienced. It is the residual diseases of living long and well, and of medicine's achievements in postponing death, that have become the principal concerns of public health in high technology societies.

The differing perspectives of clinical medicine and of public health are brought out when one compares the statements of contemporary physician authors. Thomas Lewis has written of:

> . . . patients with intractable cancers, severe rheumatoid arthritis, multiple sclerosis and advanced cirrhosis. One can think of at least twenty major diseases that require supportive medical care because of the absence of an effective technology. I would like to include a large amount of what is called mental disease and most varieties of cancer, in this category (1974:32).

Later in the same volume, Lewis states,

> We do not become sick only because of a failure of vigilence. Most illnesses, especially the major ones, are blind accidents that we have no idea how to prevent (1974:82).

Thus, while Lewis would most likely not dispute Engel's rejection of biochemical reductionism in the definition, diagnosis and treament of disease, he has overlooked a considerable body of public health research.

With particular reference to cancer and cardiovascular diseases, greater longevity, smoking and nutritional factors contribute to their ranking as the principal causes of death in the United States and in other industrialized countries. However, even when these factors are excluded, it has been persuasively agrued that, at least in the case of cancer, Lewis' focus on clinical technology may be misplaced. The role of industrial chemicals as major environmental causes of cancer, perhaps for as much as 30% to 40% of all cancers observed in the American population (Epstein 1979:27) has been plausibly argued. That the technology for controlling or replacing the forty or so known major carcinogenic pollutants is available and has been by and large poorly implemented, is more a matter of political economy than of scientific ignorance.

Sociocultural Factors in Mortality and Morbidity

My own interests, however, have been more focused on the role of sociocultural factors in health status. As can be seen in Table 1, social contributors to mortality have increased in importance throughout the twentieth century as infectious disease mortality has subsided. As compared with 1900, when accidents ranked seventh among the leading causes of death, three psychosocial cause of mortality rank among the top ten in 1975: accidents, suicide and cirrhosis of the liver. Although the overall rates are indeed lower than at the turn of the century, their proportionate contributions are magnified. When the population distribution of these causes of death is examined from the perspective of years of life lost, the impacts are again increased. Accidents, homicide and suicide accounted for 70% and 54% respectively, of deaths among men and women aged 15-24; and for 37% and 21%, respectively, among men and women aged 25-44 (U.S. Bureau of the Census 1980:74, 79).

When considering aggregate measures of morbidity, psychosocial factors emerge as highly significant. Excluding any attempt to quantify psychosomatic contributors to organic disease, Table 2 compares the rates of hospitalization for pychiatric versus all other causes. Not unitl after 1965 with the widespread use of psychoactive drugs did psychiatric hospital days fall below those of general medical-surgical utilization. These figures do not adjust for the increased use of short-term hospitalization (up by 25% over the period) because of hospital expansion, increased coverage by third party insurers and the practice of defensive medicine by physicians.

Finally, as can be seen in Table 3, declining psychiatric hospital days per 1000 persons are attributable to declining lengths of stay under de-institutionalization policies. Reductions in patient censuses have been accompanied by a 250% increase in rates of psychiatric hospitalization, the so-called revolving door pattern. Thus it appears that despite great advances in clinical practice, the aggregate data speak to a considerable contribution of psychological host factors, and of sociocultural factors external to the clinical setting, to levels of morbidity and mortality in the United States population. It seems both unrealistic and unreasonable to expect clinical practitioners or clinical institutions to undertake the modification of population-level phenomena, even though these clearly affect both the presentation and outcome of clinical interventions. It seems to me that the public health model more readily addresses these issues.

271

Table 1. The Ten Leading Causes of Death in the United States in 1900 and in 1975

Rank	1900[a] Cause of Death	Crude Death Rate per 100,000 Population	Percent of Total Deaths	Rank	1975[b] Cause of Death	Crude Death Rate per 100,000 Population	Percent of Total Deaths
	All Causes	1,719.1	100.0		All Causes	888.9	100.0
1	Influenza and pneumonia	202.2	11.8	1	Diseases of heart	336.2	37.8
2	Tuberculosis	194.4	11.3	2	Cancer	171.7	19.3
3	Gastroenteritis	142.7	8.3	3	Stroke	91.1	10.3
4	Diseases of heart	137.4	8.0	4	Accidents	48.4	5.4
5	Cerebral hemorrhage	106.9	6.2	5	Influenza and pneumonia	26.1	2.9
6	Chronic nephritis	81.0	4.7	6	Diabetes mellitus	16.5	1.9
7	Accidents	72.3	4.2	7	Cirrhosis of liver	14.8	1.7
8	Cancer	64.0	3.7	8	Arteriosclerosis	13.6	1.5
9	Certain Diseases of infancy	62.6	3.6	9	Suicide	12.7	1.4
10	Diphtheria	40.3	2.3	10	Diseases of infancy	12.5	1.4

Sources: a. Facts of Life and Death, National Center for Health Statistics, Public Health Service Publication no. 600, 1970, Table 12.

b. American Cancer Society, 1978 Cancer Facts and Figures, New York, 1979.

Table 2. Trends in Hospitalization in the
United States: Selected Years, 1960-1978

Hospital Days per 1,000 Population

Year	Non-Federal Short-Term	Psychiatric
1960	947	1491
1965	1055	1261
1970	1148	826
1972	1192	714
1974	1224	574
1976	1242	429
1978	1216	320
1978/1960, Index	127	21

Source: U.S. Bureau of the Census 1980:116.

.

Table 3. Resident Patients and Admissions to
         State and County Mental Hospitals,
         United States: Selected Years, 1950-1974

Year	Resident Patients at End of Year	Admissions
1950	512,501	152,286
1955	558,922	178,003
1960	535,540	234,791
1965	475,202	316,664
1970	337,619	384,511
1974	215,573	374,554

Source: Wiesbrod 1980.

Culture in Public Health Intervention

The public health model differs from the clinical model in that it includes the environment as an active factor in the relationship between agent and host in disease processes, with the goal of preventing disease or limiting its population level effects. The principal starting point is in the epidemiologic or environmental measurement of incidence, prevalence and exposures, in order to determine the magnitude of a health problem, the population at risk, the differential levels of risk within heterogeneous populations, and finally effective points of intervention within a system of host, agent and environment. To a very large degree, the feasibility and effectivenss of interventions are dependent upon available technology. But frequently cultural factors play a significant role in determining the success of intervention as well as the quality of measures used to indicate the need for the intervention. Several examples come to mind.

In this country, social class is highly associated with most indicators of health status. Relative incidence can often be biased because of factors affecting the reporting and recording of health status information. Thus, the true incidence of stigmatizing conditions such as venereal disease, alcoholism or child abuse is routinely underestimated among middle and upper socioeconomic (SES) groups. Conversely, economic factors tend to homogenize areas with respect to income. Thus an individual's economic performance limits residence patterns. When economic performance, resulting from psychiatric disorder is impaired, an artifactual association between social class and psychiatric illness is observed (Levy and Rowitz 1973). To consider another example, the mild neurological impairments of delayed neurological development observed in learning disabled children would likely have little effect on the life chances of a child in an illiterate society, or even an industrialized society. But slight perceptual distortion can have a severely handicapping and stigmatizing effect in a contemporary society that requires nearly uniform performance and development from an early age.

To cite several more exotic examples recounted to me by Dr. Henry Gelfand, cultural factors can effectively block prevention programs even when technology is readily available. In parts of West Africa, smallpox eradication programs were affected by local beliefs which regarded smallpox with the same moral approbation with which several venereal diseases are regarded in this country. Thus reporting of incident cases was severely impaired. During a vaccination campaign in South Africa, several Zulu communities refused to accept vaccination, due to local belief concerning etiology of the disease. The Zulu reasoned that smallpox, which was caused by devils, was not likely to be prevented by injections of fluid said to contain the remains of invisible organisms. The mode of action of the vaccine in combating the devils had to be widely explained before compliance was obtained. Similarly, a national program of spraying insecticide for malaria control in India foundered in local areas where the spraying schedule conflicted with local religious festivals. Also in India, a poster campaign to encourage control of disease-bearing flies featured a highly magnified photograph of a fly. When teams were sent out to discover why villagers were not requesting fly control, they were told that no one had ever seen one that big, but if they did they would certainly report it. It is my belief that such cultural miscommunications are also at work in U.S. society.

Cultural Perspectives on Public Health in Chicago

I would like to focus now on several examples from my own experience that illustrate that beliefs and practices in public health and public health perspectives on social problems can offer useful ways to intervene. As an example of the latter, I would like to offer a preliminary consideration of arson as a public health problem.

Arson and Public Health

There are in the criminal justice or urban sciences literature figures that summarize the amount of death and injury accrued annually from fires that are intentionally set (Moll 1974). What I will report derives from interviewing and participant observation with a Chicago neighborhood group that undertook an investigation of fires in their own neighborhood, a ten city-block area known as the Heart of Uptown. Uptown is one of the poorest pockets of the city, and one renowned throughout the city for the vastness of its problems and the savagery of its inhabitants.

Over the past seven years, over 70 Uptown residents
died in fires "caused by person or persons unknown."
That is about one death per block per year, due to
fires exclusive of those determined to be accidental.
These are preventable deaths, as I hope to show.

The neighborhood coalition undertook a study of the
"clinical course" of arson. Initially, it was
determined that any fire on a block was followed by
increasing numbers of fires in buildings on the same or
neighboring blocks. It is possible to locate blocks in
which as many as a dozen buildings are gutted at any
one time. Buildings that burned had several common
characteristics. First, they had numerous fire and
housing code violations, and extensive histories of
housing court continuances. Second, arsoned buildings
had either been unsold after several attempts through
the general listings, or alternatively, had changed
hands rapidly amongst a small network of associates,
thus artificially inflating their market price. Third,
arsoned buildings in general had several smaller fires
in porches and storage areas that resulted in insurance
reimbursement for most of the buildings' real value,
without rendering them uninhabitable. These three
characteristics describe the incubation or preclinical
phases of arson.

At some point such a building is denied further
coverage by private insurers and the building is
reinsured by the State of Illinois insurance pool.
Several more small fires may ensue, or several paper
transactions among blind land trusts as in the
preclinical phases. However, many slum tenants
recongize the symptoms and leave at this point.
Shortly before the ultimate destruction of the
building, a more serious fire and/or eviction notices
clear the property of tenants. The building is then
re-rented to vagrant or otherwise disoriented persons
for a weekly or monthly deposit. Within days the
building is burned completely in an accelerated fire.
Twelve persons died in one such fire in 1979.

Fires are more frequent in the winter due to the
strain on sub-standard heating and electrical systems.
Arsons are thus less noticeable in the winter months,
and arsonists are less likely to be seen on cold winter
nights when few people are out. The public finds it
hard to believe that people would intentionally destroy
their own property. Alternatively, it is easy to
believe that vagrants, drunks and illegal immigrants
can clumsily cause their own deaths.

Seven fires in this neighborhood, and a number of deaths, were traced to one slum owner and several associates. The neighborhood group obtained national television coverage on ABC's 20/20 news magazine for the subsequently highly disputed case of arson for profit.

Several intervention strategies were proposed by the neighborhood coalition and pursued through political channels. They recommended active investigation and prosecution of alleged arsons, increased penalities on conviction, and reform of the insurance pool to remove the profit from the crime. Additionally, block clubs were trained to recognize early symptoms and to patrol susceptible buildings. More aggressive measures, including breaking the confidentiality of blind trusts, limitations on housing court continuances and enforced divestiture of offending landlords, were proposed. I further believe that computer profiles of arson-prone neighborhoods, which combine fire calls, tax delinquency, housing court records and real estate transactions can pin-point vulnerable buildings for neighborhood or police surveillance.

An interesting footnote is that, during the period of active agitation about arson-for-profit, the alderman of the ward in which the neighborhood is located publicly disputed the existence of the problem. In the winter of 1981 a rooming house across the street from his home was burned, after following the classical clinical course. No one was killed. I have of course been speaking metaphorically, but I think it is important to consider that private insurers use epidemiologic methods in preparing risk statements on which to base premiums. Epidemiologic methods have been used fruitfully in investigations of other "accidental" causes of death, for example in highway fatalities. The problem of urban fires, and arson in particular, seems to be amenable to such analysis. In this case, the theory of arson-for-profit and the delineation of a clinical course emerge from essentially ethnographic methods of qualitative analysis.

The Control of Venereal Disease in the Gay Community

A second example of the interface between culture and health status is the transmission and prevention of venereal diseases in the gay community. I am basing this discussion on the thesis research of Norman

278

Altman, a graduate student in epidemiology. With the exception of venereal diseases, now termed Sexually Transmitted Diseases (STDs), great advances have been made in the control of communicable diseases in the twentieth century. During the five year period from 1976-1980, however, the number of reported cases of gonorrhea alone was more than twice the total number of cases of all twenty notifiable diseases reported in Morbidity and Mortality Weekly Reports (1980) by the Centers for Disease Control (CDC). Also During this period, hepatitis B (HBV), formerly "serum" hepatitis, came to be considered a venereal disease.

Noticeably higher rates for syphilis, gonorrhea and HBV have been consistently observed among male homosexuals in England and the United States than in the general population. In conjunction with a collaborative study of STD and HBV prevalence in gay men sponsered by CDC, Mr. Altman undertook supplementary surveys in the Chicago gay community in order to determine whether common risk factors associated the classical STDS, gonorrhea and syphilis, and also reliably predicted risk of acquiring HBV (Hepititis B Virus). Using questionnaires and laboratory determinations of infection or seroconversion, samples were drawn from each of three gay subgroups, the clients of a gay community sponsered STD clinic, gay bars and gay bathhouses. Although the analysis is not complete, several sociocultural factors contributing to high prevalence of STD in the gay community have been identified.

Behavioral factors affecting exposure to STD and HBV include the frequency and anonymity of sexual contacts and specific sexual practices. The degree to which infections remained untreated, and thus both prevalent and communicable, reflected cultural attitudes towards homosexuals expressed in mainstream health care settings. Of importance were survey respondents´ expressed discomfort with reporting STD symptoms to straight physicians. But of greater significance, gay males are at greater risk of asymptomatic infections than heterosexual males. Thus routine venereal disease testing as practiced in public clinics or in private practice is likely to miss many cases. Unless the patient had specifically requested multiple site cultures, which required awareness of asymptomatic disease, such infections were missed. The sexual orientation of the patient is thus critical information for routine practice, and an awkward topic for physician and patient alike. Finally, it is suggested that the apparent increase in STD rates observed in gay populations is artifactual and secondary to the more assertive use of public clinics and increased health awareness by gays in urban areas. In this example, Mr. Altman's epidemiologic survey was supplemented by ethnographic information concerning networks and subgroups in the Chicago gay community, and by survey data concerning health beliefs and health service utilization. Several specific recommendations concerning clinical practice have resulted.

The Ethnography of Drinking and Alcoholism

As a third case, since 1977, my assistants and I have been working on drinking, and associated demographic and attitudinal factors in the Lake View Community Area of Chicago. We have used both ethnographic and survey research methods, the latter based in part on Cahalan, Cisin and Crossely's (1969) well-known protocols and in part on questions derived from earlier ethnographic experience in Chicago. In particular, I anticipated that frequency of social contact might be significantly associated with drinking frequency. That proved to be the case in the sample survey which we took:

> . . . that drinkers and non-drinkers may be primarily distinguished by age and sex, and that non-drinkers are less active in all community settings than drinkers. Moreover, among drinkers, heavy drinkers report the highest levels of activity across all settings with the exception of voluntary associations, and that alcohol-related activities account for a higher proportion of the social settings in which they participate than among infrequent to moderate drinkers . . . most drinking in all drinking groups is in the company of others. The use of alcohol-related gatherings increases with reported consumption (Rodin, Morton and Shimkin 1979:14-15).

The social nature of drinking in Lake View is somewhat modified among heavy drinkers, for whom drinking has psychological significance as well:

> . . . the heavy drinker [is] a denier of problems, who nonetheless is bothered by persistent worry, or who is reacting to stressful life changes. . . . Alcohol is perceived . . . to be a potent agent for the

280

relief of anger, frustration and tension and for facilitating sociability (Rodin, Morton and Shimkin 1979:25).

The Lake View community, as with most survey approaches to the study of drinking and alcoholism, is subject both to sampling and to reporting biases. In the former, survey sampling techniques are likely to underrepresent alcoholics, and with the latter, respondents are prone to underestimate their actual drinking. For these reasons, our findings cannot be considered indicative of alcoholic attitudes and behavior. Nonetheless they do characterize the beliefs and behaviors of the larger population of normal drinkers against whom the treated alcoholic population can be compared.

One of the major problems in public health is to relate an estimate of health need based upon epidemiological data to the actual demand for services by a target population. That relationship can vary widely and for profoundly different reasons. Let me explain this, using data on chronic alcoholics in Lake View as compared with the background obtained from the sample survey.

Prolonged, very heavy drinking greatly increases the risk of dying. An excellent study by Thorarinsson (1979), included all male first admissions, in-patient or out-patient, for alcoholism in Iceland between 1951-1970, and followed nearly 3,000 men for an average of 13 years. Two-thirds of the excess mortality of the alcoholics resulted from accidents, heart disease, and suicide--all areas of particular psychosocial significance (see Table 4). American studies have obtained similar results. The contribution of alcohol abuse to hospital utilization is thus large and difficult to estimate accurately. But the implications for health service planning and utilization are apparent (Putnam 1982).

Chronic alcoholics can and do survive, often relatively well, between drinking bouts and hospitalizations. Although Chicago alcoholism has been decriminalized, the adaptations described by Spradley (1970) are much the same, with detoxification centers and hospitals substituting for jails as way stations. In Uptown, for example, the street alcoholics have an economy that is not totally unlike that of the Bushmen. They are nomadic gatherers. They have no fixed residence, but they know where resources are, and they

281

Table 4. Excess Mortality Among Male Alchoholics in Iceland, 1951-1974

Cause of Death	Number of Deaths			Excess Mortality	
	Observed	Expected	O/E*	N	%
Accident	146	36.84	3.96	109.2	34.5
Heart Disease	143	79.14	1.81	63.9	20.2
Suicide	45	10.20	4.41	34.0	11.0
Cancer	85	56.48	1.50	28.5	9.0
Pneunomia	29	8.68	3.34	20.2	6.4
Cirrhosis of liver/fatty liver	14	1.24	11.29	12.8	4.0
Alcoholism	13	1.16	11.21	11.8	3.7
Vascular lesions of Central Nervous System (CNS)	26	22.93	1.13	3.2	1.0
Other	72	39.58	1.82	32.4	10.2
TOTAL	573	256.25	2.24	316.8	100.0

* All, excluding vascular lesions of CNS, significant, p < 0.01.

Source: Thorarinsson 1979.

282

exploit them in predictable seasonal patterns. The street alcoholics are not without social support, however, although the relationships are predominantly exploitative in nature. Health providers, such as the hospitals serve as ancillary shelters. To the extent that I can determine, many street alcoholics have no strong desire to change their cirmunstances. For many of them, and as they get older, especially when they reach sixty-five and qualify for Social Security, the standard of living goes up considerably. Nonetheless, agencies feel obliged to provide alcoholism treatment services.

From a policy standpoint, the problems created are severe. The Department of Mental Health and Developmental Disabilities of the state views repeated admissions as "recidivism," which alcohol treatment agencies are directed to reduce.

Recidivism is a concept that comes out of the corrections field. Alcohol treatment is based on the premise that alcoholism is not a moral failure, but a disease. A recidivist is someone who willfully commits an offense and is repeatedly institutionalized. Cancer patients are not recidivists if a metastasis occurs. One would not classify as a recidivist a heart patient who has a re-infarct. Following a disease model, recurrences may be attributed to non-compliance. For the purpose of planning alcoholism services, then, an examination of the factors contributing to non-compliance--that is, continued drinking on the part of chronic alcoholics--is needed.

From our research, two aspects need to be considered. First is the recognition that, at a certain point, alcoholics are sufficiently deteriorated and sufficiently embedded in exploitative social networks, that the problem becomes one of maintenance in a protected environment which can encourage as much social function as medically feasible. The second is active intervention for those who have not yet established a stable way of life in the street. The pattern appears to stabalize sometime after the fifth admission to a de-tox center, at least for younger clients.

These specific problems reflect more general social service delivery policies in Chicago and in the rest of Illinois which I have examined in detail elsewhere (Rodin, Rowitz and Rydman 1982). Differences in local policies toward alcoholics, differences in sheer magnitude of population, and the availability of private insurance coverage have compartmented the flow of clients into treatment. In Chicago, alcohol treatment agencies are overloaded with chronic alcoholics leaving other types of problem drinkers virtually untouched.

The results of the studies, one of a random sample of community residents, and the other of admissions records to the detoxification center indicated rather disparate public views of the alcohol treatment system consistent with the characterization above. Among community residents, alcohol treatment options were perceived as surprisingly limited. By comparison, interviews with de-tox clients revealed a detailed knowledge of service options and preference criteria. These studies resulted in further recommendations for state authorities for re-evaluation of treatment goals for their principal clientele in the Chicago area. As with the previous two examples, a public health orientation directed us to an epidemiologic methodology and supplementation with ethnographic data to explain aggregate findings.

Anthropologists and Public Health: Potential Contributions

The three projects that I have described are not intended to be in any way representative or exhaustive of the kinds of activities that anthropologists in public health have undertaken in the United States or even in Chicago. They are indeed skewed toward an epidemiologic perspective within public health. In a recent article, Schreiber and Scrimshaw (1979) have reported on a survey of anthropologists in schools of public health. The range of research and teaching reported in this study indicates that epidemiologic work is probably a rather small component of current anthropological contributions to public health. More traditional fieldwork approaches to sociocultural problems in clinical settings appear to be the dominant mode among this small contingent. I might add that, among biological anthropologists, epidemiologic methods are more widely applied. In the last section of this discussion I will turn to a consideration of the kinds of problems in public health that might usefully be approached from an anthropological perspective, and to the kind of preparation an anthropologist interested in a public health career might consider.

There are two broad areas of public health concern that contain significant sociocultural components that have yet to be exhaustively addressed. The first is environmental regulation and the second is compliance with primary prevention and risk reduction programs. The field of environmental regulation includes a number of subspecialties, including technical aspects of monitoring and standards development. The latter do not, I believe, lend themselves to the anthropological approach. However, the implementation of regulations involves complex problems of gaining industry compliance with pollution control, occupational exposures and assessments of alternative technologies. In general, the approach to regulation has largely been punitive and, if one listens to both sides, either too costly for the industries to comply with or not punitive enough to enforce compliance. The imminent threat of loss of jobs in a shaky economy has been taken to heart by the present administration. The resolution of these difficulties requires a careful analysis of the core values and utilities observed by the public and by the interest groups involved, principally in making explicit the goals and planning processes that shape management decisions concerned with capital outlay.

The extent to which behavioral interventions or modifications of man-machine interactions can accomplish the same ends as the purchase and installation of toxic exposure control equipment requires additional study, and particularly in sorting out the relative contributions of ergonomic factors and cultural values to the acceptability of such solutions in workplaces. In considering technological alternatives, for example, to the problem of automobile pollution or rational land use practices, again the human factors approach has been given inadequate attention.

There is not a vocal demand or ample funding for such undertakings, yet these are the kinds of approaches that are considered by environmental agencies. The anthropologist's willingness to deal with the specifics of a case--for example review of an environmental impact statement, the particulars of a single plant that is to be brought into compliance, the concerns of a union in responding to health issues among the membership--is a qualification that few other social sciences share.

The second area I mentioned where anthropologists have a potential role to play is in the implementation of preventive health care. The Surgeon General's report, Healthy People (The Institute of Medicine 1979) sets out the health goals for the eighties, with areas of specific need targetted for age, sex, ethnic and social class segments of the population. It is a very interesting document, and I recommend it to you as much for the quantity of factual informantion it contains as for the anthropological value it has in illustrating the ritual process of health policy-making. It is an ambitious and idealistic volume, reflecting the myriad special interests in the public realm. Several themes emerge.

Life style factors in risk for cancer and cardiovascular disease are targeted for attention. Thus people's habits and beliefs affecting nutrition, smoking, exercise and stress reduction will be increasingly the focus of education and gentle persuasion. Maternal and child health are considered important. In part to decelerate rising health care costs, and capitalizing on middle class "self-health" and holistic health ideology, responsibility for care of the elderly, developmentally disabled, and chronically ill is likely to be increasingly returned to families. When families are gone, the least restrictive environmental guideline substitutes.

Perhaps because of our roots in overseas development work, there is quite a body of United States research on maternal and infant health. For example, Gwen Stern, the Schensuls and others have done interesting research with Mexican migrant women and parturition in Chicago. Relatively little has been done with regard to risk factor control in cancer and cardiovascular disease. Dennis Frate and Demitri Shimkin's hypertension research in Mississippi is a notable exception. There is surprisingly little research by anthropologists on the care of the disabled at home.

If one peruses the anthropological journals, rather few titles pertaining directly to public health are found. Conversely, in the public health journals, only a smattering of "cultural" studies are evident. Yet I can think of several anthropologists around the country who are now or have been actively engaged in the topical areas mentioned above. Similarly, the second and third authors of public health articles not too infrequently turn out to be master's level anthropologists.

286

My guess is that anthropologists have a toehold in public health, but these "public health" anthropologists are not a group, a quasi-group nor even a named category. Thus, a prominent medical anthropologist, David Landy, authored a fine ethnography of psychiatric aftercare facilities in 1965, but he is not considered to be "in public health" (Landy and Greenblatt 1965).

There are then, it seems to me, two general areas of applied research in preventive health that can be usefully addressed by anthropologists. The first is in discovering the contributions of cultural beliefs and practices of benefit to health services, particularly preventive services in maternal and child health, cancer screening and cardiovascular risk reduction. The second is in the examination of the role of pyschosocial factors in disease etiology. With regard to the latter, numerous researchers have attempted to measure the effects of stressful life events, crowding, unpredictability in the social environment (also, misleadingly, called social disorganization) and social subordination in contributing to disease. The role of supportive social relationships has also been investigated as a protective factor (Cassel 1974). Factors of these types have been consistently related, but at low levels of statistical contribution, to a variety of mental and organic diseases. Considerable work is still needed to refine the concepts and research designs employed. The public health field, however, is very receptive to this type of research.

There are several cautions though for the anthropologist beginning in public health. In public health the usual disciplinary boundaries are of little relevance to those contracting for or using the results of research. The finer points that distinguish an anthropologist from a sociologist or a sociologist from a social psychologist are subordinated to the direct usefulness of the research. Social research in public health must provide immediate answers to immediate questions. One does not have the luxury of a year in the field in order to identify research questions. The generalist approach is most valuable.

The generalist skills that I have found most useful have been familiarity with survey research methods, and at least modest preparation in statistical analysis. Basic courses in statistics and epidemiology are important prepatory foundations. It is most important to be aware of the federal, state and local sources of

morbidity and mortality data. Skill in presenting and
interpreting quantitative data is perhaps partially a
matter of aptitude, but it can be learned. Secondarily
it is important to master the biological and clinical
bases for the health outcomes chosen for study. An
understanding of the organizational and legal basis of
health care is also necessary. Criticism of existing
facilities cannot be well received by the users of
research if that criticism is founded on factual
errors.

Finally, though I have stated that disciplinary
boundaries are little observed in public health, the
anthropologist does have a unique contribution to make.
It is important to provide a quantitative background to
research. However, the grounding of findings in
observational research, the ability to illustrate
conclusions with detailed case material and informant
accounts and the fleshing out of statistical
relationships with the affective quality and symbolic
meaning of events to members of the group under study
are unique to anthropology. Thus the humanistic
perspective brought to the study of health and illness
is a major part of the anthropologic enterprise, and
one we ought to advocate and cultivate within the
field.

REFERENCES

Altman, Norman
1983   Sexually Transmitted Disease Risk Factor
        Identification in Gay Men. University of
        Illinois at the Medical Center. School of
        Public Health. M.S. Thesis.

American Cancer Society
1979   1978 Cancer Facts and Figures. New York.

Cahalan, Don, Ira H. Cisin and Helen M. Crossley
1969   American Drinking Practices. New Brunswick,
        NJ: Rutgers Center of Alcohol Studies.
        Monograph No. 6.

Cassell, John
1974   An Epidemiological Perspective of
        Psychological Factors in Disease Etiology.
        American Journal of Public Health
        64(11):1040-1049.

Centers for Disease Control
1981   Annual Summary 1980: Reported Morbidity and
        Mortality in the United States. Morbitiy and
        Mortality Weekly Reports 29(54).

Durkheim, Emile
1897   Le suicide: étude de sociologie. Paris:
        T. Alcan.

Engel, George L.
1977   The Need for a New Medical Model: A Challenge
        for Bio-Medicine. Science 196(4286):129-136.

Epstein, Samuel S.
1979   The Politics of Cancer. Garden City, NY:
        Anchor Books (Doubleday). (Originally Sierra
        Club Books 1978).

Foster, George M. and Barbara G. Anderson
1978   Medical Anthropology. New York: John Wiley
        and Sons.

The Institute of Medicine, National Academy of Sciences
1979   Healthy People. The Surgeon General's Report
        on Health Promotion and Disease Prevention,
        Background Papers. Washington, D.C.: DHEW
        (PHS) Publ. No. 79-55071A.

289

Landy, David and Milton Greenblatt
1965   Halfway House. Washington, D.C.: USDHEW
Social and Rehabilitation Service.

Levy, Leo and Louis Rowitz
1973   The Ecology of Mental Disorders. New York:
Behavioral Publications.

Lewis, Thomas
1974   The Lives of a Cell. New York: The Viking
Press.

MacDonald, G.
1957   The Epidemiology and Control of Malaria.
London: Oxford University Press.

McElroy, Ann and Patricia K. Townsend
1979   Medical Anthropology in Ecological
Perspective. North Scituate, MA: Duxbury
Press.

McKeown, Thomas
1979   The Role of Medicine. Princeton, NJ:
Princeton University Press.

Moll, Kendall D.
1974   Arson, Vandalism and Violence: Law
Enforcement Problems Affecting Fire
Departments. U.S. Department of Justice.
Washington, D.C.: U.S. Government Printing
Office.

National Center for Health Statistics
1970   Facts of Life and Death. Public Health
Service Publication No. 600. Washington,
D.C.: U.S. Government Printing Office.

Putnam, Sandra L.
1982   Alcoholism, Morbidity and Care-Seeking.
Medical Care 20(1):97-121.

Rodin, Miriam B., Douglas R. Morton and
Demitri B. Shimkin
1979   Social and Psychological Correlates of
Drinking in the Lake View Community. Working
paper #6. Project on Community Dynamics,
Social Competence and Alcoholism in Illinois.
Urbana, IL: Department of Anthropology,
University of Illinois.

Rodin, Miriam B., Louis Rowitz and Robert Rydman
1982   Levels of Analysis and Levels of Need: The
        Assessment of Need for Alcoholism Treatment
        Services in an Urban Community. Human
        Organization 41(4):299-306.

Schreiber, Janet M. and Susan C.M. Scrimshaw
1979   Anthropologists in Schools of Public Health.
        Medical Anthropology 3:309-338.

Spradley, James P.
1970   You Owe Yourself a Drunk: An Ethnography of
        Urban Nomads. Boston MA: Little Brown and
        Company.

Susser, Mervyn
1973   Causal Thinking in the Health Sciences. New
        York: Bantam Books, Inc.

Thorarinsson, Alma Anna
1979   Mortality among New Alcoholics in Iceland,
        1954-74. Journal of Studies on Alcohol
        40:704-718.

U.S. Bureau of the Census
1980   Statistical Abstract of the United States:
        1980 (101st ed.). Washington, D.C.: U.S.
        Government Printing Office.

Wiesbrod, B.
1980   A Cost Benefit Analysis Through Controlled
        Experiment with the Chronically Mentally Ill.
        Madison, Wisconsin: Institute for Research on
        Poverty.

Wilcocks, C.
1962   Aspects of Medical Investigation in Africa.
        London: Oxford University Press.

HOW CAN THE HEALTH PROFESSIONS USE ANTHROPOLOGY?
THE HEALTH EDUCATION PERSPECTIVE

Thomas W. O'Rourke

Introduction

The opportunity to address this issue is appreciated. While not an anthropologist by training or occupation, my sporadic exposure to the area, albeit seriously limited, has convinced me of its potential merits. This is not to single out anthropology. The thrust in health education over the past decade, as in many areas, has been to initiate and nurture linkages to other disciplines. The appearance here of a wide variety of health professions attests to this transition. Hopefully, it will continue and expand.

The underlying thesis of this presentation is that the relationship between anthropology and health education is a two-way street. Both fields can contribute to one another. For example, anthropological studies that are clinically literate can provide important information for health education orientation, planning and content. But health education can also contribute to clinical anthropology. It can indicate a variety of problems of concept, substance and techniques needing study. It can also provide a larger body of data on planned changes--and failures to change--of great importance to anthropology as a whole. Finally, because it shares many common hypotheses as vividly identified in the Shimkin-Golde introduction, it can join in more fundamental efforts to broaden the bases and applications of the entire health-social science interface.

As a point of departure, I would like to define health education, discuss this concept, indicate the factors responsible for its growing significance, temper the significance with caution and attempt to relate health education with anthropology.

What is Health Education?

As you know fadism in the health field is rampant. Today we're running, yesterday we were eating yogurt or popping One-A-Day vitamins (many of us are still doing it). Dieting is endemic in spite of the trajic demise

293

of the creator of the Scarsdale diet, and Vitamin E sales continue to be brisk despite any evidence of their purported usefulness to genital potency. Who knows what tomorrow brings? To some extent this is true within the field of health education, which formally is less than fifty years of age, but which has experienced many interpretations during that period. In the intervening years, many attempts have been made by a variety of groups and organizations, individuals--more recently a Presidential Committee--to clarify earlier definitions, to attain more precise definitions, and to achieve a standard definition of health education that is generally acceptable to those who use and to those who make possible the use of the health education process in their work. A standard definition continues to elude us. Yet its absence does not seem to detract from our individual and collective efforts to strengthen and improve health education practice and related research. Perhaps, it is as a health educator wrote for an 1947 symposium:

> Health education cannot be ´given´ to one person by another; it is not a set of procedures to be carried out or a product to be achieved; rather, it is a dynamic everchanging process of development in which a person is accepting or rejecting new information, new attitudes, and new practices concerned with the objectives of healthful living (Nyswander 1947:650).

Fortunately, because of such symposia, the concept of health education has been clarified. I would like to share two of the more accepted views. While done in the spirit of jest, you might want to label the first as an academic view and the second as an operational viewpoint. The reason will soon become apparent. Many in health education utilize the definition agreed on by the 1972-73 Joint Committee on Health Education Terminology and published in <u>Health Education Monographs</u> (1973), which views health education as:

> A process with intellectual, psychological, and social dimensions relating to activities which increase the abilities of people to make informed decisions affecting their personal, family, and community well being. This process, based on scientific principles, facilitates learning and behavioral change in both health personnel and consumers including children and youth (Joint Committee on Health Education Terminology 1973:65-66).

294

The other definition, as coined by a close colleague who ironically has long operated from an academic perch and who recently emigrated to the federal bureaucracy, is simply "any combination of learning experiences designed to promote voluntary adoption of behaviors conducive to health" (Green 1976). It should be noted that health education is not the exclusive province of the professional health educator or communicator, although they may play strategic leadership roles. Physicians, nurses, dentists, and other health professionals as well as teachers, behavioral and social scientists, out-reach workers, and consumers are all important in health education, and should be included in developing program potentials. The growth in both scope and sophistication of health education is most noteworthy. In its infancy, health education grew out of the immediate needs of institutions, primarily the schools. Historically, health education has been limited by its very applied nature. The concentration on immediate outcomes in health related behaviors and the reliance on the accepted wisdom of "medical facts" has inhibited questioning and model building. Today health education is present in hospitals, the workplace, the family and the community. As previously noted, its personnel span a wide and diverse gamut. Within this framework, health educators have made significant contributions to consumer and patient rights, patient advocacy, and in expanding the concept of the health team. Only gradually have they moved into more theoretical issues. This trend has been concomitant with the increased synthesis within health education using contributions from psychology, sociology, and anthropology to understand health beliefs, attitudes and behaviors in an effort to improve health and well being. Not surprisingly, the domain of health education has been greatly expanded. Whereas past efforts were primarily school oriented the present domain has been expanded to any populations at significant risk.

Contrary to public opinion, it should also be noted that health education is more than the provision of information. While health education includes acquiring knowledge about health matters, its purpose is the use of that knowledge. It addresses the formation of values, the acquisition of decision-making skills and the adoption or reinforcement of desirable health practices. Health education honors individuals' rights to privacy, their right to meaningful information, and their right to make their own choices.

Why Health Education?

A number of converging factors have been identified as leading to an increased awareness and interest in a stronger, more comprehensive, and more imaginative health education thrust. Among the more significant are:

1. A shift in leading causes of death and disability from acute disease to chronic conditions which generally require increased individual involvement in prevention, in recognition of illness, and in care. This shift is depicted in Table 1.

2. Increasing awareness among health professions that many health problems such as smoking, poor nutrition, over-weight, lack of exercise and recreation, abuse of drugs and alcohol, and dangerous driving involve behavior patterns and lifestyle choice which individuals can to a significant extent control (U.S. Surgeon General 1979). Much of the disease transition previously mentioned was brought about by what is generally referred to as the first epidemiological revolution. As a result of such traditional public health practices as sanitation, coupled with improvements in housing, nutrition and medical knowledge, many communicable diseases have been dramatically reduced as significant causes of mortality. Also, many of these advances required limited participation or compliance on the part of the individual. This is not the case today. For the most part, the leading causes of mortality today are the result of chronic or social diseases which are not susceptible to the classic public health intervention methods. As Dubos has indicated, these "diseases of civilization" are significantly influenced by life styles and personal health related behaviors (Dubos 1968).

Recently, former Secretary of Health, Education, and Welfare, Joseph Califano, has indicated that the current leading causes of mortality should be the focus of the second epidemiological revolution which would include attention being directed to the areas of environment, health screening and health education (Califano 1979). This latter component would focus upon changing

Table 1. Leading Causes of Death with Rates in the United States: 1900, 1925, 1950, 1981
(Rates are the number of deaths per 100,000 population)

| | 1900 | | 1925 | | 1950 | | 1981 |
Disease[a]	Rate	Disease[a]	Rate	Disease[a]	Rate	Disease[b]	Rate
ALL CAUSES	1,719	ALL CAUSES	1,168	ALL CAUSES	964	ALL CAUSES	866
1. Tuberculosis	194	Heart Diseases	185	Heart Diseases	357	Heart Diseases	331
2. Pneumonia & Influenza	184	Pneumonia & Influenza	122	Cancer	140	Cancer	184
3. Diarrhea & Enteritis	140	Nephritis	95	Intracranial Vascular Lesions	104	Cerebrovascular Diseases	72
4. Heart Diseases	137	Cancer	92	Accidents	63	Accidents	45
5. Intracranial Vascular Lesions	107	Intracranial Vascular Lesions	90	Diseases of Early Infancy	41	Chronic Pulmonary Diseases	26
6. Nephritis	80	Tuberculosis	85	Pneumonia/Influenza	31	Pneumonia/Influenza	24
7. Accidents	72	Accidents	77	Tuberculosis	23	Diabetes Mellitus	15
8. Diseases of Early Infancy	72	Diseases of Early Infancy	59	Atherosclerosis	20	Chronic Liver Disease and Cirrhosis	13
9. Cancer	64	Diarrhea & Enteritis	38	Nephritis	19	Atherosclerosis	13
10. Bronchitis	45	Syphilis	17	Diabetes Mellitus	16	Suicide	12
11. Diphtheria	40	Maternal Deaths	15	Congenital Malformations	12	Homicide & Legal Intervention	11

Sources: a. Selected from Tables 65, Vital Statitistics in Rates in the United States, 1940-1960, U.S. Department of Health, Education and Welfare, National Center for Health Statistics, 1968.

b. Selected from Table E, Monthly Vital Statistics Report, Vol. 30, No. 13, December 20, 1982, U.S. Department of Health and Human Services, National Center for Health Statistics.

the direction of our present sick-care system to a health care system, accompanied by an intensified program to reduce mortality through changes in lifestyle behaviors. Given the leading causes of mortality, coupled with the present state of medical knowledge, it appears that the greatest benefits are likely to accrue from efforts to improve the health habits of all Americans and the environment in which they live and work rather than a continuation of our present policy based upon a "medical model" approach to disease, illness and disability.

3. Acceptance by environmentalists and others that if control of many environmental hazards such as air and water pollution, occupational risks, and toxic substances are to occur, group action by informed citizens is required.

4. Concern about the high cost of health care which has resulted in efforts to recognize and prevent health problems, and to promote more effective planning and use of health care resources as ways of achieving savings and obtaining maximum benefit from expenditures. There is a widespread concern about various elements of our health care system. These elements include quality, accessibility, availability, acceptability, continuity, and costs of service. Of major immediate concern is health care costs. Total expenditures in 1982 were at a rate of approximately $300 billion per year. Per capita annual costs are now in excess of $1,200, nearing 10 percent of the Gross National Product. As Table 2 shows, the rate of growth in health care costs has been dramatic.

    It should be also noted that for most of the past decade, medical care prices outpaced increases for all other items on the Consumer Price Index; that national health expenditures have more than doubled during the 1970s and that, based on the current rate of growth, are projected by the Health Care Financing Administration to triple during this decade.

5. Recognition by health care providers that improved communication and understanding help consumers to accept their share of responsibility for both personal and community health.

Table 2.   Gross National Product and National
Health Expenditures: United States,
Selected Years 1929-1981

(Data are compiled by the Health Care
Financing Administration)

	Gross National Product In Billions	NATIONAL HEALTH EXPENDITURES		
		Amount In Billions	Percent of Gross National Product	Amount per Capita
1929	$ 103.1	$ 3.6	3.5	$ 29.49
1935	72.2	2.9	4.0	22.65
1940	99.7	4.0	4.0	29.62
1950	284.8	12.7	4.5	81.86
1955	398.0	17.7	4.4	105.38
1960	503.7	26.9	5.3	146.30
1965	688.1	43.0	6.2	217.42
1970	982.4	74.7	7.6	358.63
1971	1,063.4	82.8	7.8	393.09
1972	1,171.1	92.7	7.9	436.47
1973	1,306.6	102.3	7.8	478.38
1974	1,412.9	115.6	8.2	535.99
1975	1,528.8	131.5	8.6	604.57
1976	1,700.1	148.9	8.8	678.79
1977	1,887.2	170.0	9.0	768.77
1978	2,107.6	192.4	9.1	863.01
1979	2,368.8	212.2	9.0	942.94
1980	2,626.1	249.0	9.5	1,075.00
1981	2,925.5	286.6	9.8	1,225.00

Sources: Gibson,   R.M.:   National   Health   Care
Expenditures, 1981. Health Care Financing Review,
Vol. 4, No. 1, September 1982, pp. 1-35.

6. The growth of the consumer movement in all aspects of American society with resulting pressure for consumer involvement in all levels of health decision-making and with growing interest in self-care movements.

Thus, more than ever before, examination of the causes of ill health and of the means available for improving health status is focusing on health education as a way to achieve public health goals. The conviction is growing that the next major advances in health will come from changes in the lifestyles of individuals and from control of health hazards in the environment. In a democratic society, the educational process is a way of alerting citizens to personal and societal obstacles to good health and offers a channel for achieving needed change.

Health education can help prepare people to take greater responsibility for their own health and that of their families and communities. Through health education, individuals acquire the information, skills, and values for making responsible decisions about their personal health. Since health is influenced by environment, social conditions, institutions, and economic policies, solutions to complicated health problems often require coordinated citizen action.

The goal of health education is the health-educated consumer-citizen who adopts a health-promoting lifestyle, wisely selects and uses health care resources, products and services, and influences public policy and planning on health care issues and larger environmental matters that affect health.

Limitations of Health Education

When speaking about an area of priority interest it is commonplace to sell more than is delivered. Thus, it is necessary to temper optimism with a rather strong dose of reality. Simply, it should not be forgotten that while health education is one very promising approach to health improvement, it has only limited power to counteract the health impact of such factors as economic deprivation, poor housing, and persuasive media. For example, with respect to the latter point, it is personally amazing that smoking rates are at a twenty year low despite the annual advertising expenditure of nearly one billion dollars by the tobacco industry.

Another point I wisk to make is that advocacy of health education reflects an attractive opportunity for policy makers to "cop out" in terms of making difficult policy decisions. For example, it is easy to "blame the victim" by saying we smoke, eat and drink too much rather than instituting national policies directed toward these behaviors. It is ironic that expenditures for cigarette advertising coupled with government tobacco subsidies make the resources devoted to anti-smoking efforts miniscule in comparison. Similarly, we blame the victim and his lifestyle for high health care costs when in reality the ridiculous costs reflect the dynamics of a monopolistic and self-serving sick care system designed more to benefit the providers than the recipients. If I may digress for a moment, I would add that the impact of improved health behaviors would have no demonstrable effect on health care costs since demand is largely provider determined and the price relatively inelastic due to the noncompetitive nature of the current "sick care" system.

Application of Anthropology to Health Education

There are wide variations in the organization and administration of health programs within and between countries. It is because of this diversity that the application of anthropology becomes important. Account must be taken of a multitude of social, cultural and economic factors which vary from country to country, and even within the country or district where health education measures are to be applied. Accordingly, there can be no single formula as to how and where the health education activities fit into the whole public strategy at various administrative levels.

Use of anthropology is also essential in the planning of health education programs. The success of any program for health improvement, such as the installation of a safe water supply, or mosquito control, nutrition, or immunization programs depends on the understanding and cooperation of the people. As previously indicated, it is necessary to carefully study cultural characteristics of any given group in its environment. Ethnological studies, and the collaboration of anthropologists in the orientation, planning, and conduct of health education are always helpful, and are essential in technically less developed areas. Lack of such involvement can be disastrous. The literature is bountiful with classic examples where anthropological considerations were absent, and not surprisingly the program outcomes were disastrous.

Numerous areas of concern to health education can benefit from the inclusion of Clinical Anthropology. These could include fertility control methods, patient education, drug behavior, death education and the emergence of the hospice concept, communicable and chronic disease, accident prevention, nutritional problems such as obesity, suicide prevention, and of course, the reduction of patient and medical personnel. Essentially, the use of Clinical Anthropologgy in its application is limited only by the imagination. Possibly, this paper has helped to broaden that boundary.

REFERENCES

Califano, Joseph
   1979   Foreword. In Healthy People: U.S. Surgeon
            General's Report on Health Promotion and
            Disease Prevention. U.S. Department of
            Health, Education and Welfare DHEW (PHS)
            Publication No. 79-55071:ix-x.

Dubos, Rene
   1968   Man, Medicine and Environment. New York: The
            New American Library.

Gibson, R.M. and D.R. Waldo
   1982   National Health Expenditures, 1981. Health
            Care Financing Review, Vol. 4, No. 1,
            September 1983, pp. 1-35.

Green, Lawrence
   1976   Determining the Impact and Effectiveness of
            Health Education as It Relates to Federal
            Policy. DHEW Contract No. 5A7974-75.

Joint Committee on Health Education Terminology
   1973   New Definitions: Report of the 1972-1973
            Joint Committee on Health Education
            Terminology. Health Education Monographs,
            33:65-66.

Nyswander, Dorothy
   1947   What Is Health Education. American Journal
            of Public Health 37(6):650.

U.S. Surgeon General
   1979   Healthy People: U.S. Surgeon General's Report
            on Health Promotion and Disease Prevention.
            U.S. Department of Health, Education and
            Welfare. DHEW (PHS) Publication
            No. 79-55071.

Lillian Pickup

My name is Lillian Pickup. I have been invited to lead this discussion and comment on the preceding presentations. I am not a social anthropologist or researcher but am involved in a great many of the components needed to provide a direct service network of care. Some of these components are teaching, writing, legislative advocacy and advocacy within the health care network. My background is nursing and I am presently the program director for the Aid of Alcoholics Programs of Lutheran Social Services Incorported in the Uptown Community of Chicago.

You may be wondering rather quietly "Why is a direct service provider/non-researcher here at this conference making comments and leading a discussion?" This is a valid question: the answer can be found in part in the impetus of this conference. Practical steps toward using anthropology will involve a partnership of many academic and service disciplines. Direct service providers often are most heavily impacted by research, or desire to provide topics for research, yet are rarely involved in the planning or research process.

I have listened to various presentations over the duration of this conference. I have on the one hand found these presentations to be interesting and on the other hand found myself wondering quietly what the impact of the direct service provider in the research discussed might have been.

We have heard presentations regarding the increased incidence of venereal disease among patrons of gay baths versus patrons of gay bars. Much is being done to research the cause of this phenomenon. Socially it is the gay bath that provides the atmosphere for a casual sexual contact and most people dealing with the gay population will pinpoint this factor.

Another presentation details the attempt to deal with self help groups at Cook County Hospital. There has been little success. Cook County Hospital is crisis-oriented from patients to staff. Long term

305

problem-solving is culturally foreign to the patients and thus difficult for the staff.

Other self help presentations have dealt with Parents Anonymous and the inability to start such chapters in small communities. Why is this such a difficult undertaking? Because in some communities anonymity is not assured--not to the people who must live there--and even with Parents Anonymous we are asking people to risk coming forward to say "I abuse my child." We may need to borrow knowledge from other treatment programs such as alcoholism agencies which have found in small communities that the persons requiring treatment may need to go to another area of the state to avoid or decrease the associated stigma.

This is called common sense and reality, never overlooking the obvious. Direct service providers will often be able to provide information which may be of value in directing research projects to run more quickly and possibly in a direction that may provide immediate impact.

How can research be used, for example, as a vehicle to change treatment standards? Fine tuning projects such as were done at Cook County Hospital would have shown the crisis orientation of this grouping of patients. The Joint Commission on Accreditation of Hospitals and Illinois Public Health would then have the basis for a change in their regulations which mandate such things as group therapy, and short and long term goal setting. While group therapy, for instance, may work for some it does not work for those who function on a crisis orientation. It is difficult at best to receive licenses or accreditation without the waiver of such mandates.

Research must also find its way into the culture of the direct service provider. An example of tragic loss of impact can be found in the treatment of Native Americans today. Research done in 1940 has not even now been reflected in the alcoholism treatment network in Illinois. We are engaged in the same fight to educate service providers regarding these special needs as we were 40 years ago.

I have briefly outlined areas of need in my comments. There are more, such as how do we influence medical school curricula, interject clinical reality into administrative data gathering systems and provide realistic standards of measurement for services both present and needed? I would propose a partnership, to include many academic and service disciplines working together. Competition may be healthy--however, not when it obscures needed information. Dr. Thomas O'Rourke's presentation has opened the discussion regarding competition in health care delivery systems. We must use care that this competition not be destructive but rather a constructive partnership.

PART V

MOVING TOWARD A DISCIPLINE:

ISSUES OF DOCUMENTATION IN ANTHROPOLOGY

AND HEALTH SERVICES

FOREWORD

Demitri B. Shimkin

In the development of a new field of knowledge, few problems are more fundamental or more difficult than the creation of a comprehensive, systematically evaluated and articulated core of information. This process requires major resources over an extended period. It must also balance inherently conflicting requirements, especially those of comprehensive coverage versus quality control, and of precise definition and logical articulation versus sensitivity and originality. In Clinical Anthropology, two other sources of difficulty enter: the dispersal of basic information through a wide array of scientific journals, ephemeral reports, unpublished notes and quantitative data sets, and the variety of users, ranging from academic researchers to isolated clinicians.

Nevertheless, the importance of proper documentation for clinical anthropology must be stressed. There is literally no other way that the field can be validated and transmuted into an orderly yet productive discipline. More than this, clinical anthropologists alone have the sensitivity and experience to make critical decisions in this domain.

Documentation and the construction of a theoretical understanding of clinical anthropology are two sides of the same developmental need, which must be met simultaneously and interactively. The first goal for both documentation and theory has to be the formulation of " . . . approximate, partial, multiple, locally inconsistant or vague models" (Apostel 1961:7) that can be gradually made more consistent internally, and with other approaches such as the biomedical, its contradictions and gaps notwithstanding (Engel 1974).

In discovering what to document, two basic strategies are extant. One, which is particularly important in the early stages of disciplinary definition, is statistical. It approaches its subject as the stochastic product of an interacting body of practitioners (Radnitzky 1974). Its critical questions are: Who are the people recognized or self-designated as clinical anthropologists? What do they do? What

311

have they produced in terms of papers, books, and data sets? What studies do these works cite?

The other strategy, which arises out of the theoretical contributions of Rudolf Carnap (1939), is formal. It seeks to define the "object language" of the relevant domain--its categories, its operations, and its products as logical systems mapping exactly observable phenomena.

At the present time, efforts to develop documentation for clinical anthropology are necessarily statistical, in larger part. They reflect the work of contributors to this volume, other self-designated clinical anthropologists, contributors to such publications as Social Science and Medicine, and classic writers such as Gregory Bateson and George Devereux.

A start can also be made toward a formal strategy, using the suggestions of Golde and Shimkin (1980). Working in the areas of mental health and counselling, maternal and child health, trauma, chronic disease, rehabilitation, and community health, clinical anthropologists are concerned with diagnosis, epidemiology, intervention, and advocacy. Stress is a basic concept, which is related both to adaptive problems associated with life stages, and to social and physical mobility. Stress is intensified through distortions of perception associated with communication difficulties. The relief of stress comes through therapist-client interactions, and through the development of new adaptive capacities via learned skills and self-help. The clinical athropologist also articulates clients and client communiities with cosmopolitan medicine, especially by means of communication, conceptual translation, and brokerage. Using these and other key words as a thesaurus the vast literature of health and the social sciences can be searched both to define clinical anthropology and to trace its relationships to other disciplines, such as clinical psychology. This in turn can yield a system of categories and hypothesized relations formally defining clinical anthropology with increasing rigor.

How can these ideas be implemented? This complex group of problems is explored by the papers that follow.

Barton Clark, after reviewing the literature of "user need" studies, examines the current status of bibliographic control in anthropology in order to determine if current systems fulfill user needs, especially in the emerging area of clinical application. Richard Thompson then analyzes goals and problems in the management of quantitative data sets for Clinical Anthropology. David Klass reviews the realities and dangers of data provided to meet management needs. Then, moving to future possibilities, S.B. Sells discusses the Drug Abuse Epidemiolgy Data Center as a possible model for Clinical Anthropology, and Allan Levy sketches the potentialities of a computer based system to improve interactions in data management. Finally, Barton Clark summarizes the implications of these papers.

REFERENCES

Apostel, Leo
  1961   Towards the Formal Study of Models in the
          Non-Formal Sciences. In The Concept and the
          Role of the Model in Mathematics and Natural
          and Social Sciences. B.H. Kazemier and
          D. Vuysje, eds. pp. 1-37. Dordrecht,
          Holland: D. Reidel.

Carnap, Rudolf
  1939   Foundations of Logic and Mathematics.
          Chicago: University of Chicago Press.

Engel, George L.
  1974   The Need for a New Medical Model: A Challenge
          for Biomedicine. Science 196:129-136.

Golde, Peggy and Demitri B. Shimkin
  1980   Clinical Anthropology--An Emerging Health
          Profession? Medical Anthropology Newsletter
          12:15-16.

Radnitzky, G.
  1974   Toward a System Philosophy of Scientific
          Research. Philosophy of the Social Sciences,
          No. 4.

DOCUMENTATION IN ANTHROPOLOGY: CURRENT STATUS AND NEEDS

Barton M. Clark

Introduction

When the scientific journal was first developed as a means of communication between researchers, it is doubtful that anyone forsaw its impact upon scholarly communication. Certainly, no one would have predicted that 200 years after its inception, over 50,000 scientific journals would be published on a regular basis. Of course, these journals only represent part of the information explosion. Books, technical reports and quantitative data also contribute significantly to the phenomenon. If anthropology is to cope successfully with the information explosion, it will be essential to develop information management systems which can effectively retrieve that information which is deemed necessary by researchers and clinical users.

Fundamental to the development and evaluation of information systems for anthropology is the examination of user needs for such systems. The origins of analyzing user needs for information systems rest within the natural sciences. Only in the last three decades has there been any evaluation of user requirements within the social sciences. Brittains's classic study, Information and Its Users (1970), which summarized all of the research which had been done prior to 1970, revealed, that while many studies broached user needs, only eighteen were dedicated specifically to the user needs of social scientists.

Virtually unexamined have been the special information needs generated by the interface of the social sciences with the health sciences. Although many of the information needs expressed in the broader user studies of social scientists are obviously similar to the information needs of clinical anthropology, one can assume that some special information needs not associated with traditional academic anthropology will also arise. In particular, immediacy of information is more important in the clinical setting. Thus, technical reports and other fugitive literatures, especially of a localized nature, will often play an important role in information dissemination.

User Needs in Anthropology

As part of broader studies on user needs in the social sciences, three studies have discussed in varying degrees of detail the information needs of anthropologists. The first of these studies was John S. Appel's and Ted Gurr's "Bibliographic Needs of Social and Behavioral Scientists: Report of a Pilot Study" (1964). Comparing the ways psychologists, economists, and anthropologists utilized bibliographic services to gain access to new information sources, respondents to Appel's and Gurr's questionnaire expressed dissatisfaction with the available methods of accessing relevant information. Particular difficulty was noted in accessing fugitive literature, e.g., technical reports. In addition, anthropologists expressed a concern over the difficulty of accessing materials published outside the United State. In place of using formal bibliographic guides to answer their information needs, these social scientists resorted to retrieving new citations in the literature and from publishers' advertisements. Informal communication, including correspondence, word of mouth, and professional meetings, also contributed to accessing relevant information. Social scientists suggested that their information gathering could best be supported through a regularly published abstract journal. The service should be comprehensive with multifaceted indexing. Anthropologists indicated that information should be organized by geographical region. They also urged that language parameters be expanded to include coverage of foreign language materials (Appel and Gurr 1970:53-54).

The problem of the diffuseness of anthropological literature compared to that of other social sciences and the natural sciences was noted by Daniel (1967). Comparing the citations from selected journals, he determined the extent to which each discipline under review cited its own literature as opposed to citing literature outside of its own discipline. Using the American Anthropologist for the year 1965, Daniel found that only 56 percent of the citations in the journal were to anthropological sources. In contrast, Physical Review had a 94 percent level of citation to physics literature and the Journal of Experimental Psychology reflected an 86 percent level of citation to psychology journals.

The degree to which a journal in a discipline cites literature within its discipline is a significant indicaton of the success which a discipline-oriented bibliographic tool will have in retrieving relevant literature. The relatively high rate of citation outside the discipline that Daniel found for anthropology highlights the difficulty of developing an effective bibliographic tool for that discipline (1967:679-681).

The most comprehensive research into the nature of social science literature and its users was carried out in the late 1960´s by researchers at Bath University (England) under the direction of Maurice B. Line (Bath 1971 a,b,c,d). As part of this investigation, British cultural anthropologists were interviewed to ascertain their information gathering needs. The findings of the research were similar to those of Appel and Gurr. The accession of information tended to be a haphazard process. Citations to the literature and informal communication served as useful methods of learning about new literature. Secondary bibliographic tools, although designed to improve access to the literature, were seldom utilized to the degree to which they were intended. In part, this may be due to the low priority placed on being informed about new materials which was expressed by the anthropologists sampled (Line 1971:423).

Only two studies have dealt solely with the information needs of anthropologists. Diana Amsden (1969) surveyed seventy-six anthropologists randomly selected from Current Anthropology´s "Associates." The two most important ways the surveyed anthropologists learned about new information were from conversations with other anthropologists and from anthropological literature. Both of these methods were twice as popular for retrieving information as were indexes and abstracts. The survey also revealed a strong reliance on the literature of other disciplines. Among the major information problems identified by the sample were incomplete coverage or unsatisfactory indexing by index and abstract services. The difficulty of obtaining foreign and fugitive materials was also noted by the respondents.

Amsden suggested that what anthropology needed to help alleviate these problems was more effective bibliographic control of the literature through "a prompt cumulative, comprehensive index-abstract service" which could have the potential for computerization. In addition, a guide to the literature and bibliograhic essays should be produced (Amsden 1969:125-131).

The only other study of anthropologists'
information needs was Norman Spurling's analysis of the
faculties of the University of North Carolina and Duke
University (1973). Spurling's results are remarkably
similar to Amsden's. Again, the acquisition of
information from colleagues was a significant way to
acquire information, as were sources from
anthropological literature. In contrast, indexes and
abstracts were seldom used. Formal bibliographies
fared only slightly better. Among the information
problems identified by the sample, the difficulty in
obtaining fugitive materials and current information
were noted.

In addition to these two user studies, Clark and
van Willigen (1981) have identified user requirements
of applied anthropologists, based upon an analysis of
the literature on the needs of applied anthropology.
First, the nature of applied anthropology requires that
research be timely. Effective and rapid access to
previously collected data is, therefore, essential.
Second, accessing quantitative data is also important.
Third, most projects involving applied anthropologists
are multi-disciplinary; correspondingly, information
needs will also be multi-disciplinary. And fourth,
much of the literature which is germane to the applied
anthropologist is fugitive in nature, seldom receiving
more than limited publication.

Out of this limited amount of research certain
patterns do emerge. The acquisition of information by
anthropologists is less than systematic. Conversations
with other anthropologists play a significant role in
learning about new sources of information. The most
commonly used method of acquiring information from
published sources is from citations in anthropological
literature. Although both methods are far less
systematic than indexes and bibliograhies in searching
for new information sources, they are continually found
to be at least twice as popular, as a means for
acquiring bibliographical references.

The most often cited need for information systems
is a method for more effective bibliograhic control of
the literature. It is felt that the ideal system
should be both current and cummulative. The system
should have a multifaceted index. Abstracts should
accompany each bibliographic entry. The system would
include citations to both foreign and fugitive
literature. Although it was not specifically stated as
a need, the studies revealed the importance of

non-anthropological publications to anthropological research. An ideal system, therefore, would be able to accommodate relevant citations from non-anthropological sources.

Meeting Anthropological Needs: Indexes and Data Bases

How successfully have these needs been met by current resources? Currently there are two anthropological indexes in the English speaking world, Anthropological Literature (1979-) and Anthropological Index to Current Periodicals in the Museum of Mankind. Although both indexes provide a broad coverage of the anthropolical literature, Anthropological Index to Current Periodicals in the Museum of Mankind is limited to journal articles. Both indexes include foreign language titles.

Unfortunately, neither index is cumulative. The possibility of a cumulative index for anthropology does exist with the International Bibliography of Social and Cultural Anthropology (1955-). The International Committee for Social Science Information and Documentation, which produces the bibliography and its counterparts in economics, political science, and sociology, is developing a computer based index which would combine the indexes of all four bibliographies into a single index as well as cumulate that index. If the plan comes to fruition, it will also provide a system which would identify useful materials in other social sciences. Even with these resources, which at least partially fulfill the declared needs of anthropological researchers, old habits continue to persist. These new tools are regretably underutilized. Bibliograhic information is still obtained through informal channels and citations from the literature.

The most promising potential for overcoming the old methods of accessing information is through computer-based bibliographic systems. Currently, there are approximately fifty data bases which are relevant to the social sciences. While none of these data bases are specifically designed for anthropology, many do cover topics germane to anthropological research. In addition, data bases in the health sciences and biology will produce useful citations.

As an example, a researcher in clinical anthropology might be interested in materials on gerontology, alcoholism, or hypertension. Using an

319

online data base system, several data bases can be checked within a matter of minutes to determine if pertinent data exist; and in which data bases. The number of citations for each data base is given in Table 1. For any particular research project, further refinement through the use of additional terms would be necessary. What the test does reveal is that for a particular topic, a single data base is seldom sufficient to access all of the pertinent literature a researcher may need. Since much of the research which anthropologists pursue will be cross-disciplinary in nature, the ability to have subject searchability through numerous disciplines holds a distinct advantage over limited searching in a single discipline-oriented data base.

Beyond the standard online data bses, it is possible to develop individualized data bases, i.e., private files, either through commercial systems such as Bresearch and Dialog or through the software of a system such as the Smithsonian Institution's SELGEM system for use with a local computer. An individualized system allows the user to develop those fields deemed necessary. Besides author, title, and subject, additional fields such as type of information, e.g., data set and funding agency can be searched. Abstracts could also be produced for the file.

The advantage of a private file is that it does not have to be limited to bibliograhic entries. On-going research projects could also be included, as could descriptions of data sets. Computerized systems offer potentials which are not readily possible with manual systems, thus allowing a closer mesh between the system and the user's needs.

Applications in Clinical Anthropology

Information needs of clinical anthropologists will vary to a certain degree depending upon the work setting. Information systems, if they are to be effective, must, therefore, be cognizant of these differences. The academic researcher in universities, teaching hospitals, and other large institutions will place heavy emphasis upon document access, primarily journal and monographic literature, through libraries. Retrieval of these materials will most effectively be done through the use of bibliographies, indexes and online systems. Because time constrants in such an environment are moderate and the size of the literature

Table 1. Bibliographic Data Base Citations

Data Base	Alcoholism	Gerontology	Hypertension
Biological Abstracts	892	28	6125
Drug Abstracts	2771	0	2
ERIC[1]	743	792	60
MESH[2]	3363	402	9659
Mental Health Abstracts	7024	1377	1175
Psychological Abstracts	4092	1102	430
Social Science Citation Index	2876	750	386

1. Database of the Educational Resources Information Center

2. National Library of Medicine's Medlars database using the Medical Subject Headings (MESH) vocabulary

base is very large, the development of private computer based bibliographic files is not essential. Numerical data, however, should be accessible from existing data sets and from private files.

The needs of clinical researchers and workers in community health and allied programs, in institutional settings but with very explicit "hard" data needs usually involving definite time constrants, will, although they have the same resources as academic researchers, place a maximum value on computer based systems for the retrieval of both bibliograhic and quantitative data. They should always consider developing private files in both areas.

In contrast, researchers and clinical persons without access to large libraries, data sets, etc., will have need for specialized bibliograhies, loan services and informal information networks to provide current background and to help evaluate particular clinical and/or research needs. Among such users there will be a strong reliance on localized literature, e.g., city government reports, and report literature from comparable situations. Often information rather than document delivery would be more useful to these individuals. Computer based systems would be of limited value.

Lastly, persons who are primarily teachers at various levels will have the greatest need for careful evaluation of materials and the availability of data which is usable for texts and readings. Information systems which can provide selectivity of a broader base of data are most useful.

Therefore, for information systems for clinical anthropology to be usable they must have a successful interface between anthropology and the health sciences. The system, however, must be able to adjust to the various types of users and settings for clinical anthropology.

322

REFERENCES

Amsden, Diana
1969   Information Problems of Anthropologists.
          College and Research Libraries 29:117-131.

Appel, John S. and Ted Gurr
1964   Bibliographic Needs of Social and Behavioral
          Scientists: Report of a Pilot Survey.
          American Behavioral Scientist 7(10):51-54.

Bath University. Library
1971a   Information Requirements of Researchers in
          the Social Sciences. Bath: Bath University.

1971b   Information Requirements of Social Scientists
          in Government Departments. Bath: Bath
          University.

1971c   Information Requirements of College of
          Education Lecturers and School Teachers.
          Bath: Bath University.

1971d   Information Needs of Social Workers. Bath:
          Bath University.

Brittain, J.M.
1970   Information and Its Users. New York: Wiley.

Clark, Barton M. and John van Willigen
1981   Documentation and Data Management in Applied
          Anthropology. Journal of Cultural and
          Educational Futures 2(2-3):23-27.

Daniel, Robert S.
1967   Psychology. Library Trends 15:670-684.

Line, Maurice B.
1971   The Information Uses and Needs of Social
          Scientists: An Overview of INFROSS. ASLIB
          Proceedings 23:412-434.

Spurling, Norman Kent
1973   Information Needs and Bibliographic Problems
          of the Anthropology Departments at U.N.C.
          [University of North Carolina] and Duke
          University. Chapel Hill: University of North
          Carolina. Master's thesis.
          (ERIC ED 092 178).

QUANTITATIVE DATA MANAGEMENT FOR
CLINICAL ANTHROPOLOGY

Richard W. Thompson

Introduction: The Need for Quantitative Data
in Clinical Anthropology

During the past fifteen years there has been an
impressive development of clearinghouses and archiving
facilities for quantitative data.[1] Today most
researchers have access to a diverse array of data sets
which can be obtained and processed relatively quickly
and inexpensively. These materials range from national
census statistics to national and cross-national
epidemiological surveys and attitude polls. Generally
speaking, the data contained in these archives provide
good coverage of major socioeconomic, political and
demographic indicators for non-Communist industrialized
nations, although the coverage and availability of data
for less developed and Communist-bloc nations drops off
sharply.

Beyond these basic resources, however, an enormous
amount of quantitative data useful to clinical
anthropologists is gathered and processed each year by
anthropologists and researchers in allied disciplines.
The purpose of this discussion is to highlight some of
the challenges now faced in attempting to document and
disseminate information about data sets which might be
directly relevant to the needs of clinical
anthropologists. Initially, it seems there are three
broad areas of concern. These include: 1. identifying
the long range objectives of clinical anthropology in
order to adequately delimit the types of quantitative
data to be claimed and made available; 2. developing
standards and guidelines for researchers gathering data
relevant to clinical needs in order to insure
comparability and quality; and 3. establishing
preliminary, working plans for a limited network of
clinical anthropologists to compile a registry of
quantitative data sets and information to be made
available in the near future.

What Kind of Data Processing Should There Be?

In terms of the long-range goals for quantitative
data management within clinical anthropology, two

325

closely related priorities stand out. On the one hand, there is a need for a centralized clearinghouse, or still better, a data archiving and processing center, into which relevant quantitative data can be deposited and maintained. Closely linked with this must be a library system containing the technical reports, proposals, and data collection, processing, and data reduction operations related to each of the data sets in the archive or clearinghouse. Ideally, this facility would compile and critique published and unpublished results based on all materials deposited with the facility. In sum, we are looking toward a major undertaking with implications for vast amounts of secondary analysis and, ultimately, a resource upon which major policy makers in areas ranging from medicine to labor relations may depend. Clearly, this type of a facility should be carefully planned to achieve a maximum degree of efficiency, and usefulness, and yet remain accessible to the small user--the practicing clinical anthropologist. All of this would not only require careful planning, but most importantly, demand a well defined set of priority areas and guidelines for developing a well-integrated body of information useful to clinical anthropologists.

To a large extent, the future of this facility--if it is to emerge--will depend on how well clinical anthropologists are able to define their common interests. The initiatives by Gern and Shimkin (in this volume) in surveying research interests and applications within the field represent a major step toward defining some of these topical areas. However, considerably more is needed. Sells (this volume) has suggested establishing a priority for something he terms "an anthropological approach." This he felt would be valuable in seeking support but it seems equally important for helping us define the boundaries of the field.

At this point, it may be important to offer a note of caution in regard to rushing into this type of data archiving facility for clinical anthropology. Such a system can, if not properly thought out and constantly monitored, be too large and practically unworkable. Without well thought out priorities and proper documentation for data sets, a great deal of effort could be expended on archiving and maintaining little used or even parallel (duplicate) materials. At this point, a major effort to begin data archiving for clinical anthropology by sending requests for data sets to be deposited in some central facility is clearly premature. Without first having set out the parameters and qualifications for materials, and surveying the potential users with respect to their needs, the system could rapidly become either too generalized and unwieldy or too narrowly specialized. It is clear that considerably more effort must go into specifying the aims and objectives of clinical anthropology itself before a major push toward data archiving can be made, and conferences such as this one should provide a general framework within which this will be possible.

Data Quality Standards

Turning to the issue of standards and guidelines for including materials in a centralized clearinghouse or data archive facility, some minimal standards of quality control and comparability must be established. For anthropologists at least, comparability across data sets is most vital. In speaking of comparability, it is first a matter of being able to sort out levels or units of analysis on which variables are measured. For example, useful data for clinical anthropologists should be collected for individuals, families, households, communities and larger political units. To be usable, there should be comparative data for the relevant units at several of these "levels" so the user could easily sort out community level data from, say, household or cross-national data.

More effective comparability could be achieved through the incorporation of actual specifications detailing the overall framework and working procedures for data collection behind each data set. This should include tagging the relevant research proposal materials, technical reports in instrumentation, and field methods employed, as well as published and unpublished results. If clinicians are to effectively utilize these data sets to support a program or initiate intervention of some sort, they must know the specifics of how these data were collected, what theoretical formulations guided the researchers, what the coding and data reduction techniques were designed to accomplish, and why only certain items were selected for analysis. Thus specification of the rationale for focusing on selected portions of the data must also be incorporated in this supporting material. For the purpose of supporting practicing clinicians in the field, it is not enough just to have the codebooks and interview schedules.

327

Closely related to this is the need to contextualize the data sources so that researchers can specify exactly how materials may be comparable or non-comparable. This would include the write-up of local cultural, political and socioeconomic observations which may not be captured by the quantitative data. Looking at the Human Area Relations Files (HRAF), it is exactly the insensitivity of many cross-cultural studies to the broader context with which many anthropologists take issue. Often, variables which seem on the surface to be the same are not really comparable when the specific cultural meanings or social structures are carefully examined. What might be deemed a household, a family, or an alcoholic in Peoria cannot be assumed to be the same in south Chicago. It is necessary to specify exactly what are the local conditions operating in a community or a study area which may be relevant to understanding those variables. There may be crucial differences between the kinds of conditions that we assume and the reality, yet we may be doing secondary analysis on data that are going to have policy implications or may, worse yet, impact on individuals we are dealing with in the community.

This means that these archives would have to be tied very closely to aggregate bibliographic files. The data must be closely coordinated to the whole set of research reports, with peripheral data built up over time to accompany this data base.

Building a data base and then turning it loose to be used by the practicing clinical anthropologist without such contextualization may be not only counter-productive but could be potentially dangerous for clinical populations.

Data Attrition

Finally, turning to immediate priorities, there is a pressing need to eliminate or at least retard the rate of data attrition. By this I have in mind the loss of valuable quantitative data which occurs at the end of every project. Even with the best financial support and hard working research assistants, a great deal of data often "migrates" to disk files, tapes or is left on cards and never gets examined. Moreover, attempts to retrieve these types of data after any appreciable length of time become exceedingly difficult if not impossible. Costs to the project or to the

328

individual researcher for time and effort to make these data available to the research community are not rewarded. Project termination or the physical relocation of the project or investigator usually means the data are practically irretrievable.

At present, there is no mechanism for encouraging researchers to maintain their processed data, and what is needed now is a program or committee to coordinate the information on data resources being developed and currently available and in the hands of clinical anthropologists. This should initially proceed in two areas. The first step should be to develop a nationwide or international network of investigators interested in clinical anthropology and inform them about the needs and potentials for developing a centralized data archive. Here the objectives would be limited to cataloging the available data sets and needs of potential users and letting those with key data sets know that something will be available in the near future for maintaining their data. In other words, this effort should encourage at least some investigators to maintain their data for a few months or years longer. The second step should be to survey existing data archiving systems and establish preliminary guidelines for establishing a small "pilot" library of data sets which will be easily accessible, along with a more extensive registry of existing data sets and on-going projects which can be incorporated into the library at a later date.

Only with improved data retention can a strong substantive base be built for research application and teaching in clinical anthropology. Reworking data sets provides basic insights into the strengths and weaknesses of investigations or administrative files. More than that, the key findngs of a study often become evident only when the study has been replicated at a later date, or at another site. This has been clearly evident in the studies my colleagues and I have been making of drinking patterns and alcoholism in Illinois since 1977. It has also been evident in the investigations of the epidemiology of hypertension in Mississippi since 1969.

Conclusions

The type of centralized data archive proposed here would have a number of potential benefits which are obvious. Clearly, this facility would become an invaluable resource for secondary analysis, and, in the long run, would represent tremendous savings, since the greatest value could be extracted from even relatively small scale studies. Centralizing information on issues relevant to clinical anthropologists would further reduce the possibility that efforts are duplicated and enhance possibilities for collaboration and exchange of ideas and results. Finally, from a more practical point of view, Lillian Pickup (this volume) has already referred to the potential impact such a data center might have in terms of lending support to isolated clinical anthropologists working with local groups to influence community, state or federal policies.

NOTE

1. For a number of years data clearinghouses and archive services have been available for individuals and institutions. For a brief survey of the types of materials and services included in these sources the reader is referred to the following:

Guide to Resources and Services 1978-1979/1979-1980 from Institute for Social Research (Center for Political Studies)

University of Michigan Box 1248 Ann Arbor, Michigan 48106

Institute of Behavioral Research Texas Christian University Fort Worth, Texas 76129

REFERENCES

Chilungu, S.
  1976   Issuses in the Ethics of Research Method: An Interpretation of the Anglo-American Perspective. Current Anthropology 17:457-481.

Moles, J.
  1977   Standardization and Measurement in Cultural Anthropology. Current Anthropology 18:239-258.

SOME SOCIAL PERSPECTIVES OF BUILDING A MATHEMATICAL MODEL OF SERVICE DELIVERY IN A PUBLIC DEPARTMENT

David Klass

Introduction

About 1978 our group began to attempt a mathematical model of some elements of the Department of Mental Health and Development Disabilities, State of Illinois. The purpose was to compress the complexity of the movements of patients, from hospitals to community and back, into a manageable form. What I want to speak of is the social process involved in that attempt and its implications for data in systems of this nature. The technical aspects of our work are omitted except insofar as they inform about the social process of mathematical modeling in a large, public bureaucracy.

One must first appreciate that the data of the Department, and any manipulations of that data, become public and are translated immediately into policy and into money. For example, the Illinois Bureau of the Budget asks the Department of Mental Health for data on a regular basis. Funding to individual hospitals or to community mental health centers, or to aftercare places, etc. is made on the basis of those data. As we shall see, these facts profoundly influence the data received and how the analyses can be made.

The Complexity of Simple Facts

When we started two years ago, the first step we took was to request from Springfield a tape which contained all of the patient movement information available to the Department since 1965. The tape contained the time of the admission of the patient to the hospital, his discharge date, his age, his sex, the number of his previous admissions and his diagnosis. This information should be factual and quite simple (leaving out diagnosis), and would seem on the surface to be reasonably trustworthy. For example, the admission of a patient to a certain hospital would seem to be a very, very simple, countable thing. After we compressed the data on the tape so they became more manageable, we began, on a regular basis, to present some of our findings to a group of administrators representing all facets of the Department. We presented different formats from this tape, taking for granted that the data were what they purported to be. One day a certain incident occurred which was quite enlightening.

On this occasion we presented to the group a simple manipulation which we had made--a comparison of the 29 in-patient institutions regarding the time patients had spent in the hospital and the time spent out of the hospital before returning--a very simple output. Basically, we made some correlations between the time the patient spends in the hospital and the time it takes the same patient to return from the community to be readmitted again. What became apparent is that there was one institution whose patients returned to the hospital very quickly. An administrator of this institution was within the group. He claimed he could explain this. He had been interpreting a discharge and an admission in a way different from most of the other administrators. A discharge, to him, counted when a patient left his hospital temporarily. He would count a discharge whenever a patient left the hospital, and a readmission when the patient came back. Sometimes the patient would be out temporarily for up to seven months. He pointed out correctly that we could not compare his data with the other hospitals´ because he was defining an admission and discharge differently from the other institutions.

This incident opened a whole new arena of thought. Perhaps this administrator had thought through the best way for him to define admissions and discharges. Defined in this way, the turnover of the hospital seems very high. But perhaps he did not appreciate that the calculated length of stay of patients in the community would be decreased as our analysis showed. Our guess was that he had guessed that funding decisions were made on the basis of hospital turnover--"How many admissions and discharges do you have a year"?

We looked over the rest of the categories being reported by hospitals. We began to see that what we thought were extraordinarily concrete and well defined elements contained a certain number of hidden degrees of freedom. If the administrator was a thinking man and trying to optimize his funding he could shift the definition of some elements to what he thought would be best for his institution. This was quite a revelation to us. When inquiring into the community agency data, it also became clear that counting clients was

334

different from one community agency to another. For example, if a whole family came in with a child as designated patient, some agencies would count the child as one client, and some agencies, in a large family, would count ten clients. Another variable index was case closing. There are some community agencies that will keep cases open for years after clients finish, while others close them very quickly.

The Influence of Analytical Levels

Another issue which arose was that, even given basic elemental units that we could all agree upon in definition, how would these elements be combined in our system? Would we allow complicated mathematical operations to create a picture of each of these institutions or would we allow only simple addition and subtraction, multiplication, etc., understandable to everyone?

The issues here become very complicated and would be complicated in any system where information that is collected becomes available to the Legislature or the Bureau of the Budget. Individuals at all levels of the Department, whether they may be high level managers or individuals in community mental health centers, are acutely aware that the modelling process involves a collapsing of their whole service delivery operation into some combination of a few different elements to be shown to people responsible for funding decisions. In addition, once one has decided how to manipulate the data elements for any part of the system of service delivery, the outcome in each instance is an index of operation that remains fairly standard over time, i.e., a reification occurs. Thus agencies and institutions come to understand that an important aspect of the public peception of their operations is being determined by the mathematical operations in the model. So, not only are there "politics" in the definition of elements for the system, but there are also politics in the mathematical operations among those elements which would form the shape of each section of the Department as depicted in the model.

How then should one proceed in a mathematical modelling operation? We have tentatively agreed on the following: at least three somewhat independent elements of patient movement or cost data will be carefully defined for each aspect of the Department's operation. These will be combined in a simple arithmetic manner

335

for each section to form a "picture" of that particular section to be used for funding purposes. Three elements are used because with at least that many independent variables it becomes theoretically difficult for anyone to predict how alterations in one or another element could affect the picture of that section relative to the other sections in the system.

Summary

In sum, then, the process of creating a model for a public bureaucracy cannot escape involvement with the immediate political implications of any depiction of the bureaucracy. Administrators within such public sectors have a full appreciation of how the data issuing from their sector and any operations on that data influence funding decisions. Consequently, definitions are modified so far as possible to favor their sector's presentation. At higher levels of administration the need is for uniformity of definition so as to guide funding polices. Clearly the end results are compromised to varying degrees. These facts, which are generally true for data affecting public policy, have complex effects for researchers at clinical and institutional levels, effects which can be evaluated and offset only by the researcher's knowledge of the "social" as well as factual realities under consideration.

DATA ARCHIVES: A MODEL

S. B. Sells

Introduction

Given the importance of data sets in the development of knowledge within the social sciences and health related disciplines it is critical that a system be devised to handle this information. The Drug Abuse Epidemiology Data Center (DAEDAC) at Texas Christian University is a possible model which could be used for such a system. DAEDAC is a computerized, content-addressable literature and original data set archive in the field of drug abuse which provides information and research services and original data sets for secondary analysis and reseach to the National Institute on Drug Abuse and to the professional and scientific community interested in this area. It is an expensive project, now budgeted at around $700,000 per year, but represents a unique compendium of United States and international literature and data on the epidemiological and social science aspects of drug abuse (Texas Christian University Institute of Behavioral Research 1978; U. S. National Institute on Drug Abuse 1979).

DAEDAC represents an instrumentality to meet a need identified by two individuals working in the field. The first is the author, who wrote the initial proposal and has functioned as Principal Investigator of the project since its inception in 1973-1974. The other is Professor John C. Ball of the Department of Psychiatry (Sociology Division) of Temple University, who was a Federal official in the Special Action Office for Drug Abuse Prevention at that time, and was instrumental in the award of the initial grant. The project has been supported subsequently by the National Institute on Drug Abuse (NIDA), as a grant and more recently as a contract.

Documentation Problems in the Drug Abuse Field

John Ball and I were both concerned about a set of problems that we had perceived independently in the drug abuse field, and we proposed DAEDAC as a promising solution. The problems that we identified were of two kinds. The first problem relates to the fact that as a discipline, drug abuse is relatively new and amorphous. Journals dedicated to drug abuse reseach are few and many were only recently founded. The literature is scattered among journals in many fields--psychiatry, psychology, sociology, medicine, public health, and others. In the early to mid-1970's, also, there appeared to be a substantial number of federally supported studies for which reports were duplicated in relatively small numbers. We were concerned about the preservation, distribution, and integration of the literature, and also about the preservation of original data both as a scientific responsibility and also to enable further, secondary, research. In numerous cases it appeared that existing data sets could be utilized to investigate significant questions other than those addressed by the original authors who generated the data.

Thus, our first goal was to preserve research data, to obtain copies of hard-to-obtain reports and publications, and to codify and classify the essential information in easily retrievable form. In the course of studying the distribution of the published literature last year, I came to the conclusion that slightly over half (56%) of the drug abuse literature is published in the English language in the United States, about 20 percent in English in countries other than the United States, and 24 percent in languages other than English, including publications in more than a dozen other languages, in books and scores of journals. DAEDAC was limited initially to publications based on the United States. The scope was later extended to North America and recently, in its seventh year, DAEDAC was authorized to expand its holdings to full international scope. However, progress in acquiring much of the foreign language material has been limited by available funds.

The second type of problem reflects the opportunity to exploit new research possibilities with archival data as a result of technological advances associated with computers. With a common taxonomy by which all files in the computer are coded, it is possible to address a variety of important research problems in which 1. major parameters reported in individual studies are treated as data points in a population of studies on selected topics, and 2. multiple data sets, varying over time, population samples, or other variables are combined or compared, depending on the purpose of the research. Our experience with this type of meta-analytic research is still modest, but the indications are that this is a major new frontier for the exploitation of "data banks," the limits of which may not yet be realized.

The initial funding for DAEDAC was based principally on the first type of problem--preservation, codification, retrieval, and integration. Most of the services to NIDA staff members, state and local drug abuse administrators, research workers, and other users, have involved bibliographies, reviews of literature, special purpose analyses of selected data sets for informational purposes, and provision of selected data sets for secondary research. I have no doubt that future emphasis will also be focused on analytic strategies applied to the codified holdings of the literature and original data files.

Scope of the DAEDAC Files

With regard to the scope of the files, decisions were required at the outset in relation to the following issues: 1. languages and countries to be covered, 2. time period covered, 3. drugs covered, 4. topics to be included or specifically excluded, and 5. types of information to be included. There were additional decisions concerning policies that I will discuss later, but let me comment on these first.

Languages

Our position has always been that science and scholarship have no national boundaries. In addition, we do not subscribe to the position that if any material is worthwhile it will be available in English. However, it is a fact that cultural factors in the United States give priority to studies of United States drug use and also that the cost of acquiring and translating foreign studies is a serious consideration. For practical reasons, DAEDAC gave priority initiallly to United States literature and data and moved gradually to international coverage.

Time Period

Although drug misuse has been a problem as long as Homo sapiens has been around, we set 1960 as an arbitrary boundary for literature and data set search. This date reflects the beginning of the period defined by an upsurge in drug use in the United States, and, more particularly, in the drug research literature.

This is not an impermeable boundary, however, and our staff have been encouraged to use judgment in accessing noteworthy earlier material.

Drugs Covered

Two particular exclusions have been made, mainly to avoid duplication of other large-scale archival efforts. These are alcohol and tobacco, which are included, however, when reported in association with data on other drugs. In the case of alcohol, DAEDAC maintains a cordial relation with the Center for Alcohol Studies at Rutgers University. Initially, DAEDAC was limited to studies and data on illicit drugs, which permitted a more focused initial effort. More recently, however, the scope of the project has been extended to include licit drugs, sold over the counter and by prescription.

Topics Included

At the outset, we made a decision to restrict initial acquisitions to areas of primary importance, in order to enable the rapid development of a usable data base and to expand gradually as the earlier designated topical areas were reasonably represented in the files. In accord with this principle, DAEDAC focused initially on studies and data in the areas of incidence, prevalence, morbidity and mortality. Studies related to treatment and treatment effectiveness were among the first that were added, and, eventually, the scope was extended to virtually all aspects of medical and social science aspects of drug use, except pharmacology and toxicology, which have been specifically excluded.

Information Included and Excluded

In view of the focus on empirical-research data, we have made special provision in the DAEDAC literature file for the acquisition, coding, and retrieval of theoretical and review papers; commentary papers are generally listed in the classified bibiliography. It is recognized that some of the most important literature is included in the theoretical and review categories, and these have been coded and abstracted as far as possible. Empirical research, which is of primary concern in the literature file, is encoded in great detail, including statistical tables and relevant data that can be retrieved. Details concerning the taxonomic scheme followed and the coding manual are presented in the informational brochure referred to earlier.

Policies Concerning DAEDAC

Although not entirely germane to the structure of the archive, we adopted several policies concerning DAEDAC early on, following the strong recommendations of our excellent advisory committee, that have proven to be wise and constructive. These involve restrictions on use of the files, confidentiality of data, and ownership of data and protection of rights of contributors of data sets. With respect to the use of files, even though the documents expressing goals mentioned services to the professional and scientific community, it was decided to remove all restrictions and to provide information and services including copies of data sets, at marginal cost, to any and all persons who requested them and agreed to the conditions of use. This relieved the DAEDAC staff of the burdens of approving the qualifications of requesters and of vulnerability to charges of elitism or discrimination. There have been no instances of problems or unpleasantness as a result.

Confidentiality of data has been another touchy issue, surrounded by legal and regulatory restrictions. In this regard, two important decisions were made. First, we adopted a rigid rule that all data sets accepted by DAEDAC must be stripped of all identification data concerning individual subjects (patients, clients, prisoners, etc.) prior to delivery to DAEDAC. This has been accomplished without difficulty, usually by substituting random or sequential case numbers for names, addresses, social security numbers, and the like. Stripped of this information, most files became anonymous and the confidentiality of individually identified information was assured. Project funds were frequently used to cover the expense of such adjustments.

However, the files included data sets on general population samples and other special samples (e. g., military units) not identified as deviant, as well as treatment, criminal justice, and other deviant samples. It was felt that for these, admissions of use of illicit drugs on survey forms might require further protection against identification by profiles of other data, such as school, class, family composition, and the like. To cover this eventuality, a second rule was adopted that provided for restriction of such files, upon the request of the contributor and with the mutual agreement of the DAEDAC staff. Under this rule, it has been possible to make selected files available to investigators for secondary research, subject to the restriction that computations and analysis of data are performed by the DAEDAC staff and that the original data are not released.

The third major policy involves ownership of data and protection of the rights of contributors of data sets. The policy adopted was 1. that every data set remains the property of the contributor and can be withdrawn at any time, and 2. that users of data sets provided by DAEDAC are required to sign agreements to provide copies of papers based on them to the contributors (original authors or owners) prior to publication. The latter provision was adopted so that, in the event of reanalysis of a data set that led to conflicting results or conclusions, the original author might have an opportunity to reply. So far as I know, no cases of this type have arisen in which reply was required. These conditions have been publicized and contributors of data have been requested to sign letters of understanding concerning them at the time of data transfer. It is noteworthy that no contributor has ever raised any questions concerning use of data provided and no files have ever been withdrawn by contributors.

Organization and Structure of DAEDAC Files

DAEDAC includes two separate files, the first called the Aggregate (Literature) File, and the other, the Original Data File. For purposes of classification of reports and of original data, a common taxonomic system is employed. Each of these files is represented organizationally as a separate unit, with a supervisor and staff. The Aggregate File Unit staff includes abstractors and coders who process reports and other documents acquired for entry into the file and maintain a bibliography subfile as well as the Aggregate Data File. All three files (bibliography, aggregate-literature, and original data files) are coded by the same staff, thereby assuring greater consistency in the coding operation. The Original Data File Unit is now responsible for acquisition of data files (including negotiations with contributors), for "cleaning" of data files received (including frequency distributions on item responses or entries and tabulation of missing data), and obtaining complete documentation for each file (including copies of instruments, coding guides, and publications based on the data).

The DAEDAC organization, under Dr. Laverne Knezek, the Associate Director, also includes two librarians, one for United States literature and one for foreign literature; translators, information specialists, a systems analyst-programmer, and several analyst retrieval specialists. These specialists perform analytic and retrieval services for users of the archive, who are charged only for the marginal costs of the services performed, as well as for the Faculty-Staff Review Review Committee. The librarians are in charge of the acquisition of literature. They utilize extensive bibliographic sources, mostly computerized, to search for relevant material and prepare copies for review by the Faculty-Staff Committee. Items acquired by the librarians are included initially in the Bibliography Subfile, but subsequent disposition (full coding, classification as theoretical or commentary, with abstract or summary, or rejection as not relevant or of unacceptable quality) is the responsibility of the Review Committee, which is composed of senior members of the IBR drug research staff, several of them faculty members, and analysts assigned full-time to DAEDAC.

The Bibliograpy File, which is updated periodically, is classified, as shown in the Information Brochure, and is used also as a catalogue of the holdings of the Aggregate File. The Original Data File Unit also produces a catalogue of holdings, which includes extensive detail concerning all data sets, to aid prospective users in understanding contents and potential uses for informational and research analysis.

With regard to coding and retrieval of the literature, DAEDAC employs an alpha-numeric system that is utilized most efficiently by the staff (as opposed to uninstructed users). It is not an on-line system. It has been our position that this enables careful attention to definitions of terms and concepts and has the advantages of precision of classification and efficiency in the utilization of computer facilities. It does not provide instant output, as is claimed by on-line services, such as those that utilize key-word systems for coding and retrieval. In our opinion, the advantages of instant output must be weighed against the problems of cost and accuracy mentioned above. It is believed that most inquiries to DAEDAC are in a category of time constraint that would not be disadvantageous to the user in view of the requirement to wait for mail response, which is usually within a few days. In the rare case that is urgent, response by telephone or teletype is still available.

The DAEDAC services to users include bibliographic searches on selected topics, annotated bibliographies including tabular data and abstracts-summaries, critical reviews, provision of hard copies of publications and of instruments on file, provision of data sets, and extensive data analytic and research services requested by users. In the last-named case, the expertise of the entire IBR staff and the programming capability of the IBR research group are on call to support DAEDAC and its users.

Problems of Dissemination

In this section, I wish to discuss dissemination of information concerning the archive in order to bring it to the attention of prospective users, staffing, strategies for building the holdings, coding strategies, and some thoughts about types of material that should be included.

Promotion of the Archive

We regard the visibility of the archive as a matter of major importance, since an archive, like a library or museum, that is not utilized productively is difficult to justify. Under grant funding, DAEDAC became well known to almost every class of user over its first four years of existence. Initially there were notices in journals, descriptive articles, seminars and colloquia, and mentions in countless newsletters, catalogues, proceedings, and other informational vehicles. During the last two years of grant funding, DAEDAC published its own newsletter, the DAEDAC Database, which was mailed to an original list compiled by the staff and subsequently extended, in response to requests, to a list of over 5,500 subscribers. There was no charge for the Database, but its value can readily be documented in terms of data sets contributed and requests for all types of services.

The Database was discontinued in favor of a NIDA-distributed activities report when the funding was changed from grant support to contract. This was required under a Federal law that limits printing under Federal contracts. At the same time, the contract greatly increased services to NIDA and thus increased the usefulness of DAEDAC to officials responsible for the administration of the drug-abuse program at the Federal level. Under the present arrangement there appears to be a need for improved communication with the general community outside of NIDA both to extend awareness of DAEDAC services to all potential users and to reach potential contributors of data sets.

Staffing

With regard to staffing, the requirements for a computerized archive in a specialized field such as drug abuse are extensive and highly demanding. The most important requirements are both motivational and technical. On the motivational side, the service aspect is supreme. Every member of the staff must understand that the archive was created to facilitate research and development of knowledge concerning drug abuse, and must have a commitment to serve the interests of its users.

The technical requirements placed upon the staff include an understanding of computer operations and data base management, as well as the substantive aspects of the complex fields involved in drug abuse, which include psychology, sociology, criminology, public health, anthropology, economics-econometrics, psychiatry, and related disciplines. In DAEDAC we have been extremely fortunate in attracting a highly competent and service-oriented staff, including librarians with training in computer and data base operations and in social sciences, and analysts with a similar mix in their graduate education. Most of them have learned the technical aspects of archiving the drug abuse literature on the job, under the guidance of faculty members who work in and with DAEDAC, and professional staff members who head the various units. Our experience has indicated that, at least in the drug abuse area, this is the optimal approach.

Building the DAEDAC Holdings

During the earlier years of its existence DAEDAC was preoccupied principally with acquisition, coding, and processing of its holdings, in a effort to begin to offer services as rapidly as possible. To accomplish this, we made a policy decision to limit the topics covered in the literature, until a respectable collection was on hand, to the highest priority topics and then gradually to expand. The result has been that the literature coverage, in relation to the expanded scope, has been, and will continue for some time to be, uneven. Only recently, the scope was extended from United States literature to North American and then to international, and over-the-counter and prescription drugs were also added. These additions required initiation of retrospective searches as well as expansion of current monitoring, and also of a new translation capability to cope with foreign language literature.

The only alternative to the complexities implied in the growth process described above is to bring a collection to full maturity before offering any services. It is possible that this is actually done by commercial companies that offer "data banks" on a subscription basis, but it is unlikely that such a policy would be countenanced by a Federal sponsor. Furthermore, apart from the inconvenience of a spotty file, resulting from the arrangements for search (and also the resources available for search and in-processing), it is questionable whether there are good reasons to delay the availability of the files to serious users.

Coding Strategies

The coding manual of a literature archive is the key to what can be retrieved from it. In DAEDAC, although the general structure of the manual existed, based on the taxonomy developed early in the program, details were added as the scope of coverage grew. For example, various drug categories that were not covered earlier were added in later years. These additions were made over and above the addition of new drugs, in categories already covered, that had not been reported previously.

The adequacy of a coding strategy can best be evaluated by experience in retrieval. Obviously, requests that cannot be met because the information required was not coded furnish a basis for considering additional codes. At the same time, detail that is never called for may represent significant waste of staff time and facilities. Experience of both types can be captured and evaluated in periodic review of the system. In DAEDAC we have recently eliminated a level of detail in coding that was included originally on the basis of strong recommendations by expert advisers. We have also learned that it is not possible to anticipate every type of informational need and that decisions concerning coding strategy require practical wisdom and careful study and deliberation.

346

Identification of Suitable Material

Every archivist at some point must decide whether to limit his of her collection to certain categories of literature (and also data sets). In DAEDAC we have made every effort to be flexible and at the same time to exercise wisdom. I believe that this has worked out well, but it is difficult to be objective about one's own work. For the literature file, our search has been based mainly on the published literature (registered, but not always refereed journals, monograph series, books, and official reports in the serial literature). For the original data file, we have primarily sought data sets that were the basis of such publications, and for which adequate documentation was available. In addition, we have attempted, with some success to obtain record files from institutions (suitably edited to protect confidentiality), that offered research opportunity regardless of whether they had been analyzed and resulted in publications.

However, these general guidelines have not been followed rigidly. We have included some unpublished reports and have varied standards somewhat in the selection of material. A short time after initiation of DAEDAC, the staff concluded that some quality control was desirable, and even with very forgiving standards, the Review Committee finds it necessary to reject some material. Indeed, the current procedure, reflecting the fact that the budget does not permit us to keep up with the flow of world drug literature, has led to some priority decisions, judgments based on quality and importance in the consideration of new material. At the same time, it should be noted that standards must be flexible when applied to different subareas of a broad discipline, to different time periods and to work emanating from different countries and different parts of the world. It is not possible to write specific guidelines to be followed. The only sound alternative, which we follow at DAEDAC, involves continuing staff review and consultation. One must be willing to make changes, but not too frequently and always based on sound rationale.

Conclusions

Based on the DAEDAC model and the DAEDAC experience, I have some advice to those who are considering a data system for clinical anthropology. The following suggestions are made tentatively and with

347

appreciation of the fact that my knowledge of the field and its needs is very limited. First, it would seem wise to explore existing data bases (which appear to be available in great profusion when one initiates a search of commercially offered as well as governmentally supported sources) before undertaking the arduous task of creating a new one. I assume that certain needs may be met by DAEDAC and other archives, at Rutgers, Michigan, and Yale Universities, to mention only a few that are well-known. Once these are identified and evaluated for present and anticipated future purposes, it may be possible to plan both to fill significant gaps and to adopt a modus operandi for utilization of existing sources. Since there will necessarily be considerable lead time before a new anthropology archive might be operational, it may be desirable to encourage prospective contributors of data sets to deposit their data with one of the existing archives. Transfer to a new archive could be accomplished whenever it seems appropriate.

This leads to my second suggestion, which is to spend much time in planning. I am convinced that creative and patient planning, which should include visits to existing archives at an appropriate point, after acceptable decisions concerning the scope of the archive have been decided upon, would not only save time in the long run, but also considerable unproductive effort and expense. To the extent that critical decisions concerning the scope, content, format, and procedures of a projected data base (or bases) are made in advance, the success of the project would be enhanced.

When examining existing data bases, it is important to study their descriptive literature carefully, with particular attention to content and services provided, including costs. My experience is that descriptive titles, for archives as well as other types of material, may frequently be misleading and that the significant information may be disclosed only in the text of the brochures that are usually available.

Finally, I urge consideration of the importance of a literature file along with an original data file. The rationale for this, including the existing prospects for meta-analyses based on samples of published studies, has been presented earlier. The literature file should no longer be considered as a source only of bibliographies and topical reviews, but also for serious secondary research in which the

results of many studies become data points for
integrative analysis.

REFERENCES

Texas Christian University Institute of
Behavioral Research
    1978   Annual Report.

U.S. National Institute on Drug Abuse
    1979   Drug Abuse Epidemiology Data Center (DAEDAC):
            General Information.

COMPUTER-BASED COMMUNICATION: A NEW TOOL FOR
SCIENTIFIC INTERACTION[1]

Allan H. Levy

Computer-Based Communication and Clinical Anthropology

In the development of a complex new area, such as the application of anthropology and other social sciences to clinical and public health problems, it is extremely important to take a mid- to long-range perspective. At a minimum, such a process will take five to ten years.

Given such a time framework, the choice of strategies for data accumulation, management and retrieval must consider not merely the conditions now present in a nascent field but the proper tools for the effective handling of a rapidly growing body of materials in years to come. Unquestionably, computers will be the core of any effective future system; their use would be enhanced by the use of communication techniques of great promise that are already being tried, for example, at the Stanford University Medical School.

In the first ten years of their development, computers were primarily conceived of as instruments of immense speed and utility for numerical computations. In the next 20 years, our understanding of their potential extended: they came to be considered as instruments for the storage and retrieval of information, as storehouses of knowledge, and as tools for the manipulation and application of such knowledge. Within the last decade, we have continued to enlarge our understanding of the potential of computers. We now commonly use them as controllers of instruments; to guide airplanes, to switch power circuits, and to diagnose the malfunctions of both errant automobiles and infirm humans.

One new potential is presently emerging. This new use may have even more profound effects on our society than any of the uses with which we are familiar. The new use may eventually allow the symbiotic interaction of computers and humans in joint activities, with man and machine substituting as surrogates for each other in almost imperceptible role shifts. This new use is computer-based communication (CBC). Although it is in

351

the early formative stages, even now there is sufficient indication of its potential for altering societal interactions. Such a formidable potential mandates careful study. We should examine for its strengths, as well as for the problems that it may cause.

What is computer based communication? Fundamentally, it is the use of information processing devices intertwined with human communicators as part of a communication network. CBC involves basically simple techniques: in essence, individuals wishing to communicate with others write messages into a computer terminal. The computer stores them, notifies the intended recipient or group that a message is ready. In turn the receiver(s) will read the message, respond, forward comments to others, and thereby initiate a fresh cycle of information transimission.

Message-Mode Computer Based Communication

Computer based communication has two distinct modes of operation, message mode and conference mode. Message mode is synonymous with electronic mail, and comes closest to our present experience with communication systems. Functionally, it is a sophisticated telegraph/telephone system, embodying the most useful features of each, as well as several unique characteristics made possible by the incorporation of an information processor in the communication pathway. The advantages are:

1. Promptness: Irrespective of the distance the message must be transmitted, it will be received immediately.

2. No unnecessary interruption of normal activity: The individual receiving the message will be informed of its arrival, but does not have to immediately divert attention from current activities. Unlike a telephone call, to which the user must immediately divert all of his attention--not to do so is a prerogative of only the very arrogant or the very powerful--a computer message does not demand an immediate interruption.

3. Immediate availability: This is the converse of non-interruptibility. If a message is waiting for you, it may be read whenever you are ready; you do not have to wait for the sender to call back.

4. Permanence: The communications are machine represented, and hence may be stored permanently at the discretion of either the sender or any of the recipients.

5. Alternate outputs: The machine representation can be transferred into another form, typically printed text, suitable for permanent, nonelectronic storage and viewing.

6. Improved structure in the communication: Because the communication must be reduced to written form before transmission, those habits which govern other forms of written communication apply. In composing the message, the author will adopt some or all of the elements of written language.

Needless to say, this attribute can also properly be considered a disadvantage of computer based communication. Numerous individuals "choke up" when they are required to express even simple thoughts in writing. However, it has been our experience to date, that most individuals easily adapt to the written form of computer based communications; freed from the anxiety that their communication will be judged by "reviewers" but yet with a convenient alternative to the spoken word, their inhibitions in regard to forming the written word diminish. (It should be noted that such release of restraint does not increase the enduring literary merit of the message.)

7. Ready transferability: A message on a computer system can be sent to another recipient or group of recipients without mechanical retranscription or time delays.

8. Privacy: This is useful to recognize as a requirement as well as a potential problem. It can be considered as an asset because in any well constructed electronic mail system, careful and vigorous attention is given to ensuring the privacy of all communications. If this is not done effectively, then electronic communication will be a social evil, not a useful tool.

Computer-Based Conferencing

In the preceding section, we discussed the use of a computer based system as an enhanced message system. The real potentials of CBC do not become apparent until we consider its use as a facilitator of an electronic

conference. We should first define a conference.
Normally, a group of individuals come together at one
place, to share information and ideas between them.
Frequently they present formal short papers; other
formats are now increasingly prevalent, including
panels, poster sessions, and teaching workshops. Very
often, crowded facilities, limited time, and
constrained formats substantially reduce the value of
the conference to the participants. The limitations of
the "real" conference are well known; it is
conventional wisdom that the greatest value of a
conference is in its professionally oriented
sociability and the informal exchange of ideas.
However, the cost of this is considerable, not only in
economic terms, but also in the time of the
participants as well.

Although the technical limits of computer based
conferencing presently preclude its substitution for
the informal and social aspects of the conventional
conference, nearly all of the other defined aspects can
be approached either as well or better by electronic
means.

In a computer conference,[2] a group of individuals
(participants) agree to share information on a topic or
group of topics. Often, they plan that the product of
their conference will be a report--with a defined
beginning and end--to be published in conventional form
and distributed to others outside of the conference.
Alternately, the conference may be an ongoing
electronic exchange, in which new information is added,
comments appended, and an continuing knowledge base
established and expanded.

The techniques by which a conference operates can
be briefly summarized. A conference administrator is
appointed or selected; this individual has the
responsibility to arrange access for the individuals in
the group, provide for their training in the use of the
system, and function as a general director of the
group. Participants in the conference are drawn from
experts or others who are considered appropriate
contributors. Participants are expected to provide
information to the conference and to comment on the
contributions of others. Members of the conference (as
participants are often called) may be _full_ members; as
such they may read material contributed by others,
write texts relating to their assignments, and comment
on the material contributed by others. Some members
may be allowed to join the conference on a _limited_

basis, with access to only certain of the conference material.

A key individual is the conference coordinator. Ordinarily, a subject expert himself in the field, this individual assumes the responsibility of pointing out to other members intellectual areas of unattended concerns or unresolved considerations. The coordinator can arrange for conference members to vote on issues about which there is contention that can not be resolved by the ordinary cycles of discussion and comments. The coordinator also provides members with appropriate reminders about deadlines, and in general acts as scientist-communicator in ensuring that the conference fulfills its aims.

Finally, there is the technical consultant. This individual's contributions can not in any way be underestimated. The consultant answers the innummerable programming and system-related questions associated with the particular conferencing system in use. Each system is different and each has its own technical vagaries, and even an occasional "bug."

The Role of the Computer in Computer Based Conferencing

The computer serves to store information, both text and comments on the text. This is its most obvious function. It also acts to promptly inform conference participants as to the status of the conference as a whole. Thus one of the principal roles of the computer is handlng much of the bookkeeping that in a conventional report is associated with the editorial assistant. The computer will keep a set of markers for each participant, including notations as to number of items in the conference text, when they were entered, and which ones have not yet been seen by each participant.

In addition, the computer will have word-processing capabilities so that authors can re-organize and change their materials--which at first are actually the authors' early drafts--without the need for physicaly reentering the words into the machine.

The conference is stored in a computer file that has sometimes been termed a "notebook." There can be one or more notebooks for a conference, depending on the complexity of the topic to be considered. Each notebook consists of several "pages"; in this usage the page is not a physical one, but is conceptually closer to a chapter in a conventional book.

The notebook-comment mechanism is often supplemented by messaging between individual participants or small conference sub-groups. Sections of a proposed report can be forwarded to others not full participants in the conference for their input on a section for which they have special expertise.

A Prototype System--
The Electronic Information Exchange System

Perhaps the most highly developed computer conferencing system presently in operation in the United States is the Electronic Information Exchange System (EIES) operated at the New Jersey Institute of Technology by Professor Murray Turoff and his associates (Hiltz and Turoff 1978). This program runs off of a medium-sized minicomputer, and has been specially developed with the design goals of an effective computer conferencing system in mind. A whole variety of different conferences are underway on EIES. Its initial experiences are invaluable in pointing out the advantages and needs for further developments in the field of computer based communication. Although other systems include electronic messaging, the EIES system has been specifically planned to test and evaluate computer conferencing in the scientific community.

Passive Versus Active Computer Based Communication

The computer in the present state of most implementations acts as a passive partner. It does not add to the dialogue. It may "time-stamp" the message, keep track of when it was read by the intended recipient, inform the sender that the message has or has not been received. But it does not add to the substance of the communication. It does not add to the quality of the colloquy. Is not some further substantive intellectual contribution by the computer a feasible step? Already computers are the repositories of large stores of information in the form of data bases. Computer scientists are now working toward extending the scope of data bases to what are termed "knowledge bases." These are collections of machine based information which not only contain the raw data elements, but, in addition, contain information which

356

expresses the relationship between the data items. Problem solving programs exist which use these knowledge bases to provide logical and understandable solutions to problems difficult to resolve adequately by human cognition. A number of computer techniques have characteristics of plausible reasoning: they go through computational procedures that in their end result appear to mimic the skill of the human problem-solver.

These techniques are collectively embraced by the term "artificial intelligence." Such programs not only arrive at solutions to problems, but, equally important, the programs have the capacity to explain to a human observer how they arrived at the solution, which particular logical path they pursued to come to the end result. This ability to explain their reasoning process in a manner understandable to humans is an important reason why artificial intelligence techniques may be symbiotic--although by no means parallel-to human intelligence.

Presently, such artificial intelligence programs are not integrated into computer based communication systems. However, it is not too difficult to envision them linked in to a human-computer-human communication network.

There are many serious technical impediments to such active computer based communication. Although it is conceptually straightforward to envision the computer and its associated knowledge bases as a participant with humans in a problem solving colloquy, the actual implementation of an environment suitable for such effective interchange is not a simple task. The problems reside principally in the great flexibility and substantial imprecision of our natural language. This is in contrast to the requirements for strict precision and rigid syntax of present computer languages. Although programs that allow humans to converse with computers (using the typewriter, not the voice) have been the object of large amounts of research, in terms of both time and money, the results to date have been limited. Programs that seem to allow a natural language conversation do so in only a very limited range of discourse. In order to permit the computer to become a partner in the dialogue, substantially greater flexibility will have to be developed in natural language processing to enable the human partners in the conversation to usefully interrogate the computer and its associated data bases.

Steps Toward Active Computer Based Communication

As an initial step in developing a computer based communication system that is more than simply passive, we can allow users of computer based communication networks the opportunity to more easily access other networks. For example, in the field of medicine, a project at Stanford University (Medical Experiment-Artificial Intelligence in Medicine) (SUMEX) currently allows many workers on that system access to each other's problem solving programs, and also provides them with electronic messaging capabilities. Participants in the network have stated that the easy communication between individuals engaged in related work that the system allows has had a substantial facilitating effect. Even this first stage of computer communication has thus already given every indication of a potentiating effect on the scientific process.

The participants in this network are drawn from active scientific researchers in a specific and limited field. A logical extension of this first step might be to allow users of other networks to access both each and other problem solving networks, like SUMEX. When a scientist needs either the computational, problem solving, or stored informational resources of another computer, access should be easily available. A network of networks would be a useful first step.

The Computer as an Active Partner
in Scientific Colloquy

A further step would be for the computer and its associated knowledge bases to spontaneously generate solutions to problems or add to the conference report when it was able to do so. We are a long way from reaching that stage, but, as technically difficult as it may be, it is simply a logical extension of where we are now heading.

This step would have profound social implications; some of these are apparent at first thought, although how people would react to them is not so easily predictable. How would people react to sharing their creative activities with machines? What about the trade-off between privacy and efficiency? What about the possible feeling of being dehumanized by becoming a part of a machine-based thought system? These are all problems which our society will soon have to face. The techniques for computer based communication are all present. The first phase--passive computer communication--has already begun. The second phase will be thrust upon us. How we manage it, how we mold ourselves and our machines to a human-oriented partnership will be one of the challenges of the nineties.

Summary

Computer based communication is a newly emerging tool for improving the quality and enhancing the ease, accuracy, and utility of communication between individuals.

It is of probable importance as a tool in data management or the clinical application of the social sciences in the mid-range to long-range future. The computer acts as both a temporary storage point and as a dispatcher for messages between individuals or groups of individuals. Speed, permanence, structure, and non-interuptibility are all advantages of electronic messaging. The structure that written, as opposed to oral, communication both demands and imposes provides increased value to the communication. Computer based communication may be used for simple electronic mail, where one individual dispatches messages to either a single recipient or group of recipients. A more advanced use involves the conducting of a conference via computer. In this application, several individuals approach a common task by originating, commenting on and revising textual material directed toward a common purpose or solving a problem.

Computer based communication is presently an activity in which the computer plays primarily a clerical role in assisting human communicators. This paper discusses briefly a future potential which will see the computer playing an active role in the colloquy, providing facts, and using techniques of artificial intelligence and machine based inference to contribute to the conversation.

NOTES

1. Supported by a grant from the National Library of Medicine, National Institute of Health, DHHR, Bethesda, MD.

2. Many of the terms and concepts relating to computer conferencing have been drawn from the work of Hiltz and Turoff (1978). Their pioneering efforts in this field are at its foundation and are fundamental contributions to this field.

REFERENCE

Hiltz, Starr Roxanne and Murrary Turoff
   1978   The Network Nation. Human Communication via Computer. Reading, MA: Addison-Wesley Publishing Company.

DOCUMENTATION AND DATA MANAGEMENT:
CRITERIA FOR THE FUTURE

Barton M. Clark

The effective management of information can contribute significantly to the development of both theory and practice for anthropological approaches to health related issues. The previous papers in this section have addressed several methods for dealing with key information issues. To bring these ideas together into an effective information system it will be essential to formulate a documentation and data management plan which will provide solutions for immediate goals as well as long range ones.

The critical first step in designing an information system is to define the information paradigm of the subject. Schematically, each such paradigm might be viewed as a circle (see Figure 1).

Each paradigm will have its own system of formal and informal dissemination. Formal information systems include journal and monograph publications as well as the abstracting and indexing tools designed to retrieve the information from published sources. Interpersonal networks and conferences represent the most common types of informal information systems. Because of the common delays of publication, informal systems are often crucial to the dissemination of information.

As interdisciplinary approaches to the study of selected research and clinical problems became more common, new paradigms will be created by the overlapping of two or more subjects. Such is the case of anthropological approaches to the health sciences (see Figure 2).

Although the hachured area in Figure 2 accurately shows the domain in which one would retrieve all of the appropriate information on anthropological approaches to the health sciences, it does not reveal several critical factors relating to information systems.

First, user needs will differ from discipline to discipline: quite often in applied fields the importance of information delivery takes precedence over document delivery.

Figure 1. Information Paradigms: Isolated Fields

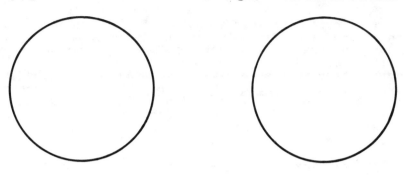

Figure 2. Information Paradigm for Anthropological
Approaches to the Health Sciences

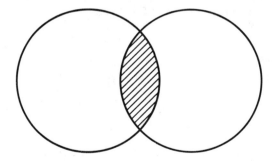

The hachured area represents Anthropological
Approaches to the Heath Sciences

Second, information handling is currently more sophisticated in some displines than in others. Online bibliographic systems such as The National Library of Medicine´s MEDLINE provide the health sciences with a level of bibliographic access which is not availiable in anthropology.

Having defined the parameters of the information system it will be imperative to ascertain those existing resources which will contribute to its activation. Identifying resources within the field will include determining primary data sources such as monographs, journals, and data sets. Useful secondary sources including indexes, abstracts, and . online bibliographic systems are particularly important to identify since the retrieval of pertinent documents can prove difficult in a cross-disciplinary subject area. Clearinghouses, research institutes, and government agencies which produce and/or disseminate relevant information are also important information nodes. The Appendix to this volume provides a preliminary assessment of resources for Anthropological Approaches to Health Sciences.

All of these steps, of course, merely identify what already exists. And though it is important to do so, it must be remembered that many of the retrieval resources were designed for either anthropology or the health sciences, and were not designed to retrieve information relating specifically to anthropological applications in the health sciences. It is, therefore, necessary, as the next step, to develop methods and criteria to meet the special information needs of this emerging field.

Short range strategies which generate specific ways of managing information unique to the interface between anthropology and the health sciences must examine approaches to the appropriate management of bibliographic, quantitative, and textual data. Accessing information will be greatly enhanced by the development of special bibliographies for researchers and practitioners. These bibliographies could be used at a later time to serve as the core of an automated bibliographic system with an extensive thesaurus, if so desired.

Because of the unsystematic development of quantitative data sets in the social sciences, it will be necessary to identify the availability of data sets which are germane to the problems of the anthropology/health science interface. It will also be necessary to establish standards of quality control for data sets to allow for a reasonable degree of compatibility between data generated from different data sets (see Thompson's and Klass' papers on this problem, this volume). Moreover, policies need to be developed to guarantee that data sets which become available for general use respect the confidentiality of informants in uniform ways.

Document or textual resource management must initially be limited to identifying libraries and other resource centers where materials are kept to insure access to these materials. Effective use of these materials would be made through the development of an information network linking individuals concerned with anthropological applications to the health sciences. For this purpose, a working group of clinical anthropologists and data management specialists needs to be formed.

Long range strategies for documentation and data management need to focus on the application of computer technology to the problems of information storage and retrieval. Bibliographic data could then be converted to a computer system which would require the development of a specialized thesaurus of subject terms in order to insure effective retrieval of appropriate materials.

The greatest potential of computer based information systems, however, is their capacity for the development of interactive electronic communication systems as well as data delivery. Computer conferencing and electronic mail systems provide a potential for information delivery which is far more rapid than either current formal or informal communication systems. With an emphasis on information delivery rather than document delivery, computer conferencing is particularly attractive to the practitioner. While for an emerging field such as clinical anthropology this prospective may appear distant, it is not premature to anticipate this mode of information handling, so that the systems developed on an interim basis do not have built-in obsolescence.

Examining the possibilities for documentation and data management, it is readily apparent that effective preliminary systems can be developed almost immediately. It is strongly urged that practitioners, researchers and teachers in Clinical Anthropology, and in the more general interface of anthropology and the health sciences act now to develop appropriate working groups, and to gain the funding needed to initiate an effective information system for this significant area of theory and practice.

PART VI

CLINICAL ANTHROPOLOGY:

CONTRIBUTIONS, PROBLEMS AND WIDER PERSPECTIVES

CLINICAL ANTHROPOLOGY:
CONTRIBUTIONS, PROBLEMS AND WIDER PERSPECTIVES

Demitri B. Shimkin and Peggy Golde

Introduction

Clinical anthropology is a small, energetic, innovative vocation. Its practitioners are young and generally cross-trained in both anthropology and health. They are centrally concerned with intervention at various levels, from the sick patient to the community at risk, in furthering human health and welfare. They manifest high levels of commitment to the people served, and exacting standards in the research services and training conducted.

Clinical anthropology is generating a promising body of theory. In this volume, Golde and Weidman, in particular, presented interactionist concepts as foundations for intervention, while Shain and Borman considered in depth the definition of disease states. The ecological rationale of the Holmes County (Mississippi) Health Research Project is detailed in Shimkin (1981).[1]

Because of these strengths, the evolving vocation of clinical anthropology has prospects far beyond mere survival, not withstanding the many difficulties of limited recognition and an adverse sociopolitical climate it faces in the United States today. Self-identity, internal structuring, recognition academically and professionally, documentation and scientific validation, choice of direction, and sheer growth to viable size are the vocation's major problems of the future. Its wider perspectives include greater therapeutic efficacy in the management of chronic diseases and in services to particular populations; increased humanizing of health services, with particular attention to problems of development and aging, chronic disease, and behavioral disorders; the productive integration of cosmopolitan health services with alternative healers, in both developing and developed countries; and the greater understanding of the impacts of differential power and of such dynamics as urbanization upon people and the societies they form, via the markers of mental and physical illness.[2]

In broadest terms, this study extends and deepens
the important volume by Eleanor E, Bauwens and her
associates (1978), The Anthropology of Health. Another
antecedent has been Linda Alexander's (1979) thoughtful
essay.

Contributions[3]

This volume and the literature covered in the
Appendix document the contributions of clinical
anthropology, expecially over the past decade, to
research, services, and training in the field of health
research.

Research

Five inter-related areas have proven to be
particularly fruitful to date:

1. The improved clinical definition of human
states, transitions, and crises. Rochell Shain and her
associates have explored the nature of tubal ligation,
not merely as a biomechanical phenomenon, but in terms
of consequences for self-image, and for sexual capacity
and enjoyment for both wife and husband. Similarly,
Miriam Rodin's work has helped refine the understanding
of American drinking practices and, with that, of
alcoholism. A decade ago, Boon and Roberts (1970)
mapped the configuration of hemophilia, in the context
of British health care, as a problem of family
functioning, educational limitation, and many other
dimensions as well as sheer survival. The works of
T.B. Brazelton (1973), Osofsky and Danzger (1974) and,
most recently, that of the behavioral anthropologist
Nancy Shand (1981) have shifted the critical questions
of birthing from child delivery as a quasi-illness to
the earliest relationships of mother and infant as
primary elements of infant functionality, bonding, and
development. These illustrations can be multiplied.
They show how the ethnography of life states and
transitions can modify existing biomedical
formulations, and lead to more appropriate strategies
of therapy or management.

2. The evaluation of sociopsychological stress.
Work on this fundamental concept has a dual
significance. It provides powerful approaches to
illness and behavioral disorders beyond simple
biomechanical formulations. It also recognizes
criteria of morbidity, such as hypertension, and,

370

ultimately, of mortality for assessing how well
societies are working for whom. Studies of stress
embody four aspects--markers of stress, antecedents of
stress, mediators of stress, and the short and long
term consequences of stress. The importance of life
changes, both sudden and expected, as precursors of
physical and mental illnes is a major point of Golde´s
analysis. This point is based on extensive research by
Malzberg and Lee (1965), Benjamin (1971), and
especially Thomas H. Holmes and his colleagues. For
example, Holmes and Masuda (1973) examine the validity
of Holmes´ scale of stressful personal events in terms
of United States and Japanese cultures, finding both
coincidences, e.g., in the extreme shock of family
deaths, and divergences. Mules, Hague and Dudley
(1977) have shown that alcoholics may have different,
less sensitive, reactions to life changes. More work
is needed on the dynamics of stress, particularly the
roles of psychosocial isolation and losses of
self-esteem. There is evidence that shared disorders
and socioeconomic difficulties (Sprague n.d.) may, at
least in the short run, be associated with heightened
competencies and well being, in the presence of felt
stress.

3. In more general terms, the conceptualization of
social environmentes as both sources and mediators of
stress. Here, the most basic, validated data come from
the investigations of the Holmes County Health Research
Project on the etiology and natural history of
hypertension (Schoenberger et al. 1975; Eckenfels et
al. 1977; Frate 1978). In that Black community,
poverty, social marginality, responsibility as head of
a household, and migration have demostrably intensified
propensities toward hypertension. Membership in
"stong" as opposed to "weak" extended families has
conversely moderated susceptibilities. Current
research on both Black and White populations in central
Mississippi is re-examining the findings of the 1970s.
In hypertension, it appears that social factors act
synergically with other factors, such as overweight,
and have particular effect at specific developmental
stages, notably late adolescence - early adulthood.

4. Emphasis on illness and health, and on therapy
and its effects as interactive phenomena involving
primary actors and relevant others in complex
sociopsychological games mediating or intensifying
pathologies. This theoretical position is explicit in
Golde´s paper, and is illustrated by Alter´s and, in
particular, Weidman´s materials. It underlies the

371

successful Mississippi experiments in the control of
hypertension by enlisting members of extended family
and church groups as de facto mediators in the
management of hypertension.

Underlying interactionism is a necessary
stochastic, systemic concept with messages as the
transitive elements, and with multiple loci of control
and control policies. All of these elements are
integral to the famous and productive theory of
schizophrenia developed by Gregory Bateson and his
colleagues (Michel 1969). On the many applications of
interactive theory and game play in psychodiagnostics
and therapy see Avedon and Sutton-Smith (1971:347-351).
Most generally, the interactivist position requires
that human states and status-transitions be examined in
contexts of relevant actors, their values, and their
communicative behavior. The interactionist position
espoused by many anthropologists is compatible with
more general ecological models (Shimkin 1966). It is
not compatible with social-structural determinism
(Mechanic 1978:25-52).

5. The development of strategies to define, and
perhaps cope with, obscure syndromes. An illustration
is Weidman's analysis of the Haitian folk disease of la
congestion. A highly significant area of needed
syndrome definition is child abuse and neglect, where
partial evidence on sequelae has developed, where
causation has been partly clarified, but where the
total syndrome and, particularly, effective
interventions need much research, including family
ethnographies. A case in point is the world of the
child in an abusing family, a world dominated by
chronic uncertainty, isolation and lack of expressive
opportunities. How does that child cope? Most likely,
through the assumption of a caretaker role (Sturges
1978). But that role carries with it the greatest
vulnerability to both heterosexual and homosexual
incest (Browning and Boatman 1977; Finkelhor 1978).
How can such a dilemma be resolved?

Services

Anthropologists have aided the development of more
responsive and effective health services in the United
States. They have fostered consumer control, the use
of indigenous health workers, self-help groups and peer
group therapies, and interactive problem solving. They
have given important technical advice and furnished
essential brokerage with communities served, for
health-services institutions.

372

1. Consumer control of health and psychological services by communities and individuals. Shimkin, Eckenfels, and Frate, Logan and Wade have illustrated the theory and practice of consumer control in Mississippi, both initially and as modified over nearly 20 years. Lepper's work with the Mile-Square Health Center in Chicago was another pioneering undertaking. More generally, anthropologists involved in the civil rights movements of the 1960s, and those active in the women's rights movement of the 1970s have been among the initiators of reforms to increase the accountability of health and pyschological services to those served (Jacobs 1979). These reforms have unquestionably worked. However, even where consumer control has been legally mandated, as in the case of predominant consumer representation on Health Services Agencies boards, it has met with intense, continuing opposition from health services providers. Accountability in regard to questions as basic as the enormous excess of hysterectomies performed in the United States is generally poor. In all, consumer control is perhaps the most difficult and most significant area of anthropological involvement in health services. Even where legal authority has shifted all formal power to health providers, a careful design of communication in health services (Frate this volume) can do much to maintain essential sensitivity to consumers.

2. Closely related to consumer control is the employment of indigenous workers as paraprofessionals and, more rarely, co-therapists. Weidman and the Mississippi group have dealt with the systematic recruitment and training of local aides; Leighton was among the first to foster the use of Navaho healers as co-therapists. The advantages of indigenous workers in reaching out to people, in understanding their needs, and in securing cooperation in diagnosis and case management have been repeatedly shown. The barriers have been prejudice and professional self-serving, coupled with insufficient attention to job analysis, progressive skill development, and team organization. There also exists a risk to those recruited of placement in dead-end jobs vulnerable to loss from the impostition of certification standards designed to serve particular professional interests. Such job pressures have often been intensified by racism.

In the United States, with a few exceptions such as Leighton's and Weidman's experiences, cosmopolitan medicine has been extremely resistant to alternative therapeutic approaches and particularly to indigenous co-therapists. Ths shift from physician to nurse-midwife in obstetrics, from birth as illness to birth as a natural event in which husband as well as wife participate, has been won only slowly and partially. In alcoholism, the limits of conventional medicine have long been evident, but lay counsellors are still utilized all too late, and with little relation to a patient's total health management. Medicine and chiropractic, although used simultaneoulsy by many, remain hostile camps. An important aspect of consumer advocacy by clinical anthropologists is the better use of alternative as well as cosmopolitan approaches for the patient's benefit.

3. The formation and maturation of self-help groups. These have been of two types, (a) multi-purpose voluntary groups, usually community organizations, that have perceived needs for health and allied services, or needs for management skills in handling health-related grants. Here, clinical anthropologists as well as other social-science and health professionals have been active for many years. (b) The specifically problem-oriented, generally single-purpose self-help groups, such as Alcoholics Anonymous and Mattachine, with their bonds of common suffering and deviant status, have avoided all but a few professionals (Sagarin 1969). The work of Leonard Borman and the Self-Help Institute is therefore noteworthy. Very important consequences in the definition of illness and deviancy, in therapeutic strategies, in advocacy, and in the roles of professionals, including clinical anthropologists, may be foreseen.

4. Technical advice and brokerage for health-services institutions. Here, anthropologists increase the efficacy and acceptability of health services by identifying perceived health problems, and acceptable and unacceptable ways of delivering health services, in relation to the key values, social structures, and environmental adaptations of the populations served. Once the data are developed, it is furthermore essential to communicate the views of services users to providers, and to develop means of reconciling differences. To be effective, this brokerage process must take place throughout the range of interrelationships, from patient/physician or nurse to community leader/hospital administrator. Weidman, Frate, and, especially, Rodin explore these problems. At an optimum level, such advice and brokerage

culminates in innovations such as the health counselling systems developed in Mississippi or the stable multi-disciplinary teams, developed by the Council on Children at Risk[4] to diagnose and recommend intervention strategies for children in identified abusing or neglecting families.

Training in the Field of Health

What kinds of data, techniques and insights can trained and experienced clinical anthropologists bring to the education of physicians, nurses, other health professionals and/or community health workers? This is an extremely complex subject embodying questions of content and method beyond the scope of the present volume.[5] Four of our papers are concerned with these problems explicitly--Friedman and Rodin in relation to medical students, and Tripp-Reimer and Isaacs in relation to nursing. Alter indirectly pleads for training in cultural relativism for social workers, while O'Rourke is attracted by anthropological theory and method as leavenings for the extreme empiricism of health educators. There is also a very large literature extant. Bluebond-Langer's (1978) poignant work on the perceptions of child leukemia patients and their families, and Williams' (1975) comprehensive survey of the special medical problems of Black people in the United States may be cited.

At this time, we suggest that the contributions of clinical anthropologists to health training may be sketched as follows:

1. In relation to content, the most significant areas are (a) sensitization to the objective and perceived realities of life, distress and healing of the patients and populations served; (b) improved communications between therapists and patients through a better understanding of patients' folk knowledge, expectations and fears; (c) improved history taking, through the identification of the special risks, e.g., of venereal disease, characterizing particular populations, of the ranges of responses that may be "normal" for given biological, ethnic or social groups, and of the special mediating factors, such as "strong" families that may modify risks; and (d) improved compliance with agreed-on-regimens, from better initial agreements and patient education, and from more efficacious outreach.

2. In terms of <u>site</u> of training, it is clear that both community and therapeutic settings are critically important. The essence of clinical anthropological insight comes through viewing the same people in both.

3. In terms of <u>method</u>, both intensive case analysis and ethnographic and survey methods are valuable. What is important is proper choice of the level of sophistication to be sought--for medical students, as Friedman suggests, limited, immediately useful approaches are a necessary start. For Public Health workers, or for Public Health Nurses, and for Health Educators, very thorough practical and theoretical instruction is more appropriate.

The acceptability of clinical anthropological training for health professionals depends in considerable part on the trainer's validating knowledge and experience in clinical settings, and on his or her sensitivity to power and status relationships in the field of health. The observations of three physicians--Drs. Johnson, Friedman and Leighton--are all relevant.

Note also should be taken of the potential value of clinically sophisticated instruction in the education of academic anthropologists. Friedman's points are well taken. Beyond understanding clinical problems and settings as influences upon roles and communications, clinical anthropologists can use data on illness and health in evaluating how well societies work for whom.

Problems of the Future

We believe that our review of the contributions of Clinical Anthropology to the field of health demonstrates that the new vocation is indeed useful. We believe also that, regardless of developments in social environment or the presence or absence of systematic efforts to solve problems of the future, Clinical Anthropology will survive, continue making contributions and develop to some degree. At the same time, we feel a knowledge, and at least partial resolution, of developmental problems could make Clinical Anthropology more useful sooner, and it might also develop service and economic opportunities for many younger people whose prospects today may be very limited, especially in academic anthropology.

Present and Future

We will introduce our consideration through the choice of three perspectives--those of a contented clinical worker, of Medicine as an institution, and of our scenario over the next decade.

Linda Alexander (1979:62) eloquently depicts the preoccupation of a contented, very busy clinical anthropologist:

> During . . . [1974-77] . . . I was happily and naively engaged in the activity of performing clinical anthropology in a medical setting, not realiziing I was having an identity problem, or challenging anthropological tradition, or contesting powerful vested interests, or contributing marginally to the enterprise at hand. I was quite ignorant of these charges and was genuinely absorbed in the enormous number of clinical problems the anthropologist may attend in a receptive and stimulating medical environment. So many possibilities existed in fact, that I had to carefully monitor my interests and establish priorities at all times.

But a major price of idyllic isolation has been the non-existence of Medical, let alone, Clinical Anthropology in the perceptions of Medicine as an organized institution. The decisive evidence for this gloomy finding is the topical description of all anthropology on p. 404 of the so-called "Tree Structure" of the United States National Library of Medicine for 1981:

Anthropology
   Anthropology, Cultural
     Archaeology
     Culture
       Acculturation
         Assimilation*
       Ceremonial
       Civilization
       Cross-Cultural Comparison
       Cultural Characterisitics*
         Cannibalism
       Cultural Evolution*
       Ethic Groups
         Blacks
         Eskimos
         Gypsies*

                    Hispanic Americans
                    Indians, Central American
                    Indians, North American
                    Indians, South American
                    Jews
                    Whites
               Ethnology
               Folklore
               Medicine, Traditional Medicine, Herbal
               Mortuary Customs
                    Funeral Rites*
                    Mummies
               Superstitions
                    Magic
                    Taboo
          Anthropology, Physical
               Craniology
               Paleontology
                    Fossils*
                    Paleodontology
                    Paleopathology
               Racial Stocks
                    Austroloid Race
                    Caucasoid Race
                    Mongoloid Race
                    Negroid Race

     *Indicates minor descriptor

This curious and extremely limited concept is
substantiated, as Clark and Borooah discuss in the
Appendix, by computer searches of a large number of
data banks. The coverage is, at best, limited and
haphazard, with such important periodicals as Human
Organization, Journal of Biosocial Science, and Medical
Anthropology being ignored.

     Given the great dependence of health researchers
and administrators on the United States Library of
Medicine and allied sources, this means that knowledge,
let alone effective use, of anthropological findings is
limited to individual contacts. One consequence is
that such health bureaucracies as the National
Institute of Mental Health do not recognize
anthropologists, in contrast to sociologists or even
chemists, as a significant constituency.
Anthropological access to research planning, training
and other funds, and to systematic job opportunities is
correspondingly small and capriciously managed.

                         378

Future prospects, as we infer from the statements by Lepper, Swartz and Tourlentes as well as our own investigations, are not bright. Over the next decade, and barring a major war or politico-economic upset, we feel that the following trends will be dominant in the United States:

1. Increased socioeconomic stratification with a growing pre-emption of public resources by the privileged. Components of this trend would include (a) an intensification of high-technology and very high cost diagnosis and surgery, with consequent continued pressures on medical costs; (b) the widened use of Health Maintenance Organizations for closed, higher income populations such as the employees of particular corporations, and within such HMOs, an expanded use of health education, preventive medicine and continued care for chronic diseases and behavioral problems; (c) a concentration of national health resources on high technology, including psychopharmacology, with reduced expenditures for services and, especially, preventive medicine; (d) reduced medical coverage for deprived populations--the aged, the poor (especially those in female-headed households), Blacks, Latinos, migrants, homosexuals, etc.; (e) extreme pressures on the resources of public and mental-health facilities serving the deprived; and (f) increasing institutional and professional rigidity, with rising standards of licensure, and hostility toward new entrants into health fields.

2. A continual growth of the population that is chronically ill, unstable and disabled. This reflects the aging of the United States population, the limited attention given to prevention and environmental safety, and the rising per capita consumption of alcohol.[6]

3. Major increases in the numbers of "non-standard" practitioners, especially religious healers, in response to the cost and failures of conventional medicine, and to the proselyting of fundamentalist sects.

4. Increased self-help group organization, including in-group therapy and case management, but also including great rises in political activism.

If these projections are at least broadly true, clinical anthropologists will have greatly enlarged potential constituencies of the deprived; may be able to develop new constituencies within Health Maintenance

Organizations and allied groups, and within self-help groups; will have intense competition and difficulties of accreditation in publicly-financed health organizations; and will have to develop skills in both technical health areas and political advocacy.

Self-Identity

The respondents to Gern and Shimkin's inquiries have clearly indicated bases for self-identity among clinical anthropologists. The field is defined by the application of anthropological concepts and techniques to the improvement of health care; the active use of research with special emphasis on cultural dimensions in health and illness, social change and its effects, and therapist/patient communications; and practical concerns with reducing barriers to health services, and with improved therapy. Those identifying with these interests need to communicate, to organize in some minimal way, and to develop initial programs. The best settings appear to be meetings of moderate size, perhaps within the context of less structured professional organizations, such as the Society for Applied Anthropology, or regionally. Only in this way can initial communications be effectively established.

All this is feasible today. The great danger evident in anthropology is divisiveness and clique formation, with concurrent proneness to generate miniscule and often ill-based orthodoxies. Anthropologists need to accept diversity in their own ranks and to embrace the tactics of varied interest groups within common structures as the sociologists and workers in public health have long been doing.

Internal Structure

It is also clear that Clinical Anthropology as a vocation unites persons of varied backgrounds, and this variation might increase substantially should anthropologically trained health workers be attracted in significant numbers. Certainly, a completely open entry and self-sorting by foci of interest and level of sophistication in anthropology and in health appear to be essential. Premature, ill-considered professionalization can only stultify. And leadership and choices of direction reflecting a diversified membership need to be systematically maintained. Structuring in terms of grades or other markers might be valid only with growth and with the development of external professional recognition. Here again, the

history of the American Public Health Association
provides useful precedents.

In contrast to our warnings against structuring
status and power, we feel that substantive and
technical interests need to be facilitated by the
formation of forums or symposia leading to productive
reports for clinical anthropologists and others
concerned. Certain directions, such as the health
needs of minorities or special groups, are clear. But
there also should be consideration of such important
questions as the ulitity, hazards and optimal
techniques of encounter and allied groups (Slavson
1947:95-106; Galinsky and Schopler 1977), relations
between cosmoplitan medicine and indigenous, including
"non-standard" healers (Taylor 1979), the assessment of
social supports in stress (Carveth and Gottlieb 1979),
and therapeutic strategies in geriatrics (Lawton 1974).

Academic and Professional Recognition

To be known and to be accepted as colleagues by
health professionals and within anthropology are
obviously essential for the development of Clinical
Anthropology as a vocation. The difficulties in
gaining such recognitin are many. They include failure
to date to form a visible group of clinical
anthropologists, and to communicate effectively the
contributions made and expectable. They involve the
resistance of governmental, professional and academic
bureaucracies to change. They reflect a national
reluctance to face issues of social justice. Yet there
are feasible approaches to resolving these questions,
in time and with sufficient intelligent effort.

Of greatest importance is recognition and support
of Clinical Anthropology, as both sound and needed in
health care, by the medical profession. There are many
physicians of high competence and status who are deeply
concerned with the social and ethical discussions of
medical practice, research and teaching. This is
evident from the presentations of our eight
participants, particularly Drs. Lepper and Swartz. But
physicians need convincing that the interesting ideas
of our field can be effectively and systematically
incorporated into medical routines, in the way, say,
that clinical psychologists have become recognized
partners for psychiatry.

There is no royal road to gaining this essential
recognition. But anthropologists should known that an

important part of the innovations in our country's social medicine, broadly defined, is being financed by the Robert Wood Johnson Foundation. The list of grant recipients (Robert Wood Johnson Foundation 1981:51-77) is a virtual directory of concerned and active health-services institutions ranging from the School of Medicine at UCLA, to the Nebraska Commission on Aging, and the Surry County Family Health Group, Inc., of Surry, Virginia. Here is a network which clinical anthropologists as individuals and Clinical Anthropology as a vocation should seek to enter.

Nursing is involved in Clinical Anthropology today. Eleanor Bauwens (1978) and her associates have communicated how nursing uses anthropology with skill. Continuing ties between the two fields are the function of the Council on Nursing and Anthropology, a 126-person group of nurses, of whom more than half have graduate degrees in anthropology (Dougherty and Bolton 1980).

Clinical anthropology also shares both a therapeutic orientation and many theoretical positions with Social Work. An excellent illustration is the social work concept of the Life Model, which places case management strategies in both an interactional setting and as a problem of cumulated life-transition stresses impinging upon maladaptive personal relationships and communications (Germain and Gitterman 1980). More extensive relationships between the two fields have yet to be developed, a situation largely true for relationships with various health-oriented disciplines such as clinical psychology.

But what about legitimacy vis-a-vis academic anthropology? Medical anthropology, i.e., social (rarely, biosocial) anthropology with a light admixture of comparative health systems, psychiatry, and clinical familiarization, has become widely although not universally accepted. Stonger professionalism in the area of health, exemplified by the program at the University of California, San Francisco, meets resistence in many departments of anthropology, since it cannot be accomplished without the surrender of much customary content. And that brings up the threat of disciplinary fragmentation.

Two answers to this somewhat illusory problem exist. One, already indicated, is a view of anthroplogy--like other complex disciplines--as a confederation of specialities totally mastered by no

382

one person. The other, which is a basic need for anthropology, is more involvement in abstraction and methodology which, paradoxically, can unify vast areas of nominally different pure and applied problems into fewer but more productive categories and algorithms.

Documentation and Scientific Validation

The activation and interactions of a network of mutually recognized clinical anthropologists need to be consolidated by the growth and ready availability of professional resources. Barton Clark, Richard Thompson, David Klass, and Allan Levy have particularly dealt with these issues. There is a need for an armament of technical supports: rosters, bibliographies, report files, statistical data bases, technical manuals, texts, seminars, workshops, courses, training centers and allied means accessible to practitioners and students as well as high-level researchers. Elements of such an armament exist, as Clark and Borooah show; how to transform them into a unified body of resources presents difficulties, which are magnified by the small scale of use that is likely to prevail, at least for some time to come. Moreover, while in past days much aid could be expected from governmental and private agencies for the accumulation of these resources, a more extensive self-help effort will certainly be essential now. The task, in general, is difficult but do-able.

Choices of Direction

In our opinion, the field of Clinical Anthropologgy has three potential ways of growth. It can seek to become a tightly defined, technical profession like Clinical Psychology; it can be an auxiliary skill for health professionals, like Master of Public Health training; and it also has a possibility for developing first-level practitioners, like those with Bachelor of Social Work degrees. Each course of action, and each combination of courses, has corresponding advantages and disadvantages.

Tight professionalization at the doctoral or even post-doctoral level is critically important for strong research and innovation in practice. It is also the best avenue for the development of status and incomes. Specialized training for health professionals--say, a two-year M.S.--provides a good complement for a body of advanced students from anthropology. But it would have to be quite standardized to meet the expectations and sometimes the requirements of health professions. The M.D.-Ph.D. level of joint professionalism would be invaluable for technical leadership.

A very different perspective is opened by the training of first degree workers, to be prepared for defined kinds of positions in community health and other, largely local, settings. This is a level of application which Anthropology as a field has largely ignored. Yet it is likely to be especially important in meeting the needs of deprived groups and health organizations for "social technicians." The work now being conducted by Frate and his colleagues in Mississippi and by Weidman in Florida provides important leads to how such training could be conducted and how such training could, in part at least, be designed for presentation at Community Colleges. Allied to this could be the incorporation of clinical anthropological training in the in-service education of mental health and public-health workers in primary care. Such developments would, we feel, be extremely desirable. But we know that to undertake them well would take some years of careful preparation by academic institutions, by service agencies (such as the Department of Mental Health and Human Disabilities in Illinois) and community and self-help groups.

Should such an evolution take place, the relationships of Clinical Anthropology to the parent discipline would be profoundly changed.

Growth

An extremely important characteristic of anthropology, let alone clinical anthropology, is its miniscule size as a profession--perhaps 10,000 persons, including graduate students. As Gern and Shimkin have estimated, clinical anthropologists numbered about 500 in 1980.

In startling contrast, total employment in health occupations in the United States in 1979 slightly exceeded 4.8 million persons. The basic data are presented in Table 1. It shows an immense body of opportunities, even in such relatively small occupations as Pharmacy. It shows also that most health workers are women, and the proportion of whom are Black is relatively high. Here are people who may need what anthropology has to offer; they provide a moral challenge, not a means to gain high status and income.

384

Table 1. Health Employment in the United States, 1979

Occupation	Number of Persons in Thousands	Percent Female	Percent Black
Total Employment	4,812	74.5	15.9
Physicians, dentists and related	787	11.9	7.9
Physicians*	431	10.7	9.5
Dentists	131	4.6	4.6
Pharmacists	135	24.4	9.6
Registered nurses	1,223	96.8	11.4
Therapists	207	72.9	11.6
Health administrators	185	48.1	7.0
Health technologists and technicians	534	69.5	11.4
Clinical laboratory	217	71.9	15.7
Radiology	104	73.1	7.7
Health service	1,818	90.4	24.9
Health aides and trainees	281	87.5	22.4
Nursing aides	1,024	87.5	30.6
Practical Nurses	376	97.9	18.6

*Includes medical and osteopathic physicians.

Source: U.S. Bureau of the Census 1980:109.

385

This juxtaposition of occupational sizes shows that, if clinical anthropologists are successful in demonstrating to the health field that they have valuable, perhaps necessary, skills for the delivery of health services, then Clinical Anthropology must be prepared to grow beyond any academic visions. Such a growth has taken place in both Clinical Psychology and in Social Work.

Let us review the key data here not because either field represents a close model for anthropological emulation but because both are well studied and show many areas of potential future decision making.

Clinical Psychology. While exact data are unavailable, there are currently over 40,000 clinical psychologists employed in the United States (Table 2). The critical growth of the profession took place between 1926 and 1961, especially in the years immediately after World War II. A summary of statistics on growth in membership in the American Psychological Association gives the basic picture (Bibace et al. 1965:106).

Table 2. Growth in Membership:
American Psychological Association

| Year | Number of Members | Changes | |
		Period	Percent Increase
1926	535	–	–
1931	1,267	1926/31	+ 135
1936	1,987	1931/36	+ 57
1941	2,937	1936/41	+ 48
1946	4,427	1941/45	+ 51
1951	8,554	1946/51	+ 93
1956	14,509	1951/56	+ 81
1961	18,948	1956/61	+ 31

By 1961, clinical psychologists accounted for 36 percent of the psychological profession. Only 27 percent were employed in educational institutions; 13 percent were self-employed; 2 percent were in private industry; and the remainder were in various therapeutic institutions, especially State mental hospitals (Bibace et al. 1965:111-114). The growth of Clinical Psychology was stimulated by World War II and, particularly, the perceived needs of the Veterans Administration and the United States Public Health Service. These agenices not only funded training but also placed pressures on trainers to systematize programs and accreditation standards. A series of conferences, beginning with the Boulder (Colorado) Conference in August 1949 defined Clinical Psychology in administrative terms.

In subsequent years, clinical psychologists have strongly emphasized the development of tests, particularly verbal ones, of psychic functioning, as well as therapy largely on a one-to-one basis. Psycholanalytic approaches and behavior modification have been predominant modalities (Reisman 1966). The issues of social stress and social change remain peripheral (Rabin 1974).

Social Work. Formal, college-level training in social work began in 1898 with the Summer School of Philanthropic Workers in New York but made little headway until the passage of the Social Security Act in 1935. By 1941, 1900 workers who had completed a two-year course in medical social work in an approved school or had equivalent training through experience, or a combination of work and experience, belonged as professional members in the American Association of Medical Social Workers (Fink 1942:29, 296-297, 341). By December 1976, membership in the National Association of Social Workers, primarily holders of the M.S.W. degree, numbered 70,046. Of these members, 56 percent were in government agency employment and 3 percent in private practice; 40 percent were in direct services, with the remainder in planning, administration, etc. Eight thousand members were registered clinical social workers. Nearly seventy percent of the entire membership was female; however, at the doctoral level, two-thirds were male (Meyer and Siegel 1977). While social work has been continually concerned with better standards and professionalization, and has begun to enter into the needs of industry (Ozawa 1980) as well as deprived clients, it remains deeply committed to social justice. Cooper´s (1977) excellent article is illustrative.

Should the demand for clinical anthroplogists increase in some relation to the histories of Clinical Psychology and Social Work, academic departments of anthropology will face the choice of basic changes or of seeing training move to other disciplines incorporating anthropology, as has been evident in Education.

What kinds of consequences might come from real growth?

An increase in numbers to, say, 5,000 clinical anthropologists, means subspecialization, on one hand, and standardization, on the other. At that level, employment would begin to be routine. Rather than the specially tailored use of exotic skills, Clinical Anthropology would have to represent predictable skills in defined areas and restaints of activity in others. The range of skill levels would also increase, from the high level researchers to some analogues of social work case workers or practicing clinical psychologists, persons able to use a well-defined inventory of techniques in specified settings and in routine cases.

Should Clinical Anthropology approach the scale of, say, Clinical Psychology or Social Work--a profession of 40,000 persons or more--its internal bureaucratization and other changes would be indeed profound. Today's individualism would be a romantic memory.

Growth and standardization, if attained, carry risks of intellecutal stultification and loss of responsiveness to the values and needs of the people served. To offset such risks, to maintain Clinical Anthropology as a dynamic enterprise, it would be essential to retain a strong research orientation with attendant skepticism and attention to observed realities. There would be a need for good feedback between field and academe. Complementary to intellectual rigor is the need for continued ethical sensitivity. Is what is being done efficacious? Could it be harmful? And finallly, it would be vital to retain openness--in regard to varying approaches, different patterns of training, etc.--and with it, the dynamics of health variation and constructive disputations.

Wider Perspectives

The significance of a viable and productive Clinical Anthropology far exceeds any potential growth of such a vocation. For anthropology, in its commitments to field work, to grass roots inquiry, and to problem resolution in the terms of the people affected, has an essential catalytic role both disturbing and creative. It is highly likely that, in this country, Clinical Anthroplogy will have increasing impacts upon clinical practice in medicine, nursing and other health fields, and in the organization and structuring of community health, including one form or other of health maintenance organization. A foreseeable area of change is an improved relationship between professional health services and self-help groups.

Beyond this, clinical lessons are likely to emerge into changes in health policy, better defining services needed and unneeded, mechanisms for access to appropriate care, and the prevention of destructive sociopsychological stresses. In such applications to policy, the contributions of clinical anthropologists would emerge from analyzed experiences, and provide counter balances to the aggregative concepts of political scientists and medical sociologists.

Finally, few limits can be put on the potential contributions of clinical anthropologists to that majority of the world's population for whom cosmopolitan medicine remains too costly and inaccessible, and from whom good health must be sought through the enhancement of indigenous resources and skills. Such studies as Marchioni's (1977) brilliant analysis of the improvement of Jamaican children's diets through an apparent retrogression--more subsistence gardening--point out ways how macro-level policy implications can emerge from micro-level clinical research. The many goals which lie beyond-- the Himalayas of a future applied anthropology--have been well sketched by Thomas Weaver (1973) and his colleagues.

389

NOTES

1. For a more general approach to health in human ecology see Moore et al. (1980). Note also, for the entire field of anthropology, the identification by Mandelbaum (1978:25) of four key postulates--"holism, fieldwork, comparative method, and micro level to macro level theorizing."

2. An insightful treatment of the complex relationships between social systems and health/illness roles is given by Mechanic (1978:53-92). This problem is well explored, in a British context, by Morris (1970).

3. We must stress that many of the developments covered in this section have broad multi-disciplinary histories. Game theory, invented by John Von Neumann, the eminent mathematician, and applied to a wide gamut of problems from those of military strategy and economics onward is an illustration. Our study does show, however, that the developments cited have been both significant elements of the theory and practice of Clinical Anthropology, and objects of anthropological innovation.

4. The Council on Children at Risk, formerly directed by Catherine Alter, M.S.W., and now by Roy A. Harley, M.A., is charged with recommending the specific handling of serious child abuse and neglect cases in the Rock Island, Illinois, area by the State of Illinois Department of Child and Family Services. For this purpose it uses Family Diagnostic Teams consisting of a physician, clinical psychologist, social worker, and anthropologist. Each family is systematically interviewed and tested by the Team in procedures averaging about 15 hours of professional time. About 50 such reports are prepared annually.

    The analysis of 30 of these diagnostic reports covering that number of families and 80 children up to age 17 disclosed that, for this entire group, over one-half of the children were coping poorly or extremely poorly. Some 35% of the total were in the ages 6 through 11, with girls predominating. Physical and emotional neglect, physical abuse, and sexual abuse contributed in equal proportions to these children's stresses. The intervention strategies recommended have sought to minimize family dissolution by combining required parental therapy and intensive family monitoring by protective workers.

5. For a more extensive study of training issues in Clinical Anthropology see Golde (n.d.).

6. Per capita alcohol consumption in the United States in terms of U.S. gallons of absolute alcohol annually has risen from 0.6 in 1920-1930, to 1.5 in 1950-1960, to 1.8 in 1970-1974, with further rises since then. It is now at the highest level since 1835, and about half the level of 1800-1830. It is about the same level as Canada, the United Kingdom and Sweden. The highest consumptions are in France (4.5 gallons), Italy (3.6 gallons) and Germany (3.2 gallons); the costs in cirrhoses of the liver and other sequelae correspond (Rorabaugh 1979:225-239).

REFERENCES

Alexander, Linda
1979 Clinical Anthropology: Morals and Methods. Medical Anthropology 3:61-108.

Avedon, Elliot M. and Brian M. Sutton-Smith
1971 The Study of Games. New York: John Wiley.

Bauwens, Eleanor E., ed.
1978 The Anthropology of Health. St. Louis: C.V. Mosby Co.

Benjamin, Bernard
1971 Bereavement and Heart Disease. Journal of Biosocial Science 3:61-67.

Bibace, Roger, James F.T. Bugenthal, Stuart Cook, Sol Gerfield, Donald Klein, Ija N. Korner, Joanne Powers, Alan O. Ross, Charles R. Strather and C.L. Winder
1965 Pre-Conference Materials Prepared for the Conference on the Professional Preparation of Clinical Psychologists. Washington, D.C.: The American Psychological Association, Inc.

Bluebond-Langer, Myra
1978   The Private Worlds of Dying Children.
         Princeton, N.J.: Princeton University Press.

Boon, R.A.   and D.F. Roberts
1970   The Social Impacts of Haemophilia.   Journal
         of Biosocial Science 2:237-264.

Brazelton, T. Berry
1973   Neonatal Behavioral Assessment Scale.
         Clinics in Developmental Medicine 50:1-66.

Browing, Diane H.   and Bonny Boatman
1977   Incest: Children at Risk.   American Journal
         of Psychiatry 134:69-72.

Carveth, W. Bruce and Benjamin H. Gottlieb
1979   The Measurement of Social Support and Its
         Relation to Stress.   Canadian Journal of
         Behavioral Science 11:189-188.

Cooper, Shirley
1977   Social Work: A Dissenting Profession.   Social
         Work 22:360-67.

Dougherty, Molly C.   and Margie E. Bolton
1980   Directory of Nurses, Anthropologists, and
         Others with Interest in Nursing and
         Anthropology.   The Council on Nursing and
         Anthropology (CONAA).   Gainesville, FL:
         College of Nursing, University of Florida.

Eckenfels, E.J., D.A. Frate, E.W. Logan, K.E. Nelson,
J.A. Schoenberger, D.L. Shumway and R.C. Roistacher
1977   Endemic Hypertension in a Poor, Black, Rural
         Community: Can It Be Controlled?   Journal of
         Chronic Diseases 30:499.

Fink, Arthur E.
1942   The Field of Social Work.   New York: Henry
         Holt.

Finkelhor, David
1978   Psychological, Cultural and Family Factors in
         Incest and Family Sexual Abuse.   Journal of
         Marriage and Family Counseling 4:44-49.

Frate, Dennis A.
  1978   Family Functioning and Hypertension in a
           Black Population. Ph.D. Dissertation.
           Department of Anthropology. University of
           Illinois at Urbana-Champaign.

Galinsky, Maeda J. and Janice H. Schopler
  1977   Warning: Groups May Be Dangerous. Social
           Work 22:89-94.

Germain, Carel B. and Alex Gitterman
  1980   The Life Model of Social Work Practice. New
           York: Columbia University Press.

Golde, Peggy
  n.d.   The Status and Potential of Clinical
           Anthropology.

Holmes, Thomas H. and Minora Masuda
  1973   Life Changes and Illness Susceptibility. In
           Separation and Depression. John P. Scott and
           Edward C. Senay, eds. pp. 161-186.
           Washington, D.C.: Publication No. 94,
           American Association for the Advancement of
           Science.

Jacobs, Sue-Ellen
  1979   "Our Babies Shall Not Die", A Community's
           Response to Medical Neglect. Human
           Organization 38:120-133.

Lawton, M. Powell
  1974   Social Ecology and the Health of Older
           People. American Journal of Public Health
           64:257-260.

Malzberg, Benjamin and Everett S. Lee
  1956   Migration and Mental Disease. A Study of
           First Admissions to Hospitals for Mental
           Disease, New York, 1939-1941. New York:
           Social Science Research Council.

Mandelbaum, David G.
  1978   The Potentials of Anthropology. In
           Anthropology for the Future. Demitri
           B. Shimkin, Sol Tax and John W. Morrison,
           eds. pp. 24-41. Research Report No. 4,
           Department of Anthropology. University of
           Illinois. Urbana, Illinois.

393

Marchioni, Thomas J.
1977   Food and Nutrition in Self-Reliant National
         Development. The Impact on Child Nutrition
         of Jamaican Government Policy. Medical
         Anthropology 1:58-79.

Mechanic, David
1978   Medical Sociology: A Selective View. 2nd ed.
         New York: Free Press.

Meyer, Henry J. and Sheldon Siegel
1977   Profession of Social Work: Contemporary
         Characteristics. In Encyclopedia of Social
         Work. John B. Turner, ed. 17th issue
         2:1067-1081. Washington, D.C.: National
         Association of Social Workers, Inc.

Michel, Karl M.
1969   Schizophrenie und Familie. Beitrage zu einer
         neuen Theorie von Gregory Bateson, Don
         D. Jackson, Jay Italey, John H. Weakland,
         Lyman C. Wynne, Irving M. Ryckoff, Juliana
         Day, Stanley J. Hirsch, Theodore Lidz, Alice
         Cornelison, Stephen Fleck, Dorothy Terry,
         Harold T. Searles, Murray Bowen, Ezra
         F. Vogel, Norman Bell, Ronald D. Laing and
         J. Foudrain. Frankfort am Main: Suhrkamp
         Verlag.

Moore, Lorna, G., Peter W. Van Arsdale,
JoAnn Glittenberg and Robert A. Aldrich
1980   The Biocultural Basis of Health. St. Louis:
         C.V. Mosby Co.

Morris, J.N.
1970   Uses of Epidemiology. Second Edition.
         Edinburgh: E. & S. Livingtone.

Mules, J.E., W.H. Hague and D.L. Dudley
1977   Life Change, Its Perception and Alcohol
         Addiction. Journal of Studies on Alcohol
         38:487-493.

National Library of Medicine
1980   Medical Subject Headings--Tree Structures,
         1981. Library Operations. Bethesda,
         Maryland: National Library of Medicine.

Osofksy, J.D. and B. Danzger
  1974   Relationships Between Neonatal
          Characteristics and Mother-Infant
          Interaction. Developmental Psychology
          10:124-130.

Ozawa, Martha N.
  1980   Development of Social Services in Industry:
          Why and How? Social Work 25:464-470.

Rabin, Albert I., ed.
  1974   Clinical Psychology: Issues of the Seventies.
          Lansing: Michigan State University Press.

Reisman, John M.
  1966   The Development of Clinical Pshchology.
          New York: Appleton-Century-Crofts.

Robert Wood Johnson Foundation
  1981   Annual Report 1980. The Robert Wood Johnson
          Foundation, P.O. Box 2314, Princeton, NJ
          08540.

Rorabaugh, W.J.
  1979   The Alcoholic Republic. An American
          Tradition. New York: Oxford University
          Press.

Sagarin, Edward
  1969   Odd Man In. Societies of Deviants in
          America. Chicago: Quadrangle Books.

Schoenberger, J.A., M. Corder, E.J. Eckenfels,
D.A. Frate, E. Logan, K.E. Nelson, W. Peltz,
R.C. Roistacher and D.B. Shimkin
  1975   Hypertension in Holmes County, Mississippi.
          In Epidemiology and Control of Hypertension.
          O. Paul, ed. New York: Stratton.

Shand, Nancy
  1981   The Reciprocal Impact of Breast-Feeding and
          Culture Form on Maternal Behavior and Infant
          Development. Journal of Biosocial Science.
          13:1-17.

Shimkin, Demitri B.
1966   Adaptive Strategies: A Basic Problem in Human
          Ecology. In Three Papers on Human Ecology.
          Mills College Assembly Series, 1965-66.
          Oakland, CA: Mills College.

1981   Systems Analysis: A Promising Focus for
          Biosocial Research. Journal of Biosocial
          Science 13:127-137.

Slavson, S.R., ed.
1947   The Practice of Group Therapy. New York:
          International University Press.

Sprague, Carolyn A.
n.d.   Economics, Coping and Psychological
          Well-Being Among Middle-Class Americans.

Sturges, Jane S.
1978   Children's Reactions to Mental Illness in the
          Family. Social Casework: November 1978,
          530-536.

Taylor, Carl E.
1979   Implications for the Delivery of Health Care.
          Social Science and Medicine 13B:77-84.

United States Bureau of the Census
1980   Statistical Abstract of the United States,
          1980 (101st edition). Washington, D.C.:
          U.S. Government Printin Office.

Weaver, Thomas (general editor)
1973   To See Ourselves. Anthropology and Modern
          Issues. Glenview IL: Scott, Foresman & Co.

Williams, Richard A.
1975   Textbook of Black-Related Diseases. New
          York: McGraw-Hill.

APPENDIX

INFORMATIONAL RESOURCES FOR CLINICAL ANTHROPOLOGY

Romy Borooah and Barton M. Clark

A bibliography may be many things but it is never complete. There are always citations which elude the compiler. Even if this were not the case, as soon as a bibliography is sent to the publisher it has stopped growing although the production of new citations continues. Ideally, then, a bibliography attempts only to be representative of a larger whole. We hope that is what we have accomplished with this bibliography.

The basis of this bibliography was threefold: sources on Clinical Anthropology suggested by Drs. Peggy Golde and Demitri Shimkin; the research contributions of participants in the network of clinical anthropologists; and articles and chapters in series and works to which clinical anthropologists contributed, or which they cited frequently. Serial and book coverage extended, with some exceptions, back to 1970. In all, the initial list comprised about 500 items. It was reduced, first by including only those materials available for detailed examination at the University of Illinois; second, by minimizing redundance, a maximum of five items being set, for example, for each author; and third, by the preferential selection of contributions clearly presenting both methods and data. The final coverage gives, we feel, a sound representation of the ideas and work of clinical anthropologists, with a highly selective complement of other items. It provides, in our opinion, a useful first step in research and more advanced teaching in Clinical Anthropology.

In a developing area of the social sciences such as Clinical Anthropology, it is often difficult to determine the boundaries of a subject which is inclined to draw from a wide spectrum of sources. This is particularly true in an area which utilizes resources from both the social sciences and the health sciences. The bibliography attempts to reflect this diversity if only in a highly selective manner.

The primary division of the bibliography is by "Anthropologists" and "Related Health Oriented Researchers." The purpose of this division is to identify not only the different topics and approaches of research carried out by clinical anthropologists but also to identify representative research in other disciplines which can significantly contribute to Clinical Anthropology. Both lists are arranged alphabetically by author but are numbered sequentially from 1 to 180 as a single list. The majority of citations are post-1970.

In addition to providing standard bibliographic data for each entry, keywords and phrases are supplied for each entry. These terms are based upon those terms used by the authors. An index to these terms is provided at the end of the bibliography. It is designed not merely to facilitate use of the sources cited but especially as an intitial thesaurus substantively defining Clinical Anthropology.

The bibliography should serve only as a starting point in one's search for resources in Clinical Anthropology. An examination of the bibliography reveals that while a large and diverse number of journals publish on Clinical Anthropology, a small number of journals provide the core, e.g., Human Organization, Journal of Biosocial Science, Social Science and Medicine. Regular examination of these journals will provide one with additional resources.

Numerous indexes in the social sciences and health sciences can also serve as a method of retrieving useful information. Social Science Citation Index, Psychological Abstracts, and Index Medicus are particularly pertinent. There are, however, limitations to the effectiveness of the thesauri of the indexes. Social science indexing tools tend not to use a satisfactory vocabulary for the health sciences while the health science indexes are often inadequate in the development of social science terminology. In addition, several useful social science journals are not indexed in some of the medical indexes.

Because of the permutations which are possible with computer based bibliographic systems, they offer a more effective manner of updating resources than their paper counterparts. Since no single bibliographic data base effectively covers Clinical Anthropology, it is usually necessary to search several data bases. The proliferation of data bases suggests the utility of consulting the annually updated <u>Computer-Readable</u> <u>Bibliographic</u> <u>Data</u> <u>Bases</u>: <u>A</u> <u>Dictionary</u> <u>and</u> <u>Data</u> <u>Source</u> <u>Book</u> (Williams et al. 1976-) for available data bases and descriptions of contents of the data bases.

Much more difficult of access than textual materials are social science data sets. Now more and more frequently put into machine-readable form, they still tend not to have a wide circulation. Use is often limited and must be determined by the holding agency. For this reason we have not chosen to include citations to any data sets in the bibliography. A compendium of resource centers possessing social science data sets is the <u>Encyclopedia</u> <u>of</u> <u>Information</u> <u>Systems</u> <u>and</u> <u>Services</u> (Kruzas and Sullivan 1978).

The federal government is the major producer of readily availble machine-readable social science data sets. Two useful resources for determining availability are the <u>Directory</u> <u>of</u> <u>Computerized</u> <u>Data</u> <u>Files</u>, <u>Software</u> <u>and</u> <u>Related</u> <u>Technical</u> <u>Reports</u> (U.S. Department of Commerce 1976) and the U.S. Bureau of the Census´ <u>Directory</u> <u>of</u> <u>Data</u> <u>Files</u> (1979). Next to the federal government, the Inter-University Consortium for Political and Social Research supplies the largest number of diverse files (1980-81).

Numerous specialized data archives hold materials which are of particular interest to clinical anthropologists. Two particularly useful centers are the Drug Abuse Epidemiology Data Center, on the campus of Texas Christian University, and Rutgers´ Center for Alcohol Studies Documentation and Publications Division.

REFERENCES

Inter-University Consortium for Political
and Social Research
1980-81 Guide to Resources and Services: 1980-81.
      Ann Arbor: University of Michigan, Institute
      for Social Research.

Kruzas, Anthony and Linda U. Sullivan
1978   Encyclopedia of Information Systems and
        Services. 3rd ed. Detroit: Gale Research.

U.S. Bureau of the Census
1979   Directory of Data Files. Washington, D.C.:
        U.S. Government Printing Office.

U.S. Department of Commerce
1976   Directory of Computerized Data Files,
        Software and Related Technical Reports.
        Washington, D.C.: U.S. Government Printing
        Office.

Williams, Martha et al.
1976-   Computer-Readable Bibliographic Data Bases: A
        Dictionary and Data Source Book. Washington
        D.C.: American Society for Information
        Science.

BIBLIOGRAPHY: ANTHROPOLOGISTS

1. Aamodt, Agnes, M.
    1978   The Care Component in a Health and
            Healing System. In The Anthropology of
            Health. Eleanor E. Bauwens, ed.
            pp. 37-45. St. Louis: C.V. Mosby.

            concept of care, healing system,
            sociocultural matrix, values and beliefs

2. Abernathy, Virginia
    1976   Cultural Perspectives on the Impact of
            Women´s Changing Roles on Psychiatry.
            American Journal of Psychiatry
            133:657-661.

            change, cultural perspectives,
            psychotherapy, self concept, sex role
            stereotypes, women

3. Ablon, Joan and William Cunningham
    1981   Implications of Cultural Patterning for
            the Delivery of Alcoholism Service: Case
            Studies. Journal of Studies on
            Alcoholism, Supplement 9.

            alcoholism, case studies, cultural
            patterning, ethnicity, health care
            planning, health service delivery, Irish
            Catholic, values

4. Agar, Michael
    1977   Growing Through Change: Methadone in New
            York City. Human Organization
            36:291-295.

            drug addiction, drug usage pattern,
            methadone, street drug proliferation

5. Aguilar, Ignacio and Virginia N. Wood
    1976   Therapy Through a Death Ritual. Social
            Work 21:49-54.

            cultural factors, death, folk medicine,
            institutionalization, Mexican Americans,
            mourning, psychosocial adjustment,
            psychotherapy, therapeutic community

401

6. Albrecht, Gary L., ed.
   1976   The Society of Physical Disability.
           Pittsburgh, PA: University of Pittsburgh
           Press.

           adaptive-coping behavior,
           interdisciplinary perspective, physical
           diability, rehabilitation, self
           definition, societal reaction

7. Albrecht, Gary L. and Paul C. Higgins
   1977   Rehabilitation Success: The
           Interrelationships of Multiple Criteria.
           Journal of Health and Social Behavior
           18:36-45.

           health service institutions, physical
           disability, rehabilitation success,
           social functioning

8. Alexander, Linda
   1979   Clinical Anthropology: Morals and
           Methods. Medical Anthropology 3:61-107.

           applied anthropology, diagnosis, ethics,
           medical anthropology, social
           intervention, therapy

9. Angrosino, Michael V.
   1978   Applied Anthropology and the Concept of
           the Underdog: Implications for Community
           Mental Health Planning and Evaluation.
           Community Mental Health Journal
           14:291-299.

           applied anthropology, community health
           services, community orientation,
           community support, health service
           evaluation, policy recommendations

10. Ball, Michael, Richard A. Wunderlich,
    and Jai Swyter
    1972   Problems in Treating Obesity. American
           Family Physician 6:86-92.

           case management problems, obesity,
           practitioner-client relationship,
           psycho-behavioral factors, treatment

11. Becker, Gaylene
     1980   Growing Old in Silence. Berkeley:
             University of California.

             aged, aging, anthropological
             perspective, deaf, social functioning,
             support groups

12. Bennet, Linda A., Margaret Locke,
    Thomas W. Maretzki, Robert Straus and
    Hazel H. Weidman
     1982   Symposion: Reconsidering Appropriate
             Roles for Medical Anthropologists in
             Clinical Settings: Case Studies.
             Medical Anthropology Newsletter
             14:18-26.

             anthropologist role, clinical
             anthropology, clinical research,
             clinical setting, medical anthropology

13. Bluebond-Langer, Myra
     1978   The Private Worlds of Dying Children.
             Princeton: Princeton University Press.

             child, death, parent-child interaction,
             role play, socialization, terminal
             illness

14. Blumhagen, Dan
     1980   Hyper-tension: A Folk Illness With a
             Medical Name. Culture, Medicine and
             Psychiatry 4:197-227.

             explanatory model, hypertension, illness
             behavior, illness belief system

15. Boon, R.A. and D.F. Roberts
     1970   The Social Impact of Haemophilia.
             Journal of Biosocial Science 2:237-265.

             child illness, chronic disease,
             educationally disadvantaged, family
             burden, haemophilia, parents' needs

16. Borman, Leonard D.
    1970   The Marginal Route of a Mental Hospital
            Innovation. Human Organization
            29:63-69.

            health institution reform, health
            service delivery, hospital patient,
            mental hospital, practitioner-client
            relationship, support groups

17. Caudill, William
    1958   The Possibility of a Clinical
            Anthropology. Chapter in his The
            Psychiatric Hospital as a Small Society,
            pp. 345-370. Cambridge MA: Harvard
            University Press.

            culture, interpersonal relations, life
            stages, personality, practitioner-client
            relationship, psychotherapy,
            socialization

18. Chrisman, Noel J.
    1977   The Health Seeking Process. Culture,
            Medicine and Psychiatry 1:351-377.

            health culture, health seeking behavior,
            health service ultilization, illness
            history, sick role, symptom
            identification

19. Chrisman, Noel J. and Thomas W. Maretzki, eds.
    1982   Clinically Applied Anthropology.
            Dordrecht, Holland: D. Reidel Publishing
            Company.

            anthropologist role, clinical
            anthropology, clinical practice,
            counseling, health science setting,
            teaching

20. Clark, Margaret
    1970   Health in the Mexican-American Culture.
            Berkeley: University of California
            Press.

            bilingualism, change, health culture,
            Mexican American, role of health worker,
            socioeconomic environment

21. Clausen, Joy P.
    1979   Humanizing Health Care. In Family
            Health Care. D. Hymovich and
            M. Barnard, eds. pp. 235-242. New
            York: McGraw-Hill.

            health culture, health service delivery,
            humanistic health care, patient care,
            practitioner-client relationship,
            sociocultural and psychological needs

22. Cohen, Carl I. and Jay Sokolovsky
    1979   Clinical Use of Network Analysis for
            Psychiatric and Aged Populations.
            Community Mental Health Journal
            15:203-213.

            aged, ex-mental patients, inner-city
            populations, network analysis, social
            networks

23. Comaroff, Jean
    1976   A Bitter Pill to Swallow: Placebo
            Therapy in General Practice.
            Sociological Review 24:70-96.

            client expectations, diagnosis, general
            practice, placebo theory, role of healer

24.
    1978   Medicine and Culture: Some
            Anthropological Perspectives. Social
            Science and Medicine 12B:247-254.

            anthropological perspectives, health
            culture, health-illness concepts,
            medical paradigms, role of illness

25. Conklin, Elizabeth
    1978   Final Report of the San Diego County
            Battered Women's Pilot Project. San
            Diego, CA: San Diego County, Equal
            Opportunity Management Office.

            battered women, epidemiology, legal
            assistance, police intervention,
            protective services,
            social-psychological background

26. Cosminsky, Sheila
    1977   Alimento and Fresco: Nutritional
            Concepts and Their Implications for
            Health Care. Human Organization
            36:203-207.

            adaptability, biomedical-ethnomedical
            systems, Guatemala, health culture,
            nutrition

27. Council on Children at Risk
    1978   Child Abuse in Scott County: A
            Statistical Report and Plan of Action.
            Moline, IL: Council on Children at Risk.

            child abuse, epidemiolgy, prevention,
            treatment services

28.
    1979   Child Abuse in Rock Island County: A
            Statistical Report and Suggested Plan of
            Action. Moline, IL: Council on Children
            at Risk.

            child abuse, community response,
            epidemiology, health service delivery,
            health services available, health
            services needed

29. Damon, Albert
    1975   Biological Anthropology as an Applied
            Science. In Physiological Anthropology.
            A. Damon, ed. pp. 360-367. New York:
            Oxford University Press.

            adaptation, applied science, biological
            anthropology, health ecology, human
            ecology, urban environment

30. Dougherty, Molly C.
    1972   The Nursing Role in Health Care Planning
            and Implementation: A Cultural Approach.
            Nursing Forum 11:311-322.

            health care planning, nurse's role,
            practitioner-client relationship,
            subcultural patient

31.
    1976   Health Agents in a Rural Black
               Community. Journal of Afro-American
               Issues 4:61-69.

               Blacks, health culture, health seeking
               behavior, health service delivery,
               indigenous health worker, rural
               community

32. Dube, K.C. and Narendra Kumar
    1972   An Epidemiological Study of
               Schizophrenia. Journal of Biosocial
               Science 4:187-195.

               caste group affiliation, drug use,
               epidemiology, India, marital status,
               occupational status

33. Eckenfels, Edward, Dennis A. Frate,
    Eddie W. Logan, Kenrad E. Nelson,
    James A. Schoenberger, David L. Shumway
    and Richard C. Roistacher
    1977   Endemic Hypertension in a Poor Black
               Rural Community: Can It Be Controlled?
               Journal of Chronic Disease 30:499-518.

               Blacks, chronic disease, community
               health services, etiology, hypertension,
               indigenous health worker, rural
               community

34. Evaneshko, Veronica and Eleanor Bauwens
    1976   Cognitive Analysis and Decision-Making
               in Medical Emergencies. In Trancultural
               Health Care Issues and Conditions.
               M. Lenniger, ed. New York: F.A. Davis.

               cognitive analysis, decision making,
               health culture, illness categorization,
               medical emergency

35. Fabregia, Horacio, Jr.
    1974   Disease and Social Behavior: An
               Interdisciplinary Perspective.
               Cambridge, MA: MIT Press.

               decision theory, disease concepts,
               health care, illness behavior,
               interdisciplianry perspective, social
               medicine

36. Ferguson, Frances N.
    1976   Stake Theory as an Explanatory Device in
              Navaho Alcoholism Treatment. Human
              Organization 35:65-78.

              acculturation, alcoholism, community
              attitudes, community involvment, Navaho,
              Stake theory, treatment response, values

37. Foster, George
    1977   Medical Anthropology and International
              Health Planning. Social Science and
              Medicine 11B:527-534.

              developing countries, disease concepts,
              health care planning, indigenous health
              care system, international cooperation,
              medical anthropology

38. Foulks, Edward F.
    1980   The Concept of Culture in Psychiatric
              Residence Education. American Journal
              of Psychiatry 137:811-816.

              cultural psychiatry, culture concept,
              health practitioner training/education,
              psychiatry

39. Foulks, Edward F. and Solomon H. Katz
    1975   Biobehavioral Adaptation in the Arctic.
              In Interrelations in Population
              Adaption. E.S. Watts, F.E. Johnston and
              G.W. Lasker, eds. The Hague: Mouton.

              adaptation, anxiety, Arctic Eskimo,
              Arctic hysteria, epilepsy, malnutrition,
              stress

40.
    1977   Nutrition Behavior and Culture. In
              Malnutrition, Behavior and Social
              Organization. L.S. Green, ed.
              pp. 219-231. New York: Academic Press.

              adaptation, Arctic Eskimo, Arctic
              hysteria, cultural response,
              industrialized West, malnutrition,
              stress

408

41. Frate, Dennis A.
     1978   Family Functioning and Hypertension in a
               Black Population. Urbana, IL:
               University of Illinois, Department of
               Anthropology, Ph.D. Thesis.

               Blacks, family interaction,
               hypertension, psychosocial stress, rural
               community

42. Frate, Dennis A., Joel B. Cowen,
     Allison H. Rutledge and Michael Glasser
     1980   Behavioral Reactions During the Post
               Partum Period: Experiences of 108 Women.
               Women and Health 4:355-371.

               husband's support, insomnia, maternal
               age, maternal health, postpartum
               depression, women

43. Frate, Dennis A. and Dennis Hoffron
     1977   The Medical Management of Elderly
               Patients: The Health Team Approach.
               Paper presented at the annual meeting of
               the American Public Health Association,
               Washington, D.C.

               aged, chronic disease, economic
               problems, emotional break-down,
               isolation, mobility

44. Garrison, Vivian
     1977   Doctor, Espirtista or Psychiatrist?
               Health-Seeking Behavior in a Puerto
               Rican Neighborhood of New York City.
               Medical Anthropology 1:65-91.

               health culture, health seeking behavior,
               indigenous health resources,
               psychophysiological disorders, Puerto
               Ricans, urban community

45.
  1978   Support Systems of Schizophrenic and
          Non-schizophrenic Puerto Rican Migrant
          Women in New York City. Schizophrenia
          Bulletin 4:511-564.

          community health services, ethnicity,
          interpersonal relationships, mental
          health, Puerto Ricans, rehabilitation,
          schizophrenia, support organizations,
          therapy, urban community

46. Gomila, Jacques
    1978   Differences sexuelles dans les relations
            malade/therapuete. Prealables d'un
            anthropologue. Social Science and
            Medicine 12:223-231.

            attitude to health, Canada, cultural
            characteristics, health service
            delivery, mental health,
            practitioner-client relationship,
            therapist

47. Graves, Theodore D.
    1973   The Navaho Urban Migrant and his
            Psycholigical Situation. Ethos
            1:321-342.

            adaptive behavior, epidemiology, mental
            health, migrant, Navaho, psychological
            situation, urban migrantion

48. Harwood, Alan
    1981   Ethnicity and Medical Care. Cambridge,
            MA: Harvard University Press.

            ethnicity, health care delivery, medical
            anthropology, medical care, minority
            groups, professional-client relations

49. Haynes, Terry L.
    1977   Some Factors Related to Contraceptive
            Behavior Among Wind River Shoshone and
            Arapahoe Females. Human Organization
            36:72-77.

            American Indians, birth control,
            contraceptive behavior, female,
            fertility, religious influence, values

50. Heggenhougen, H.K.
    1979   Therapeutic Anthropology: Response to
            Shilo's Proposal. American
            Anthropologist 81:647-651.

            child health, "culturogenic" distress,
            diagnosis, individual pathology,
            therapeutic anthropology

51. Jacobs, Sue Ellen
    1979   "Our Babies Shall Not Die": A
            Community's Response to Medical Neglect.
            Human Organization 38:120-133.

            community health services, ethnic
            minorities, maternal health, mortality
            rate, pre/post natal care, self-help
            efforts

52. Johnson, Thomas M.
    1976   Sociocultural Factors in the Intergroup
            Perception of Health Problems: A Case of
            Grower Attitudes Toward Their Migrant
            Workers. Human Organization 35:79-83.

            child health, epidemiology, health
            culture, health service utilization,
            intergroup relations, sociocultural
            matrix

53. Katz, Solomon H. and Anthony F.C. Wallace
    1974   An Anthropological Perspective on
            Behavior and Disease. American Journal
            of Public Health 64:1050-1052.

            adaptation, anthropological perspective,
            change, child health, disease,
            ethnomedicine, holistic models, human
            ecology, human ecosystems

54. Kaufman, Lorraine and Albert H. Schrut
    1975   The Parenting Process Project: An
            Experimental and Clinical Application of
            Psychoanalytical and Anthropological
            Perspectives. ERIC Document ED131941.

            anthropological perspective, child
            development, counseling, discussion
            groups, family interaction, parent-child
            relationship, parent counseling,
            psychoanalytical perspective

55. Kay, Margarita
    1978   Clinical Anthropology. In The
            Anthropology of Health. Eleanor
            E. Bauwens, ed. pp. 3-11. St. Louis:
            C.V. Mosby.

            anthropological methods, clinical
            anthropology, education, health, health
            care models, health culture

56. Keefe, Susan Emley
    1982   Help-Seeking Behavior Among Foreign-Born
            and Native-Born Mexican Americans.
            Social Science and Medicine
            16:1467-1472.

            help-seeking behavior, intraethnic
            variation, Mexican American

57. Keith, Jeannie
    1980   "The Best Is Yet to Be": Toward an
            Anthropology of Age. Annual Review of
            Anthropology 9:339-364.

            Africa, aged, Asia, cognition, cultural
            context, ideology, interpersonal
            relations, role

58. Klein, Janice
    1978   Susto: The Anthropological Study of
            Diseases of Adaptation. Social Science
            and Medicine 12B:23-28.

            adaptive-coping behavior, child health,
            culture specific illness, epidemiology,
            health culture, sociocultural and
            psychological factors, susto

59. Kleinman, Arthur
    1978   Clinical Relevance of Anthropological
            and Cross-Cultural Research: Concepts
            and Strategies. American Journal of
            Psychiatry 135:427-431.

            case management, clinical psychiatry,
            cross cultural research, diagnosis,
            ethnomedicine, heatlh illness concepts,
            mental health, practitioner-client
            relationship

60. Kleinman, Arthur, Leon Eisenberg and B. Good
    1978   Culture, Illness, and Care. Annals of
            Internal Medicine 88:251-258.

            clinical concepts, cross cultural
            research, elicitation process,
            health/illness concepts, indigenous
            health care systems

61. Klepinger, Linda
    1979   Paleopathologic Evidence for the
            Evolution of Rheumatoid Arthritis.
            American Journal of Physical
            Anthropology 50:119-122.

            ankylosing spondylitis, chronic disease,
            disease evolution, etiology,
            paleopathology, rheumatoid arthritis

62.
    1980   The Evolution of Human Disease: New
            Findings and Problems. Journal of
            Biosocial Science 12:481-486.

            demography, disease, epidemiology,
            infectious disease, migration,
            nutrition, paleopathology

63. Koss, Joan D.
    1980   The Therapist-Spiritist Training Project
            in Puerto Rico: An Experiment to Relate
            the Traditional Healing System to the
            Public Health System. Social Science
            and Medicine 14B:255.

            public health sytems, Puerto Ricans,
            therapist-spiritist communication,
            traditional healing systems

64. Leighton, Dorothea C., John S. Harding,
    David B. Macklin, Allister W. McMillan
    and Alexander H. Leighton
    1963   The Character of Danger: Psychiatric
            Symptoms in Selected Communities. New
            York: Basic Books.

            ecology, psychiatric epidemiology,
            socio-cultural disintegration,, symptom
            identification

413

65. Leininger, Madeline
    1970   Nursing and Anthropology: Two Worlds to
             Blend. New York: John Wiley.

             anthropological perspective, culture
             concept, nursing, practitioner-client
             relationship, transcultural health care

66.
    Witchcraft Practices and Psychocultural Therapy
             with Urban U.S. Families. Human
             Organization 32:73-83.

             acculturation stress, transcultural
             psychotherapy, United States, urban
             community, witchcraft practices

67.
    Culture and Transcultural Nursing: Meaningg and
             Significance for Nurses. In Cultural
             Dimensions in Baccalaureate Nursing
             Curriculum. pp. 85-110. New York:
             National League of Nursing, NLM
             Pub. 15-16662.

             health-illness concepts, humanistic
             health care, nursing education,
             transcultural context, transcultural
             nursing

68. Leslie, Charles, ed.
    1978   Theoretical Foundations for the
             Comparative Study of Medical Systems.
             Social Science and Medicine 12B:65-138.

             comparative models, disease history,
             health care systems, health culture,
             medical paradigms

69. LeVeck, Paula
    1974   Developmental Reactions in Young
             Adulthood. In New Dimensions in Mental
             Health-Psychiatric Nursing.
             M.E. Kalkman and A.J. Davis, eds.
             pp. 129-154. New York: McGraw Hill.

             child development, developmental
             reactions, mental health, psychiatric
             nursing, role diversification, stress,
             youth

414

70. Lex, Barbara W.
    1974   Voodoo Death: New Thoughts on an Old
              Explanation. American Anthropologist
              76:818-823.

              autonomic tuning, death,
              neurophysiological research,
              psychophysiological disorders, voodoo
              subculture

71. Lipson, Juliene G.
    1980   Consumer Activism in Two Women's
              Self-Help Groups. Western Journal of
              Nursing Research 2:393-405.

              consumer participation, self-help
              efforts, women

72. McDermott, Walsh, Kurt W. Deuschle and
    Clifford Barnett
    1972   Health Care Experiment at Many Farms.
              Science 175:23-31.

              disease management, disease pattern,
              health action program, health ecology,
              mortality, Navaho, poverty, rural
              community

73. Macgregor, Frances Cooke
    1960   Social Science in Nursing: Applications
              for the Improvement of Patient Care.
              New York: Russel Sage Foundation.

              context of illness, nursing education,
              practitioner-client relationship, social
              science approaches, sociocultural and
              psychological factors

74.
    1978   Facial Disfigurement. In Disability and
              Rehabilitation Handbook.
              R.M. Goldenson, ed. pp. 389-395. New
              York: McGraw Hill.

              case management, epidemiology, facial
              disfigurement, psychosocial
              implications, rehabilitation

75. Maduro, Renaldo J.
     1975   Voodoo Possession in San Francisco.
               Ethos 3:425-447.

               acculturation stress, adaptive
               strategies, altered states, Blacks,
               transcultural psychotherapy, voodoo
               subculture

76. Maduro, Renaldo and Carlos F. Martinez
     1974   Latino Dream Analysis: Opportunity for
               Confrontation. Social Casework
               55:461-469.

               acculturation stress, dream analysis,
               interpersonal relations, Latino,
               psychotherapy

77. Mars, G.
     1975   A Social Anthropological Approach to
               Health Problems in Developing Countries.
               CIBA Foundation Symposium 32:219-235.

               Africa, anthropological approaches,
               Asia, developing countries, health care
               planning, health service delivery

78. May, Jude Thomas, Katherine Knoop Parry,
     Mary L. Durham and Peter Kong-ming New
     1980   Institutional Structure and Process in
               Health Services Innovation: The Reform
               Strategy of the Neighborhood Health
               Center Program. In Assessing the
               Contributions of the Social Sciences to
               Health. Meyer H. Brenner, A. Mooney and
               T.J. Nag, eds. pp. 117-139. Boulder,
               CO: The Westview Press (for the American
               Association for the Advancement of
               Science).

               health institution reform, neighborhood
               health center, social welfare programs

79. Miller, Nancy Brown
    1970   Utilization of Services for the
              Developmentally Disabled by American
              Indian Families in Los Angeles. Los
              Angeles: University of California at Los
              Angeles, Dept. of Anthropology, Ph.D.
              Dissertation.

              American Indians, cultural
              characteristics, developmentally
              disabled, health service utilization,
              patient-client relationship,
              transcultural health care

80. Muecke, Marjorie
    1976   Health Care Systems as Socializing
              Agents: Childbearing, The Northern Thai
              and Western Ways. Social Science and
              Medicine 10B:377-383.

              childbirth practices, comparative health
              care, Euro-American, health culture,
              socialization, Thailand

81. Newman, Lucile F.
    1981   Social and Sensory Environment of Low
              Birth Weight Infants in a Special Care
              Nursery: An Anthropological
              Investigation. Journal of Nervous and
              Mental Diseases 169:448-455.

              anthropological investigation, clinical
              management, human interaction, nursing,
              premature infants, sensory environment,
              social environment

82. Polgar, Steven
    1962   Health and Human Behavior: Areas of
              Interest Common to the Social and
              Medical Sciences. Current Anthropology
              3:159-205.

              health action programs, health culture,
              health personnel, health status, human
              behavior, social science

83. Polger, Steven and Frances Rothstein
    1970   Family Planning and Conjugal Roles in
            New York City. Social Science and
            Medicine 4:135-139.

            Blacks, birth control, conjugal roles,
            pelvic exam, poverty, Puerto Ricans, sex
            domination, urban community

84. Reynolds, David K. and Norman L. Farberow
    1976   Suicide: Inside and Out. Berkeley:
            University of California Press.

            case management, hospital patient,
            mental hospital, participant
            observation, practitioner-client
            relationship, suicide

85. Rodin, Miriam B., Douglas R. Morton and
    Demitri B. Shimkin
    1981   Beverage Preference, Drinking and Social
            Stress in an Urban Community.
            International Journal of the Addictions
            17:315-328.

            alcoholism, beverage preference,
            drinking behavior, psychosocial stress,
            urban community

86. Ruybal, Salley D., Eleanor E. Bauwens
    and Marie-Jose Fasla
    1975   Community Assessment: An Epidemiological
            Approach. Nursing Outlook 23:365-368.

            community health assessment,
            epidemiological approach, nursing,
            nursing education, problem
            identification

87. Schafft, Gretchen E.
    1980   Nursing Home Care and the Minority
            Elderly. Journal of Long Term Care
            Administration 8:1-31.

            aged, Blacks, nursing home, patient care

88. Schoenberger, James A., Marion Carter,
    Edward J. Eckenfels, Dennis A. Frate,
    Eddie Logan, Kenrad Nelson, William Peltz,
    Richard Roistacher and Demitri B. Shimkin
    1975   Hypertension in Holmes County,
            Mississippi. In Epidemiology and
            Control of Hypertension. Paul Oglesby,
            ed. pp. 485-501. New York: Stratton
            Medical Book Corp.

            Blacks, epidemiology, hypertension,
            poverty, psychosocial stress, rural
            community

89. Shand, Nancy
    1981   The Reciprocal Impact of Breast-Feeding
            and Cultural Form on Maternal Behavior
            and Infant Development. Journal of
            Biosocial Science 13:1-17.

            breast-feeding, cultural practice,
            infant development, Japanese, maternal
            behavior, United States

90. Shiloh, Ailon, Peggy Golde, Demitri B. Shimkin,
    Hazel H. Weidman, Lorraine Kaufman,
    Howard F. Stein, Thomas Maretzki,
    Toni Tripp-Reimer, John C. Russell
    and Clifford R. Barnett
    1980   Open Forum: Clinical Anthropology.
            Medical Anthropology Newsletter 12(1).

            clinical anthropology, heath care,
            medical anthropology, therapeutic
            anthropology

91. Shimkin, Demitri B.
    1968   The Calculus of Survival. Medical
            Opinion and Review 11(10):47-57.

            adaptive strategies, cybernetics, game
            theory, globalism, socialization, United
            States, U.S.S.R.

92.
        1970   Man, Ecology, and Health. Archives of
                Environmental Health 20:111-127.

                comparative health care, environmental
                stress, health education, health
                research, health trends, human ecology,
                United States

93.
        1972   Mortality in Mississippi 1963-1967: A
                Search for Environmental Factors in
                Disease. Man-Environment Systems
                2:125-128.

                Blacks, disease, environment, health
                ecology, migration, morbidity,
                mortality, rural community

94.
        1981   Systems Analysis: A Promising Focus for
                Biosocial Research. Journal of
                Biosocial Research 13:127-137.

                adaptation, biosocial research, human
                ecology, rural community, systems
                analysis, urban environment, values

95. Snyder, Alice Ivey
        1978a   Midlife Crisis Among Submariners' Wives.
                In Military Families. Adaptation to
                Change. E.J. Hunter and D.S. Nice, eds.
                pp. 142-154. New York: Praeger.

                adaptation, marital separation, mid-life
                crisis, role stress, self definition,
                sex roles, women

96.
        1978b   Periodic Separation and Physical
                Illness. American Journal of
                Orthopsychiatry 48:637-643.

                blood pressure, depression, E.N.T.
                disorders, health awareness, marital
                separation

97. Sokolovsky, Jay, Carl Cohen, Dirk Berger
     and Josephine Geiger
     1978   Research Networks of Experimental
             Patients in a Manhattan SRO Hospital.
             Human Organization 37:5-15.

             ex-mental patients, interpersonal
             relations, isolation, network analysis,
             rehabilitation, schizophrenia, support
             organizations

98. Stein, Howard F.
     1979a   Rehabilitation and Chronic Illness in
             American Culture: The Cultural
             Psychodynamics of a Medical and Social
             Problem. Journal of Psychological
             Anthropology 2:153-176.

             chronic illness, cultural context, group
             psychodynamics, health/illness concepts,
             rehabilitation, sick role, stigma,
             United States

99.
     1979b   The Salience of Ethno-psychology for
             Medical Education and Practice. Social
             Science and Medicine 13B:199-210.

             comparative epistemology,
             ethnopsychology, health practitioner
             training/education, psychocultural
             context

100. Swyter, Jai
     1976   Dignified Death: An Ideal. Military
             Chaplains' Review. Spring:1-8.

             aged, Arctic Eskimo, cultural practice,
             death, dying, environmental adaptation,
             euthanasia, hospital patient, medical
             ethics

101. Van Der Bruggen, H.
     1976   Arabian Mohammedan Patient: Various
             Anthropological Aspects of Nursing
             Care. SOINS 21:93-97.

             anthropological perspective, Arab,
             ethnic groups, Islam, nursing care

102. Vermeer, Donald E. and Dennis A. Frate
1979   Geophagia in Rural Mississippi:
          Environmental and Cultural Contexts and
          Nutritional Implications. American
          Journal of Clinical Nutrition
          32:2129-2135.

          Blacks, cultural context, environment,
          geophagy, hyperkalemia, hypertension,
          nutrition, rural community, sex
          differences

103. Von Mering, Otto
1962   Disease, Healing, and Problem Solving:
          A Behavioral Science Approach.
          International Journal of Social
          Psychiatry 8(2):137-148.

          adaptive behavior, decision making,
          healing system, illness categorization,
          problem solving, societal reaction,
          symptom identification

104.
1970   Medicine and Psychiatry. In
          Anthropology and the Behavioral and
          Health Sciences. O. Von Mering and
          L. Kasden, eds. pp. 272-292.
          Pittsburgh, PA: University of
          Pittsburgh Press.

          context of study, disease pattern,
          disease pattern change, health/illness
          concepts, medicine, psychiatry

105. Watzlawick, Paul, John H. Weakland
and Richard Fisch
1974   Change: Principles of Problem Formation
          and Problem Resolution. New York:
          W.W. Norton.

          conceptual framework, group
          psychodynamics, problem solving,
          psychology of change

106. Weakland, John H.
     1979   The Double-Bind Theory: Some Current
               Implications for Child Psychiatry.
               Journal of Child Psychiatry 18:54-66.

               child, cybernetic causal model,
               double-bind theory, family therapy,
               hyperactivity, psychopathology

107. Weidman, Hazel Hitson
     1979a   Falling Out: A Diagnostic and Treatment
               Problem Viewed from a Transcultural
               Perspective. Social Science and
               Medicine 13B:95-112.

               acculturation stress, adaptive-coping
               behavior, Bahamians, Blacks, diagnosis,
               falling-out, health culture, seizure,
               transcultural perspective

108.
     1979b   The Transcultural View: Prerequisite to
               Interethnic (Intercultural)
               Communication in Medicine. Social
               Science and Medicine 13B:85-87.

               acculturation, ethnicity, health care
               systems, intercultural mediation,
               transcultural health care,
               transcultural perspective, urban
               community

109. Wilson, C.S
     1978   Contributions of Nutrition to
               Anthropological Research. Federal
               Proceedings 37:73-76.

               cultural practice, developing
               countries, ethnic minorities, nutrition

110. Wood, Corrince Shear
     1978   Syphilis in Anthropological
               Perspective. Social Science and
               Medicine 123:47-55.

               anthropological perspective, disease
               history, disease transmission,
               etiology, prehistoric evidence,
               syphilis, venereal disease

111. Abad, Vincent, Juan Ramos and Elizabeth Boyce
     1974   A Model for Delivery of Mental Health
              Services to Spanish-Speaking
              Minorities. American Journal of
              Orthopsychiatry 44:584-595.

              bilingualism, folk healing, health
              service delivery, mental health
              services, Puerto Ricans, service
              utilization, Spanish-speaking
              minorities

112. Anthony, E. James
     1969   The Mutative Impact on Family Life of
              Serious Mental and Physical Illness in
              a Parent. Canadian Psychiatric
              Association Journal 14:433-453.

              child development, chronic illness,
              family crisis, genetic expectations,
              mental health, parent illness, role
              performance

113. Bard, Morton and Joseph Zackes
     1971   The Prevention of Family Violence:
              Dilemmas of Community Intervention.
              Journal of Marriage and the Family
              33:677-682.

              community development, crisis
              intervention, family crisis, family
              violence, law enforcement, police
              intervention, values

114. Barmettler, Donna and Grace L. Fields
     1975   Using the Group Method to Study and to
              Treat Parents of Asthmatic Children.
              Social Work in Health Care 1:167-176.

              asthma, child illness, chronic illnes,
              group counseling/therapy, parent-child
              interaction, parents' needs

424

115. Benjamin, Bernard
     1971   Bereavement and Heart Disease. Journal
             of Biosocial Science 3:61-67.

             bereavement, chronic disease, emotional
             stress, heart disease, mortality rate,
             widowhood

116. Brazelton, Berry
     1979   Behavioral Competence of the Newborn
             Infant. Seminars in Perinatology
             3:35-44.

             affective communication, behavioral
             competence, child development, culture
             change, infant behavior

117. Brazelton, Berry, Edward Tronick
     and Lauren Adamson
     1974   Early Mother-Infant Interaction from
             Parent-Infant Interaction. CIBA
             Foundation Syposium 3.

             behavior expectation, disturbed
             interaction, infant attention pattern,
             infant behavior, mother-infant
             interaction

118. Cain, Lillian Pike
     1973   Casework with Kidney Transplant
             Patients. Social Work 18:76-83.

             adaptive coping behavior, child,
             chronic illness, family crisis, kidney
             transplant, therapeutic intervention

119. Carlson, Bonnie E.
     1977   Battered Women and Their Assailants.
             Social Work 22:455-460.

             assistance seeking behavior, battered
             women, demographic characteristics,
             drug/alcohol abuse, service delivery
             recommendations, socioeconomic
             background, stereotypes

120. Cassel, John
     1964   Social Science Theory as a Source of
             Hypotheses in Epidemiological Research.
             American Journal of Public Health
             54:1482-1488.

             disease causes, disease theory,
             epidemiological research, multiple
             causes, social science

121. Cobliner, W. Godfrey, Harold Shulman
     and Vivian Smith
     1975   Patterns of Contraceptive Failures: The
             Role of Motivation Re-examined.
             Journal of Biosocial Science 7:307-318.

             abortion repeaters, birth control,
             contraceptive failure, contraceptive
             practice motivation, reality appraisal

122. Cohn, Anne Harris
     1979   Effective Treatment of Child Abuse and
             Neglect. Social Work Journal
             24:513-527.

             child abuse, health service evaluation,
             neglect, policy implications, treatment
             services

123. Coulehan, John L.
     1980   Navaho Indian Medicine: Implications
             for Healing. Journal of Family
             Practice 10:55-61.

             community health, health culture,
             homeostasis, indigenous health care
             systems, Navaho, sociocultural and
             psychological factors

124. Creswell, William, Warren Huffman
     and Donald Stone
     1970   Youth Smoking Behavior Characteristics
             and Their Educational Duplication.
             Urbana: University of Illinois.

             addiction, anti-smoking education,
             behavior modification, school
             attendance, smoking behavior, youth

125. David, Ann C. and Elizabeth H. Donovan
     1975   Initiating Group Process with Parents
             of Multihandicapped Children. Social
             Work in Health Care 1:177-183.

             child, group counseling/therapy,
             multihandicapped, parents' needs,
             physical disability, psychosocial
             problems

126. Dimsdale, J.E., J. Eckenrode, B.M. Kaplan,
     Frances Cotten and S. Dornbusch
     1979   The Role of Social Support in Medical
             Care. Social Psychiatry 14:175-180.

             community health, disease transmission,
             health care systems, morbidity,
             mortality, social networks

127. Dupont, Robert and Mark Greene
     1973   The Dynamics of a Heroin Addiction
             Epidemic. Science 181:716-722.

             addiction, demography, law enforcement,
             narcotics, prevention, treatment

128. Engel, George L.
     1977   The Need for a New Medical Model: A
             Challenge for Biomedicine. Science
             196:129-136.

             biomedicine, grief, medical paradigms,
             mental health, psychosocial factors,
             systems theory

129. Epperson, Margaret M.
     1977   Families in Sudden Crises: Process and
             Intervention in a Critical Care Center.
             Social Work in Health Care 2:265-273.

             accident victims, family crisis,
             shock-phase process, trauma centers,
             treatment

130. Fenwick, Rudy and Charles M. Barresi
     1981   Health Consequences of Marital Status
               Change Among the Elderly: A Commparison
               of Cross-Sectional and Longitudinal
               Analysis. Journal of Health and Social
               Behavior 22:106-116.

               aged, institutionalization, life
               changes, marital status, perceived
               health

131. Finkelhor, David
     1978   Psychological, Cultural and Family
               Factors in Incest and Family Sexual
               Abuse. Journal of Marriage and Family
               Counseling 4(4):41-49.

               alcoholism, child abuse, community
               attitudes, conjugal bond, family
               interaction, incest, isolation, poverty

132. French, Lawrence A. and Jim Hornbuckle
     1980   Alcoholism Among Native Americans: An
               Analysis. Social Work Journal
               25:275-285.

               alcoholism, American Indians, federal
               social policies, marginality

133. Gaensbauer, Theodore J. and Karen Sands
     1979   Distorted Affective Communications in
               Abused/Neglected Infants and Their
               Potential Impact on Caretakers.
               Journal of Child Psychiatry 18:237-250.

               affective communication,
               caretaker-infant bonding, child abuse,
               child development, infant behavior,
               neglect, personality traits

134. Goffman, Erving
     1969   Strategic Interaction. Philadelphia:
               University of Pennsylvania Press.

               calculation conduct, game theory, human
               behavior, interpersonal communication,
               strategic interaction

135. Good, Byron J. and Mary-Jo Delvecchio Good
      1981   The Meaning of Symptoms: A Cultural
              Hermeneutic Model for Clinical
              Practice. In The Relevance of Social
              Science for Medicine. Leon Eisenberg
              and Arthur Kleinman, eds. pp. 165-196.
              Dordrecht, Holland: D. Reidel
              Publishing Co.

              clinical practice, cultural hermeneutic
              model, cultural patterning, symptom
              expression

136. Gotom, Musa Dimka
      1975   Towards an Indigenous Model for
              Pastoral Counseling and Care, Based on
              Some Socio-Cultural, Anthropological,
              and Theological Presuppositions of
              Certain Nigerian People. Claremont,
              CA: Claremont, School of Theology,
              Ph.D. Dissertation.

              community health, community
              orientation, disease concepts,
              indigenous health care system,
              interpersonal relations, pastoral
              counseling, sociocultural matrix

137. Gove, Walter R. and Jeannette F. Tudor
      1973   Adult Sex Roles and Mental Illness.
              American Journal of Sociology
              78:812-835.

              anxiety, hospitalization, mental
              health, psychophysiological disorders,
              psychosis, sex roles

138. Grossman, Leona
      1973   Train Crash: Social Work and Disaster
              Services. Social Work 18:38-44.

              accident victims, aftermath reactions,
              behavior under stress, crisis
              intervention, social work role

139. Hatfield, Agnes
     1978   Psychological Costs of Schizophrenia to
               the Family. Social Work 23:355-359.

               chronic illness, family burden, family
               crisis, family interaction, mental
               health, schizophrenia, support service
               recommendations

140. Henderson, George and Martha Primeaux, eds.
     1981   Transcultural Health Care. Menlo Park,
               CA: Addison-Wesley.

               ethnic groups, health-illness concepts,
               nursing, transcultural health care,
               United States

141. Hessler, Richard M.
     1977   Citizen Participation, Social
               Organization and Culture: A
               Neighborhood Health Care Center for
               Chicanos. Human Organization
               36:124-134.

               community health, community
               organization, decentralization, health
               care systems, health service
               recommendations, Mexican American,
               neighborhood health center

142. Hinckle, L. et al.
     1968   Occupation, Education, and Coronary
               Heart Disease. Science 161:233-245.

               chronic disease, education, heart
               disease, mobility, occupation, risk,
               social status

143. Holmes, Thomas and Minoru Masuda
     1973   Life Change and Illness Susceptibility.
               In Separation and Depression.
               J.P. Scott and E.C. Cenay, eds.
               pp. 161-186. Washington, D.C.:
               American Association for the
               Advancement of Science Publication 94.

               illness susceptibiltiy, life changes,
               life event scale, mental health,
               psychosocial stress

144. Jurmain, Robert D.
     1977   Stress and the Etiology of
             Osteoarthritis. American Journal of
             Physical Anthropology 46:353-365.

             American Indians, Arctic Eskimo,
             Blacks, chronic disease, degenerative
             disease, lifestyle, osteoarthritis,
             stress, systemic factors

145. Kaplan, David M., Aaron Smith, Rose Grobstein
     and Stanley E. Fischman
     1973   Family Mediation of Stess. Social Work
             18:60-69.

             adaptive coping behavior, chronic
             illness, clinical management, family
             crisis, family mediation, stress

146. Kessler, David et al.
     1973   Assessing Health Quality--The Case for
             Tracers. New England Journal of
             Medicine 288:189-193.

             community health, health assessment,
             health care system, systems analysis,
             tracer

147. Kessler, Ronald C., Roger L. Brown
     and Clifford L. Broman
     1981   Sex Differences in Psychiatric
             Help-Seeking: Evidence from Large-Scale
             Surveys. Journal of Health and Social
             Behavior 22:49-64.

             health problem recognition, health
             seeking behavior, mental health,
             psychiatric morbidity, sex differences

148. Knapp, Vrinda S. and Howard Hansen
     1973   Helping Parents of Children with
             Leukemia. Social Work 18:70-75.

             child illness, chronic illness, family
             crisis, leukemia, parents' needs,
             support organizations, therapy

149. Kress, Helen
        1975   Adaptation to Chronic Dialysis: A
                 Two-Way Street. Social Work in Health
                 Care 1:41-46.

                 adaptation, chronic disease, dialysis,
                 practitioner-client relationship,
                 psychosocial stress

150. Lane, Helen J.
        1975   Working with Problems of Assault to
                 Self-Image and Life-Style. Social Work
                 in Health Care 1:191-198.

                 chronic illness, hospital patient, life
                 style change, psychosocial problems,
                 self image assault, therapeutic
                 intervention

151. Lawton, M. Powell
        1974   Social Ecology and the Health of Older
                 People. American Journal of Public
                 Health 64:257-260.

                 adaptation, aging, ecological model,
                 environment, therapy

152. LePontois, Joan
        1975   Adolescents with Sickle Cell Anemia
                 Deal with Life and Death. Social Work
                 in Health Care 1:71-80.

                 adolescents, chronic illness, death,
                 group counseling/therapy, psychological
                 stress, sexuality, sickle cell anemia,
                 vulnerability

153. Levine, Blaine S. and Amado M. Padilla
        1980   Crossing Cultures in Therapy:
                 Pluralistic Counseling for the
                 Hispanic. Monterey, CA: Brooks-Cole.

                 acculturation stress, health culture,
                 health service delivery, Hispanics,
                 transcultural psychotherapy

154. Like, Robert and James Ellison
     1981   Sleeping Blood, Tremor and Paralysis: A
             Trans-Cultural Approach to an Unusual
             Conversion Reaction. Culture, Medicine
             and Psychiatry 5:49-63.

             Cape Verdeans, conversion reaction,
             folk belief system, professional-client
             communication, symptom management,
             transcultural approach

155. Li-Repac, Diana
     1980   Cultural Influences of Clinical
             Perception: A Comparison Between
             Caucasian and Chinese-American
             Therapists. Journal of Cross Cultural
             Psychology 11:327-342.

             Chinese Americans, clinical
             perceptions, cultural bias, therapist

156. Malcolm, L.A.
     1970   Growth of the Asai Child of the Madang
             District of New Guinea. Journal of
             Biosocial Science 2:213-226.

             Asai of New Guinea, child, child
             development, environmental adaptation,
             growth pattern, growth rate,
             malnutrition

157. Morice, Rodney
     1978   Psychiatric Diagnosis in a
             Transcultural Setting: The Importance
             of Lexican Categories. British Journal
             of Psychiatry 132:87-95.

             Australian Aborigines, lexical
             categories, professional-client
             communication, psychiatric diagnosis,
             transcultural setting

158. Morycz, Richard K.
     1980   An Exploration of Senile Dementia and
             Family Burden. Clinical Social Work
             Journal 8:16-27.

             aging, chronic illness, family burden,
             isolation, senile dementia, social work
             intervention

159. Mulder, H.C. and T. Suurmeijer
     1977   Families with a Child with Epilepsy: A
              Sociological Contribution. Journal of
              Biosocial Science 9:13-24.

              child illness, chronic disease,
              epilepsy, family interaction, health
              seeking behavior, social assistance

160. Munakata, Tsunetsugu
     1982   Psycho-social Influence on Self-Care of
              the Hemodialysis Patient. Social
              Science and Medicine 16:1253-1264.

              hemodialysis patient, psychosocial
              factors, self-care behavior

161. Neumann, Alfred, Samuel Opusu-Amaah and
     Daniel A. Ampopo
     1976   Integration of Family Planning and
              Maternal and Child Health in Rural West
              Africa. Journal of Biosocial Science
              8:161-173.

              birth control, birth control
              acceptance, child health, family
              planning, maternal health

162. Parry, Joan K. and Nancy Kahn
     1976   Group Work with Emphysema Patients.
              Social Work in Health Care 2:55-64.

              chronic disease, emphysema, group
              counseling/therapy, life change, peer
              support, psychosocial problems,
              therapeutic counseling

163. Rabkin, Judith G. and Elmer L. Struening
     1976   Life Events, Stress and Illness.
              Science 194:1013-1020.

              empirical studies, life events,
              multicausal model, multidimensional
              perspective, stress

164. Radelet, Michael L.
      1981   Health Beliefs, Social Networks and
                Tranquilizer Use. Journal of Health
                and Social Behavior 22:165-173.

                anxiety, community health, drug use,
                health/illness concepts, social
                networks, tranquilizers

165. Rosenfield, Sarah
      1980   Sex Differences in Depression: Do Women
                Always Have Higher Rates? Journal of
                Health and Social Behavior 21:33-42.

                biological explanations, depression,
                mental health, sex differences, sex
                roles

166. Russel, John C.
      1983   Responsibilities of Anthropological
                Researchers in Psychiatric Clinical
                Settings. Human Organization 42:63-69.

                anthropological research,
                anthropologist role, clinical setting,
                psychiatric disorder

167. Sadler, Patricia O.
      1977   The "Crisis Cult" as a Voluntary
                Association: An Interactional Approach
                to Alcoholics Anonymous. Human
                Organization 36:207-210.

                Alcoholics Anonymous, alcoholism,
                "crisis cult" model, interactional
                model, voluntary association

168. Schmidt, Ruth Laila
      1983   Women and Health Care in Rural
                Pakistan. Social Science and Medicine
                17:419-420.

                health care systems, health needs,
                health planning, Pakistan, rural
                community, treatment seeking, women,
                women doctors

435

169. Scott, Clarissa
       1978   The Theoretical Significance of a Sense
                 of Well-Being for the Delivery of
                 Gynecological Health Care. In The
                 Anthropology of Health. Eleanor
                 E. Bauwens, ed. St. Louis, MO:
                 C.V. Mosby.

                 gynecology, health care delivery, well
                 being

170. Serrano, Alberto C., Margot B. Zuelzer
     and Don D. Howe
       1979   Ecology of Abusive and Nonabusive
                 Families. Implications for
                 Intervention. Journal of Child
                 Behavior 18:67-75.

                 adaptive-coping behavior, child abuse,
                 crisis intervention, family
                 interaction, multidimensional
                 perspective, protective services,
                 stress

171. Seyle, Hans
       1976   The Stress of Life. Revised ed. New
                 York: McGraw Hill.

                 adaptation, chronic disease, history of
                 concept of stress, psychophysiological
                 implications, stress

172. Snow, Londell F. and Shirley M. Johnson
       1977   Modern Day Menstrual Folklore: Some
                 Clinical Implications. Journal of the
                 American Medical Association
                 237:2736-2739.

                 folk medical belief, health care
                 provision, low income, menstruation,
                 patient behavior, transcultural setting

173. Snowden, Robert, Peter Eckstein
     and Denis Hawkins
       1973   Social and Medical Factors in the Use
                 and Effectiveness of IUD´s. Journal of
                 Biosocial Science 5:31-49.

                 birth control, birth control
                 acceptance, IUD, IUD use effectiveness,
                 patient-client relationship,
                 sociocultural and psychological factors

174. Steffensen, Margaret S. and Larry Colker
     1982   Intercultural Misunderstanding About
              Health Care: Recall of Descriptions of
              Illness and Treatment. Social Science
              and Medicine 16:1949-54.

              communication problem, health care
              delivery, health-illness concepts,
              illness-treatment concepts

175. Stock, Robert F.
     1976   Cholera in Africa. London:
              International African Institute.

              cholera, chronic disease, disease
              diffusion, disease pattern, epidemic
              disease, medical cartography, systems
              model

176. Strauss, Milton et al.
     1977   Behavioral Concomitants of Prenatal
              Addiction to Narcotics. In Annual
              Progress in Child Psychiatry and Child
              Development. S. Chess and A. Thomas,
              eds. New York: Brunner.

              addiction, child, chronic disease, drug
              addiction, maternal drug addiction,
              narcotics, pre/post natal effects,
              psychomotor development

177. Stubblefield, Kristine S.
     1977   A Preventive Program for Bereaved
              Families. Social Work in Health Care
              2:379-389.

              adjustment, bereaved family,
              bereavement, death, mental health,
              psychosocial stress, social work
              intervention

178. Sturges, Jane S.
     1978   Children's Reaction to Mental Illness
              in the Family. Social Casework
              59:530-536.

              adaptive coping, child development,
              family crisis, family interaction,
              mental health, personal conflict, role
              behavior

179. Trotter, Robert T., II and Juan Antonio Chavira
    1978   Discovering New Models for Alcohol
              Counseling in Minority Groups. <u>In</u>
              Modern Medicine and Medical
              Anthropology in the United
              States-Mexico Border Population. Boris
              Velimirvic, ed. Washington, D.C.: Pan
              American Health Organization.

              alcoholism, counseling, folk health
              care system, Mexican American, minority
              groups, treatment models

180. Walker, Philip W.
    1980   Recognizing the Mental Health Needs of
              the Developmentally Disabled People.
              Social Work Journal 25:293-297.

              developmentally disabled, health
              service development, mental health
              services, stress, therapeutic
              intervention

indigenous health care
  system
  37, 60, 123, 136

indigenous health
  resources
  44

indigenous health worker
  31, 33

individual pathology
  50

industrialized West
  40

infant attention pattern
  117

infant behavior
  116, 117, 133

infant development
  89

infecticus disease
  62

inner-city populations
  22

insomnia
  42

institutionalization
  5, 130

interactional model
  167

intercultural mediation
  108

interdisciplinary
  perspective
  6, 35

intergroup relations
  52

international cooperation
  37

interpersonal
  communication
  134

interpersonal relations
  17, 45, 57, 76, 97, 136

intervention, crisis
  see crisis intervention

intervention, police
  see police intervention

intervention, social
  see social intervention

intervention, therapeutic
  see therapeutic
  intervention

intra-ethnic variation
  56

Irish Catholic
  3

Islam
  101

isolation
  43, 97, 131, 158

IUD
  173

IUD use effectiveness
  173

Japanese
  89

kidney transplant
  118

Latino
  76

law enforcement
  113, 127

THE UNIVERSITY OF ILLINOIS

DEPARTMENT OF ANTHROPOLOGY

RESEARCH REPORTS

1 *Interim Report on Preliminary Site Examination Undertaken in Archaeological Section A of FAI 255 South of Business 40 in the Interstate Portion of Area S-34-4 of the Cahokia Site, St. Clair County, Illinois.*

Charles J. Bareis   (1967, 18 pp. + 9 maps)

OUT OF PRINT

2 Sak lu'um *in Maya Culture: and its Possible Relation to Maya Blue.*

Dean Edward Arnold   (1967, 53 pp.)

OUT OF PRINT

3 *Research Toward the Development of Predictive Models for Archaeological Site Distribution in the Kaskaskia River Drainage.*

Andrew C. Fortier   (1978, iv + 84 pp.)

OUT OF PRINT

4 *Anthropology for the Future.*

Demitri B. Shimkin, Sol Tax, and John W. Morrison, editors

(1978, vii + 294 pp.)

$6.00

5 *How Midwesterners Cope: the East Urbana Energy Study.*

Carolyn A. Sprague and Demitri B. Shimkin   (1981, v + 164 pp.)

$4.00

6 *Archaeology in the American Bottom: Progress Report of the Illinois FAI-270 Archaeological Mitigation Project*

Charles J. Bareis and James W. Porter, editors   (1981, xiv + 227 pp.)

$5.00

Order from Department of Anthropology, 109 Davenport Hall, University of Illinois, 607 South Mathews Street, Urbana, Illinois 61801. Payment must accompany order, be payable to "University of Illinois", be in U. S. currency check or money order, and include postage and handling costs of 85¢ per item.